RESISTANCE

RESISTANCE

HOW WOMEN SAVED DEMOCRACY FROM DONALD TRUMP

Jennifer Rubin

WILLIAM MORROW

An Imprint of HarperCollins*Publishers*

HarperCollins books may be purchased for educational, business, or sales promotional use. For information, please email the Special Markets Department at SPsales@harpercollins.com.

FIRST EDITION

Designed by Elina Cohen
Illustration by Vi-An Nguyen

Library of Congress Cataloging-in-Publication Data has been applied for.

ISBN 978-0-06-298213-1

21 22 23 24 25 LSC 10 9 8 7 6 5 4 3 2 1

For democracy's defenders

"I stand on their shoulders. Others stand on mine. I know my responsibility."

—Nancy Pelosi on the suffragettes, from her
2019 *Time* 100 interview

"Women belong in all places where decisions are being made. . . . It shouldn't be that women are the exception."

—Associate Supreme Court Justice Ruth Bader Ginsburg
on the elevation of Sonia Sotomayor

CONTENTS

PART 2: WOMEN REMAKE POLITICS

PREFACE

Especially for women, Donald J. Trump's 2016 election came as a bolt out of the blue, a jolt that left them personally wounded, fearful, and angry. They had expected so much better from the American electorate. Demagogues had run for president before but had been kept at bay. Huey Long, George Wallace, and Father Coughlin never came close to winning national elections. Nevertheless, tens of millions of voters had embraced an abjectly ignorant, racist, and unfit huckster. His negative attributes had not disqualified him in their eyes but rather they endeared him to them.

His election unnerved the daughters of the 1960s and 1970s, who had seen uneven but forward progress for women on so many fronts. The election of a man nostalgic for the unliberated 1950s undermined their faith in their fellow Americans' judgment and tolerance. The assumption that one could rely on the common sense of the American people now seemed farcical. Past gains women had once imagined permanent, such as access to safe abortions, seemed suddenly fragile. Women's confidence that legal, social, and economic advances provided a floor below which American women could not fall was called into question. The promise that women were on a path to full inclusion and equal power in all aspects of American life? That suddenly seemed like a pipe dream. In the face of this calamity, women did what they always do: They gathered to talk and commiserate, to bolster one another, to share their stories, and to begin planning. With remarkable speed, a grassroots resistance, not made exclusively but certainly primarily of women, began to sprout.

When the shock of election night wore off, millions of women faced daunting challenges: to actively engage as citizens; to elevate women's place in American politics; to continue to fight against Trump's policies; and to decry his outrages, scandals, and lies. Women exasperated by Trump's election ran for office by the hundreds. Others volunteered, raised money, or protested. In whatever role they played over the next four years—volunteer, activist, candidate, donor, protester—women refused to allow Trump's presidency to become the new normal.

At the same time the grassroots opposition was sprouting, key women power players in the Democratic Party started to pick up the pieces after a devastating loss, infuse their organizations with new purpose, harness the energy from the grassroots, and deploy their fundraising dollars and expertise to dislodge Trump. They channeled women's anger over the confirmation of Justice Brett Kavanaugh in 2018; their outrage over southern states' abortion bans; their horror over the grotesque mistreatment of migrant families and children; their indignation over the constant assaults on democracy; and their grief over the passing of Supreme Court Justice Ruth Bader Ginsburg in 2020 into a defiant movement to deny Trump a second term.

Meanwhile, in some corners of the Republican Party, lifelong conservatives were mortified that the party of Abraham Lincoln had united behind someone whose character and views represented a repudiation of everything that had attracted them to the GOP. To the shock of anti-Trump Republicans, fellow members who had once extolled the GOP as the party of ideas countenanced Trump's hostile takeover of the party and, worse, began to rationalize and defend his noxious views. Many craved access to

Trump's administration and sought jobs in an executive branch led by a dangerous narcissist.

While the Republican Party devolved into a cult of personality, millions of American women, both Democrats and Republicans, aghast at the 2016 election results, set out on a personal and political journey that began even before the Women's March on January 21, 2017, the largest single day of protest in American history. Democratic women not only ran but triumphed in the 2018 midterm House races. Republican women did the same in 2020. Women candidates joined the presidential race, battling persistent media bias and gender stereotypes, and confronted many less qualified men on the debate stages. Hillary Clinton had not been the last woman to compete for the presidency but the first for a major party. Her losing candidacy benefited the more politically adept and diverse women candidates who followed her—and enabled the election of a barrier-breaking woman vice president in 2020.

The Trump era was a time of a personal triumph and political awakening for many women and the birth of a mass movement largely headed and fueled by women. It scrambled many women's assumptions about people on the other end of the political spectrum, forged new friendships, and encouraged the formation of new networks. Women reinvigorated the Democratic Party and threw the Republican Party back on its heels. The political storm that gained steam over four years proved as powerful as the women's movement of the 1970s and as consequential as the 1960s civil rights movement.

Trump's shocking victory provoked millions of women to elevate the importance of politics in their daily lives—to the extreme detriment of the party Trump took over. Women's political involvement soared, and their partisan identification shifted in dramatic ways, affecting the composition of Congress, the makeup of the parties, and the language of politics. Ironically, Trump prompted many White women to prioritize gender over race. His election added impetus to political organizing among Black women, long the backbone of the Democratic Party, and among Native Americans.

In the aftermath of Trump's defeat, we can now fully appreciate how millions of women transformed their own lives and recaptured our democracy from the clutches of an authoritarian bully. Defeat is an orphan, the saying goes, but victory in this case had millions of mothers. Their story is what follows.

RESISTANCE

PART ONE

FROM DEJECTION TO ELATION

CHAPTER 1

THE NIGHTMARE BEGINS

The *New York Times* "needle," an omnipresent election tracking device on the *Times*' website, drifted away from Hillary Clinton in the direction of real estate mogul and reality TV star Donald Trump. Gosh how strange. Perhaps the exit polling was out of whack or big metropolitan counties with Democratic voters had not checked in. Sitting in the *Washington Post*'s offices, I felt a sense of panic begin to rise.

By early evening on election night 2016 Trump had won Florida and—what?!—Michigan and Pennsylvania were too close to call. The needle fell farther into the red. Eighty-one percent probability of a Clinton win became 40, then 20. My first reaction, akin to the news of a natural disaster or grave illness in the family, was denial. It cannot be. We all saw Trump on the *Access Hollywood* video bragging about sexually assaulting women. America could not elect this man. The needle must be wrong. If only.

When I left the *Washington Post*'s offices on K Street just after ten p.m. the DC streets were empty and oddly quiet. Waking up the next morning, I momentarily grasped at the notion that it had been a horrible nightmare—or a news reporting screwup that put the Florida 2000 vote-counting debacle to shame. I had written a column "breaking up" with the Republican Party in the spring of 2016 and then poured my energy into my *Washington Post* opinion pieces and TV appearances to alert my fellow Americans of the dangers of electing Trump. The irony did not escape me that in the one presidential election in which I was rooting for the Democratic presidential nominee, the party blew what seemed to me and millions of other voters to be an entirely winnable race.

I had been certain that Trump, if elected, would degrade our public discourse, attack democratic institutions, and govern recklessly. I saw from the start of his campaign a dangerous demagogue, someone who deployed the same tricks all despots and wannabe despots use—the Big Lie, the scapegoating of outsiders, the appeal of a strongman who says "I alone can fix it." I was never convinced, however, that my thesis would be tested in the real world, let alone that the outcome would be far worse than I had dared imagine. In the wake of the election, I felt sick, and my sense of doom deepened that American democracy would be stress-tested as never before. I was even more despondent that previously "normal" Republicans had supported him. With his victory, Republicans could be expected to support Trump, rationalize his outrageous conduct, and pursue noxious policies he had described in the campaign. I steeled myself for the likelihood that Republicans would countenance reckless and even illegal behavior.

The GOP's victory in 2016 was particularly devastating to thousands of Republican and Republican-leaning women like me who had crossed party lines to vote for Hillary Clinton—certainly more devastating to us than any prior *defeat* a GOP presidential nominee had suffered. In past presidential elections, I had voted for the losing Republican presidential candidate more than once— President George H. W. Bush in 1992, Sen. John McCain in 2008, and Mitt Romney in 2012. These were decent, honorable men who deeply believed in democracy and at critical junctures in their careers had put country above party or personal gain. However, I had never feared democracy would be endangered by their defeats. Now I felt the country was in peril.

Like many who would wind up in the Never Trump camp—the informal gaggle of Republicans and ex-Republicans who would not assent to Trump's takeover of the GOP—I once had identified with moderate Republicans who were dedicated to victory in the Cold War, expanded opportunity, free trade, and robust legal immigration. In November 2016 that party seemed as extinct as the Whigs. During the campaign I watched in horror as prominent, widely respected Republican politicians and opinion leaders succumbed to careerism, tribalism, and flat-out fabrication. Living through a political *Body Snatchers* experience, I had witnessed one conservative "intellectual" and politician after another, one "respectable" publication after another, rationalize, defend, and then laud a detestable figure who repudiated principles and positions that once animated these same Republicans' political lives.

I had experienced firsthand Trump's misogynistic wrath during the campaign. On December 1, 2015, I wrote a column for the *Washington Post* in reaction to his demand that CNN pay $5 million to charity for his appearance at a Republican presidential debate. "The most obvious explanation for putting forth an utterly ridiculous demand is to induce the other side to reject it," I surmised. "In this case, that would give Trump, who has done worse in each successive debate, an excuse to beg off. Why is he scared of debating his competitors?" I suggested that "he has run out of one-liners" and "cannot talk extemporaneously at length (at least not rationally) about policy issues, especially foreign policy, where he has blundered in the past." This evidently struck too close to home. Trump tweeted, "Highly untalented Wash Post blogger, Jennifer Rubin, a real dummy, never writes fairly about me. Why does Wash Post have low IQ people?" Instead of covering the MAGA crowd's bullying from afar I was now in the middle of it, a target of his base who hurled vulgar insults by email and social media. The hate email and tweets, often threatening and anti-Semitic, rained down on me. It was a preview of what was to come for me and for scores of women when the most powerful man in the world publicly singles you out and implicitly encourages his supporters to harass and threaten you. Friends and colleagues joked that this was a sign I was "relevant"; I did not see it that way. I felt under siege, and worse, despondent about the presence of so many unhinged if not deranged Americans.

I did not know on that dreary 2016 election night and in the days that immediately followed that millions of women shared a mixture of dread and disorientation. I had no idea their reaction to the 2016 election results would spawn a new spirit of defiance and an era of political activism. At the time, all I could feel was a sense of disorientation. I felt unmoored to either party, convinced the Republican Party had no loyalty to the country, the Constitution, or the truth. As never before, I was deeply worried about American democracy. I had thrown my all into making the case against Trump and now felt as if it had been for naught. Like virtually all mainstream media commentators I had not for a moment imagined Trump might win. It turned out I was not alone in struggling to process what had just happened.

On election night, in living rooms and at watch parties around the country, the results triggered common sensations of shock, horror, and loss for millions of women. Women shared a feeling of alienation from a country they had misjudged, a sense for the first time in their lives that American democracy was as fragile as some European countries in the 1920s and '30s. Dazed paralysis eventually would give way to anger and then to mass action. But election night itself was brutal.

Two women, both major movers in the Democratic Party and the progressive movement, went to New York to take part in Hillary Clinton's victory celebration at the Javits Center on election night 2016. They traveled from Washington, DC, to be with donors, old friends from the Clinton years, and other progressive leaders to watch the historic election results come in. Within hours of Donald

Trump's victory announcement, they were forced to put aside or at least contain their own emotions and figure out how thousands of activists, donors, campaign operatives, and think-tank scholars would readjust to the new political reality.

One was Neera Tanden, longtime adviser to Hillary Clinton and a principal architect of the Affordable Care Act (ACA) in the Obama administration. She was rumored to be Clinton's future Health and Human Services secretary and already cochaired the Clinton transition. Raised by a single mother who for a time after a divorce relied on food stamps and public housing, Tanden deeply believed the Democratic Party was a friend of ordinary people and a backstop when personal tragedy struck. An Indian American who had lived the American dream, she also understood that America, despite its flaws, was a haven for immigrants. Political junkies might recognize the dark-haired, impeccably dressed progressive from her TV appearances, but her full-time job was heading the Center for American Progress (CAP), the progressive think tank and its adjacent political arm. For her, Trump's victory threatened the values and endangered the people she held most dear. Moreover, her most significant professional achievement, helping craft the Affordable Care Act in the Obama White House and shepherding it through Congress, was now at risk. Indeed, the entire architecture of the New Deal and the Great Society, from Social Security to Medicaid, was in jeopardy. The seminal Supreme Court cases protecting women's access to abortion, gay marriage, and unions' ability to organize could be swept away with a Republican president and Senate and the judges they would put on the bench.

On election night 2016 Tanden watched, along with tens of millions of ordinary voters, as things went from bad to worse for Clinton. "By eight o'clock Florida looked not so great," she recalled. Shock set in as states fell to Trump. She found it "stunning on multiple levels." It was not just that Democrats could lose the election, but that people "could vote for this guy." Like millions of women she asked herself, "What's happening to America?"

She needed to catch the two a.m. train back to DC to explain the election results to her children and to hundreds of staffers at CAP. She would have to gather devastated employees to reorient them and transform CAP into the face of the opposition. She realized on the long, dark, and depressing train ride home that to sustain the fight and preserve Democrats' past achievements, any sense of despondency and fatalism had to be staunched. Having just overseen a CAP study of the aftermath of Hungary's elections in which right-wing nationalist Viktor Orbán triumphed, Tanden knew how a demoralizing loss to a wily demagogue could shatter the opposition.

There would be no high-fives for the hundreds of thousands of volunteers and staffers who had spent two years on the Clinton team, no revelry with veterans of the Clinton and Obama administrations, no inside gossip about who would be taking what jobs. This was a lonely and surreal experience for someone who had been anticipating triumph. Tanden would not be returning to the capital victorious, a Cabinet or senior staffer ready to expand upon Obama's legacy. She would be on the outside, with few tools at her disposal to influence the new administration. As shaken as she was, she knew others were depending on her. She had a think tank, donors, and the entire progressive movement to worry about. If she crumbled, she could not very well expect all of them to carry on.

Tanden recognized she could not sugarcoat the results when she spoke to her employees at CAP the Wednesday after the election. She candidly acknowledged the devastating loss and warned that the new administration would "assault every one of our values and people will be under attack." Tanden told her employees, many obviously despondent, "We have to be the voice of people who are going to feel under attack." A tearful lesbian Latina CAP staffer spoke up to say she was angry but also scared being in a country in which someone like Trump could win. Tanden looked out on the sea of a couple hundred crestfallen people, many young people facing their first huge political disappointment. She told them, "We all have to protect each other and stand up for each other. Part of this mobilization will defend to the death the values that ensure she is as American as anyone else." The organization was about to recast itself as a leader of the resistance to Trump.

Before Trump, I regarded Tanden as among the most astute center-left insiders. We differed on an array of issues, but she was no extremist. She hewed to the facts, believed in America's international leadership, and understood government is about creating consensus to improve Americans' lives. Over the course of the next few years, often over drinks at the restaurant across from CAP's offices—later forced to close in the 2020 pandemic—I discovered my politics were more aligned with Democrats who defended our democracy than with Republican Trump worshippers. We provided a sounding board, and often a reality check, for one another. She provided insight into the pitched battles against Trump and a window into a party that had always been "the other side." I offered what insight I could about the group of disaffected and/or former Republicans with whom I navigated the Trump years.

The other woman who traveled to New York to the Javits Center on Election Day 2016 was Ilyse Hogue, president of NARAL Pro-Choice America, the most prominent abortion rights advocacy group in the country. Hogue was a lifelong Democratic activist with experience acquired at a wide array of progressive groups, including MoveOn.org and the anti–Fox News watchdog group Media Matters for America. Her devotion to the abortion rights fight stemmed from personal experience, which she bravely described to the entire world at the 2016 Democratic National Convention in Philadelphia.

In a fiery red dress, she told the audience in the arena and at home that years ago she found out she was pregnant but at the wrong time in her life. She explained that she made "the decision that was best for me, to have an abortion and get compassionate care at a clinic in my own community." She noted that she and her husband were now the proud parents of twins. With a slight quiver in her voice she declared, "It's not as simple as bad girls get abortions and good girls have families. We are the same women at different times in our lives—each making decisions that are the best for us." This was personal. She knew firsthand how vital it was to give women control over their own lives.

On election night 2016, she was in a suite at the Javits Center with Khizr and Ghazala Khan, the Gold Star couple whom Trump had attacked after their appearance at the Democratic National Convention. As the election results came in, Hogue had to excuse herself so as not to cry in front of the couple, whom she knew had so much more to lose and would be even more devastated than she. She got a call from feminist author Rebecca Traister to come down to the floor of the Javits arena. "They are going to punish women," Rebecca Traister said, anticipating the right-wing backlash against women. "We have to go home right now," Hogue told her husband. As her panic level rose, she marveled that her husband seemed so calm and composed. Worried about her mother and mother-in-law, who were sitting with her young twins back home, and the devastating effect on pro-choice forces, she also took an early-morning train back to DC.

Onboard the Amtrak train rattling its way back to Washington, DC, Hogue could not ignore the enormity of the task ahead. Pro-choice forces would need to come to terms with a new legal reality that women would face in the Trump era. The dream of a solid progressive majority on the Supreme Court was gone for now. Instead of planning for a new liberal justice to replace the deceased Antonin Scalia, she faced the task of holding the line on abortion rights, fending off confirmation of right-wing judges, and finding a new slate of pro-choice women candidates for state and federal races. There were dozens of urgent issues that demanded her attention, but she understood how critical it was to focus her organization on the Supreme Court and to prevent activists, donors, and candidates from spinning their wheels on dozens of different issues. The prospect that funding would dry up, activists would go down without a fight, and poor women and women of color—who are those most affected when abortion access is restricted—would suffer were almost too horrible to contemplate.

Back in Washington, DC, quite a different group of women were watching the returns come in on election night. Sarah Longwell, who was the national board chair of the gay rights group the Log Cabin Republicans, was with her first son, three months old at the time, and her wife at a friend's house with other couples who had young children. She was a rising star on the right, well-known in political circles for her sarcastic wit. She was a product of the Midwest and looked the part, eschewing makeup and fussiness, favoring tweed jackets. As the child of two intellectually curious lawyers, she grew up in central Pennsylvania reading the works of renowned conservative intellectuals and attending public school in her early years and then a private prep school in Harrisburg, Pennsylvania, before attending Kenyon College, where she worked on the conservative newspaper.

For her, politics was about ideas, and the Republican Party was the party that championed personal responsibility, defended freedom against despots, and understood the power of free markets. Throughout her college years and early career, she had been intellectually comfortable in the GOP. That was tested when she worked as a communications aide on a book tour for former Pennsylvania senator, social conservative, and antigay provocateur Rick Santorum, who in 2004 some conservatives viewed as a presidential contender. She traveled with him to book signings and media stops, watching gay protesters scream at Santorum, who previously had caused an uproar by equating homosexuality with bestiality.

At one event, two mothers with a preteen daughter were at the protest line, carrying a sign "My Two Moms Took Me Bowling." Her heart sank. Longwell had been struggling to come out to her friends and family at the time, and the sight of this small, precious family shook her. There she was on the other side of the protest line, standing shoulder to shoulder with an infamous homophobe.

She vowed to come out to those in her life, including her conservative colleagues, many of whom were vocally against gay marriage. She promised herself she would find some way to champion gay rights within the Republican Party. Eventually, she became the first woman to hold the position of national board chair of the Log Cabin Republicans.

By nine p.m. at Longwell's election night gathering, the crowd had thinned out and one woman from each couple had departed with the young children. As Longwell later recalled, "Things were becoming strange." She furiously texted back and forth with a friend, Republican operative Tim Miller, who had worked on former Florida governor Jeb Bush's presidential campaign, as they tried to make sense of the returns. At some point he told her simply, "He's going to win." She remembered the mood in the room. "It was like a wake. It was a bunch of people with heads in their hands." Many of those who remained were ex-smokers but someone went out to get a pack of cigarettes. She took one and went out on the front porch. There she saw neighbors on their porches up and down the street doing precisely the same thing. The neighbors exchanged glances, implicitly asking, *What is going on?*

The day after the victory of the Republican nominee, Longwell was deeply unnerved and began soul-searching. What had she been missing in her party, and what had she gotten so wrong about her fellow Republicans? Horrified by Trump, she now began to acknowledge that while not all Trump supporters were racists, too many of her Republican colleagues simply did not care that he was a racist. For a time, she tried to convince herself that Republicans in Congress would restrain Trump. His proposed Cabinet had a few good, stable figures like former generals James Mattis and John Kelly. Surely, she thought, they would reel in the novice president.

Watching the Trump inauguration, however, she shared former president George W. Bush's reaction that Trump's belligerent, dark speech was "some weird shit." Later all she could recall was "how dark it was." Still, it was just a speech so maybe his actual performance would not be so bizarre, she hoped. Then, a week after the inauguration, Trump announced the Muslim ban barring the entry of anyone from a list of Muslim-majority countries. She realized she was on the opposite side of the political divide from her fellow Republicans who had made peace with Trump and even cheered the virulently bigoted policy. Deep in her bones she understood, "This is wrong." Then came Trump's inability to condemn the neo-Nazi march in Charlottesville in August 2017. That severed her connection to the Trumpified GOP. "I was out," she decided. What was not clear was what she would do next. Like many Republican women, Longwell had to choose: Withdraw from the fray or fight back? The decision would be made more difficult because she would be confronting and challenging people she previously respected and worked alongside throughout her political career.

On election night, armchair pundits and news junkies across America tried to gauge what was happening. For most women, politics was not a profession or advocation but an interest, one which heightened in presidential election years. Among them, Abigail Spanberger, at home in suburban Virginia with her husband and three kids, was stunned. Years earlier, she had followed her father into law enforcement, eventually working at the CIA as an undercover agent. The blond, slim woman with a dry sense of humor was not the portrait of an undercover agent that people raised on James Bond movies would envision. Contrary to the image of a daring, risk-seeking spy, Spanberger was controlled, preternaturally calm, detail-oriented, and unwilling to leave anything to chance. And yet when Florida went for Trump, she burst into tears.

When the Brexit vote had occurred earlier in 2016 a friend from the UK had told Spanberger how embarrassed she was for her country. Britain had chosen to follow a self-destructive leap into populism and anti-immigrant fearmongering. Now the shoe was on the other foot and on the other side of the Atlantic. Spanberger, as her friend did, felt her country had lost its way. Spanberger had not served her country to see America retreat into isolation under an "America First" banner nor to allow a foreign power to interfere in our elections.

After leaving the CIA in 2014 she had decided to continue her family tradition of public service. However, she never thought of herself as a politician. She later recalled that running for office was not yet on her radar screen. In her mind, politics was something other people did, but she now understood that her priorities and attention might need to focus beyond local philanthropy and volunteer work. She surely had no idea she would soon be a star in the 2018 freshmen House class and in the center of the impeachment storm.

Like Spanberger, scores of women around the country who had seethed over Trump's verbal assaults on women and minorities and experienced near-constant rage over his attacks on the country's core values were stunned. They nevertheless did not become paralyzed. To the surprise of both political parties, the mainstream media, and even themselves, previously politically inactive women across the ideological spectrum became energized in a way America had not witnessed in decades.

They marched, they organized, they became donors, they ran for office, they made new alliances, they "persisted," as Senate Majority Leader Mitch McConnell of Kentucky complained when Massachusetts Senator Elizabeth Warren refused to sit down and be quiet as instructed on the Senate floor. Defeating Trump became the animating principle of their lives. Moreover, they did this together, with other women, and in the process found validation and a sense of community. The predilection, an instinct more than a strategy, to seek consolation and comfort in relationships prompted them to reach out to other like-minded, unnerved women. Unconsciously, they had begun the shift from spectators to political activists.

I had a different role as a journalist. I would have to chronicle the attacks on American democracy and track the fierce resistance Trump had engendered. I was gloomy for a time, but as I watched women travel from despair to anger to activism, I felt a sense of pride and admiration. These women had not given up; in fact, they had turned their lives around, reinvented themselves. If they did not sink into despair, I could not either. Instead, I could tell their story, the story of how they would help change American politics as they changed their own lives and the lives of other women. In doing so I would also find new allies among principled Democrats and former Republicans fighting Trump in the courts and on the campaign trail. I would also meet and befriend a flock of women lawyers who would become household names on TV as legal commentators on impeachment and Trump's assault on the rule of law. One, Mimi Rocah would run for and win the race for Westchester County district attorney. Another, Maya Wiley, would go on to run for New York City mayor in 2021.

I was both observing and participating in a great awakening, a hinge moment in history when fundamental change and political realignment are possible. My first task was to fully understand why the push to put a woman in the White House failed in 2016.

CHAPTER 2

WHAT WENT WRONG?

I had always believed that sooner or later a woman inevitably would win the presidency. I erroneously assumed that electing a woman would be easier than electing an African American man, as the country had done in 2008 and 2012. Therefore, as historic as Clinton's 2016 campaign was, at the time I was far less focused on her status as the first woman nominee of a major party than I was on just how she was going to defeat Trump. What mattered to me was not her gender but her ability to save both women and men from a bully whose "Lock her up!" chants and incitements to punch out protesters gave his campaign the unmistakable air of an authoritarian movement. In my eyes, she was an imperfect means to a critical end, namely beating Trump. A Republican presidential victory would be a tragedy from my perspective for the country and for my values; I did not then appreciate how Clinton's failure would have significant ramifications for other women's future presidential aspirations.

From the perspective of many American women, the potential for a woman president in 2016 was a long overdue event at an urgent moment. A Clinton win would mean the youngest generation of girls would never know an America that had invariably elected male presidents. She not only could break the highest political glass ceiling, but she could bolster women far beyond the White House. It was widely expected, based on her track record of hiring women in the Senate and State Department and on her campaigns, that she would name a record number of women to high positions in the executive branch, to the courts, and to advisory boards and councils. During the campaign she told MSNBC's Rachel Maddow at a town hall, "I am going to have a Cabinet that looks like America, and 50 percent of America is women, right?" No woman had ever held the job of secretary of treasury nor defense nor served as director of the CIA or National Intelligence. Clinton had the potential not only to increase the number of women but place them in barrier-breaking positions. Once there, her appointees could open the path for other women to rise. She could also be an example to leaders in the private sector that a woman was entirely capable of reaching the highest executive post in the country and overseeing a huge and complex organization, the federal government. To women who felt their progress in both the public and private sectors had stalled, her victory offered the potential to shock the system, unleashing opportunity and erasing lingering doubts that women could not handle the most critical, powerful positions in their field.

To be sure, in the decades before the 2016 election, American women's lives had changed dramatically. American women in the twenty-first century stand on the shoulders of their predecessors: the suffragettes of the 1920s, such as Alice Paul and Carrie Chapman Catt who finally won the decades-long battle for the right to vote, and the leaders of the 1970s "second-wave" feminism, championed by Gloria Steinem, Betty Friedan, and, in the courts, by Ruth Bader Ginsburg. Just fifty years ago, women faced a world in which they were denied employment in many fields and could be fired for getting pregnant. Federal court judges, state and local officials, and members of Congress were virtually all White men. Before 1970 a grand total of three women had held a governorship, and neither major party had seriously considered putting a woman on its presidential ticket. Prior to 1970 only ten women had ever served as a US senator.

By 2010, women had surpassed men in associate, bachelor's, and master's degrees. Women went from just 38 percent of the workforce in 1960 to 59 percent in 2010, and for married women, from 32 percent to 61 percent. Nevertheless, by 2016 women's progress had plateaued and reactionary forces had made alarming inroads. The Population Reference Bureau reported in 2014 that women's labor participation rate had declined slightly and a sizable gap "between the median earnings of men ($50,033) and women ($39,157)" persisted. Women were still concentrated in low-paying jobs, the study found, "but even for the same job, women earn significantly less than men. Women make up about 46 percent of those working full-time in management, business, and finance jobs but their median earnings in those positions are only about 74 percent of men's earnings."

The glass ceiling was real. Among the Fortune 500 CEOs, only fifteen were women in 2010. One study found, "In 1980, there were no women in the top executive ranks of the Fortune 100 companies; by 2001, 11 percent of those corporate leaders were women." At major law firms four-fifths of equity partners were male in 2018. In the start-up world, only 2 percent of venture capital funding went to female founders in 2017. Women held only 38 percent of university tenure-track positions in 2016. Women's frustration understandably grew with the snail's pace of progress in the private sector.

The political realm was only marginally better. It had taken from the onset of the women's revolution in the 1970s until the so-called Year of the Woman in 1992 for women to make significant gains in national politics. According to Susan Carroll of Rutgers University's Center for American Women and Politics, "The women's movement put a message out there to society that had not been there before, that women's interests were not always the same as men's interests." That realization would prompt more women to enter politics and more women voters to support women candidates.

Following the Anita Hill–Clarence Thomas Senate Judiciary hearings in 1991, chaired by then Senator Joe Biden, a critical mass of women finally entered Congress. In 1990 there were thirty-two women in the House; after the 1992 election, the number shot up to fifty-four along with a record seven women in the Senate. The number of women over the next two decades slowly crept up, but the increase was overwhelmingly among Democratic women. After the 2016 elections, eighty-one Democratic women sat in Congress compared with only twenty-nine Republican women; only six of twenty-three women in the Senate were Republicans.

Meanwhile, in statewide elections (e.g., governor, lieutenant governor) the number of women remained flat or, in some cases, declined. After the 2016 election, the Center for American Women and Politics reported, "In contests for statewide elective executive offices, the number of women who will serve in 2017 is 75 (32D, 42R, 1NP), compared with the 2016 figure of 75 (33D, 41R, 1NP), or 24 percent of the 312 positions." Despite success in winning congressional seats and in attaining state and local posts, neither major party had a competitive female presidential candidate until 2008, and until 2016 neither had ever nominated a woman for president. No woman had been elected vice president; no woman of color had ever appeared on a presidential ticket.

If it was hard for Democratic women to advance through the political ranks it was nothing compared to what Republican women encountered. It was not until the Republicans lost the House majority in 2018 that a concerted effort, largely by women candidates and politicians themselves, raised and recruited Republican women, with remarkable success. Unsurprisingly, a big part of the difference came down to money. Democratic candidates enjoyed an enormous advantage over their Republican counterparts largely thanks to one critical entity: EMILY's List. (There is no "Emily";

it is an acronym for "Early Money Is Like Yeast.") Founded in 1985 to elect pro-choice women, by 2008 EMILY's List had raised over $200 million. In 2012 alone it raised more than $4.6 million for candidates and spent more than $7.7 million in independent expenditures, largely money to be used for third-party ads; in 2014 those numbers increased to more than $4.7 million and $8.1 million, respectively. In the 2016 cycle those numbers passed *$6.6 million and $33 million.*

EMILY's List was the biggest but by no means the only PAC aiding Democratic women. In 2012, Sen. Kirsten Gillibrand (D-NY) founded Off the Sidelines to promote women candidates and advocate on issues critical to women. The PAC not only endorsed and raised money for women candidates but championed issues affecting women, such as sexual assault in the military, childcare, and equal pay. In 2014, Off the Sidelines spent nearly $3 million for women candidates. By 2018, the Off the Sidelines PAC gave money to nearly forty women running in House, Senate, and gubernatorial races.

It was also a matter of will. Republican voters were increasingly White and male, and any pressure to diversify from the small cadre of elected women historically had met with derision. Republican donors, overwhelmingly White and male, did not comprehend the value in recruiting and supporting women. It was little wonder, then, that women members were scarce on the Republican side of the aisle. Going into the 2016 election, not a single Republican woman had ever sat on the Senate Judiciary Committee. No woman had ever occupied a seat in the Senate Republican majority leadership. No Republican woman had ever held the position of House speaker or minority or majority leader or whip. Without women in leadership and without a commitment to advance women, the gap between Republican women and Democratic women in office became a chasm.

If an educated, well-informed, and capable Republican woman with some interest in politics wanted to run for office, there were very few ready-made groups and resources to guide her through the process. "EMILY's List has been around for decades," former New Hampshire GOP Senator Kelly Ayotte recalled in an interview with *Roll Call*. Until 2018, however, the support structure for Republican women was virtually nonexistent. "There's been a Republican woman problem for a while," Kelly Dittmar, a political scientist at the Center for American Women and Politics, told the *New York Times* in 2018, a year in which the Republican House freshman class had a single woman. If a Republican woman had a political family to support her or a record in local government, she might be able to make the leap to higher office, but such women were few and far between. In the Senate, Kansas Republican Nancy Kassebaum, who had held office for roughly two decades, was the daughter of Alf Landon, a former governor and presidential candidate. Kay Bailey Hutchison from Texas had multiple terms in the House and a stint as state treasurer before running for the Senate. In the House, a common route for Republican women was to replace a deceased spouse, which occurred fifteen times for Republican women. Outside of those avenues, it was an uphill climb for non-wealthy Republican women.

As a result, there was a visible contrast in the chambers of Congress. On the GOP side of the aisle one could see an ocean of White men in dark suits, a fitting microcosm of a party that railed against the demographic changes sweeping the country; on the Democratic side, brightly colored women's suits and dresses and many non-white members (both male and female), broke up the visual monotony.

Election of a woman president in 2016, therefore, presented the potential to boost appointment of women to the executive and judicial branches, to elevate women in business, and to reexamine barriers that still prevented women from enjoying full equality. Regardless of ideology or party, women would have a champion in the White House concerned about equal pay, healthcare, and childcare.

Losing that opportunity, one they were so certain had finally arrived, was crushing. Rebecca Traister wrote in her book *Good and Mad*, "The election of Donald Trump over Hillary Clinton for the presidency of the United States in 2016 may have felt like a stinging, agonizing shock to many of us who lived through it . . . We'd allowed ourselves to be taken in by the lie, by the illusion that we had come farther than we had." The *New York Times* painted a vivid picture of reaction to the election in Cambridge, Massachusetts. "It was visceral. Women felt gutted, shocked, appalled, afraid. The prospect of celebrating the election of the nation's first female president had been crushed by a man whom many women viewed as sexist." Across the country, the *Mercury News* reported from California's Bay Area, "Hillary's Defeat Crushes Many Women's Hopes."

The response was understandable. Millions of women found it infuriating that the archetypal example of a more qualified woman losing to a less qualified man—no, make that an utterly and obviously *un*qualified man—prevailed. Clinton's obvious advantage over Trump in expertise was indicative of the double standard voters set for women candidates. As political scientists Georgia Duerst-Lahti and Madison Oakley explain, in political fights to establish qualifications and leadership qualities, "expertise has been central to women's advancement in public life. In fact, since women began to enter the public realm in the 1970s, they have relied upon expertise as a rational response to sexism, often having higher and better credentials than their male counterparts."

Clinton's victory was supposed to vindicate the efforts of millions of women in the workplace who had frequently outworked their male peers and taken on more criticism, which was often nothing more than thinly disguised sexism. Clinton, the quintessential A student—diligent and expertly prepared and who had patiently waited her turn—would finally be rewarded, they believed. Those of us who believed America was, with all its imperfections, a meritocracy hoped to see our faith vindicated when one of the most prepared candidates in history beat one of the least. When that confidence was dashed, her defeat seemed all the more dispiriting. Clinton's former campaign communications manager Jennifer Palmieri wrote in 2018, "We had lived our lives playing by a certain set of rules, and they had failed us. We didn't know what to make of it at first. Could it be that women are meant to go only so far in the world?"

It seemed that all those years toiling in politics worked against Clinton, a terrifying takeaway for women who put their heads down and worked for years hoping to advance in their careers. In Trump's telling and in many media portrayals, Clinton's expertise and longevity in public life were a burden, a sign she was an insider, part of the "swamp," and a defender of the status quo. Her rejection horrified many women who thought working within the system would earn recognition and advancement. Women's traditional advantage in being viewed as more honest and trustworthy than men was undercut by Trump's "Crooked Hillary" refrain, by the media's obsession with her email scandal, and by comparatively minimal coverage of the far more numerous and serious allegations against Trump. In one study, Kelly Dittmar of the Center for American Women and Politics wrote: "A review of network evening newscasts revealed that while just 32 minutes of presidential campaign coverage between January 1 and October 21, 2016, was given to in-depth policy coverage, 100 minutes was allocated to covering Clinton's emails." While the press obsessed over her emails, Trump's own scandals got scant attention.

Worse, Trump skated by on the ill-conceived notion that lack of political experience was a positive trait. *USA Today* described his final weekend of campaigning before the 2016 election: "As it rolled up to a hangar in eastern North Carolina on the campaign's final weekend, the theme from *Air Force One* blaring away, Donald Trump's supporters waved signs and snapped cellphone photos while eagerly awaiting the presidential candidate's final argument—one that targets the American political system generally and Hillary Clinton, in particular." The report continued, "'To all Americans I say it's time for change,' Trump told his backers while echoing themes he has used for more than 16 months on the campaign trail. 'It's time for new leadership.'" Voters ate it up, buying the line that we could run government like a business. Only someone with no idea how government worked, apparently, could clean it up. Clinton, in this mindset, had wasted decades learning policy, meeting world leaders, and passing laws.

In assessing how she could lose to an unqualified huckster, Clinton tended to blame then FBI director James Comey, who eleven days before the election came forward with "new" information about her emails found on longtime aide Huma Abedin's laptop. That discovery would later prove to be inconsequential, but the damage to Clinton had been done. In her memoir Clinton argued, "If not for the dramatic intervention of the FBI director in the final days we would have won the White House." Polling did show her numbers dropped at that point, and in a close race it could have been the difference between winning and losing.

Aside from the particulars of the candidates and Comey's intervention, the obvious reason for her loss remained: gender. Palmieri observed about Clinton's concession speech in 2016, "Fundamentally it wasn't about the words she used in her concession speech but what she represented. She was no longer a woman pushing to be president. She was a gracious loser putting the needs of her country above her own. It was the role of Hillary as an ambitious candidate that troubled us." An ambitious woman, an outspoken and unapologetic feminist, simply rubbed a lot of male voters the wrong way. It was telling that voters were often at a loss to explain exactly what about Clinton they disliked so. She was "awful" or "terrible," but rarely did they cite a mistake made as secretary of state or a failure as New York's senator. If anything, voters antagonistic to her campaign—egged on by Trump—cast back to the Bill

Clinton presidency and its assorted scandals, which ranged from firing travel office employees to the Whitewater banking dustup. To many women, these reactions sounded like excuses, not well-considered reasons to vote for Trump.

What Palmieri called "an unconscious but pervasive" gender bias was not the sole reason for her loss, but certainly played a role, perhaps a pivotal one. If Trump had been running against a man, he would never have lurked creepily behind his opponent during a debate, hyped a bout of the flu as evidence of her frailty, and constantly referenced the candidate's spouse's infidelities. The irrational vehemence of her critics in the media and the microexamination of every action—from how she interacted with the public at a Chipotle lunch stop to her failure to make one more campaign swing in Wisconsin—suggested something beyond ordinary politics was at play.

Even the media treatment after her loss was telling. Pundits and politicians bristled whenever she voiced her views on the election, be it on Twitter or in an interview. This kind of reaction was unique in presidential politics. At an event at Rutgers University, Clinton observed, "That began to happen after the election. . . . I was really struck by how people said that to me—you know, mostly people in the press, for whatever reason—like, 'Oh, you know, go away, go away.'" She added, "They never said that to any man who was not elected. I was kind of struck by that."

The Center for American Women and Politics reported that gender was a concern for at least some voters, pointing to "an August 2016 Associated Press piece [which] found that nearly 30% of those surveyed reported a woman president would not be tough enough to handle a military crisis or keep the country safe from terrorism, and just over 20% were skeptical about a woman president's ability to make hard decisions." Moreover, polling from the Public Religion Research Institute "showed Trump supporters much more likely than Clinton voters to say that men and women should 'stick to the roles for which they are naturally suited,' that society has become too soft and feminine, and that society today seems to 'punish men just for acting like men.'"

Clinton's loss could not be explained as just a bad year for Democrats. There remained a gap between how voters regarded a woman running for a legislative seat and one running to be chief executive. Democrats added two women to the Senate and added ten to the House. Some portion of voters, it seemed, felt comfortable with women in legislative seats, but not for the job of commander in chief.

It was not just women who were flummoxed by Clinton's loss; the entire political establishment and the media struggled in the days and weeks following the 2016 election to figure out why their expectations, seemingly reinforced by public polling, had been dashed. The polls were wrong, sort of. National polls in fact were remarkably accurate; Hillary Clinton *did* win the popular vote by more than three million votes or 2.9 percent. Trump however pulled an inside flush in the Electoral College, winning Michigan and Wisconsin in the Upper Midwest and the Rust Belt (Ohio and Pennsylvania). Had Clinton grabbed about 78,000 more votes in Michigan, Wisconsin, and Pennsylvania, she would have won.

Women certainly *did* support the first major party female nominee, but not by a sufficient enough margin to boost Clinton to victory, and not consistently among subgroups of women. Clinton won the overall women's vote (54 to 41 percent), but it was on the strength of her support from Black women (94 percent), the Democratic Party's most reliable voters. Among Hispanic women she did well, but not well enough (69 to 25 percent) to make up for lost ground among other voters; President Obama had won 76 percent of these voters in 2012. Exit polls showed White women voted for Trump by a margin of 52 to 43 percent. Clinton did better than Obama (who lost this group 42 to 56 percent), but she could not deliver a majority of the White women's vote for Democrats, even with misogynist Donald Trump on the ballot.

Subsequent analysis delivered a more nuanced understanding of the White women's vote. Using a postelection survey report of 2016 voters who had cast ballots, the Pew Research Center in 2018 found Trump did win among White women, but not with a majority and by a much narrower margin than had been originally reported. The revised figures showed Trump won White women by a 47 to 45 percent margin. Nevertheless, even if the White women's vote for Clinton was slightly bigger than had been originally thought, there remained a sizable gap in her support between White and nonwhite women. White women were still a critical part of the Republican coalition.

In particular, *evangelical* White women, like evangelical White men, saw Trump as a culmination, not a departure from the past. Since President Reagan, the evangelical culture warriors had cast their lot in with the GOP, which had delivered on conservative judges, gun rights, and "religious liberty" (code words for allowing religious groups or individuals to deny services or benefits based on their religious objections). Trump had his list of conservative-approved Supreme Court nominees, talked a good game on guns, and channeled his base's anger at an increasingly secular world. Trump's complaint about saying "Happy Holidays" instead of "Merry Christmas" was a dog whistle to these voters, both men and women, to signal that he cared about keeping America a Christian nation.

Evangelical White women had marinated in the same toxic brew of right-wing media that White men had been soaking in. Decades of watching Fox News and listening to conservative talk radio preaching fear of immigrants, the horrors of the Clintons, and the supposed rise of anti-Christian bigotry had a powerful effect. Rather than provide a counterweight for a perceived liberal bias, conservative media became a comfy refuge, an alternative reality. The right-wing media bubble stoked animus toward elite universities and antagonism toward mainstream media. In the universe of hermetically sealed conservative media, Trump was coming to rescue them from civilizational destruction—or at least give them a tax cut. In short, tens of millions of White women prioritized religion and race over gender and responded to Trump's message of White grievance.

In retrospect, demographics looked even more decisive and Clinton's shortcomings as a candidate less so than they did in the immediate aftermath of her loss. And four years later we learned that no matter who the Democratic Party nominated, a whole lot of pro-Trump Whites would turn out in crucial states to "own the libs" or to try to return to a bygone era when White men were dominant. The presence of so many stalwart Republicans, including about 70 percent of White evangelicals, were a potent force in American politics, one Trump expertly transformed into a cultlike following. It was not clear *any* Democratic candidate in 2016 could have beaten someone who so expertly inflamed White voters. Nevertheless, postelection analysis tended to focus on Clinton's personal faults and pervasive sexism as the reasons for the Democrats' defeat. Presidential politics in American has become a game of inches; Clinton had simply come up a smidgen short. Few commentators, however, were willing to acknowledge that their entire evaluation of the race and the role of gender would have evaporated if less than forty thousand people in three states switched from Trump to Clinton.

THE RESISTANCE TAKES ROOT

In the immediate aftermath of the 2016 election, women insiders, grassroots activists, and politicians stunned and shaken by Trump's victory moved from mourning to action, from disbelief to determination. The speed with which they did can be attributed to the connectivity afforded by social media and women's affinity for collaboration and relationship-building. Rather than stew alone in anger or fall into depression, women reached out to their female friends, neighbors, and colleagues, sensing they would find personal solace and political solutions in communities in which they already belonged or would build themselves.

Over at EMILY's List, CEO Stephanie Schriock arrived at work the Wednesday morning after the election. At forty-seven, the tall, striking blonde with a booming laugh had taken the reins of EMILY's List, one of the most influential organizations in the progressive world, in 2010. In that role she headed an entity responsible for recruiting and training thousands of pro-choice women to run for office and raising millions of dollars each election cycle. Understandably, the election results were devastating for Schriock.

Having just returned to DC from a horrifying election night in

New York, she turned over in her sleep-deprived brain the events of Tuesday. She had taken the train up to New York on Tuesday afternoon, ready for a historic celebration. Even before arriving in New York, however, a well-connected Democratic woman from Michigan approached Schriock. "We have a problem in Michigan," she had told Schriock. Schriock nervously asked, "The kind of problem that we are going to lose Michigan?" The answer was ominous: "I don't know." Schriock navigated the rest of Election Day with a knot in her stomach, carrying a sense of potential doom. That evening she attended an event for donors and activists in New York with Guy Cecil, chief strategist for the pro–Hillary Clinton presidential super PAC, off-site from the Javits Center. There, she received a frantic call to come back and reassure top donors and party leaders. "But what am I going to tell them?" she had asked. Well, Virginia thankfully had come in for Hillary Clinton. She had motored around a room of donors with a forced smile planted on her face, "Virginia is fine! Virginia is okay!" But beyond that, things were not fine.

As the evening wore on shock, disbelief, and a sense of doom set in. She huddled with a small group of progressive leaders including Cecile Richards, the longtime president of the Planned Parenthood Federation of America, to begin assessing the enormity of the task ahead, starting with how they could reassure their staff, donors, and volunteers to resist despair and stay in the political fight.

When Schriock entered the EMILY's List offices that Wednesday morning, she saw a mess: the floor and desks littered with empty cups, newspapers, and other remnants of a long election night. The smell of stale, uneaten food wafted through the office. Some employees had left early Tuesday night, others had never gone home. The place had the feel of a wake. Some staffers were in tears, many of them sitting or standing in small groups trying to regain their composure. It felt to her like "death." She recognized that staffers, especially the young and idealistic women starting their careers, needed the space to grieve. However, like Tanden at CAP, she felt the urgency to keep moving forward and help her staff remain focused and productive.

She issued two directives to her staff that morning: Clean up the office and get breakfast, a hot breakfast, for everyone. Give them nourishment and something productive to do. That would begin the process of working their way through what still seemed like an awful dream. The first few days would be "like walking through fog" for Schriock and her troops. Schriock pulled her staff from their stupor, avoiding recriminations as to which women did (women of color) and did not (White) support Clinton. She had to focus on motivating her staff and the entire pro-choice movement to come together and prepare for the Trump presidency.

After an election, especially a presidential election, political policy and advocacy groups usually see donations drop to near zero. Indeed, in past years EMILY's List set aside money in its budget to get through the lean postelection months when donors were drained of cash and energy. Nevertheless, to the amazement of the staff, online donations poured in—to the tune of $500,000 on the Wednesday, Thursday, and Friday following the election. This was unprecedented for a political organization—and it was not just the money.

Unbeknownst to senior staff for several weeks after the election, calls from women wanting to run for office had been flooding the organization. The front desk had directed them to the website for EMILY's List where after several clicks, they could find a page to sign up for training to run for office. After Thanksgiving, Schriock's digital staff reported that at this link, which they rarely monitored because it was hard to access, over a thousand women had signed up for training. Buoyed by that stunning figure, Schriock and her staff began to shake off their lingering depression and anxiety.

Schriock's team had been genuinely fearful that all the work over the years encouraging women to run for office would be smashed by Clinton's loss. Schriock realized, "We could not have been more wrong. That one thousand would turn into over five thousand." Now they had the unexpected opportunity to find, train, and elect even more pro-choice women.

In the 2018 cycle, EMILY's List would go on to train over 5,400 women—30 percent of the women trained by EMILY's List since it was founded in 1985—through more than fifty Run to Win in-person trainings and webinars in twenty-five states including Virginia, Texas, Michigan, Maine, California, New York, and Washington, DC. The recruitment and self-recruitment of viable, trained women would need a fundraising effort on a scale even they had never seen. Otherwise, all this effort and enthusiasm would be wasted.

Over at CAP's offices a few blocks away, Neera Tanden understood by early Wednesday morning that progressives had to "reorient" themselves following the election. There would be no Democratic administration to transition to, but rather a colossus—a united Republican Congress and president—dead set on rolling the clock back not only on the Affordable Care Act but the entire Obama administration's legacy on race, gender, gay rights, the environment, and immigration. CAP was an ideas factory but it also had a political action arm, CAP Action Fund. The latter provided a critical hub for a host of progressive groups and causes to coordinate resources, messaging, and tactics. Progressives needed an organized and strategic effort to push back on the new administration. There was no other logical choice, no group but CAP with the heft, money, and personal connections to lawmakers, donors, and activists cultivated through its leaders' decades of experience in Democratic politics. Lawmakers on the Hill would answer their calls; reporters and TV producers would seek them out for comment; and leaders from critical groups ranging from organized labor to hospital associations would trust their data and political judgment.

With impressive speed, major Democratic-aligned entities, including organized labor, immigrant rights groups, women's rights activists, and health care advocates, came together after the election to focus on the Affordable Care Act. Since the president-elect and the Republican leadership in Congress had signaled repealing the ACA would be first on their agenda, Democrats had to begin there. Some advocates were already suggesting "negotiating" over the future of the ACA. Tanden, who had watched Trump transform himself from a failed businessman to reality TV show star to "birther" conspirator in the Republican Party and had followed Republican conservatives in Congress for decades, would have none of it. She told individual groups they could do as they pleased, but she knew Trump would play "domination politics." She cautioned, "If you go into this White House and start negotiating, he's not just going to take the ACA, but he's going to take Social Security, Medicare and Medicaid." She bluntly warned, "It's not like he's just going to take the ransom [the ACA]. He's going to go kill all our children," meaning the entire social safety net. This fight would not end in a negotiated surrender but rather in victory—either for Trump or for them.

By mid-December, CAP's political arm "rebranded." The term "resistance" was already in common use in social media to describe the Trump opposition. It seemed both sufficiently contemporary (lingo familiar to anyone who had ever seen a *Star Wars* movie) and serious (as in the French Resistance during World War II) to serve as the new identity for CAP and for the left more generally.

In a memo entitled "The Path Forward," CAP Action declared, "America did not sign off on a radical-right agenda with Donald Trump's election, and progressive leaders should remember that. . . . The challenge of Trump is that he will offer many targets; as he did throughout his campaign, Trump will continue to pit Americans against Americans. Progressives must defend against these divisive attacks. Indeed, protecting civil rights is a central progressive value, and we cannot ignore it." CAP Action set the terms of debate. "Progressivism that cedes an inch on civil rights is not worth fighting for. But progressivism that ignores the economic needs of the struggling and striving will not be successful either." The memo continued: "As we chart a path forward, economic and democratic renewal must be the cornerstone of both an affirmative progressive policy agenda and an effective response to Donald Trump's disastrous policies." The battle lines were drawn on Trump's domestic agenda.

On the list of worries for progressives, the courts ranked high. The Supreme Court seat left vacant after the death of Scalia—and kept empty by Senate Majority Leader Mitch McConnell's refusal even to grant a hearing for Judge Merrick Garland's confirmation—was a precious commodity for both sides in the abortion debate. With the expected election of Hillary Clinton, NARAL's Hogue and other abortion rights advocates were poised to secure a progressive majority on the Court and give older liberal justices the opportunity to retire and be replaced by a like-minded justice, if they so wished. Instead, activists who had spent forty-five years defending *Roe v. Wade* and its legal progeny could barely comprehend "losing" that seat. Worse, they strongly suspected that aging Justice Anthony Kennedy, appointed by Republican Gerald Ford, would take the opportunity to retire during a Republican administration to allow a Republican president to fill his seat. In addition, one of the aging liberal justices might pass away, opening yet another seat. In particular, they nervously eyed Ruth Bader Ginsburg, praying the diminutive eighty-three-year-old icon, who already had survived two bouts of cancer, could power through four years of Trump.

Hogue held an out-of-office retreat with senior NARAL staff on November 13, 2016. In her mind, if NARAL did not focus on one key issue it would "die a thousand cuts." Other groups could take the lead on health care or executive branch appointments, but NARAL had to lead on the courts.

The Scalia seat would be extremely hard to keep from the clutches of the right wing, but it was impossible *not to fight*. Hogue reasoned that if there was only a 20 percent chance to block a far-right nominee it was worth it. From the start of the administration she understood that the real prize, the fifth vote to uphold abortion rights currently held by Associate Justice Anthony Kennedy, would be where the last stand to defend legal abortion would unfold. Hogue understood that Democrats and progressives did not have a history of coordinated fights on SCOTUS seats. If they did not start to build a campaign infrastructure and come out swinging, the next open seat—which would shift the balance on the Court—would be even harder. "We knew we had to start to play the long game immediately," Hogue recalled. The Scalia seat would be the dress rehearsal for the main event that they were nearly certain would come with the retirement of Kennedy.

To prepare for these Supreme Court fights, NARAL had to engage its members, educate the public, encourage Senate Democrats to hold their ground, and reiterate to pro-choice Republicans that protecting abortion rights was essential. It meant getting its message about the fragility of abortion rights out to the media and the public at large. And it required they research every judge on Trump's list of potential Supreme Court candidates. By Inauguration Day, NARAL had the "book," the bible of research on and the opinions of all twenty-one candidates on Trump's list of Supreme Court judges preapproved by the conservative Federalist Society and blessed by anti-choice forces.

While Democratic insiders like Tanden, Hogue, and Schriock planned how to navigate the Trump era, ordinary women in towns, cities, and rural areas in every state were working through the shock and anger of the election and deciding on their next steps. If politics had never been front and center in their lives, if they had treated it like a spectator sport or shied from electoral politics in favor of policy advocacy, that all had to change. It was an all-hands-on-deck moment. That shift in personal engagement was happening on both small and large scales.

Leah Greenberg, a staunch progressive who had worked on the Hill, in the State Department, and at a nonprofit organization focusing on human trafficking, and her husband Ezra Levin, who had also worked on the Hill and in the nonprofit world, launched, almost by accident, a national progressive behemoth.

Thanksgiving for Leah Greenberg and her husband in 2016 was in Austin, Texas, with relatives. She and her husband met up with friend Sara Clough who ran a Facebook group of progressives. Talking to Clough around the kitchen table in Austin they mulled what to tell despondent progressives. Their Democratic friends and colleagues were restless. Since the election all sorts of progressive Facebook groups buzzed with election postmortems. The chatter on the left ranged from despondent to angry. Mostly, people had questions. What would they now do? How do they fight off the expected assault on the progressive agenda? The conversations became circular: *The situation is intolerable. The moment requires action. The problem is overwhelming and disorienting. We are paralyzed. Rinse and repeat.*

Greenberg and her husband had watched the emergence of the right-wing Tea Party during the Obama years with a mixture of disdain and awe. Greenberg had to give the right its due—these people had figured out how to use the election of Barack Obama as fuel to light a right-wing fire. Progressives said it was all "astroturfing," a top-down operation orchestrated by characters like the Koch brothers. Greenberg knew otherwise. "This was grassroots," she conceded in the wake of the 2016 election. The Tea Party's adept manipulation of patriotic imagery and ideals to call fellow Americans to action intrigued her. Tea Party leaders had gone back to America's founding documents to rally fellow citizens and instill a sense of mission. They had adopted symbols of the past—reviving the eighteenth-century Gadsden "Don't Tread on Me" yellow flag, for example—and taken to quoting *The Federalist Papers*. The Tea Party's focus was on traditional themes like limited government, but their adherents were laser-focused to take down Obamacare as a symbol of the pernicious role of big government.

The left had no organization or mechanism of that kind—*yet*.

Policy advocates for every progressive cause from the environment to abortion were plentiful. Democrats had ideological warriors and PACs, donors and think tanks. MoveOn.org pioneered online organizing and first incorporated social media as a vital campaign tool. However, the left lacked a political mechanism to channel the Resistance's burgeoning anxiety and disappointment in the wake of the election into an effective operation that could engage in direct action. Viewing the Democratic Party apparatus as ineffective at best and generally misguided in its stale, top-down messaging operation they needed a dynamic, easily mobilized organization.

Bombarded by emails from emotionally wrought friends and colleagues, Greenberg reasoned that she and her husband should give their Facebook and real-world friends a guide to help them find constructive things to do, whether it was registering voters or pushing lawmakers on key issues. They put together a twenty-three-page guide, a how-to book, with substantial help from a friend who had experience in labor organizing. What to call it? Well, they needed a united effort that put fine ideological distinctions and disagreements aside. They could not splinter on racial or gender lines and needed a patriotic theme. And thus, they called it "Indivisible"—as in the Pledge of Allegiance's "one nation, indivisible under God."

Greenberg and Levin initially had no grand ambition to redraw the political landscape or change the face of activism, just the desire to give a few Facebook groups a way to channel energies and avoid despondency. After some drafts and redrafts incorporating the ideas of a few dozen friends, Greenberg launched the guide as a Google Doc in mid-December 2016. "Five groups," she recalled. That was the goal. If five Facebook groups found this helpful and used it as a guide for activism that would be a success. Levin sent out a tweet to circulate the guide asking, "Please share w/ your friends to help fight Trump's racism, authoritarianism, & corruption on their home turf."

Within hours the Google Doc crashed. The couple's in-box

overflowed. Greenberg remembered the heady excitement when they recognized how far their work had traveled. She recalled her elation: "They were using the guide in Alaska!" Soon, the mainstream press caught wind of Indivisible. The *New Yorker* came for an interview and heralded their effort in a story entitled "The Crowdsourced Guide to Fighting Trump's Agenda." Another surge in interest followed. Rachel Maddow featured the guide on her show in early January 2017. Again, sign-ups soared. They were far from certain in the 2016 election aftermath that Trump's election could ignite progressives the way Obama's election lit up conservatives, but here were signs of the hunger on the left to do *something*.

The guide gave step-by-step instructions for forming local action groups, holding meetings, and finding causes and candidates to target. The Indivisible document candidly acknowledged that the group was "looking to replicate the Tea Party's success in getting Congress to listen to a small, vocal, dedicated group of constituents." It continued: "The guide is intended to be equally useful for stiffening Democratic spines and weakening pro-Trump Republican resolve."

Indivisible had no real organization for weeks after the guide was released, only Greenberg, her husband, and a few DC friends manning emails. The enterprise soon became unmanageable as a part-time endeavor. Both decided to quit their jobs and devote all their energies to the project. The idea was terrifying, if only because Greenberg and Levin had no guarantee they could survive financially. The couple sent out a fundraising plea to the then 17,000 Indivisible users. Seventy thousand dollars came back. Relieved, they figured that this might just work.

They set up a nonprofit entity, started posting for key staff jobs, and began to build an organization. The initial flood of money allowed them to initiate professional fundraising and grant-seeking. By the end of 2017, they estimated local groups had sprouted to reach possibly 1.5 million people. A year after Trump's election, Indivisible had forty paid staffers, a $12 million budget, and a veritable army of progressive activists, mostly women. And all of this inspired from a kitchen table in Austin and a single Google document.

It soon became obvious to Greenberg and her husband that about three-fourths of the Indivisible activists were women. While women are disproportionately Democratic in affiliation, a gender gap this large was striking. The core animating sentiment for the group in Greenberg's eyes boiled down to a simple idea: "This isn't the country I thought it was." She saw women, and specifically women who were far more secure than Dreamers or LGBTQ members in the military or other groups targeted by Trump, develop a deep sense that our democracy was horribly broken. For the first time in many of their lives, they worried their own position in society was at risk. These women, particularly those with school-aged children, imagined one day getting the "Well what did you do in the Trump era?" question from their children. The compulsion to do *something*, to call out the bullying, and to reaffirm that America was a welcoming nation was a common refrain running through diverse groups, among people of different ages and geographic regions.

For someone like Susan Griffin in Huntsville, Alabama, who had never been involved in politics, Indivisible was a lifeline. Watching Rachel Maddow in January after the election she heard about Indivisible and went to the website to sign up. She decided to schedule a meeting at a local hotel. She texted six friends. Five hundred people showed up. While the Democratic Party had been a disorganized and ineffective "mess" in Alabama, Griffin realized progressives like herself were not entirely isolated. From a local women's march on the day after the inauguration to the battle over the Affordable Care Act to the protests over child separation, her group became a nimble, fearless presence in the Huntsville area. She teamed up with Historically Black Colleges and Universities (HBCUs), the local NAACP, the Southern Poverty Law Center, and immigrant rights groups to pursue their progressive values. "We'd work with anyone" was her mantra, whether that was lending a sound system to a high school group organizing a gun safety event or partnering with HBCUs to register students to vote. She and her group, which grew to two thousand members on Facebook, got out of their comfort zone, traveling to poor Black areas where no one had ever shown up to register voters. They visited bus stops and local clinics to find released ex-felons and help them regain their voting rights. She recalled, "Every single person in Indivisible and at events, to a person, felt their spirit was fed" when they engaged in direct action. The time when she thought politicians had the "secret sauce" or had the luxury to ignore voters was over. Griffin's forces learned "not to hesitate to approach local officials." She discovered that politicians were "just people." She realized, "They are just like us. We have not just the right but the duty and the obligation to contact our leaders." The mystique of all-knowing and competent politicians had faded.

Outside of Indivisible, women were also organizing on a neighborhood and local level. In cities and suburbs around the country, woman spent the weeks just after the election commiserating with friends and neighbors. Women began to process the election results and consider what it meant for their lives. At playgrounds watching their children, in office lunchrooms, at church, and on social media they turned to one another. Republicans who had broken with the GOP, Democratic women who had never engaged in politics, and women who had never registered with a party tried to make sense of the results and wrestle with the realization they had been sleepwalking through democracy's demise.

In a leafy neighborhood of Los Angeles, for instance, Jennifer Levin was among those women who received a political wake-up call on election night. She had first gotten her feet wet in political activism on gun control issues but certainly did not see herself as a full-time activist. On election night, like so many others, she had gone to a friend's house where a small group of women had gathered with their daughters, all decked out in white (the color of suffragettes), ready for a jubilant victory party. As she later recalled, "It was the worst party ever, like a wedding that didn't happen." The results shook her to her core. She spent the next few days writing down her feelings, pouring out her anger at herself and others who had let this happen. She began to shoot off emails to friends, announcing when she was going to a local political event or volunteer at a local shelter or food bank. Someone in her circle learned about Center for Popular Democracy, an umbrella organization founded in 2012 to encourage political activism for progressive causes.

Levin and five of her friends dialed into a national conference call and were blown away. Women from Alaska to Alabama were on the call. Levin was shocked so many people could so easily find ways to channel their political energy. The six texted one another during the call. *Can you believe this? Is this all there is to becoming a full-time activist?* "Boy, it turned out to be a low barrier to entry," she later recounted.

From six people, Levin's group grew to two thousand. They needed a name for what they did, which was meet up with friends to do public service. And so, Hang Out, Do Good was hatched. They found comfort in just being together, in getting out of their tony neighborhoods. Levin saw with her own eyes the racial and economic divide in a city where wealthy Whites had access to good schools and jobs, could rely on friendly police, and enjoyed plentiful retail outlets. What she simply took for granted, she now realized were the benefits of "White privilege." Soon Levin and her allies were helping on campaigns, volunteering in immigrant communities, and going to places in their own city they had never ventured before. Levin's group became a fixture at first-time women candidates' events and were among the thousands of women volunteering for House campaigns.

A similar phenomenon was taking place in Virginia's Seventh Congressional District, where former CIA agent Abigail Spanberger lived. Carol Catron, who had occasionally volunteered for Democratic campaigns in the past, had invited about thirty people to her house a few days after the election to commiserate and get their bearings. One of those guests knew Kim Drew Wright, a poet and author, who had put together a pro-Clinton group (Women for Clinton and Cocktails) during the campaign and was now gearing up for the Trump years. The two groups merged, forming the Liberal Women of Chesterfield County (LWCC), made up of women and an occasional spouse. Generally, the members previously were uninvolved in politics; now they were determined to fight back against the administration. They soon organized chapters, some by the elementary school their children attended, and others by policy topic such as abortion rights or family separations.

Her group worked furiously over the next few years marching and protesting, attending town halls, canvassing, and postcard writing for Democratic candidates, setting up candidate forums, and finding individual causes to support. Catron confessed that in the past she knew about federal offices but not the slew of local elected officials. By 2019 she knew them all. Moreover, in 2019, Democratic candidates competed up and down the ballot for offices from state senate to city clerk for the first time in local and state elections. This was democracy, the sort of citizen-led involvement the Founders had envisioned.

Women in different parts of the country, who had been spurred to enter the world of activism and politics in the Trump era, had similar experiences. They learned that politics was not something other people with specialized insight did. Politics is what *they* did now. People already in politics did not have any specific expertise, and in some cases knew less than these women and their friends did. The notion that politics must be left to "experts" and political insiders melted as women discovered just how lacking in imagination and focus many of these elected officials were. Nevertheless, for millions of women, their interest in political activism might not have blossomed and endured if not for a historic event, one that held out the promise of a mass movement and national political change: the Women's March on January 21, 2017.

CHAPTER 4

MARCH FORWARD

If Trump's election provided the match, the Women's March added fuel to the burgeoning anti-Trump movement's fire. The Women's March was more than a discrete, uplifting experience. Just as Martin Luther King Jr.'s 1963 March on Washington featuring his "I Have a Dream" speech became the civil rights movement's iconic event, the Women's March proved to be a seminal moment for the women of the Resistance. It demonstrated the breadth and intensity of women's outrage and signaled the start of a new period of citizen activism. Participation in the march galvanized individual women, both those who attended and those who watched on TV, into a unified movement larger than their own neighborhoods.

The idea for the march started in Hawaii, on Facebook. Teresa Shook, a retired lawyer, put a post on the Pantsuit Nation Facebook page the day after the election inviting women to participate in a march. Ten thousand people had signed up by the next morning. A journalist and activist, Vanessa Wruble ran with the idea and dubbed it the "Women's March," a deliberate reference to the 1963 event. Cochairs Tamika Mallory, Bob Bland, Carmen Perez-Jordan, and Linda Sarsour soon joined. (In later years, Mallory and Sarsour's anti-Semitic comments made them toxic to the group, forcing them out of leadership roles at the organization that continued to run annual marches.)

The 2017 march unleashed a political tsunami. Millions of women worldwide donned pink hats and carried homemade signs. Trump's inaugural crowd was underwhelming while the turnout for the Women's March shocked the political world. As the *New York Times* reported, the march in DC alone attracted three times the number of people as the inauguration. By one count, there were over 650 marches occurring around the country. The *Washington Post* found the best estimate for participation was over 4.1 million people nationwide or nearly 1.3 percent of the total population had attended a march. (That is roughly the entire population of Oregon and larger than the population of twenty-four states.)

Washington insiders initially had been skeptical about a march. Few if any Democratic officials or leaders of established progressive groups knew who was running it. If they were going to hold this thing a day after the inauguration, where were they going to get hotel rooms? Who was going to come to this? Professional politicians and consultants had little confidence that a ragtag operation could turn out a significant crowd under the circumstances.

Even the newly elected Democratic Senator Kamala Harris of California, one of the four who would appear onstage to speak at the march, had done some gut checks with colleagues. Newly elected women lawmakers called one another. Are you going to this thing? Senator Harris asked her female colleague if this was "something." A lot of elected leaders shrugged and seemed skeptical. Neither Harris nor her women colleagues anticipated this would be a historic date. "No one knew anything because it was so organic," she later recalled. It seemed that the civil rights movement had come full circle. Harris's mother marched in the 1960s; now her mother's best friend from Berkeley attended the Women's March—with her granddaughters—to watch Harris. She could sense this was a possible inflection point. "Anyone watching this could see this had momentum," Harris observed. "The challenge [was] to sustain it."

EMILY's List executives and other progressive leaders confessed later they had not seen the potential for success. Slowly, however, it dawned on them that something out of the ordinary was happening. A friend of EMILY's List CEO Schriock from the Department of Homeland Security called her to say this was going to be a *really* big deal. Schriock asked, "What, like 200,000?" No, her friend laughed. "You don't have so many buses for 200,000 people." More like half a million would arrive by bus. Schriock was flabbergasted. Word about the march circulated in progressive networks; the buzz started to build and attract her interest. After years of extolling fellow citizens to get involved in politics and to tell politicians what they wanted, professional politicians were nevertheless shocked when an immense, authentic grassroots movement rose up to do just that. In their minds, the march could not be *that* big because no one they knew in official DC had been in on the ground floor planning it.

Schriock and her team debated whether and how EMILY's List should become involved more directly in the march. They decided that on the day after the march, EMILY's List would hold a training session for prospective candidates at a DC hotel. It seemed improbable that women who had been marching all day and partying all night would get up at eight a.m. to meet for four hours of training in a hotel basement. Nevertheless, they figured that for a small investment they might reach out to a few hundred women. They still worried the turnout would be even lower but planned to cut down the space if the turnout was small. Instead, over a thousand women showed up, and organizers were forced to stop letting in attendees. That morning Schriock and her team watched slack-jawed as women streamed into the room. The attendees' enthusiasm and excitement were infectious. Yes, here was confirmation that women who had flocked to the march did not see it as a one-day event, but as the start of a new stage in their lives.

The organizers' original plan was to have no elected women speak. Schriock advised the organizers that it was critical to show that elected women were with the marchers and were still relevant to the battles ahead. They did not need a lot of women, she counseled, just a few. EMILY's List helped broker the appearance of four women—Rep. Maxine Waters (D-CA) and Senators Tammy Duckworth (D-WI), Kamala Harris (D-CA), and Kirsten Gillibrand (D-NY)—to speak onstage at the main DC march. Two would eventually run for the presidency, two would be included on the short list for vice president. One would make history.

Like many progressive leaders, Schriock wanted desperately to get out of the pre-inauguration maelstrom of Washington, DC. Schriock traveled to Miami on the Friday before the march for a progressive gathering to discuss and coordinate their strategy for the Trump years. With the billionaire Koch brothers' right-wing confabs as a model, progressive money man and Media Matters founder David Brock gathered 120 activists at Miami's Turnberry Isle for panels, speeches, and fundraising to plot out their game plan for the next four years. Progressive lawyers such as Norman Eisen put together a litigation strategy for progressive activists and Democratic state attorneys general, which would be the inspiration for dozens of suits against the Trump administration. If nothing else, the gathering raised the morale of progressive activists and cemented their conviction that for the next four years whatever internal differences they had would be set aside in the common effort to thwart Trump's agenda, win back Congress, and oust him from the presidency. On Schriock's flight back to DC, to her amazement, the plane was packed with women in pink hats. The mood was joyous and rowdy. Recalling her trip, she exclaimed, "A party plane to DC?! This might be a 'thing' after all."

The march proved to be a life-changing event for thousands and perhaps millions of women. Weeks earlier, Sarah Schulz in Midland, Michigan—just like so many other women—was sitting dumbfounded on her couch on election night after sending her kids to bed. Born in Flint, Michigan, she had spent time in New York but moved back to Midland about ten years earlier after losing her job. She had been politically interested but not personally involved. The 2016 race, however, caught her attention. She was a Clinton supporter, excited by the possibility of a woman president and aghast at Trump's candidacy, if for no other reason than her fear that her eleven-year-old daughter would experience a misogynist president who would do and say anything to gain power. She and her daughter had studied the issues and followed the candidates; Schulz's Facebook group exchanged news items and tracked the race's progress.

As election night dragged on, the celebratory cake she and her daughter purchased sitting on the table uneaten, she sat transfixed long after her family went to bed. Finally, she took her cell phone to bed, toggling back and forth from one news site to another, until Michigan was called. It was over. She woke up the next morning still in a state of disbelief. She had to break the news to her daughter, who knew how strongly Schulz felt about Trump. Her daughter asked, "Are we going to be all right?" A parent could reassure her child, but Schulz and the women in her Facebook group who had followed the race were in tears and turmoil.

The days after the election were both disorienting and reaffirming for Schulz. She and some of her Facebook friends were despondent, but most of all stunned. How did this happen? What had they missed? Years later Allison Wilcox, one of the original members of the Midland group, would recall in a column for her local paper, "We were in shock that the America that had elected Barack Obama in 2008 and 2012 had somehow become the America that had elected Donald Trump in 2016. We felt that Trump had won by appealing to people's fears and prejudices, and we wanted to resist that." In those first days and weeks they found strength in their collective grief. "We wanted America to continue its forward progress, striving to live up to the ideals in our founding documents—especially the ideals of equality and justice, regardless of gender, religion, skin color, or economic status," Wilcox said. "We came out because we believe that women's rights are human rights and human rights are women's rights."

The women decided to meet at the local church to console one another and think this through. Eighteen women showed up, which in a conservative town pleasantly surprised Schulz. The first meeting was cathartic as they shared their bewilderment but also their surprise. Schulz mused that many of them had felt alienated in an overwhelmingly Republican city. Did their neighbors, the carpool moms and soccer dads, really buy what Trump was selling? How could the country have embraced a bully and a bigot? Talking with other women going through the same range of emotions was reassuring, providing confirmation they were not alone in the Trump era. As they talked, they became more determined to not simply throw up their hands and retreat to private life. They promised to meet again soon.

The group kept meeting for a couple weeks, but the members soon decided they needed a plan. They needed to *do* something. Schulz liked to say that "the antidote for despair was action." Fortunately for her band of friends and for hundreds of thousands and then millions of women, the march was a ready-made event for them, the first chance to publicly *do* something.

Schulz's group hooked up with a similar group in Saginaw County to rent buses for the trip to the march in DC. Their group of eighteen had grown to one hundred. As they departed, a local march was setting up in Midland, which came as a shock to the progressive women who imagined there were no other Democrats in their conservative town. The simple discovery that some of their neighbors and work colleagues were progressives did much to bolster the spirit of these and other self-organizing women.

It was hard for Schulz to explain to family and friends why she was going. She struggled to respond when they repeatedly asked what she hoped to accomplish at the march. Ultimately, she decided, she needed to figure out what she was going to do in the Trump era. Trump, in her mind, was a symptom of something deeper that had gone wrong. "Here I was, an able-bodied person who could make the trip," she told herself. She would go and figure out the "why" of her journey along the route. Like so many thousands of women, the march took on the feel of a pilgrimage, a leap of faith, and an effort to find something bigger than oneself to latch on to. The trip took on a festive air as dozens upon dozens of women in cars, trucks, trailers, and buses—people just like them—were on the road, all going to the march. She felt reenergized simply to be doing something, literally putting one foot in front of the other.

The size and scope of the march took her breath away. This was the inspiring experience she needed to gain a sense of mission, although she would be hard-pressed to define precisely what that mission would look like. The high point of the march for Schulz, ironically, was the local march back in Midland, which was four hundred people strong. Certainly, there were more like-minded citizens in her town than she had thought. She returned home, grew her network, dubbed the Women of Michigan Action Network, to two thousand people. The group's cofounder Jen Ciolino told the local high school newspaper in February 2017, "A number of us had experienced, some of the, as I would say, the emboldened hate that came out as a consequence of the election rhetoric." She shared, "My own family was directly targeted. I have a mixed-race family, we were targeted while we were coloring the sidewalk in front of our church." She recalled the "hateful, racial slurs yelled at us, along with Trump's name yelled at us," adding, "This was here in Midland. We were fearful of what kind of policy [he] was going to drive and what kind of rhetoric was there going to be."

A YEAR LATER Schulz told her local paper the *Midland Daily News* she was running for state representative in the Ninety-eighth District. "I never considered running for office until over a year ago," she said. "More and more and more I've considered it since the last presidential election." She explained, "I'm a mom, a wife and a businesswoman. I'm here to try and fix the system that is so broken and harmful." She lost by only about 1,500 votes in a Republican stronghold. She ran again in 2020. However, with a much larger turnout in a presidential year, she lost by about 8,400 votes.

Other women just dipping a toe into full-time activism had similarly inspiring experiences at the Women's March. Carol Catron from Virginia's Seventh Congressional District went up to DC the night before the march with her sister and son. They stayed with another sister and in the morning went to the Metro to ride to the march location. They were astounded by what they saw. It took them one and a half hours to get through the line that had backed up onto the escalator. On the ride, the Metro driver told his passengers over the PA system how proud he was of them and assured them they were making a difference.

When Catron's group arrived at the L'Enfant Plaza Metro stop a huge cheer went up from the crowd outside as if the home team had just scored a winning touchdown. The same enthusiastic welcome greeted each new train packed to the gills with marchers.

Catron heard over and over again from women attending the event, especially older and married women from heavily Republican districts: "I thought I was the only one." The march provided Catron and others affirmation that they were not isolated. Instead, they felt they were participating in something outside their own circle of friends, helping to transform apolitical or barely political women into full-time activists. By 2019, Catron would go to so many marches, she would sometimes forget which cause was on which day. She joked she periodically had to ask herself, "So, wait, what am I protesting on Friday?"

Only in retrospect did women recognize the march's long-term impact not only on themselves but on the country. Groups of women from churches, clubs, and schools, mothers and daughters and even some grandmothers, entire offices of workers, and blocks of neighbors found themselves in a similar spot, eager to do something to reaffirm they were not going to give up despite a devastating election loss. The march was both a way to heal and a way to move past the election into the Resistance, which for many would become a full-time avocation or job.

In my reporting for the *Washington Post*, women whom I interviewed told me at the time they "wanted to be with other women" and felt compelled to do "something." Others sensed it was history in the making and did not want to miss it. Still others wanted to show their daughters that the message of empowerment and independence they had been raised on was more than just words. Some just wanted to demonstrate that they had not been cowed into silence; they would be in the streets, in the voting booths and on the trail themselves.

Years later, Speaker Nancy Pelosi recalled, "They marched and [then] they ran, they voted. Everybody had her own story." The impact of the march was so great, Pelosi believed—as Harris did—because "it was spontaneous, and it was organic." While women had their own top issues, be it the environment or gun control or health care, they discovered their shared values and discovered their own "why"—the reason for their determination to organize, to become activists, and to run for office. The march embodied one of Pelosi's favorite sayings: "We don't agonize. We organize."

For women who had not been politically engaged or uninvolved for years the sense of affirmation that they were not alone was critical. Randi Weingarten, head of the American Federation of Teachers, had been organizing all her adult life. This was different. The march told millions of women who would never have otherwise met that they were not the only one feeling the urgency of the moment. "They were not only not alone in the country; they weren't alone in Anchorage" (or whatever city they had come from). "The first women's march was a reaction to the cruelty of Trump," already in evidence, Weingarten sensed, something that transcended normal political divisions.

As I watched pink-hatted women gather and march in unbelievably large numbers, I felt a surge of pride. As bad as things had gotten, millions of women were not giving up. I was in awe of their organizational prowess that allowed them to pull off not just one enormous DC spectacle but marches in cities and towns across the country. I would not don a pink hat nor form a political network but I could cover those who did. I could track the rising female stars in the Democratic Party. And I could, like these women, find common cause with fellow Americans who in the past might have been on the other side of some policy argument. I joked that I longed for the day when I could argue with progressives about the appropriate top marginal tax rate. All that seemed so small and irrelevant when democracy's future hung in the balance. I had to expand my circle of contacts and sources, reset my own expectations about grassroots politics, and recognize that the reaction to Trump was itself a once-in-a-generation phenomenon.

Without this dramatic, massive event the day after the inauguration, the anti-Trump counterrevolution that followed might never have gotten off the ground—and it might not have stirred some Republican women to rethink their political affiliation. While most Republican women in the House and Senate and in right-wing advocacy groups fell into line behind Trump, a small but influential group of women in media and in political consulting and even some who had worked on losing presidential campaigns in 2016 realized they no longer felt at home in Trump's GOP. The march reassured them they had not lost their minds; there was in fact something terribly wrong in our politics. And still, the question remained for anti-Trump Republicans, as it did for Democrats, whether they could convert an impressive onetime expression of angst into the beginning of something consequential.

CHAPTER 5

THE FIRST BIG BATTLES OF 2017

Throughout 2017, the Resistance to Trump operated on multiple levels. At times, these efforts overlapped and reinforced one another. The Democratic Party and allies like the Center for American Progress (CAP) waged the fight in Congress to preserve the Americans with Disabilities Act (ADA), other groups such as the American Civil Liberties Union (ACLU) litigated against the administration, and new entities like Indivisible operated in their own lane.

The Resistance engaged sooner than many of its participants expected. Just a week after the inauguration, Trump issued his first iteration of the Muslim travel ban he had promised his supporters during the campaign. With little planning or interagency cooperation and a vaguely worded executive order, panic and mass confusion played out in airports all over the country. Something else was present—throngs of ordinary Americans protesting the exclusion of immigrants from majority Muslim countries, a cruel and ill-conceived measure that swept up students, doctors, grandmothers, college professors, former translators for the US military, and refugees. With the help of intense media coverage, the protests grew. Politicians came out to airports, as did immigrant rights groups and their lawyers. Spurred by scenes of distraught visitors and buoyed by the outpouring of concern from ordinary Americans, still others joined the throngs for three days of protest in late January 2017.

Indivisible's leadership seized the opening to organize its members, provide guidelines for lawful protest, and show the face of the Resistance. Indivisible relied upon local groups around the country to get the word out to their newly energized activists. Back in DC, Indivisible founders and volunteers fielded hundreds of questions via emails and texts. Questions about the ban and requests for help were coming in faster than the skeletal staff of volunteers at Indivisible's headquarters could respond. They were "fanatical," as Leah Greenberg put it, about responding to all the inquiries. They were building a bottom-up organization, so their primary task was to keep people engaged; that meant the group's leadership needed to show their members the organization was responsive and supportive. Greenberg and the Indivisible leadership decided to hold a conference call to get out some basic information and hear from immigration experts to explain the exact contours of the ban, explain the legal challenges that would follow, and provide advice on peaceful protest. To their amazement, some thirty-five thousand people joined the call. It took thirty minutes just to get everyone on the line.

Sure enough, thousands of protesters appeared at airports in Dallas, Boston, Phoenix, Detroit, Birmingham, and elsewhere. In Syracuse, Indivisible members turned out a thousand people at the airport. The Herndon-Reston, Virginia, group turned out hundreds at Dulles International Airport. Indivisible groups called on activists to protest at offices of lawmakers, including North Carolina Republican Senator Thom Tillis. Activists from Metairie Indivisible, Indivisible New Orleans, the Lower Ninth Ward, and other progressive organizations gathered outside Louisiana Republican Senator Bill Cassidy's office, drawing local news coverage. San Francisco Indivisible could soon boast that after thousands attended the Women's March in DC, throngs of their members engaged in airport protests. These Indivisible activists then used social media to spread word that they had begun to "meet regularly with our Members of Congress and make thousands of phone calls to their offices to pressure them to do everything in their power to counter the policies and politics of Trumpism." Activists soon learned each event was an opportunity to gain news coverage and collect contact information about who their members were and what they wanted to do. The protests themselves encouraged discussions among members not only about immigration but a range of progressive issues.

The spontaneous protests were infectious. For its members, mostly women, this was their first true protest experience. Some had participated in the Women's March in DC or in marches in their home states, but that was a far cry from swarming airports and facing off against security forces amid a sea of cameras and microphones. "Aayah Khalaf, a Muslim American, was sitting at home watching the protest on television when she and her friend studying from Egypt decided to join the rally," CBS News reported. "It was her second time joining a protest. The first one was the Women's March. 'It's not just against Muslims. It against environmental rights and human rights overall. I think everybody has to stand up against this,' said Khalaf, 29." *Rolling Stone* reported, "Some protesters make last-minute signs with pizza boxes. At one point, a car pulls over to hand curbside protesters a box of Dunkin' Donuts hot chocolate through the window." Scenes of jammed airports played on local news outlets, spurring people literally to get off the couch, hop in the car, and join the protests. The *New York Times* reported on about forty Muslim ban protests, many attended and advertised by Indivisible chapters in local communities. Indivisible was also among the groups organizing a huge rally in Lafayette Square across from the White House.

Susan Griffin, the Huntsville, Alabama, activist, took a group to the Huntsville International Airport, one of her group's first events. She had never been engaged in any political events until her bus trip to a women's march in New York City. This was the first of many events relating to the administration's immigration policies that would command her interest. Griffin believed deeply that "these are issues where [you] have to be willing to fight for people like you." This kind of effort played out in dozens of communities and showed the breadth and determination of the Resistance.

This early call to action helped local group leaders assess the most effective ways to communicate with their members; members learned how to deploy quickly and protest peacefully. The media and country learned there were plenty of Americans willing to turn into self-directed citizen activists. For those women who were new to political activism it was a heady experience.

More important, it was their first taste of success. Local and national media covered their events, while progressive legal groups sent lawyers to the airports and filed suits. When a federal court in Brooklyn blocked the first version of the ban and allowed people who arrived with visas to enter, they had their first tangible victory. *Mother Jones* called it a "stunning defeat" for Trump. A federal court in Massachusetts soon followed. The ACLU, which pursued four of five initial cases, crowed, "Our courts today worked as they should as bulwarks against government abuse or unconstitutional policies and orders. On week one, Donald Trump suffered his first loss in court."

I watched, like most of the country, with a mixture of amazement and pride. Here were ordinary people standing up to their government on behalf of people they did not know and would likely never have met if not for the political provocation provided by the administration. It was hard not to be thrilled at the prospect that ordinary people were not giving up but were instead, some for the first time in their lives, becoming active citizens.

In addition to protests at airports, Indivisible groups also started to show up at both Republican and Democratic senators' offices on issues beyond immigration. While there, they implored senators not to confirm Trump's unqualified and extreme nominees. If they did not win those confirmation fights, they certainly gained practice, learned to recognize the senators' staff, and engaged with local media. They also had put lawmakers on notice that there would be accountability for their votes.

In the first months of the Trump presidency, there was one essential battle that dominated the raft of progressive worries about the new administration. Virtually every establishment Democrat and progressive grassroots leader knew that if the administration succeeded in repealing the Affordable Care Act (ACA)—or if Trump had instead kicked off his term with a popular, bipartisan measure like infrastructure—the Resistance might crumble. When Trump took aim at the one issue that was absolutely certain to galvanize the Resistance, they recognized the stakes could not be higher.

As early as December 2016, Democratic activists and members of Congress knew health care would be the first and perhaps most critical fight in the new administration. Trump met with congressional Republicans leaders within weeks of his election and signaled that repealing the ACA would be their first initiative. This came as no surprise, since Republicans had spent the last seven years promising to rip it out root and branch. Now flush with victory, Republicans plunged forward.

At a policy meeting among progressive groups, CAP's head, Neera Tanden, and other progressive leaders "gamed" out the chances of holding on to Obama's health care legacy. They put their chances at fifty-fifty. Had Trump reached out to Democrats to negotiate the terms of surrendering the ACA, it might have been hard to keep red state Democratic senators in the fold and might have cooled the passion of activists. With Trump defiantly pushing ahead with a Republicans-only initiative, however, the Democrats had an objective they thought all Democratic lawmakers and activists could agree on: preserving health care coverage for tens of millions of Americans.

Until the Trump era, Tanden's greatest professional achievement arguably had been enactment of the ACA. Now, when it came time to prevent the demise of the historic legislation Tanden was arguably the linchpin, the leader of a wide array of Democratic groups who held the line on repealing the ACA.

The first order of business was to keep red state Democrats on board. Tanden and Minority Leader Charles Schumer worked the phones talking to red state senators like Jon Tester from Montana, Claire McCaskill from Missouri, and Heidi Heitkamp from North Dakota. Trump had won in all three states, and senators from all three would be on the ballot in 2018. However, all were Democrats who passionately supported the first guaranteed health care system for able-bodied, non-senior adults. Tanden knew the popular perception is "to see all these guys like weather vanes," but here principle outweighed any short-term partisan considerations. They were fully aware support for the ACA might cost them their seats, yet none could imagine allowing the Trump tide to wash over them and sweep vulnerable Americans out to sea. While Tanden and Schumer kept their conversations with red state lawmakers going, the Service Employees International Union (SEIU) put up ads in defense of the health care act in December. There was then no turning back from an all-out war.

CAP, SEIU, and the other coalition members such as Families USA and Protect Our Care (which even before the election had raised money to run ads in defense of the ACA) would be the critical inside players. They first did their homework. Tanden and her colleagues talked to Never Trump Republicans and to ordinary Trump voters. They ran focus groups and conducted polling. They learned that unlike the DC Republicans, Trump voters in red states and elsewhere enjoyed the benefits of the ACA, including the expansion of Medicaid. They had voted for Trump because they actually believed they would get a *better* health care plan. Once the progressive health care coalition learned that many of his voters received subsidies through the ACA or accessed Medicaid benefits, they could plan out a strategy to not only rally Democrats but to motivate Trump's own voters to oppose the ACA's repeal.

Tanden was convinced, contrary to conventional wisdom, that

Trump had not created a post-truth political environment. She believed and constructed a strategy on the premise that "facts really matter." The health care coalition carefully monitored each Republican proposal, calculated its impact on seniors, on rural Americans, and on others who had benefited from the ACA. Experts and analysts did the number crunching; the political operation would figure out how to weaponize that data.

CAP's experts could collect and analyze proposals and break down the effect of various schemes on individual states. This data, however, had to get to activists and the media if the progressive coalition was going to cajole lawmakers into preserving the ACA. CAP's solution was to create a Google Doc, which it made available to the press, Democratic-aligned groups, and activists to illustrate the harm done to Americans in individual states and congressional districts if the ACA were to disappear. That document would be downloaded more than *eight million* times. Development and promulgation of that document may have been the single biggest factor in beating back repeal of the ACA.

When the Congressional Budget Office came out with an analysis that twenty-two million people would lose health care under the House Republicans' plan, CAP and its coalition partners got the word out to progressive groups and the media. They had experts available (including Tanden) to go on TV and talk to journalists about the bill's impact. CAP and other experts pumped out the findings on social media. Sure enough, the next day on the front pages of local newspapers from Oklahoma to Ohio, headlines blared that millions would lose their health care if the Republican plan passed. Trump voters, like the rest of Americans, began to grasp that their own health care was at risk. If cuts to rural hospitals went through, they would close—leaving residents without a nearby hospital and their localities without a significant employer. If Medicaid funding failed to keep up with inflation and population growth, their elderly relatives' nursing home care would decline. And if the changes eliminated subsidies for people who were able to buy their own health care insurance plans for the first time, they might once again be priced out of the market. In short, what otherwise would have been an abstract political argument, now became personal—and frightening.

The health care coalition could estimate just how many people in Maine or Alaska would be harmed. Twenty million nationwide who would lose coverage was a statistic, but it would be radioactive news when local news reported fifteen thousand voters getting kicked off their insurance in a specific congressional district or ninety thousand in a small state.

When two of the Republicans most likely to vote against repeal, Senators Susan Collins of Maine and Lisa Murkowski of Alaska, read their home state newspapers, they saw headlines and TV ads blaring that Medicaid cuts would ravage opioid treatment programs and senior care. The *Portland Press Herald* in Maine carried headlines like "Move to Repeal Affordable Care Act 'Just Inviting Chaos,' Maine Leaders Say," while the *Bangor Daily News* warned in July, "The current Senate legislation would repeal parts of Obamacare, roll back its expansion of the Medicaid government health care program for the poor, eliminate most of Obamacare's taxes and replace Obamacare insurance subsidies with a system of tax credits to help individuals buy private health insurance." In Murkowski's home state, the *Anchorage Daily News* reported, "If Congress were to repeal portions of the Affordable Care Act supporting the individual market and Medicaid expansion, roughly 54,000 Alaskans would be without health coverage within two years."

Tanden also recognized Republicans were making a fateful mistake. In constructing the House bill, Republicans added caps on Medicaid expenditures, which would amount to massive cuts in available funding over time. Tanden knew that if voters understood Medicaid did not cover only poor people but seniors in nursing homes, addiction treatment, and acute care for newborns, the bill would face a storm of protest. When Republicans released their plan, CAP and its allies worked furiously to push that information out to the states.

In addition, the health care coalition came to understand the impact Medicaid cuts would have on rural hospitals. "Rural hospitals serve millions of Americans, including some of the nation's most vulnerable populations. In emergency situations, their close proximity can save lives," CAP's website explained in July. "Even in nonemergencies, rural hospitals are often the center of health care delivery systems where community members can access a full range of health care and social services. Yet the Senate's Better Care Reconciliation Act (BCRA), which would repeal the Affordable Care Act (ACA) and drastically cut federal support for the Medicaid program, would disproportionately harm rural hospitals and the communities they serve."

The Associated Press soon echoed the warning ("Rural Hospitals Face Uncertainty with Health Care Proposals") as did *Forbes* ("Obamacare Repeal Could Cripple Rural Hospitals and Lead to More Closures"). Democratic and Republican lawmakers from rural regions and states knew how critical these hospitals were to rural communities. Cut Medicaid and/or the ACA and the rural hospital would have insufficient reimbursements to keep open. Once a local hospital shuttered, whole towns could collapse. In Montana, for example, a critical red state Democrat Jon Tester told a home state paper, the *Billings Gazette*, that the repeal measure was a "dangerous bill that will raise rates, kick hardworking folks off their health plans and shutter rural hospitals." And sure enough "The Montana Hospital Association strongly opposed Republicans' attempt in July to repeal ACA." Likewise, the rural hospital issue became critical for Murkowski. *Vox* reported, "Alaska struggles with the highest health care costs in the country. But it expanded Medicaid to cover its poorest residents and saw tens of thousands of people sign up for private coverage. The consequences of repealing the law were, in the end, too much for Murkowski to take." The impact of Medicaid cuts on rural hospitals became a defining issue for many lawmakers from rural red states.

While CAP managed the inside game, Indivisible burst onto the scene with grassroots activism for the health care fight. Greenberg and her team did not believe at the onset that they could pull off a win in the ACA battle since Republicans controlled both houses of Congress and the White House. However, they knew it was essential that progressives fight every step of the way and leave it all on the field. If they did not, the entire premise of the organization—political change is possible from the grassroots—would be eviscerated. Even if they fought and lost, they would ensure their voices were heard, force lawmakers to look over their shoulders, and show their members what collective action looked like. Their mantra became: "The ACA is everything."

Many local Indivisible groups wanted to organize sit-ins in members' offices. Indivisible initially did not want to promote these out of concern they would turn off average Americans, but when members took matters into their own hands and began sit-ins on their own, Indivisible offered advice and support. An Indivisible group from Ohio came down to stage a sit-in at Ohio Republican Senator Rob Portman's offices. Indivisible's policy director Angel Padilla and other Indivisible leaders joined them.

As attention turned to the Senate, Indivisible launched the website Trumpcare to direct members to key lawmakers whom they could call or visit. They issued requests each day to direct calls to specific members. Local groups organized hundreds of local rallies in key states.

Indivisible chapters in every state implored their members to let their voices be heard. Minuteman Indivisible in Lexington, Massachusetts, visited lawmakers' offices and held a protest when Speaker Paul Ryan came to town. Indivisible groups in Michigan announced a final push in the summer to rally support for the ACA and pressure lawmakers. In Maine, Indivisible groups were up and running as early as February and would keep pressure on Collins, a key Republican, through the final vote. In state after state, ordinary citizens were enlisted to put the screws on lawmakers.

This was direct democracy in its purest form. Among the people making the calls, showing up at lawmakers' offices and town halls, and turning out for protests, a large percentage were college-educated women between thirty-five and fifty-five, many with young children. These women had health care coverage for themselves, but they were concerned other families would lose theirs.

Outside of Indivisible, engaged networks of women also joined the ACA fight. In Chesterfield County, Virginia, Carol Catron and her Liberal Women of Chesterfield County recognized health care as the first big fight of the new Trump era. A large number decided to attend the second and last town hall in May held by Republican representative David Brat of Virginia's Seventh Congressional District. Brat seemed to have perfected the art of keeping his constituents at bay. The event was hosted by state Senator Amanda Chase at a megachurch in a very Republican part of the district. Voters needed a ticket to attend and just to get into the parking lot. Attendees had to present photo ID and the ticket before passing by multiple police cars stationed outside the event. Some in Catron's group organized a "die in" protest across the street to highlight the concerns of people with preexisting conditions.

Catron had her ticket and passed through the Brat security phalanx. She entered, thinking only the truly devoted Brat supporters would attend. The reality was quite different. The town hall organizers instructed the crowd not to interrupt, not to carry signs, and not to demonstrate. "This is *my* town hall," Chase declared at one point. That did not work. The crowd was angry and ignored Chase's threats to sit down and shut up or face expulsion. Catron could feel the tension rising in the room. Chase tried to tell a story about how she and Brat had met. The crowd grumbled. Around Catron, a bunch of women sarcastically began chanting, "We don't care!" To Catron, Brat seemed to laugh off their anger. This was a wake-up call: Some of these Republican lawmakers were arrogant and deeply out of touch with their own voters.

The first critical votes on the ACA came in the spring. After failing to garner the necessary votes and pulling the bill from the

House floor Republicans regrouped and finally passed its bill in May. They celebrated their win at the Rose Garden. It was a rookie move, creating video of lawmakers celebrating their "accomplishment" of taking away health care.

The action then moved to the Senate. The health care coalition had target lists for Senate Republicans (as they had for the House) with names of Republicans they thought were persuadable, including Rob Portman of Ohio and Shelley Moore Capito of West Virginia. At one time the Senate list reached as many as ten people, including very right-wing members like Sen. Rand Paul who thought the bill did not go far enough in privatizing health care. The hope Paul and other extreme anti-government right-wingers would hold true to their libertarian convictions quickly faded.

The Monday before the critical Senate vote the Capitol was abuzz with news that Arizona Republican Senator John McCain, who had been at home for brain cancer treatment, was coming back to the Hill. Tanden and her team foraged for any information on his vote. Was he there for the Defense appropriations bill or was he there to cast a history-making vote against his party's single most important legislative initiative? Coalition members launched calls to Arizona's governor and the Arizona Chamber of Commerce, who would oppose the bill primarily because of the effect on rural hospitals. That, the coalition leaders hoped, would provide some cover to McCain to vote against the bill. There was no news to be found however about McCain's decision.

Thursday night, Tanden was at CNN's studios for an 11:30 p.m. appearance in advance of the decisive ACA vote scheduled for the early morning. She got a call from Senator Schumer's chief of staff Mike Lynch, who told her they were going to lose. He urged her to call the coalition partners. They had lost Portman, Shelly Moore Capito, and others. Tanden asked about McCain. "I don't know where McCain is," Lynch responded. Tanden shot back, "That may be, but do you know how he's voting?" "But Neera, boatloads of Democratic tears have been cried waiting for John McCain to do the right thing." Tanden asked her team if she should alert her partners. They decided if the news was bad, everyone would know soon enough. They decided to wait. Tanden and her team grasped at straws. A TV shot caught McCain with a Cheshire cat grin going into the Senate elevator. Well, that might be positive, right? McCain certainly did provoke buckets of Democratic tears, but this time tears of joy after his historic thumbs-down on the Senate floor.

The Resistance had secured the bare minimum number of votes to defeat the repeal, with no margin for error. They had kept enough pressure on Collins and Murkowski to prompt them to defy intense pressure from the White House and right-wing activists who threatened to challenge them when they next came up for reelection. They pumped up the rural hospital issue that was important to McCain and to red state Democrats. Remarkably, they kept every Democrat on board, including red state moderates who would put their own careers at risk.

The Resistance was ecstatic that, although it was now undermined by the Trump administration's regulations and neglect, the ACA would remain in place. More important, this battle became the first tangible way to "beat Trump." The anger and disappointment from the election had been turned into a positive: an extraordinary upset win. The vote meant *everything* to those toiling in the Resistance. "The most psychologically important thing for the Resistance was that people actually believed there was hope in humanity," Tanden later recalled. Here was a single act of "decency" that would provide hope and keep enthusiasm high. In her eyes it was a huge lift, "fundamental" to shoring up the ground troops.

Moreover, arguably the greatest legislative upset in modern American politics confirmed Indivisible's theory of political change. With smart advocacy and granular data, Americans at the grassroots could change the agenda and indeed the entire balance of power in American politics, even with the White House and both houses of Congress in GOP hands.

CHAPTER 6

WARM-UP ELECTIONS FOR 2018

Democrats saw two chances in 2017 to mount what amounted to dress rehearsals for the 2018 midterms. The first came in Virginia, which along with New Jersey holds its statewide and state legislative races in "off-off" years, that is odd-numbered years. Off-off elections were a legacy of Jim Crow, a deliberate attempt to depress turnout and give outsized voting strength to older, White voters, who vote regularly, in comparison to younger, poorer, and nonwhite voters who are less likely to turn out. That was a pattern the Democrats had to break if they were going to pick up seats in the state legislature and win the governorship. They also recognized that an impressive victory would serve as a model for congressional midterms, when Democrats across the country also would have to register irregular voters and get to the polls to overcome Republicans' reliable and largely White turnout.

Virginia Democrats in 2017 had reason for optimism, including recent state voting history. They had a run of three consecutive Democratic governors and other statewide officeholders, a winning streak that reflected the state's tilt from red to blue. The Democratic shift was in large part due to the recent population surge in more liberal Northern Virginia and the influx of high-tech workers from other states and abroad. Over the last decade a steady flow of white-collar government employees and government contractors had moved to the suburbs and exurbs of Washington, DC. Between Washington, DC, and Dulles International Airport, a corridor of new office buildings employed thousands of these workers, who in turn drew doctors, lawyers, accountants, and other professionals to the area. By the early 2000s Virginia was a divided state: the burgeoning Democratic population in Northern Virginia, and then everything else—a combination of rural Whites, small-town conservatives, and African Americans. Northern Virginia was more diverse, more progressive, and more affluent, in keeping with the New South springing up in places like the greater metropolitan Atlanta area and in the Raleigh-Durham-Chapel Hill region. With each election the population advantage in Northern Virginia increased the share of Democratic votes, resulting in GOP losses in local races in the DC suburbs and in statewide races. Quite simply, Republican politicians were becoming an endangered species thanks to demographics.

The "New Virginia" recoiled in horror when a neo-Nazi march in Charlottesville in 2017 resulted in the death of a young woman. The more progressive Virginians, especially those who were not born in the state, had no sympathy for racism dressed in Confederate garb. Trump excused the neo-Nazis, telling American there were "very fine" people on both sides. Virginia Republicans clung to Trump, defending his statements and continuing to insist Confederate monuments around the state remain. That provided plenty of motivation for Democrats to beat back the scourge of the far right.

Republican Ed Gillespie barely squeaked by in the gubernatorial primary against Corey Stewart, a right-wing activist who made preservation of Confederate statues a top issue. Gillespie, a moderate Republican who had served in the George W. Bush administration and served as chairman of Mitt Romney's presidential campaign, soon discovered the dilemma of Republicans in the Trump era: To get the president's support and stoke the enthusiasm of an increasingly extreme Republican base, Republicans had to veer far right. In a Democratic-leaning state that would make winning a general election even more difficult.

Gillespie faced off against moderate Democrat and well-liked physician Ralph Northam who beat the more progressive Tom Perriello in the primary. Gillespie, under pressure from the right wing, began running ads picturing ominous Hispanic gang members who he claimed endangered the lives of state residents, a dog whistle if not a bullhorn directed at his party's increasingly nativist base. Media outlets and Democratic politicians voiced outrage and condemned Gillespie for trying to be Trump's mini-me. Northam, a moderate Democrat who stressed jobs and health care, became increasingly confident that Gillespie's approach and mimicry of Trump would backfire, helping Democrats capture suburban White voters, especially women, and rack up wins with a batch of women candidates on the ballot. He and every other Democrat running for statewide office won going away.

Below the statewide races for governor, lieutenant governor, and attorney general, Democrats hoped the tide sweeping Republicans from office in the Northern Virginia suburbs and in other densely populated areas of the state would continue to rise. The leftward shift in Northern Virginia had not yet taken out several well-liked, moderate Republican members in Northern Virginia. Pockets of Republican support kept state legislative districts around Richmond in the GOP column. Democrats thought this was the year to finally break the GOP stranglehold in the House of Delegates. Democrats fielded a slate of new faces, a record number of women, including Danica Roem, a transgender woman who ran against a right-wing, antigay Republican; two Latinas; two Asian American and Pacific Islander women; and a lesbian. *USA Today* reported on the connection to the Women's March:

"Right after, I felt I needed to do more," said Hala Ayala, a single mother of two and cyber security specialist running for a delegate seat representing an area including Prince William's County. "At the march you could stare into one another's eyes and see where they've been. It was almost intolerable," said Ayala, who's been a volunteer and community organizer but never run for office. Like Ayala, a number of the women running for the first time are minorities.

Kathy Tran, the first Vietnamese woman elected to the House of Delegates, told NBC News she was motivated to run by Trump's election and the xenophobic forces he had unleashed. "What we're seeing is on one hand the rise in nativism and anti-Semitism and racism, which has an opening and a voice to speak up," Tran said. "I think, on the other hand, we're going to see immigrants and communities of color and LGBTQ communities and women speaking up much more loudly and much more strongly."

These candidates were part of a record number of women seeking office—forty-three Democrats, one Republican, and one independent. This did not happen by accident. At EMILY's List, Schriock saw the opportunity in the Virginia races not only for big Democratic wins but for big wins for *women* candidates. With the Women's March still fresh in her mind, she told her team, "We are not going to let those women down." They made a full-court push to recruit, train, and support pro-choice women. With a philosophy "recruit widely, target smartly" they worked strenuously to get women into the primaries and through to the general election. Especially on the female candidates' campaigns, women powered the volunteer effort. Even on a rainy weekend before the election, Schriock was amazed to see how many canvassers were out and how much fun everyone seemed to be having. These were the "joyful warriors" she liked to see in the field. Volunteering for a friend on the campaign trail, Abigail Spanberger was amazed by the enthusiasm and the number of grassroots participants, many of them women.

Local groups such as Indivisible NoVa West (the western part of Northern Virginia) fully engaged. They worked as door knockers, phone bank callers, and postcard writers, all of whom could be deployed to key districts. Indivisible brought on experienced organizers to help local groups connect with campaigns and provide advice and software tools for candidates and local activists. This was the first real campaign for Indivisible forces aside from a few stray special elections. It therefore provided a test as to whether their members could be as effective in a state election as they had, say, in the ACA fight. To do that they had to expand the campaign map, finding viable candidates for as many races as possible.

Democratic insiders had vastly underestimated the potential gains. Democrats swept all the statewide races and flipped an unheard of fifteen seats in the House of Delegates, including three of the four in Spanberger's area in the Richmond suburbs and eight in Northern Virginia. Eleven of the fifteen women who won had been backed by EMILY's List. Hala Ayala and Elizabeth Guzman, a native of Peru, won their races and became the first two Latinas in the state legislature. With her win, Roem became the first transgender person to serve in public office and the first in Virginia's state legislature.

In looking at the results, many analysts concluded a strong governor with coattails helped to flip a record number of legislative seats. The turnout, particularly in North Virginia, was off the charts, and the women's vote there and around the state was stunning. Northam barely lost the male vote (48 to 50 percent) but won an astounding 61 percent of the women's vote to Gillespie's 39 percent. His victory would have been impossible without that surge of women voters. Northam won White women college graduates handily (58 to 42 percent) and White women regardless of education by only three points. Northam won a higher percentage than Hillary Clinton among both groups. The media saw that impressive win and, reasonably, concluded he helped sweep in a slew of new Democratic lawmakers, including women.

Schriock later recalled, "I don't think that was what was going on." She saw a swarm of women House of Delegates candidates fire up an army of women volunteers who were eager to deliver a verdict on the GOP, and on Trump specifically. They were out in the field door-knocking in inclement weather, making a personal connection with voters. Hundreds upon hundreds of volunteers, including Catron's LWCC group, registered new voters, worked the phone banks, and recruited their neighbors and friends. Schriock saw a volunteer network that had not existed a year earlier. She reasoned that these women may have boosted Northam, not the other way around.

She and some savvy Democratic insiders took away another lesson. The women who won were not the sort of conventional, milquetoast candidates whom the party had fielded in the past. Democrats nominated a fleet of diverse, nontraditional candidates willing to take on Republican incumbents. In the Sixty-Eighth District Democrat Dawn Adams campaigned with her wife. In the Seventy-Third, anthropology professor Debra Rodman was not the genteel, coiffed Virginia politician voters in her area were accustomed to seeing. A friend of Abigail Spanberger's, Melissa Dart who ran in the Fifty-Sixth, was a mother of three including a special-needs child, who took progressive stances on Medicaid expansion, LGBTQ rights, raising the minimum wage, and increasing spending on mental health. The prevailing notions of how a legislator had to sound, look, and dress seemed to evaporate. Instead of running White male contenders, barely distinguishable from Republicans in their policy positions and who had lost year after year, Democrats won with diverse women and newcomers to politics, many of whom were more progressive than previous Democratic candidates. Even in socially conservative Virginia, the definition of "electable" was shifting, although few in the mainstream media took notice.

Every one of the Democratic women elected in House of Delegate races in 2017 held her seat in 2019, and Democrats added two more state senate seats and six more delegates. That resulted in two "firsts": The first woman (and first Jewish) speaker of the House of Delegates, Eileen Filler-Corn, and the first African American majority leader elected in the state senate, Charniele Herring. Democrats achieved and held historic gains, and it was women who delivered them.

A year after the 2016 debacle, I felt relieved that the Democrats had staged a historic victory *somewhere*, filled the ranks of the state legislature with diverse women, and mobilized women volunteers on the ground. In advance of the 2018 midterms Democrats also were assembling a slew of women candidates, many of whom had never run for office or considered themselves particularly political. While the national media continued to visit the Rust Belt diners, pointing out that Trump's hard-core White male supporters were still with him, they seemed oblivious to the rise in the ranks of women candidates. What they missed, I was convinced, was a revolution in the suburbs and the intensity of anti-Trump animus, especially among women.

There was one more 2017 election, the Alabama Senate race. At first blush the contest seemed like a slam dunk for Republicans in a state that had not elected a Democrat to the US Senate in twenty years. However, this time the race took place in the midst of the #MeToo movement, an ostensibly nonpolitical movement with political consequences that knocked the legs out from under the Republican nominee.

Throughout 2017 women, including high-profile politicians and entertainers, had been stepping forward with a series of stunning, stomach-turning revelations of sexual assault and harassment in media, business, politics, and sports. It was an ongoing story, which dominated the headlines. Although a group by the same name was founded by an African American woman, Tarana Burke, in 2006, the phrase took on new meaning in the Trump era. Women responded to the serial scandals by sharing stories of their own harassment experiences on Twitter, using the hashtag #MeToo. Once actress Alyssa Milano and other celebrities used it, the name stuck.

Trump's pick for attorney general, Alabama Republican Jeff Sessions, later an irritant to Trump in special counsel Robert Mueller's investigation of Russian interference in the 2016 election, opened up the Senate seat for a December special election. While the nomination and confirmation of a pro-life, anti–criminal justice reform, and anti-immigration hawk to the post of attorney general was distressing for Democrats, Sessions's elevation did provide them with a shot, albeit a long one, to pick up a Senate seat. Republican Luther Strange appointed by Alabama's Republican governor held the seat temporarily but had to compete in a special election in 2017, the winner to serve until 2020.

Few Democrats saw much of a chance to pick up a Senate seat in one of the reddest states in the country. Republican insiders, including Senate Majority Leader Mitch McConnell of Kentucky, were pleased to back Sessions's replacement Luther Strange, a solid and amenable Republican with conventionally conservative views. However, the controversial, radical former judge Roy Moore—who had suggested 9/11 was divine punishment; joined birther conspirators in questioning President Obama's origins; refused to take down the Ten Commandments from his courtroom despite a court order; called for banning Muslims from public office; and demonized gays—won the nomination in the August primary to the chagrin of Republican senators. They dreaded the prospect of a gadfly and extremist joining their ranks. Trump nevertheless backed him.

Just weeks before the election an earthquake rocked the race. In November 2017, the *Washington Post* reported on multiple women's allegations that Moore had propositioned and/or sexually assaulted them when they were teens. Meticulous reporting discovered his creepy behavior had been so disturbing that he may even have been banned from a local mall. Nevertheless, there he was as the Republicans' Senate nominee in what should have been a slam-dunk election.

The detailed coverage of these women's experiences would have been powerful under any circumstances. Coming after weeks of coverage of #MeToo incidents and with a president in the White House who bragged on the *Access Hollywood* tape ("When you're a star, they let you do it. You can do anything. . . . Grab them by the p---y. You can do anything"), the story electrified the country and enraged millions of women activists. Moore was yet another reminder that while a slew of powerful men had been toppled in the #MeToo era, Trump, despite the *Access Hollywood* tape and more than a dozen complainants of sexual assault and harassment over the years, had attained the country's highest political office and the loyalty of the Republican base and officeholders.

Moore had been a prosecutor with enormous personal influence in the community at the time he had preyed on young women and girls, but his path to the court and to the Senate nomination had never been hindered. His rise was reminiscent of Trump's success as a real estate developer and ultimately as a presidential candidate; he was never held accountable for his conduct. For many voters, women especially, here was their opportunity to deny Moore the Senate seat, to vindicate the stories of his victims, and, perhaps, to send a message to the #MeToo-in-chief that his political days were numbered.

In Alabama, women told the media they were "embarrassed" and experienced "nausea and disgust" over the reports. AL.com's editorial board declared, "We each know someone in our lives who is a survivor of sexual assault or child abuse. Many of us are still searching for the words needed to tell our own stories and some may never find that voice. This election is about them." The editors implored readers: "A vote for Roy Moore sends the worst kind of message to Alabamians struggling with abuse: 'if you ever do tell your story, Alabama won't believe you.' Or, worse, we'll believe you but we just won't care." The editorial concluded, "Alabamians must show themselves to be people of principle, reject Roy Moore and all that he stands for."

This was now a national referendum on the credibility of #MeToo victims, a test as to whether even in an overwhelming pro-Trump state, women's anger over Trump and abuse by other powerful men could upset the political equation. Trump and the Republican Party generally stood by Moore or at least avoided comment. Mitch McConnell, who weeks earlier had demanded Moore step aside, had lost his nerve to defy Trump by early December. "I'm going to let the people of Alabama make the call," he said lamely on ABC's *This Week*.

Trump went one step further, campaigning for Moore in the Florida Panhandle right next door to Alabama. He told the crowd, "The future of this country cannot afford to lose a seat in the very, very close United States Senate." If Republicans lost the seat, they would drop to just fifty-one votes, barely enough for a majority and putting them at risk of losing more votes when moderates broke with the party, as they had done on health care. And, as if that were not clear enough, he added, "We need somebody in that Senate seat who will vote for our Make America Great Again agenda. So, get out and vote for Roy Moore."

Meanwhile, Indivisible's Alabama organizations had gone into overdrive when the revelations about Moore's past conduct broke. Local groups composed of primarily White women teamed up with African American groups to stage events, canvass neighborhoods, and make sure they reached irregular voters who never had seen a door knocker in their neighborhoods. Residents who both parties regularly ignored seemed grateful, and a little shocked, that anyone had come to ask for their vote.

In Huntsville, Alabama, Susan Griffin and the majority of her mostly female group had little to no experience in campaigning. In retrospect she realized their inexperience was a "blessing and a curse"—a curse because they did not know what they were doing and a blessing because they otherwise might not have entered the political fray. She readily conceded, "We didn't know any better." What was clear for her and her members is that "Roy Moore was such a gift because he was so repulsive." Week after week Indivisible volunteers from out of state would come into town to help them door knock and register voters in support of Democrat Doug Jones, a former prosecutor best known for his prosecution in the early 2000s of two KKK members for the 1963 bombing of the 16th Street Baptist Church in Birmingham that killed four Black girls.

Her group regularly went to both Alabama A&M and Oakwood University, two HBCUs, to team up with student groups, staff, and faculty, as well as the local NAACP, to register students in what had previously been low-turnout areas. This was thanks to state rules that made it difficult for college students to register and vote. Their new registration numbers reached into the hundreds, and then the thousands.

The Jones-Moore election results were shocking. Jones pulled off an upset, winning the state 50 to 48.3 percent. Women of color made the difference. Jones won women voters 57 to 42 percent—on the strength of nonwhites—and lost male voters by nearly the same margin. Women were 51 percent of the turnout, giving Jones a bigger pond of voters in which to fish for votes. Jones won 98 percent of Black women voters, 86 percent of nonwhite college grads, and 90 percent of nonwhites without college degrees. He won 78 percent of the heavily African American Seventh Congressional District.

This was a critical lesson for Black women activists, particularly in the South. NPR reported, "Black voters made up 29 percent of the electorate in Alabama's special Senate election, according to exit polling. That percentage is slightly more than the percentage of Black voters in the state who turned out for Barack Obama in 2012." Democratic National Committee chairman Tom Perez declared, "Black women led us to victory. Black women are the backbone of the Democratic Party and we can't take that for granted. Period." Savvy Democrats tucked away the important lesson: Even in the South, if they listened to and inspired them, Black women would do the hard work to deliver their red states.

In the Deep South, however, Republicans—even with a candidate accused of child molestation—maintained their grip on White women (winning 63 percent), college-educated White women (52 percent), and non-college-educated White women (73 percent). Moore got 90 percent of Republicans, although there were cracks in the base among key groups of voters. In the suburbs, which Moore barely won (51 to 47 percent), the *Washington Post* reported that enthusiasm for Moore was depressed. "Every single county swung left compared to 2016, with some moving more than 15 points. Moore lost 12 counties that Trump won." The report continued, "Typically reliable and sizable Republican wins in the rural north and south of the state evaporated into razor thin margins." Between a lackluster turnout of Whites and an increased turnout and margin in Black areas, "Jones was able to eke out a 21,000-vote victory, while Republicans normally win by more than half a million votes." Some Democrats hoped that White voters in the South who were not yet ready to entirely abandon the Trumpified GOP might not bother showing up at the polls. They would have done well to remember that the White vote lagged when Trump was *not* on the ballot.

In Georgia, African American Stacey Abrams, who had been organizing low-income and African American voters for three years, watched with interest. Shortly after the Supreme Court in the *Shelby County v. Holder* case gutted the preclearance provision of the Voting Rights Act, which required states with a history of voting discrimination to get approval from the Justice Department before making voting changes, she set up the New Georgia Project. Anticipating a wave of voter suppression measures she thought it essential to register and turn out hundreds of thousands of new voters, many Black, poor, and young. She raised a few million dollars and got to work. Despite then secretary of state Brian Kemp's allegations of "voter fraud," she made steady progress in searching out and registering new voters. As Reuters reported, "Aiding these efforts are seismic changes in the formerly agrarian state's population . . . as newcomers flocked in from out of state, including liberal Whites and people of color." It sounded a lot like the demographic changes that turned Virginia from red to blue. With throngs of new voters and intense outreach in both urban and rural areas to voters that both parties had previously ignored, she eyed a governor's race for 2018. This would be a chance to demonstrate not only her own political drawing power but the development of a more progressive and diverse voting majority she referred to as the New American majority.

For Democrats around the county, the question going into 2018 was whether they could duplicate 2017 results—staging upsets in Republican enclaves and winning with a slew of diverse women in the midterms to capture the majority in one or both houses of Congress. Democrats had miraculously saved the ACA, but they needed a majority in at least one house of Congress to get control of committees to investigate administration scandals and to block Trump's agenda. If both houses remained in GOP hands, Trump's cavalcade of corruption would go unchecked and his party surely would mount another assault on health care and the social safety net. Without significant Democratic wins they feared new efforts to deport the Dreamers and more tax cuts for the rich that would drain the Treasury of revenue for domestic spending.

Democrats needed to remember the key lessons of the past year: Don't assume some Republican seats cannot be flipped; recruit political novices; portray Democrats as the defenders of the little guy; and emphasize health care. Most of all, make certain to appeal to women, especially Black women. If they failed to wrest at least one house away from GOP control, they might be looking at a string of legislative defeats and the horrible prospect of a second Trump term.

CHAPTER 7

REPUBLICAN WOMEN CHART A NEW COURSE

Trump's election impacted a significant segment of Republican women just as profoundly as it did the Democratic women who felt compelled to self-organize or run for office. Republican women and ex-Republican women, both the Never Trumpers and those who reluctantly voted for him in 2016, anticipated a Clinton win in November 2016 just as most Americans did. I was among those women who hoped that a Republican defeat would serve as a long-overdue wake-up call to the party.

Many White women who chose to stick with Trump were among those voters convinced that Trump would not win. A CNN poll in late October 2016 showed about 70 percent of voters expected Clinton would win. A similar poll conducted by the *Washington Post* and ABC found roughly six in ten voters were convinced she would win. In polls and interviews voters nevertheless said they want to "shake up" Washington. The networks exit polls showed a large plurality of voters wanted someone to bring about change (39 percent), not someone with experience (22 percent) or good judgment (20 percent). As Reuters described the election result, "Fed up with Washington and feeling left behind, supporters of

Republican Donald Trump upended the U.S. presidential race, electing a political newcomer they say offers the country a shot at dramatic change." If he somehow did win, many Republican women
had hoped he would mature in the job and that reliable, "respectable" conservatives would tether him to a traditional Republican
agenda of fiscal sobriety, low taxes, and strong national security.

I had been hoping since 2012 that the party would shape up.
After Mitt Romney's loss that year, the party put out the so-called
autopsy report under the guidance of the then Republican National
Committee chairman Reince Priebus, later Trump's first chief of
staff. The report all but acknowledged the party's reputation as a
club of uncaring White plutocrats. It warned that a male-dominated,
White party would be wiped out by the country's growing diversity. Recognizing that President Obama had won women by eleven
points and single women by "a whopping 36 percent," the GOP
vowed to advance women in leadership roles, to combat the notion
Republicans were waging a "war on women," to encourage and
train women to run for office, and to really listen to women for
a change. It made dozens of recommendations such as embracing
"comprehensive immigration reform," creating a new organization
to "increase the Party base by promoting the inclusion in the Party
of traditionally under-represented groups and affiliations," investing in Hispanic outreach and media, establishing "a presence in
African American communities and at Black organizations such
as the NAACP," and seeking to "implement programs to connect
with female voters and help female candidates."

The autopsy report tried to counsel Republicans that they could
not rely solely on White voters and that efforts to rely on a shrinking demographic were bound to fail. These were simply words on a
page. Within the party—donors, activists, and voters themselves—
there was no groundswell of support either to diversify its candidates or to rethink its positions on immigration, racial inequality,
or criminal justice reform.

Rather than follow the sound advice in the autopsy, the GOP

doubled down on its dependence on White evangelicals and male voters. Trump's entire Make America Great Again movement was a message to White evangelicals, especially men, who resented the rise of minorities and women in the workplace, felt disrespected by "elites," and feared secularism would undermine their cultural domination. In the 2016 primary, Trump defeated candidates like Florida Senator Marco Rubio who preached the sort of inclusive message the autopsy report promoted; Trump demeaned Carly Fiorina, making clear that insulting a woman's appearance was acceptable in conservative circles. Jeb Bush ran on immigration reform. But Trump won the nomination, leaving advocates of a more inclusive approach on the defense or silenced altogether. Fearmongering about immigrants was in; inclusion was out.

Republican media stars like Ana Navarro explained in a piece for CNN why she had felt compelled to vote for Clinton. "I voted against Donald Trump because I am a Republican. I accept that Trump duly won the Republican nomination. But I do not accept that he represents Republican values—not the ones I grew up respecting." Defeat Trump and her party might be rescuable. Katrina Jorgensen, leader of a South Carolina young Republicans group, expressed a similar sentiment. "Candidates, staff and volunteers have already walked away from Trump, and there's no question it will keep happening. If Trump gains a greater control of the party, these people might even be forced out," she warned in an op-ed for the *Guardian*. She concluded, "Only a loss by a wide margin would send a clear message to the Republican party: this is the wrong choice for America." The only way to save the Republican Party *she* admired was to crush Trump.

The assumptions that Trump would lose or that the party would restrain him were faulty; Trump did win, and the party establishment fell in line behind Trump. Elected Republicans became an adoring phalanx that enabled his worst ideas, tolerated his financial corruption, and reinforced his most malicious viewpoints. The Trumpification of the GOP that flowered during Trump's presidency made clear he was not an invader but rather the true leader of a party willing to change its personality, its class identity, and its intellectual ethos.

Once Trump won, there was no getting around it: The GOP had gotten worse, not better, for women and people of color. Many conservative women in the anti-Trump boat felt stranded, alienated from the party and the conservative ecosystem—and more than a little sheepish that conservatives who were once touted as policy wonks and thought leaders were falling in line behind Trump. Conservative women in media and think tanks or who simply embraced conservative policies had assumed the party was serious about its principles. They got a rude awakening. Instead of advocating for American leadership in the world based on universal human values, Trump promoted "America First" and fawned over dictators. Rather than extol equal opportunity, he fomented bigotry. Instead of defending free markets, he pursued cronyism and protectionism. Instead of supporting legal immigration, he demeaned immigrants and used them as a scapegoat for his base's economic problems. Flouting the party's rhetoric on "family values," Trump, a twice-divorced philanderer, encapsulated the negative qualities evangelicals supposedly denounced. The same social conservatives who had decried Bill Clinton's infidelities deified the former real estate mogul. Some Republican women struggled to understand how the party had arrived at the point of giving up its core positions for the sake of embracing someone who had bragged on the *Access Hollywood* tape about sexually assaulting women.

The Republican Party's relationship with women had been complicated over the last few election cycles, to put it mildly. The gender gap—the difference between male and female support for a party's candidates—grew dramatically over a series of elections. Women consistently favored Democrats; men favored Republicans. As the gap widened in the 1980s and 1990s, the number of women Democratic officeholders increased while Republican women's numbers fell. Even earlier, however, a gender shift in the 1960s and '70s had taken place with the defection of White *men*, particularly in the South, from the Democratic Party to the Republican Party. Scholars Ruy Teixeira and the Brookings Institution's Alan Abramowitz wrote in 2008,

> During the Sixties, these new demands on the welfare state came to a head. Americans' concern about their quality of life overflowed from the two-car garage to clean air and water and safe automobiles; from higher wages to government guaranteed health care in old age; and from access to jobs to equal opportunities for men and women and Blacks and Whites. Out of these concerns came the environmental, consumer, civil rights and feminist movements of the Sixties.

That meant White men started to reach the conclusion that "the Democratic Party simply had less to offer them in this environment. As a result, these men, most prominently in the South, naturally migrated to the Republican Party."

When women broke heavily for Democrats, their candidates won comfortably. Bill Clinton's victory in 1992 was fueled in large part by women who strongly favored him over George H. W. Bush (45 to 38 percent). In 1996 Clinton lost the male vote but coasted to victory with a seventeen-point margin among women. When Republicans could narrow the gender gap, as George W. Bush did in 2004 by winning 48 percent of the women's vote, they could secure a victory.

Meanwhile, *non*-evangelical White women increasingly gravitated to the Democratic Party beginning in the Ronald Reagan years. The move coincided with the polarization of American politics and the deepening ideological divide between the parties. Reagan's more muscular foreign policy and his ideological framework—"Government is not the solution to our problem; government is the problem"—did not sit well with millions of women disinclined to favor confrontational international relations and anti-government animus. Reagan's assertion in 1986 that the "nine most terrifying words in the English language are: 'I'm from the government and I'm here to help'" was poorly received by women whose major domestic policy concerns have long centered on issues such as education and health care.

White women have never been monolithic, however. Geography and religion play an extraordinarily important role in differentiating the voting patterns of White women. It was among evangelical White women, especially in the South, that Republican identification had remained particularly strong. Activated by right-wing leaders like Phyllis Schlafly who derided feminists and played to stay-at-home mothers who felt looked down upon by their peers, women joined men in the ranks of politically active White evangelicals whose influence in the GOP grew dramatically beginning in the 1980s. That influence has been exaggerated by their high turnout and unwavering loyalty to the GOP, with about eight in ten reliably voting Republican. Between 2000 and 2020, White evangelicals made up about 26 percent of the electorate while their numbers in the general population dropped to about 15 percent.

In her research, Angie Maxwell, director of the Diane D. Blair Center of Southern Politics & Society, stressed the important differences between evangelical women and non-evangelical women, and between women in the South and in the rest of the country. "Trump won 57 percent of White women with no college experience outside of the South," she explained. "In the states of the former Confederacy, that number jumps to 68.9 percent." She found, "Overall, in 2016, about 35.3 percent of these non-college-educated White women identify as Christian fundamentalists. But there is a huge regional distinction again. In the South, that number is 49.9 percent; outside of the South it is 29.9 percent." In the presidential elections leading up to Trump, according to pollster Celinda Lake, Republicans carried non-college-educated White women by margins ranging from eighteen to twenty-one points.

Evangelical White women, like their male counterparts, saw Trump as their champion, a warrior against the decline of White Christian Protestants and "traditional families." These voters feared the diminishment of their demographic majority and cultural and political domination. Trump might have been a jerk, but he was *their* jerk, inveighing against foreign trade deals, cheap labor, and what they saw as infringement on their religious liberty. He would deliver on judges, rail against elites, and protect them from what they viewed as an onslaught of immigrants. Penny Nance Young, head of Concerned Women for America, conceded in an essay for CNN that many women "don't like their choices, but they are sticking with Trump." With the Supreme Court majority hanging in the balance, she argued, "They are practical women acting on a binary choice. They find the election of Clinton so distasteful they are willing to support a less than noble leader." One researcher interviewing evangelical women in California found: "Rather than just representing the Republican party, Trump reproduces emotionally driven evangelical narratives, including the imperative to return the US to its rightful (White) Christian heritage. For many White evangelical women, accustomed to hearing these narratives in their churches, Trump's language is resonant and familiar." They would remain loyal to Trump and the GOP while non-evangelical White women, mostly in the North, fled from the GOP.

Even in the pre-Trump Republican Party, a segment of non-evangelical White women in the Northeast, Midwest, and West, especially married and affluent women, had remained loyal to the GOP for decades. Republicans pitched to women who had joined the White flight to affluent suburbs by stressing concerns like crime, school busing, and high taxes. The "soccer moms" whom Republicans successfully courted became shorthand for suburban White women worried about terrorism in the years directly following 9/11.

White suburban women for decades had kept the internal machinery of the Republican Party humming. Women volunteers, often organized through Republican women's groups, had worked as door knockers, poll workers, phone bank callers, and in dozens of other functions at every level of party organization. Among voters, Republican women as late as 2000 (when George W. Bush won 44 percent of all women) and 2004 (when Bush won 48 percent of women voters) were a vital part of the GOP's winning presidential coalition. In large part their loyalty to the GOP stemmed from antipathy toward the left wing of the Democratic Party, which they viewed as proponents of high taxes and hostile toward religion and stay-at-home mothers.

If Reagan had jump-started the gender divide and the migration of non-evangelical White women to the Democratic Party, Trump's presidency would vastly expand this gap. Aside from southern White evangelicals, millions of women recoiled from the misogynistic bully. Many college-educated White women soon discovered they had more in common with Democratic women of color than they did with loyal White Republicans. Many Republican, college-educated White women who had been active in Republican politics were particularly put off by Trump's demeanor, language, and willful ignorance. Much of what Democrats had been saying about Republicans' disrespectful attitudes toward women and racism toward nonwhites turned out to be true.

Anti-Trump Republican women's participation in the Resistance took many forms. Two young Republicans who had been policy and political activists in the party, Jennifer P. Lim and Meghan Milloy, met over drinks at the St. Regis hotel in DC during the 2016 Republican primary season with a few friends. Appalled by Trump's racism and disregard for true conservative principles, they decided to organize women on Facebook under the banner of Republican Women for Hillary. To their astonishment, hundreds of Republicans, mostly women, from all over the country joined. CNN was among the first media outlets to discover them and reported, "Faced with a choice between Clinton and Trump, some Republicans have begrudgingly agreed to support him while others are simply opting out of the election. But for these women who founded the group (and one man who has joined in solidarity), Trump's bombastic style, offensive rhetoric toward women and minorities, slapdash policy 'suggestions' risk destroying the party." Even *Marie Claire* magazine tracked them down for an in-depth interview with Lim ("Why I, a Republican, Am Voting for Hillary Clinton"). With a huge lift from the media, their group grew to about a thousand people.

Lim was invited to speak on the final night of the 2016 Democratic National Convention in Philadelphia. Expressing her angst over a potential Trump presidency, she told the cheering crowd she had supported the GOP in the past because of its principle that "liberty, equality and individual rights that cannot be taken away." Since the Trump GOP had abandoned those commitments she was voting for Hillary Clinton.

She was not alone. Mindy Finn, an up-and-coming Republican star and respected political consultant, had run in 2016 as vice president on an independent conservative ticket with Evan Mc-Mullin, a former CIA agent and ex-Hill staffer. Finn's petite stature and restrained, deliberate demeanor masked her dogged work for conservative candidates and causes. McMullin-Finn's quixotic presidential effort served as an outlet for disaffected Republicans unwilling to give up on their conservative values or vote for a racist, unfit Republican nominee. Together with McMullin, Finn had helped knit together a grassroots organization of hundreds of thousands of discouraged Republicans and independents across the country. After the election in which she anticipated Trump's defeat, she fully intended to use the organization as a launching pad for a movement to reform and revitalize the GOP.

By late afternoon in Utah on Election Day she saw that this game plan was not going to pan out. Finn thought of herself as an election "nerd," who knew how to count votes and how to read exit polls. As Florida fell to Trump, she said aloud, "This is not good." Young staffers and volunteers began to cry or stare in disbelief.

She had a speech prepared for what she had thought would be an inevitable Clinton win. She furiously began to rewrite her remarks. She needed to shift gears to help the volunteers, voters, and staff process the demoralizing results. Set to speak before McMullin, she struggled to find a way to be positive, to point to a future that was not unremittingly gloomy. There was no use trying to disguise how bleak things appeared with a racist, sexist man with authoritarian impulses heading to the White House, backed by a Republican House and Senate.

In such dire circumstances, she told the crowd that their mission to reject right-wing populism and defend conservative values (truth, the rule of law, human rights) was even *more* important. In a Trump administration it would be critical to defend the rights of women, the safety of immigrants, and the pillars of democracy. In one evening, she went from disbelief to panic to determination that her campaign effort would not be wasted. Instead of an engine to reform the GOP from within, she and McMullin had unintentionally erected a beachhead on the right to oppose the Trumpified Republican Party that had imbibed his nativist, know-nothing brand of populism.

Finn saw Trump take over their party and Republican men "fall in line like sheep." She sadly concluded, "This was not my party. This was not the party I grew up in." Worse, maybe it *was* the party she grew up in, and it took Trump to peel off the thin veneer of decency to reveal its underlying character and bigotry. She candidly acknowledged, "I felt betrayed. I felt embarrassed. I felt regret about investing so much time in advocating for, in carrying water for men who I believed had my back." She would have to help create a sane center-right movement to wean Republicans from a party that had lost its ethical, constitutional, and policy bearings.

After the 2016 election, Finn and her former running mate reconstituted their presidential operation as a nonprofit group, Stand Up Republic, which sought to advocate for values like truth, the rule of law, and equal protection under the law. The Alabama Senate race provided a unique opportunity for them to weigh into an election contest that Republicans normally would have won without breaking a sweat. Here was the test as to whether women, even in the Deep South, could hold politicians accountable based on the evidence right in front of their eyes. McMullin and Finn put in $500,000 for independent ads on Doug Jones's behalf. Their investment, while not enormous, paid off with Jones's narrow win.

Finn and McMullin were part of an informal alliance of Republicans who broke with Trump, often using the hashtag #NeverTrump on Twitter. It included conservative think-tank scholars, consultants, former officeholders, pundits, foreign policy gurus, and activists. They did not all agree on policy matters or even on whether the Republican Party should be obliterated entirely. However, they did share a determination to limit Trump's influence on the party, block his assault on democratic institutions, and ultimately defeat him at the polls. More important, they were determined to reinforce the guardrails of democracy against increasingly authoritarian Republicans. Some remained Republicans, others considered themselves independents and still others reregistered as Democrats. If I no longer felt at home in the Republican Party, I certainly felt welcomed and supported by this loose grouping, people who like me inveighed against Republican hypocrisy and cried foul when Trump attacked the courts, insulted immigrants, ingratiated himself with dictators, and engaged in massive financial conflicts of interest.

Sarah Longwell, who spent election night in despair with her wife and newborn, was then a senior vice president at a right-leaning communications firm. To understand what had occurred and construct a strategy she knew she and like-minded, disaffected Republicans had to start with research. At the meetings and think sessions after the election she met other horrified conservatives including then editor for the *Weekly Standard* William Kristol, former chief of staff to Vice President Dan Quayle. Kristol had been a regular on Fox News in its less Trumpified days and remained a respected pundit and policy wonk throughout the Reagan and Obama years. He had regularly spoken out about Trump before the election to warn that the GOP would not stand up to him. "The Republican establishment turns out to be really as weak and as lame as Donald Trump said," he said in a May 2016 interview on CNN. "They are basically capitulating to Donald Trump." After the election Kristol was often the voice of sobriety, if not gloom, telling other Republicans to expect the worst from Trump and not to count on Republicans to stand up to him. He publicly admonished Republicans for failing to condemn Trump on the Muslim ban in late January 2017. He tweeted, "Hey, Republicans in Congress (and out): Try uttering the simple statement, 'On this I disagree with President Trump.' It's not that hard." It turned out to be impossible, and Never Trumpers continued to discuss how to react to Trump and a party gone over to the dark side.

After one of the many "What is to be done?" sessions with Never Trump Republicans, Longwell cornered Kristol. She asked, "Don't you think we should do something not just talk?" She wanted to figure out what Republicans had been thinking and what opportunity there was for pushback against Trump. Kristol agreed, and with his buy-in she knew the media and potential funders would take their cause seriously. She pitched to donors for some research money and set out to conduct a series of focus groups with some of the women who had voted with Trump in 2016 but might be persuaded to dump him in 2020.

In her focus groups with reluctant Trump supporters, Longwell was shocked to see just how much faith they had lost in all institutions. If you said Trump was a liar and narcissist, they would respond, "All politicians are liars and narcissists." If you said he was engaged in self-dealing, they would retort all politicians were corrupt. Whether political nihilism was their excuse to support an amoral president with populist appeal, or whether cynicism truly had overtaken these soft Trump supporters, they felt no remorse for their votes in the immediate aftermath of the election. There still was good news, however. Although Trump's approval was high among Republicans, many reluctant Trump voters were open to a primary challenge in 2020. Longwell therefore decided to focus on voters who were "soft" Trump supporters. Over time she would direct her considerable strategic and ad-making talents to swaying this segment of the electorate. She figured she could educate reluctant Trump voters, and thereby convince them that Trump's faults were much greater than they had imagined. Then they might just abandon him in 2020, provided the Democratic nominee was not Hillary Clinton.

To save her party, which she still thought possible, she needed a vehicle to advocate for Republican resistance to Trump. Together with Bill Kristol she founded Defending Democracy Together, an umbrella organization for groups such as Republicans for the Rule of Law. As its executive director Longwell used her communications and advertising experience to oversee an impressive video and TV ad campaign that at critical points in his term sought to push back against Trump.

Not only were these ads conceived and produced by Republicans, but the stars were Republicans themselves. Longwell hit upon a winning formula: Take an issue Republicans had supported for years, run clip after clip of a Republican at the time defending that position, and then challenge Republicans to stick to past positions rather than turn themselves upside-down to stay in Trump's good graces. "It was beyond hypocrisy," Longwell explained. "This was the total absence of shame. No one was willing to hold them accountable." The process of abandoning long-held beliefs in order to placate Trump was "not a bug but a feature" of the Trumpified GOP, Longwell decided. There were no beliefs in the Trump era. All that was asked of Republicans was whether they stood with Trump on matters large and small, no matter the facts or the circumstances, or whether they retained any past principles. As a seasoned Republican, Longwell knew where these Republicans had stood on various issues because that was where *she* had and still stood on traditional conservative values and ideas. It was Trump loyalists' own views that had been kicked to the curb for the sake of Trump sycophancy.

Longwell launched a couple dozen ads in the next couple of years, spending millions on discrete TV ad buys, followed by cheaper digital ads. These were so effective that network and cable TV programs regularly picked them up, giving them more visibility. Some went viral, and Republican politicians who appeared in the ads felt obliged to respond, usually by insisting these inconvenient reminders did not come from "real Republicans." In fact, Longwell was the real Republican who embraced values the party once advocated; she just was willing to call out Trump toadies for abandoning them.

During the Russia investigation she focused on Trump's knuckling under to Vladimir Putin and sought to defend special prosecutor Robert S. Mueller III, imploring Republicans to prevent his firing. One of her group's first and most effective ads came just at the time Mueller was appointed special counsel. Trump and his Republicans began attacking Mueller's character, claiming he was a flunky for Democrats and asserting (spuriously) he was disqualified by conflicts of interest. In fact, Mueller was a Vietnam veteran and former FBI chief who had devoted his entire life to public service. But *Longwell* did not have to say it; she found clips galore of *Republicans* attesting to his fine character during the time of his FBI confirmation. Back then, he was an absolute "straight shooter" and declared an honorable man by Mitch McConnell, Paul Ryan, and Mike Pence—before they decided in the age of Trump that Mueller was an ethical disaster.

The ad went viral after it ran during the first James Comey interview with ABC's George Stephanopoulos. Later, from the Mueller report we learned Trump was, in fact, considering firing the special prosecutor. The image of Mueller as a war hero and honorable public servant in Longwell's ads may have helped him retain public support and thereby keep his job. After the Mueller report came out, her ads focused on explaining the findings of his investigation to the country.

Longwell bird-dogged Republicans over the next few years, invariably digging up videotape of them taking exactly the opposite position they had migrated to for the sake of defending Trump. If Republicans allowed Trump to grab executive power—to build his wall for example—she found clips of them condemning Obama's own power grabs. When Trump's emoluments and self-enrichment became an issue she again went to the video. Vice President Mike Pence was one Republican who provided fodder for Longwell's ads.

Pence during the campaign had attacked the Clinton Foundation repeatedly for its ties to foreign governments and firms, arguing that it was essential to keep candidates far away from foreign influence. Now he was working for a man who used his office to arrange for foreign leaders, American politicians, and dignitaries to stay at his properties and who had pursued a Trump Tower deal in Moscow during the campaign. Longwell's job was to underscore these kinds of 180-degree turns.

Longwell also helped launch *The Bulwark*, an online news and commentary site with fiery podcasts that became a refuge for Never Trumpers. As publisher and contributing writer, she took on Trump apologists and enablers in Congress and the media. She and other Bulwark writers named the hypocrites, lampooned the goofy arguments of intellectually dishonest conservative journalists, and skewered the spinelessness of elected Republicans. During the 2017 and 2018 cycles Longwell reiterated the necessity of preserving the Constitution and putting checks on Trump through *The Bulwark*, TV appearances, and social media. To do that, she knew, Democrats needed to win at least one house of Congress in 2018. She would lend a hand to help the most reasonable Republicans (e.g., Rep. Will Hurd in Texas) survive in 2018 but she rooted for a Democratic majority.

Rooting for Democrats became easier when she discovered the background and agenda of many first-time Democratic candidates, including many impressive women. She happened to be in Ohio in 2018 doing a focus group so dropped in to see a conference of the moderate Democratic group Third Way. In attendance were a batch of eager new female candidates. "These guys are so awesome," she realized. "These are not the AOCs [Alexandria Ocasio-Cortezes]. They were totally pragmatic moderates." Many had military backgrounds and had moderate positions not all that different from hers on issues like Russia or trade. As someone with a fondness for checks and balances anyway she said to herself, "It wouldn't be the worst thing in the world to see a bunch of these women in Congress."

Some in the Never Trump camp ventured into the den of Trump-adoring crowds to deliver unpleasant truths. Mona Charen, an author and conservative pundit who had impeccable Republican credentials going back to her years as a speechwriter for First Lady Nancy Reagan, was among the most visible. Her writing and advocacy in the pro-life movement, critique of liberal academia, and analysis of the collapse of traditional families and civic institutions were suddenly at odds with the party's present embrace of Trump. She wrote in March 2016, "Everything Trump says and does is a form of self-medication for a damaged soul. His need to disparage others, to glorify himself, and to be the 'strong man' could lead to disastrous judgments by the man in charge of the nuclear codes." Charen recoiled when Trump whined that a "Mexican" federal judge (Gonzalo Curiel, an American of Mexican descent) could not be fair to him in a civil trial or when Trump insulted the Gold Star mother who had appeared at the Democratic National Convention. ("If you look at his wife, she was standing there, she had nothing to say, she probably—maybe she wasn't allowed to have anything to say, you tell me," Trump sneered.) Throughout 2016 and 2017 she continued to speak and write in opposition to Trump's lack of conscience and decency—and Republicans' willingness to rationalize it. "[The] Republican Party used to be a party that claimed to believe that character was important, that character mattered," she said in an NPR interview in October 2016. "They said that again and again in the Clinton scandals. . . . We've even abandoned that. We don't even have the decency to be hypocrites here. We just simply have so many Republicans, not all but so many Republicans have simply said, no, that whole character thing—never mind. It really doesn't matter at all. And that's a huge loss for the country."

To her chagrin, Trump prevailed and she confronted the Brave New World of Republican hypocrisy. Charen had for years been a panelist or speaker at the annual Conservative Political Action Conference (CPAC) held in Washington, DC. It was a gathering of some of the most ideologically ferocious right-wing groups and speakers with a bent toward brash advocacy and high-wattage attacks on the left. Like the rest of the conservative ecosystem, CPAC became a cheering section for Trump and Trumpism, growing more extreme and more enamored of right-wing populism with each year of his presidency.

The activists at these events come from various factions of the GOP. The Young Republicans, nearly all White males who often dress in suits, prowl the hallways and gape at the conservative stars. The occasional costumed character in Revolutionary garb strolls through the exhibit halls. Rows and rows of conservative media fill the back of the main convention room, a reminder for the GOP that rightwing media is as much an organizing and messaging operation as the party itself.

Charen was invited to speak at CPAC, to her surprise. As she later wrote, her views on Trump's cronies at the time were "no secret" given that she had been publicly excoriating Trump and his minions for over two years. She recalled, "I knew the crowd would be hostile, and so I was tempted to pass." Nevertheless, she understood the importance of challenging the Trump enablers, forcing Trump's cheerleaders to confront their departure from their professed values and addressing the trend of authoritarianism, misogyny, and racism in the GOP. Asked to speak on a panel about #MeToo, she saw this as a perfect opportunity given a book she had written, due to come out in June that year, which took on the "hookup" culture and deterioration of intact families.

With about ten minutes left on the panel, Charen later recalled in the *New York Times*, "The moderator threw a slow pitch right over the plate. She asked us about feminist hypocrisy." This was certainly in Charen's wheelhouse. "Ask me that at a cocktail party and I will talk your ear off about how the very people who had lectured us about the utter venality of workplace sexual harassment throughout the 1980s became suddenly quiescent when the male-factor was Bill Clinton," she wrote. However, the moment called for something different. It was evident to her that intellectual and moral credibility depended on holding Trump to the same standard the right had applied to President Bill Clinton. She knew she was about to rouse a political mob and steeled herself for the response. Charen castigated her party as hypocritical for seeking to impeach Clinton but standing by figures like Trump and Roy Moore. She declared, "You cannot claim that you stand for women and put up with that." She watched it begin to dawn on the other conservative women panelists that something was not quite right. As she continued, the unease on the panel and in the room morphed into irritation and eventually anger that someone not entirely within the Trump tribe had entered their domain.

Boos and heckles rained down on her. She also denounced CPAC's invitation to French nationalist Marion Maréchal-Le Pen, who echoed the views of her notoriously fascistic grandfather, Jean-Marie Le Pen, once head of the National Front. Charen called the invitation a "disgrace." Again, the boos rang out. She had to be escorted out of the building by security. She left shaken but satisfied.

If Never Trump Republicans were to establish their credibility and hold the party to account for its hypocrisy, then confrontation with true believers was inevitable. In the days after her memorable CPAC appearance, Charen recounted the incident on numerous radio and TV shows. For the Trumpian cult, she was one more betrayer of the faith. Nevertheless, her appearance and the coverage it generated suggested she and others on the right could reach conservative women and men who had followed their past work. She had credibility on the right as someone who fought in the trenches for conservative causes and watched with horror as Republicans lined up behind a president who made Bill Clinton look like a Boy Scout. Charen, along with other Never Trump cohorts, could expose the soulless, lawless nature of the GOP. She and the rest of the Never Trump movement understood the task for conservative dissenters was not just to shame their former colleagues, but also to show the rest of the political world that not all Republicans had succumbed to Trump's right-wing populism.

Never Trumpers' advocacy would inspire ridicule and anger from Republicans still in the Trump fold. Those of us who refused to countenance Trump's lies and reminded Republicans of the views they had abandoned were pilloried by what we came to refer to as the anti-anti-Trump Republicans—Republicans too sheepish to attack Trump and earn the scorn of their party but desperate not to defend an unfit president. They whined that Never Trumpers were irrelevant—yet wrote column after column denouncing us. They accused us of being Democrats for having the temerity to demand that not only Trump but his Republican enablers in the House and Senate, who were endangering the republic and savaging democratic institutions, had to go. Their pitched fits were both a source of amusement to Never Trumpers as well as confirmation that to some degree we had pricked the conscience of these Republicans, who only a few years ago were willing to drum out of the party anyone who did not meet their tests of conservative ideological purity.

A group of right-wing activists and pseudo-pundits operating under the banner of "the Americans Principles Project"—which I found laughable since their only consistent principle was slavish loyalty to Trump—wrote to the *Washington Post* in October 2018 objecting that I was not a "real" conservative. They demanded a pro-Trump Republican be hired. "Anyone following Rubin's writing closely at this point would rightfully find the claim that she is 'conservative' laughable," they asserted. "And yet, she is still regularly touted in the media as a conservative voice—and by your own paper as 'reporting from a center-right perspective.'" Given that these were the people who jettisoned past conservative positions I still adhered to on everything from the "rule of law" to American international leadership to free trade to belief in objective reality, I found their whiny objections risible. I refused to respond and thereby give them the satisfaction of getting my attention and access to my wider audience, which dwarfed their own. I continued routinely skewering in columns and TV and radio appearances those who fancied themselves "conservatives" but abandoned conservative ideals to rationalize Trump's racist outbreaks and authoritarian mindset. If anything, this sort of hypocritical outrage spurred me and other Never Trumpers to double down on our indictment of the Republican Party and the group of spineless pundits who enabled a dangerous, lawless president. Their howls signaled we were making a difference and making them squirm. We were getting through to some segment of Republicans or former Republicans who began to recognize that the GOP was essentially a right-wing mob, untethered to principles.

For Never Trump women activists like Longwell, Lim, Mallory, Finn, and Charen, the 2016 election turned into a revelation about the shared interests, if only temporary, with many mainstream Democrats. The policy differences seemed inconsequential in the face of a threat to democracy itself. I too found commonality with Democrats in the fight to defend rational discourse, objective reality, and democratic values. These were people, I soon discovered, I had more in common with than I had imagined.

CHAPTER 8

A NEW GENERATION OF DEMOCRATIC WOMEN

As Republican women struggled with their new political reorientation, a brand-new crop of Democratic women decided it was time to become participants, not merely observers, in America's political life.

Abigail Spanberger left the CIA in 2014 with no plan to run for office. For whatever job or activity that lay ahead, Spanberger needed to declassify her résumé, which could not reveal too much information about her time in the CIA. She could say she was stationed in Europe, but not reveal the specific country—although she had a degree from a German university. She wanted future employers and organizations to know her real job, not her "cover job." As she freely admitted, she was utterly mediocre in her cover job, doing the bare minimum to keep employed, while she remained focused on her intelligence work.

Even before the 2016 election, Abigail Spanberger decided she wanted to join Emerge, a nationwide organization with state chapters devoted to helping women run for state and local office but also to help deepen their advocacy skills and political involvement. She needed the sense of "mission" the CIA provided her, and she wanted to meet other women who were politically inclined. Spanberger downloaded the Emerge program's questionnaire, which asked whether she would ever run for office. Her mother had run for school board, but she had not seriously considered running herself. She wrote down that maybe one day, perhaps in the next Virginia state election cycle (2019), she would run for state senate. After the interview required for admission to the group, the political juices started flowing. As she later recalled, her attitude went from "Hey, this is something I'd like to do" to "I MUST do this!"

A woman candidate already had been recruited for Spanberger's Virginia House of Delegates district for 2017, where the incumbent was retiring, and others were already running in districts adjacent to hers. Spanberger figured she would help with the Democratic campaign in her own and adjacent districts. However, Spanberger's focus changed dramatically in early 2017. She attended a town hall held by her congressman, Freedom Caucus member Rep. Dave Brat, the lawmaker who had so turned off Catron and her group. Brat was gung ho for the recently announced travel ban from Muslim-majority countries, telling the crowd how necessary this was and how terrific Trump was as president. Spanberger watched in amazement. Not only was this policy initiative blatantly racist and cruel, but as a matter of national security, she knew from her CIA background, this was dangerous and counterproductive. *We would be fueling Muslim fundamentalists' propaganda and alienating countries whose help we would need. She* could do a better job than this guy, she realized. She had falsely assumed that as an elected leader he would have access to information ordinary citizens did not and would possess unique expertise. To her surprise, Brat, like plenty of incumbents, was far less informed than she and other educated voters.

The recognition that many incumbents had no special knowledge or background and, she suspected, were less hardworking and capable than herself, was hardly unique to Spanberger. As hundreds and thousands of women for the first time attended town halls, went to lawmakers' officers, or watched C-SPAN hearings attentively, they got an up-close view of their elected representatives. Coming away unimpressed, hundreds of women made the decision to run for local, state, and federal office.

Spanberger began to consider a congressional race against Brat and quickly figured out that midterm elections do not begin in midterm years. The process of recruiting candidates, laying out a national game plan, and fundraising for the 2018 midterms began early in 2017. Women who had just weathered the shock of the election had to decide quickly whether to run for office and then figure out how to do it. For the next few months, Spanberger and her husband discussed a possible congressional race. It would not be easy. No Democrat had won the district in fifty years and no woman had ever won there. Trump had carried the district in 2016. On a personal level, they had three school-aged children and understood the time commitment a campaign would require. Nevertheless, they agreed that if they wanted to do this, they would go full out, committing to winning and sacrificing money and family time. In April she finally made the decision to run and in July 2017 announced her candidacy for Congress.

Spanberger was one of many first-time women candidates running in 2018. Democrats nominated a total of 158 first-time candidates, both men and women. Martha McKenna, a Democratic consultant, told *Politico*, "When a state legislator runs for Congress, that's a formula we know. But when a nurse or a mom or a young veteran decides to run, their campaign looks and feels different, and in 2018, there's a lot of power in that."

Fortunately, there was an infrastructure in place to help Spanberger and others. Throughout 2017 and 2018 many progressive groups sought to boost Democratic women candidates at the local state and federal level. EMILY's List was the best known, but Off the Sidelines, She Should Run, Get Her Elected, Ignite, Higher Heights for America, and Emerge (for state and local races) were among the organizations willing to do everything from funding women to helping them find key staff to providing training for first-time candidates to simply making political connections with other women. This infrastructure would be critical if Democratic women were going to be successful.

While Spanberger was sketching out her run in Virginia, out in California, Irvine School of Law professor Katie Porter was undergoing a similar process.

KATIE PORTER HAD watched the 2016 presidential election returns at a local community center in Orange County, California—once the home of so many Ronald Reagan Republicans. The curly-haired, fast-talking, and witty academic had gone through a hellish divorce with an abusive spouse in 2013. When she sought a restraining order to keep him away from her and her children, he retaliated demanding an order against *her*. The judge ruled for her and denied her ex-husband's frivolous request. For a legal academic, originally from Iowa, her position at Irvine School of Law—which was growing in prestige—in a place where winter coats were unnecessary was almost ideal. On election night, she had eagerly awaited the returns.

She already had been picked to join the Hillary Clinton transition team and planned to fly to DC on the Friday after the election for both a law conference and the transition start-up. On Election Day, she nevertheless felt unsettled, all too aware that back in Iowa plenty of people enthusiastically had supported Trump. She spent election night at a community center, packed with families waiting to cut into the sheet cake bought to celebrate Clinton's expected win. The liberal crowd grew hushed as the night went on. "The men bailed early on," Porter recalled. The women hung around late to cry, to hug, and to console one another.

Porter was certainly not considering entering elective politics. She had from time to time considered public service, but never as a candidate. She had testified on the Hill, done some training for the

Federal Trade Commission, and watched her mentor at Harvard Law School, Sen. Elizabeth Warren, and her state's attorney general, Kamala Harris, both go off to the Senate.

Porter did not think she was "electable." She was a single mom with three kids. She was "solidly" middle class, without personal or family wealth. Besides, she liked being appointed, picked for things, on her merit. With the election of Trump however she felt that she and her peers had let the country down. They failed to take the Trump threat seriously and had not worked hard enough to elect Clinton. They had become detached from a great number of their fellow Americans. She later confessed she felt that she and many of her female peers had been asleep at the switch while Trump whipped up his supporters into a frenzy.

Porter still had the conference to attend in DC so on the Friday after the election she boarded the plane, crying most of the way across the country. The stewardesses did not bother to inquire why she was so upset. After all, here was a woman flying alone from California to DC days after the election of Trump. They *knew*. Porter went to her conference, walked around the Capitol, and headed back home. Perhaps she would run in two to four years, when her kids were older. Her boyfriend told her he "didn't get it." He pointed to people they knew who had run for office and won. Why not get ready *now* to run? She had no good excuse to postpone a possible race.

In the weeks after the election, she began to seriously consider the idea of running for Congress. She made plans to talk to her mentor. Warren was out in Los Angles right around Thanksgiving, just a few weeks after the election. Porter drove up to meet her and they sat down to talk.

She told Warren she had three ideas. First, she could expand her expertise and start teaching tax law, for example. Warren smiled weakly. "Well, tax is interesting. What's your second idea?" Porter said she might become a law school dean. Warren made a face. In her blunt style she said, "That's a god-awful idea." Herding around academics and playing university politics? That was a waste of Porter's skills and would drive her to distraction. Warren asked, "What's your third idea?" Porter had intentionally left this one for last, hoping Warren would hop on board with the first or second choice. Well, she told Warren, she could run for Congress. Warren was intrigued and peppered her with questions about her district, held by a low-key, undistinguished, and very conservative woman, Mimi Walters. What did the district look like? What were the numbers in the 2012 presidential election? Porter, as was her style, had done her homework and was prepared to answer Warren's questions. "I like this idea," Warren said firmly. "This is good." She promised she would be with Porter "every step of the way" and told her she had to learn something new—a new fact, a new perspective, a new insight—every day in politics. Both the promise of help and the opportunity for intellectual growth appealed to Porter. Warren was right on both counts. As things would turn out, her encouragement of Porter was among Warren's most important contributions to the Resistance.

In early April, Porter formally declared her candidacy. She had no personal wealth, no family money, but she had contacts from Warren and Harris who could provide advice. She got invaluable fundraising advice, as she recollected: "Download your phone contacts, make an Excel spreadsheet, fill in what you think people can give and then start calling." As a bankruptcy expert Porter felt sheepish about asking for large donations. At the time she worried, "What if they could not really afford this?" Nevertheless, she put her head down and started calculating what she thought each person on her list might offer. She texted old high school friends, friends of friends, and anyone else she knew, however slightly. Porter at first recognized she was "wildly bad" at asking for money. Many of the potential donors were constituents, so she felt obliged to converse with them, listen to their ideas, and hear their problems. As a result, her pace was glacial. She learned that fundraising could be lonely and isolating; outside of money-raising events, "It was just yourself, your phone, and the list of donors," she discovered.

Porter nevertheless was more fortunate than most first-time candidates. She was the first Democrat to declare for the race, and with a strong push from Warren, EMILY's List decided to back her. Not only would this provide her with periodic infusions of cash—dubbed "magic money"—but EMILY's List gave the race itself legitimacy. The incumbent was a woman in a very Republican district, but now with EMILY's List in the race, it was not considered a lost cause. After six or seven months her personal fundraising was tapped out, but after appearing on the EMILY's List fundraising mailer $60,000 poured into her campaign coffers.

She also saw a torrent of women political activists arrive to help. Jennifer Levin's group Hang Out, Do Good regularly drove down to Orange County from Los Angeles to fill the ranks of volunteers and to attend one event after another. They became a familiar sight at her campaign appearances. They provided Porter with a visible example of women's new spirit of activism, and Porter's gutsy rookie race gave Levin's group confidence they were doing something constructive. Women had always figured prominently in the ranks of campaign volunteers, but in the 2018 midterms, the numbers and the level of commitment of women was off the charts. Porter selected an all-female senior campaign team.

At the beginning it was Porter and her aide Nathan Click in the car ten hours a day. He initially laid his surfboard across the front passenger and back seats; Porter sat in the back. After a time, Click tied his surfboard to the roof of the car, allowing her to sit up front. This was not the sort of sober sedan that usually ferried congressional candidates about, but the somewhat comical surfboard-toting car reinforced her profile as an unconventional candidate.

In her heavily Republican district, she often did door-knocking at "mixed" households. It was not unusual for the wife to be supportive of her while the husband remained in the Republican camp.

At times, the husband opened the door and said he was not giving her a cent while the wife peered over his shoulder, silently signaling she was all in with Porter. At other homes, the man said he was Republican (or voting for a Democratic opponent) but would graciously agree to get his wife.

BACK ON THE East Coast, former Marine pilot Amy McGrath, now an instructor at the Naval Academy in Annapolis, Maryland, was also inspired to shift careers and transform her life. On election night she had blithely assured their German au pair who was nervous about Trump's anti-immigrant talk. "Don't worry, he'll never get elected," McGrath glibly declared. As the results came in, she felt a sinking feeling, a sense of dread. She was deeply disappointed in her fellow Americans and shaken to her core. This is not the America she had signed up to serve in battle.

She had wanted to be a fighter pilot ever since she learned the job existed. When her mother discovered her interest, she was compelled to tell her daughter that girls could not do the job. Why? Her mother said, "It's the law." McGrath retorted, "Change the law." Her mother explained it was not that easy. That kicked off a discussion about civics and government and sparked a lifelong interest in the intersection of national security policy and politics. McGrath wrote to lawmakers urging that they change the law barring women fighter pilots. Some went unanswered. Some were dismissive, or even rude. As luck would have it, just as she was applying for college in her senior year of high school, the law changed. In a stroke, she got her shot at the career and life she always wanted.

After graduation, deployment, and ninety bombing missions in Afghanistan, she took an assignment as a congressional fellow with Democratic congresswoman Susan Davis from San Diego, where she eagerly plunged into the minutiae of public policy. She studiously avoided politics in the military, yet she found herself time and again in sympathy with Democrats on the budget, on Don't Ask, Don't Tell, and on other issues. She prided herself on sticking to the facts and resisting partisanship, but she quickly concluded that when it came to Republicans, "These guys were full of shit."

By 2016, she was teaching basic government at the Naval Academy, finally stationed in the same location as her husband, who was also in the military. The day after the election she went to work. All around campus midshipmen walked in stunned disbelief, as if a natural disaster had occurred. She had to be strictly neutral about anything smacking of politics, but she began asking herself how she was going to respond. As she turned the results over and over in her mind, she felt the compulsion to return to her home state of Kentucky, a deep red state where Trump had won going away. "I could not understand it, I did not get it," she recounted. Did Americans not know about his stance on issues, about his ethical failings? Were they bamboozled or had Americans lost their sense of civic responsibility? If she returned, perhaps she could grasp why these people had voted for Trump. Maybe in some other role she could defend her country, although she had not yet figured out what that role might be.

Every two years former members of Congress, both Democratic and Republican, came to her class to talk about government service. One of those who had visited was former Kentucky Democratic congressman Ben Chandler. At the time, politics was not on her radar screen. "So, we talked about Kentucky and horses," she later recounted. He did give her his card with the typical offer to call him if she ever needed anything. Now, in the wake of the election, rifling through her desk, she found the card and decided to email him. "I just started typing," she remembered. Without knowing exactly where she was heading, she drafted a long message to Chandler. It soon turned into a cathartic exercise that left her sobbing. *What is happening to the country? What has happened to Kentucky? If I came back to Kentucky, being a former Marine, could I make a difference?* Within two hours, Chandler emailed her back, "I think if you came home, you'd make a difference." He promised to help her. Like many American women, the shock and horror brought on by Trump's election propelled her to leap into the political arena.

She moved her family back home to Kentucky's Sixth District and started to figure out how to run for office. A neophyte in politics she thought, "How hard could it be, right?" As she was moving a household and her small children, she quickly learned everything she did not know. Fundraising, advance work, polling, media appearances, campaign finance laws, staffing—she had never dealt with any of it. It was not Marine boot camp, but she and her husband went to candidate camp to learn the basics of operating a campaign. She got a crash course in some of the nuts and bolts of campaigning, but her biggest discovery did not come from the classroom. Her casual meeting with Kentucky congressman Ben Chandler back at the Naval Academy turned out to be a lifeline. Through Chandler she found a campaign manager who in turn found the man who became one of the most important figures on her campaign, Mark Putnam.

The lanky, gray-haired campaign adman had seen a video of her appearance at a local veterans' group. With years of campaign experience under his belt, he knew she was a remarkable talent. Her presence and posture gave away her military background and she had none of the pretense and arrogance that afflicts many candidates. She was down-to-earth, the mom in the car pool lane. And she was funny. She just happened to have been a Marine pilot and a quick learner.

Putnam agreed to put together a video to launch her campaign that summer. The only problem was she needed to raise $35,000 to make it. She called friends and relatives in her large, extended Catholic family. Everyone gave money, Republicans and Democrats alike. Somehow, she scraped together enough. It was blazing hot on the day of filming, which also coincided with the day she was moving into her new house with her husband and kids. The idea was to shoot on a runway near parked aircraft, highlighting her military career. Putnam asked her to bring her leather bomber jacket. "Good grief," she thought to herself. Of all the days to ask for *that*. "It was buried somewhere" in all those boxes strewn across the house, she figured. She rummaged through one box after another until she found and plucked it out. Out on the runway it felt like 110 degrees. Putnam said, "Listen, you're never going to survive three hours in the sun with that. Just forget it." McGrath would have none of that. Not only had she turned the house upside down looking for it, but one does not tell a Marine you are never going to be able to do something. "Brother, I am going to wear it," she told him. Through hours of filming, the jacket stayed on.

The video went out on August 2, 2017, and almost immediately she began to hear from her family and political figures that she was "trending"—which at the time she did not completely understand. The video was a sensation, the image of a woman fighter pilot—in that bomber jacket—ready to serve her country, this time in politics, was enthralling. The money flooded into her campaign. McGrath began calling donors to thank them. Shocked, they would tell her "No one ever thanked me for giving money." McGrath would respond, "No one ever gave me thousands of dollars before."

Thanks to the viral video and a huge fundraising haul, her race caught the attention of the media. The cable news networks started calling for interviews. Untrained in TV, her appearance might be a disaster, but the opportunity ultimately was too good to pass up. Some interviews went well, others were rocky. Like everything else in this experience, she got better and more comfortable with time. McGrath's was a campaign of firsts.

She found she enjoyed town halls, where she would ask the crowd for a show of hands to indicate how many had never worked on a political campaign before. About three-quarters of the hands would pop up. She would reply, "Me too!" Never donated? About 85 percent never had. She would repeat, "Me too!"

She drew a tough primary challenger in the person of Lexington mayor Jim Gray. He was wealthy and therefore could fund his own campaign, which made him the Democratic Congressional Campaign Committee's favored candidate. The first poll showed her thirty points down. As 2017 ended McGrath could see that in her district—about 40 percent urban, 60 percent rural—urban women were angry and anxious over Trump's election. Out in the rural areas, many seemed relatively unconcerned about Trump. What was also apparent is that while Gray had the establishment support, McGrath had the newcomers to politics. At a campaign field office opening event in Frankfurt attended by about 125 people, an older woman approached her. She told McGrath she knew everyone who is anyone in the state Democratic Party and yet she didn't know a soul there. That told McGrath she was injecting new blood into the party; Gray could get the old monied Democrats and she could get everyone else. Perhaps Democrats had tired of electing rich White guys.

CHAPTER 9

THE 2018 BATTLES

While the Resistance staved off the ACA repeal and triumphed in off-off year elections in 2017, Republicans still controlled the White House and both houses of Congress. The Republican Party had further devolved into a Trump cult. Inept and/or corrupt executive branch officials were confirmed (and many like Secretary of State Rex Tillerson, Health and Human Services Secretary Tom Price, and Interior Secretary Ryan Zinke were fired or forced to resign), and the torrid pace at which right-wing federal district and appeals court judges were confirmed in the Senate never waned. The daily assault on Americans' sanity and values, usually by tweet, prompted some to conclude that "nothing mattered"; in essence, that the Resistance was a failure and Trump was "winning." The only sure way to thwart Trump's agenda and to conduct real oversight was to win one or both houses of Congress. Democratic donors, activists, politicians, and voters pursued that overriding and immediate objective for 2018.

Although the economy was not as strong as it had been under President Obama, unemployment was still low, and wages were beginning to inch up. Republicans, reliant on White non-college-educated men's seething resentment to fuel their reelection, never bothered to craft a message specifically for women. It was a one-size-fits-all pitch: The economy is strong; immigrants will take your jobs and kill your children if Trump does not stop them.

If the midterms revolved around the economy, Democrats would have a tough time convincing the average voter to flip one or both houses of Congress to serve as a check on Trump. If, however, the election was about Trump's failed effort to repeal the ACA, Speaker of the House Nancy Pelosi was certain the voters would look to her party to prevent Trump from taking their access to health care. She pounded away at that message at the beginning of the year when she excoriated Republicans for allowing more than three million additional Americans to lose insurance coverage. "Over the past year, the Trump Administration has spitefully tried to undermine the Affordable Care Act by eviscerating funding for ACA open enrollment advertising, deliberately creating massive confusion around ACA enrollment availability and making constant threats to cut off key ACA payments," she said in a blistering statement. She warned that Republicans would "double down on their sabotage efforts." And she kept up the drumbeat all the way to Election Day, when she bluntly declared at a news conference, "This election is about health care." At every turn she tried to discourage Democrats from getting off track. As she said in an appearance in Texas in September, "I just say to the candidates, [Republicans] would like to think that we're out there going for impeachment, shutting down ICE, all kinds of things, and that serves the president's purpose."

On its face, it was a message aimed at men and women alike but polling consistently shows that most women are responsible for the health care choices for their families. In a race in which Democrats needed to flip suburban seats where many college-educated women resided, this message had particular resonance. She made clear that impeachment, for which some members were already agitating in the wake of the Mueller report, was not to be the focus. She stuck to her message that the facts would guide them on impeachment.

. . .

THE MIDTERM YEAR started out with a burst of activism in, of all places, red states in the form of teacher strikes that began in February 2018. If teachers were involved that meant women were involved. In excess of 75 percent of public school teachers are women, and among women voters education, along with health care and other family issues, consistently ranks high on their list of priorities. Teachers in West Virginia faced a hike in health care premiums, which essentially reduced their pay to 2012 levels. They organized on Facebook, went out on strike, and successfully rolled back the premium increase. Strikes followed in other, primarily red states such as Arizona, Oklahoma, Kentucky, and West Virginia—and then spread to purple and blue states in places like Colorado, California, and Washington. It wasn't explicit, but gender discrimination was often the subtext.

As *Time* magazine reported, "Teaching has long been dominated by women, and experts say the roots of its relatively low pay lie in sexism." At some point, no matter how much they loved their students, teachers simply could not make ends meet. The *Post* reported that the teacher walkouts helped make 2018 a record-setting year for work stoppages, with over 485,000 strikers. "The labor unrest wasn't a result of prominent unions in manufacturing, such as United Automobile Workers, or transportation, such as Teamsters," the *Post* noted. "It was driven by a wave of teacher strikes that spread from West Virginia (35,000 workers) to Oklahoma (45,000) and Kentucky (26,000). Within months, 267,000 more teachers in Arizona, Colorado and North Carolina staged walkouts."

In some cases, the experience launched strike activists into policy and political roles. Carri Hicks, a schoolteacher from Oklahoma, was inspired to go into politics and would launch a winning state senate campaign. In Arizona, teacher Kathy Hoffman, incensed by Trump's election and the paltry school funding, ran a shoestring campaign as a Democrat and won the race for Arizona's superintendent of education, one of about three hundred members of the American Federation of Teachers who ran for office,

60 percent of whom won, in 2018. Likewise, the National Education Association could boast 1,194 Democratic and 585 Republican members, more than 56 percent women, who ran for state house or senate seats. About 58 percent of these candidates won. In addition, the teachers' strikes prompted EMILY's List to reexamine the political map. Strikes in red states raised the visibility of potential midterm opportunities that might not otherwise be on Democrats' radar screens.

EMILY's List chief Schriock, for example, spotted Kendra Horn in Oklahoma, a lawyer with experience on the Hill and who cofounded Women Lead Oklahoma, an advocacy group to connect women in public roles. She would be an ideal candidate herself for Congress and received EMILY's List's backing. When Michael Bloomberg's political operation, the Independence USA PAC, asked Schriock late in the campaign where they might stage a stunning upset Schriock pointed to Horn. Bloomberg took the advice and spent heavily on her. Horn went on to win.

While health care was the top-line issue on which Democrats would run, a series of other issues developed during 2018 that had special importance to women. Conservatives would joke during his presidency that President Barack Obama did more to help organize and unify the right than anything conservatives could do. In the Trump era the same could be said of Democrats. Without him, his serial assaults on the American psyche and institutions, the Resistance might have collapsed. Indeed, the worse his behavior and the more outrageous his policies became, the more women recoiled and the stronger the Resistance became. That was certainly true when it came to guns and immigration.

The February 2018 slaughter at Marjory Stoneman Douglas High School in Parkland, Florida, terrified students, teachers, and parents as no single incident had since the Sandy Hook massacre in December 2012, when twenty-six people, including twenty children between the ages of six and seven, were murdered by a lone gunman. The day after Sandy Hook, Shannon Watts activated a Facebook group to seek tougher gun laws. The group, eventually named Moms Demand Action, affiliated with Everytown for Gun Safety, Bloomberg's organization. Within a few years there were Moms Demand chapters in every state, increasing pressure on lawmakers to support commonsense gun legislation in 2018 and beyond. What made Parkland arguably more impactful than the numerous incidents in the five and a half years since Sandy Hook were the articulate teenage survivors who were proficient in social media. These young people took it upon themselves to infuse the gun safety movement with a new level of defiance, anger, and commitment.

As parents and students around the country wiped away tears, stared in disbelief at the news coverage, and carried on frightening conversations about active shooters with their own children, a group of self-possessed teenagers grabbed Americans' attention. David Hogg started filming and interviewing students while the shooter was still loose. Like a veteran reporter he told CNN, "If I was going to die, I wanted to die doing what I love, and that's storytelling. And this is a story that needed to be heard. . . . At least our echoes, our voices would carry on and possibly make some action." He and classmates such as Alex Wind and Emma González became household names and frequent guests on cable TV news. *Time* magazine reported,

> Most of these kids cannot vote, order a beer, make a hotel reservation or afford a pizza without pooling some of their allowance. On the surface, they're not so different from previous generations of idealistic teenagers who set out to change the world, only to find it is not so easy. Yet over the past month, these students have become the central organizers of what may turn out to be the most powerful grassroots gun-reform movement in nearly two decades.

About a month after Parkland, they staged a massive gathering of at least five hundred thousand people, dubbed the March for

Our Lives, in Washington, DC. Nearly nine hundred local protest events were held around the country. This was the largest student-directed protest since the Vietnam War. Hollywood celebrities collectively donated millions of dollars to pull off the event, and progressive groups like Indivisible pitched in to help organize and publicize it, raising interest for a student walkout from schools around the country on April 20. González, transfixed the country when she paused during a speech and remained silent for the same period of time it took the gunman to slaughter seventeen people. "Since the time that I came out here, it has been six minutes and 20 seconds," she said. "The shooter has ceased shooting, and will soon abandon his rifle, blend in with the students as they escape, and walk free for an hour before arrest."

Meanwhile a sophomore girl, fifteen-year-old Lane Murdock, came home from school in Connecticut on the day of the Parkland shooting. "I was feeling numb," she recalled. She had been a self-described "theater and art" kid and not someone who saw herself as a political activist. She went on the Change.org website and without envisioning any grand impact called for a school walkout on April 20, 2018, the nineteenth anniversary of the Columbine school shooting. The call for action went viral and international, casting her into the media spotlight and forcing her to learn how to put together a mass action in two months. The petition accumulated over 270,000 signatures. The National School Walkout Twitter account accumulated more than a hundred thousand followers in five days. Indivisible reached out to her, providing resources and advice. Some 2,600 schools would participate. Like women of all ages activated by a political event, Murdock recounted that her life divided into "pre" and "post" walkout. On a national tour later that summer to speak to student groups, she came to the attention of the gun safety group founded by former congresswoman Gabby Giffords, who had been seriously wounded and permanently disabled in a mass shooting outside a supermarket in Arizona. Soon

Murdock progressed to the status of "senior fellow" and began to train other student advocates.

Measuring the precise impact of the gun safety furor in the summer of 2018 is problematic. At the most basic level, those who attend rallies, according to a *Washington Post*-KFF poll from April 2018, were more likely to vote. Moreover, nearly two-thirds of gun control rally-goers were Democrats or leaned Democratic and 70 percent disapproved of Trump. Gun safety events, like the Women's March, provided a way to engage and activate anti-Trump voters, making them more likely to participate in other campaign-related activities, such as phone-banking, door-knocking, and fundraising. Trump initially promised students and parents from Parkland he would back gun safety measures. "We're going to be very strong on background checks," he told them at a White House sit-down. "We're going to go strong on age of purchase and the mental aspect." After talking to the NRA, he unsurprisingly backed down and refused to support even widely popular proposals like expanding background checks. He left gun safety activists even more enraged.

The Parkland shooting and renewed attention to mass gun attacks did not affect men and women equally. Women voters well before Trump came along tended to be more Democratic and progressive than men. On guns in particular, women, even Republican women, have historically been more amenable to gun restrictions. A CBS poll in 2000, for example, showed 78 percent of women (vs. 62 percent of men) favored stronger gun laws with 91 percent of women (vs. 78 percent of men) favoring child-safety locks on guns. In December 2012, after the Sandy Hook massacre, a *Washington Post*-ABC News poll found that "women are more apt to support stricter gun control than are men, by a 12-point margin, 59 vs. 47 percent."

In October 2018, about eight months after the Parkland shooting and a month before the midterms, Gallup showed 61 percent of

Americans favored stricter gun control. The gender gap was stark: 71 percent of women and 51 percent of men favored stricter laws. Here was an issue that mobilized anti-Trump forces, but women in particular.

IN ADDITION TO the gun issue, Trump's inhumane treatment of immigrants, especially of children, may have been the single biggest factor in galvanizing Republican women to turn on their party and in motivating millions of Democratic voters to volunteer and turn out in the midterm election. This was the kind of event, not unlike the #MeToo movement, that transcended politics and shocked the conscience of Americans regardless of party.

The trouble began when Attorney General Jeff Sessions on April 6, 2018, announced a "zero tolerance" policy, which meant all unauthorized border crossers would be prosecuted. Sessions issued an edict to all US attorneys that "a crisis has erupted at our Southwest Border that necessitates an escalated effort to prosecute those who choose to illegally cross our border." That entailed detaining them, holding them in custody, and eventually deporting them. Implicit in this order was the need to forcibly separate minors from their parents so the latter could be held indefinitely while the children, pursuant to the Flores Settlement Agreement, could not be held for more than twenty days. As the Center for American Progress correctly anticipated, "The *Flores* safeguards were put in place to protect children from spending prolonged periods of time locked up in horrendous conditions that are decidedly detrimental to their safety and well-being. However, the administration's latest plan could sidestep this effort, resulting in thousands of vulnerable children and their families spending prolonged periods of time in unlicensed detention centers."

Despite Sessions's announcement, Kirstjen Nielsen, the secretary for Homeland Security, testified before a House committee that there was no separation policy. This was the first in a series of disastrous public performances by Nielsen, who came to epitomize the coldhearted, inhumane bureaucratic machine that treated migrants fleeing their violence-torn home countries as criminals who irresponsibly brought their children long distances. News of the separation policy began to dominate the headlines, and Democrats in Congress and on the midterm campaign trail inveighed against a cruel, abusive policy. The administration's self-made human rights disaster took on the atmosphere of a sadistic farce. In mid-June, Sessions defended the Trump administration's separation policy in front of a group of Christian clergymen. He proclaimed, "I would cite you to the Apostle Paul and his clear and wise command in Romans 13, to obey the laws of the government because God has ordained them for the purpose of order. Orderly and lawful processes are good in themselves and protect the weak and lawful." White House Press Secretary Sarah Huckabee Sanders reiterated this coldhearted sentiment: "It is very biblical to enforce the law."

Religious groups did not see it that way. Official pronouncements came from Methodist, Catholic, Jewish, and other religious groups decrying a policy that resulted in the deaths of a number of children and long-term trauma to hundreds of others. Religious leaders condemned the administration's policy for mistreating, abusing, and traumatizing families instead of "welcoming the stranger," as the Bible decreed. Clergy reminded their parishioners of Jesus's words: "I was hungry and you gave me food, I was thirsty and you gave me drink, I was a stranger and you welcomed me."

By mid-June, the Department of Homeland Security disclosed that a couple thousand children had been separated from their parents, and worse, that there was no plan to reunite them with their families. Criticism mounted from the media and human rights groups, yet Nielsen continued to insist she was justified in arresting and separating families. She point-blank refused to apologize. Trump eventually was forced to declare that the administration would no longer separate families, but the arrests continued and the public could see that the administration, even under court order to reunite families, was reckless, disorganized, and mean.

The child-separation policy proved to be hugely unpopular, but especially among Democrats and women. In July 2018, a Quinnipiac poll showed 66 percent of voters opposed the policy. Among Democrats that number soared to 91 percent. Seventy percent of women (versus 61 percent of men) and 65 percent of White women (versus 55 percent of White men) opposed the policy. Women seemed to have a more acute, visceral reaction to the scenes of crying, desolate children than men. That emotional reaction bridged what had been a partisan divide. A news story that transcended partisan politics resonated as a moral and human issue of decency and put a wedge between Republican politicians and those White women voters who in the past might have stuck with the GOP on purely partisan grounds.

In Chesterfield County, Virginia, the reaction to child separation among Carol Catron and her group of activists was typical of many at the time. They found this the most "unbearable" of all the actions of the Trump administration. Individual women did what they could to go to the border or to raise collections of clothes and toys for refugee children. Women simply could not fathom intentionally inflicting psychological damage on young children. The *Richmond Times-Dispatch* reported on a rally in June featuring Democratic Senator Tim Kaine and attended by scores of women. "We've let this country get to the point where children have been separated from their parents and we still don't know how or when they'll be reunited," activist Jencey Paz told the crowd. "We need to be better allies. We need to care about the reunification of families, and we need to care about stopping violence and incarceration forced on them after they've been reunited."

The child separation policy was of such importance that at NARAL Ilyse Hogue went to her board to receive permission to go beyond her normal policy mandate that was limited to abortion and reproductive rights. She knew it was necessary to confront the separation policy as an example of gross hypocrisy by a party that seemed to care only about "life" *before* birth. This was the most compelling example imaginable of the pro-life movement's disregard for women and children. Moreover, NARAL's members and donors were becoming irate and engaged on the issue; NARAL was obliged to follow.

For NARAL, Hogue's decision meant coordinating with other progressive voters to stage rallies, go to Capitol Hill, write and call lawmakers, and raise the issue with candidates out on the campaign trail, some of whom took the opportunity to go to the border or to detention facilities to call attention to the plight of the children.

Indivisible also made the issue a high priority. Indivisible's leaders knew from the group's start that their members could not fully engage on every issue. Early on they had set priorities, one of which was to fight "issues that would harm the most vulnerable communities." That certainly applied to immigration policy, persecution of minorities, the plight of those given temporary protection from the Obama administration's Deferred Action for Childhood Arrivals (DACA), and the Muslim ban. As Indivisible put it in its founding documents, "While recognizing that all Americans are at risk under Trump, there are communities in this country that are particularly at risk. These include immigrants, Muslims, people of color, women, LGBTQ persons, the disabled, and many others. We firmly believe that an attack on one is an attack on all. It is our duty as Americans to stand indivisible with individuals and communities that are being targeted by the Trump administration." The Resistance drew strength from opposition to Trump's cruelty—making the movement a moral as well as political crusade. Nothing, then, could be more essential than opposing a policy that tore toddlers from their parents' arms, kept beleaguered children in horrible conditions, and shipped them off around the country with no plan to reunite them with their families.

The local Indivisible chapter in San Antonio, for example, teamed up with a slew of groups (RAICES, United We Dream,

Texas Organizing Project, SATX Indivisible, and SA Stands) as well as politicians and faith leaders to hold rallies, protests, marches to the border, and vigils. The same occurred in Fort Worth, Houston, and other Texas cities and towns as well as Indivisible groups throughout Arizona, California, and other Southwest states.

Indivisible's system of local action, focused on pressure from lawmakers' own constituents and engaging with local media, once again proved effective, helping to raise awareness around the country. They also reached out to officeholders and presidential aspirants such as Sen. Elizabeth Warren to keep voters' focus on the issue.

There were activists who joined multiple groups and worked with whomever was most active in their area. Laurie Woodward Garcia, an activist in South Florida, was entirely apolitical until six months before the 2016 election. An irregular voter, she became alarmed by the racist messages coming from Trump and his supporters. She volunteered for the Hillary Clinton campaign. When Clinton lost, she told her family, "I'm going to find out who's responsible for this." She turned into a political whirlwind. A friend and fellow Clinton volunteer had found out about Indivisible, which Woodward Garcia also had learned about from the news. Soon she was all in, not only with Indivisible but with MoveOn.org, United We Dream, and a local Muslim caucus (although not Muslim, she joined them for a lobbying day in Tallahassee). She soon became a self-proclaimed immigration activist.

She found her local Democratic Party disorganized, unresponsive, and tone deaf. She organized her own local progressive group, about a hundred strong, mostly women with a female leadership team. Her group went up to DC for a Dreamers protest, closed down a street, and proudly got themselves arrested. Back home she started to visit an Immigration and Customs Enforcement (ICE) intake facility in Miramar and was horrified by the conditions and the neglect of children. She told the local CBS affiliate, "The first thing I tell people when I go out there, I'm going out there as a mom, a pissed off mom. . . . We need to hold them accountable." She returned again and again over the next year. With fellow activists she continued her work through the 2018 midterm elections, canvassing, texting, calling, and traveling even to rural areas where few Democrats ever campaigned to get out the vote.

Protests generated wall-to-wall TV coverage, which, in turn, served as free TV ads for progressives and progressive causes. Trump's domination of cable TV news in the 2016 election cycle, worth billions of dollars in ad time, helped him capture the Republican presidential nomination. Starting in 2017, it was progressive, anti-Trump protests that generated free media coverage, a boost to Democrats who embraced the rally attendees' causes.

Trump's xenophobia did not abate, and in a last desperate attempt to rally his base before the midterms he engaged in nonstop fearmongering about immigrants. He fixated on a "caravan" of immigrants—men, women, and children desperate to escape violence in Central America—even though it was hundreds of miles away from the border when he raised the issue. The right-wing echo chamber of Fox News and talk radio reverberated with unsubstantiated allegations that criminals and even terrorists were among the refugees. But if Trump's railing against the asylum seekers engaged his own base, it also served as a reminder to Democrats and women in particular of his racism and arguably his most abominable action to date, the separation of small children from their families. Trump was whipping up the hard-core, anti-immigrant voters in his base. With each tweet and angry denunciation, however, he was alienating suburban women and college graduates, both male and female. Unintentionally, he did Democrats' work for them by narrowing his base of support while energizing and broadening the opposition. In particular, he managed to reinforce women voters' determination to oust his allies in the midterms.

Trump's cruel, inhumane treatment of innocent women and

children at the border worked to his own detriment as did his refusal to part company with the National Rifle Association by supporting sensible gun control, even in the face of one mass shooting after another, often perpetrated by individuals spouting the same White nationalist rhetoric Trump deployed. At the Pittsburgh Tree of Life synagogue, the attacker decried Jews for helping to bring immigrants to America; in the fall of 2018 the owner of a van covered in pro-Trump messages and photos targeting prominent Democrats was arrested for sending explosive devices to liberal donor George Soros, whom right-wing Republicans regularly demonized, and to Democratic politicians and media outlets that Trump scorned. Trump's actions helped pry loose independents who may have voted for him in 2016 but were increasingly wary of his rhetoric and unhinged conduct. Polls in normally conservative districts in Orange County, California, and in New Jersey showed Democratic challengers opening up wide leads with independents. "Soft" Republicans and most especially, college-educated White women, also soured on him. These issues intensified Democrats' enthusiasm and helped engage Democratic donors. It was in this atmosphere, with progressive wind at their backs, that a flock of women newcomers prepared to deliver a significant blow to Trump and the Republican Party, although a final complication for anti-Trump forces popped up just weeks before the election.

CHAPTER 10

A FINAL CURVEBALL

Hogue and other progressive organization leaders got the news in June 2018 they had dreaded, the announcement that Justice Anthony Kennedy would retire. Kennedy, who demonstrated in his last term that he often sided with the four other Republican-appointed justices, was no darling to the left. However, his presence on the Supreme Court was critical as the fifth vote to protect abortion rights. For decades, activists like Hogue had counted on Kennedy to preserve the constitutional right to abortion. Without his vote, the Democratic-appointed justices who consistently voted to preserve the constitutional protection for access to abortion would be outvoted 5 to 4. Hogue's entire career in progressive politics and decades spent marching, fundraising, lobbying, and speaking out on behalf of women's right to legal abortion could be wiped out by fifty-one members of the US Senate elevating a new anti-abortion justice to replace Kennedy.

Hogue and other pro-choice activists knew everyone on Trump's preapproved court list was anti-*Roe* and had to be vigorously opposed. However, when Trump selected Brett M. Kavanaugh, a pugnacious conservative lawyer during the George W. Bush years who then sat on the DC circuit court, Hogue saw vulnerability. Unlike Justice Gorsuch who was smooth, gracious, and judicial in temperament, Kavanaugh was a brash partisan who had worked with Kenneth Starr on the Bill Clinton impeachment fight and later in the Bush White House.

Since Trump was elected, Senate Majority Leader Mitch McConnell of Kentucky had devoted his political capital and energy to refashioning the federal courts at every level. His aim was nothing short of a transformation of both the Supreme Court and the lower courts. By installing ideologically conservative judges devoted to curtailing abortion, striking down gun safety laws, limiting the scope of federal power, and expanding religious conservatives' exemptions from laws governing other Americans, he could solidify a conservative legal regime that would withstand the vicissitudes of electoral politics. If the country as a whole would not support the social agenda of the right, he would install judges to do the right's bidding. McConnell showed just how savvy an operator he could be in the summer and fall of 2018. Instead of letting the Senate go home for an extended recess in August, he kept the Senate in session. This not only handicapped Democrats running for reelection who were anxious to get home to campaign but insulated Republican and red state Democratic members from the sort of raucous town halls and protests that helped doom efforts to repeal the ACA in 2017. While pro-choice organizing continued, the media lost interest in the story. Without a flashy confrontation in August there was little "electricity" heading into the hearings. McConnell publicly boasted to the media that "I have discovered that occasionally I can get more cooperation, for example when I canceled the August recess." McConnell was convinced that "there's no question that nothing unifies the Republicans like the courts."

Along with the rest of the country, Hogue learned in the fall of the bombshell allegation by Dr. Christine Blasey Ford that Kavanaugh had sexually accosted her at a party when they both were teenagers. For weeks rumors had circulated that there was a "problem," which Hogue suspected might be sexual, although she knew nothing more than the general public. She was on the phone outside

NARAL's office when she learned the news. Her initial thought was: "This is it. He's a goner." That optimistic take was fleeting. She soon realized that the old rules of conduct no longer applied. Republicans would not be shamed into pulling the nomination.

The hyper-politicization of the Supreme Court nominations did not begin nor end with Kavanaugh. Progressive and conservative groups for decades have come to see Supreme Court confirmation fights as pitched policy battles on everything from abortion to the Second Amendment to affirmative action. However, the Kavanaugh scandal introduced a raw emotional issue, namely the right of victims of sexual abuse to be heard and taken seriously.

THE ALLEGATIONS OF sexual misconduct against a nominee of a president who himself had collected an extraordinary number of sexual predation complaints over the years *and* the confirmation's proximity to the critical midterm elections heightened what even in normal times would be an emotionally charged event. Democratic activists worried this might threaten their prospects for victory in the midterms by waking up heretofore unenthusiastic Trump voters. However, they also saw one final opportunity to galvanize women's opposition to Trump and his party.

Direct from the president's mouth, the message to White men was that *they* were victims. He told reporters in early October, "Well, I'd say that it's a very scary time for young men in America when you can be guilty of something you may not be guilty of. This is a very difficult time." In this mindset, women who had been harassed and assaulted were not the primary concern; it was men— like him—who had been accused of sexual assault who were potential victims. Coming after the wave of revelations from #MeToo victims this seemed absurd and downright infuriating to women and many men. Women, not men, constituted the overwhelming proportion of victims. The incidence of false sexual assault claims was no higher than for other crimes. But Trump was a professional victim himself—of the press, of liberals, of the intelligence community, and of insufficiently loyal Republicans. He was second to none when it came to instilling resentment, anger, and a sense of victimhood among White males, the most privileged segment of the population.

Making the prep-school-educated, Ivy League alumnus, and federal court judge Kavanaugh into a victim was no easy trick. Nevertheless, demonizing real victims and convincing his supporters that privileged Whites were in peril was what Trump did best. In casting wild accusations that this was all a left-wing conspiracy, suggesting therefore that Dr. Blasey Ford was lying or confused, and in mocking her, Trump gave voice to his resentful mostly White male base and played to its penchant for conspiracy theories.

At a rally, Trump went even further. He cruelly mocked Blasey Ford: "How did you get home? 'I don't remember.' How'd you get there? 'I don't remember.' Where is the place? 'I don't remember.' How many years ago was it? 'I don't know.' " Senate Judiciary Committee chairman Lindsey Graham of South Carolina sniffed that her "emotional accusation" had not been "corroborated," as if her own testimony was insufficient.

Hogue, an avid social media user, was infuriated by Trump's rhetorical assaults and frequently dashed off tweets to condemn the Republicans' dismissive and insulting tone. Women's access to abortion was not the only issue on the line; the confirmation fight now was about respect for the mostly female survivors of sexual abuse and families who had endured the aftermath of these traumatic events.

Hogue found skepticism even among *progressive* donors. Did they really want to put all their eggs in a basket held by a single woman accuser? Despite skittishness among her donors and allies, Hogue had no option but to fight for every Senate vote. She kept up a steady drumbeat against Kavanaugh in the media and encouraged NARAL forces on the ground to make their voices heard.

Pro-choice activists continued to check in with red state Democrats, trying to keep the defections to zero. Sen. Heidi Heitkamp of North Dakota was in the middle of a tough reelection campaign. Politically, it would have been smart for her to support Kavanaugh. However, the issue of sexual assault was personal. As attorney general in her state, she developed expertise in the area and a deep emotional connection to the survivor community. She was especially sympathetic to Native American women in her state who experienced sexual assault at a much higher rate than the general population. And on a personal level, Heitkamp's mother had been the victim of sexual assault as a teenager. To the relief of pro-choice activists, she declared she would vote against Kavanaugh. She would lose her race a few weeks later.

The hearings also became a stage for two women senators who outside their home states were not yet well known. On a Senate Judiciary Committee devoid of Republican women, Democrats had four women: ranking member Dianne Feinstein and Kamala Harris, both of California, Amy Klobuchar of Minnesota, and Mazie Hirono of Hawaii. The most dynamic and charismatic was Harris, a freshman senator and the only African American woman in the Senate at the time (the second in history) and the first to represent California. Harris had cut her teeth as a district attorney and then as state attorney general. She was perfectly situated to take on Kavanaugh and she did, with some success. When Kavanaugh continued to boast of his many female law clerks and supporters, Harris cornered him, "Do you agree that it is possible for men to both be friends with some women and treat other women badly?" He conceded the point.

In perhaps her most memorable exchange she grilled Kavanaugh on abortion rights. She asked if he knew of any laws "that the government has power to make over the male body?" He seemed flummoxed and a long pause ensued. "I'm happy to answer a more specific question, but . . ." She gave little ground: "Male versus female." Kavanaugh floundered, asking if she meant medical procedures. She repeated the question. He finally gave up. "I'm not aware of any right now, Senator," Kavanaugh conceded, ending his torment. Her point was made: Conservative justices were willing to regulate the most intimate choices women make in a society in which women's reproductive rights are uniquely burdened. It was a story she later would rely on during her presidential run. For many Americans this was their introduction to Senator Harris.

In an interview with CNN the following year, Brian Fallon, executive director of Demand Justice, a progressive legal group, remarked that "the Kavanaugh experience proved that she has the mettle to be aggressive and not back down to Republicans." He added, "The person that rose to the occasion was Harris."

Just as the Kavanaugh confirmation battle helped introduce Harris to a national audience, it also lifted the profile of another former prosecutor, Sen. Amy Klobuchar. One academic study credited her as the most productive senator, even when she was in the minority party. Klobuchar had the reputation of a worker bee, a lawmaker determined to pass bills. She had prosecuted sexual assault and abuse cases as a district attorney and championed women's rights in the Senate. And even more relevant to the Kavanaugh hearings, she also had experienced firsthand the behavior of an alcoholic, her father. As the issue of Kavanaugh's drinking habits became a matter of discussion, Klobuchar planned her questions.

Her star turn came in a memorable confrontation with Kavanaugh:

KLOBUCHAR: So, you're saying there's never been a case where you drank so much that you didn't remember what happened the night before, or part of what happened.

KAVANAUGH: It's—you're asking about, you know, blackout. I don't know. Have you?

KLOBUCHAR: Could you answer the question, Judge? I just—so you—that's not happened. Is that your answer?

KAVANAUGH: Yeah, and I'm curious if you have.

KLOBUCHAR: I have no drinking problem, Judge.

KAVANAUGH: Yeah, nor do I.

KLOBUCHAR: OK, thank you.

Kavanaugh felt compelled to apologize later. Nevertheless, Klobuchar's steely poise under fire was an indication that while she may have lacked the name recognition of other Senate stars, she possessed some formidable rhetorical skills. The hearing made clear she was tenacious with a talent for delivering a crisp rhetorical blow, a skill that would come in handy as she positioned herself for a possible presidential run.

Despite Harris's and Klobuchar's impressive performances, Hogue needed Republican senators to buck their party and oppose Kavanaugh's nomination. Sen. Susan Collins of Maine, one of a handful of persuadable Republicans, was met day after day with protesters both in her home state and in DC, including many from the community of survivors of sexual assault and the pro-choice movement who had trusted her for years to resist the anti-abortion pull of her party. She refused to say which way she was leaning, keeping pro-choice activists on edge until the final vote. Only later would activists find out that her vote was never really in doubt. Indeed, the barrage of voices demanding she live up to her pro-choice self-labeling only served to annoy her and compel her to dig in her heels.

Hogue did not speak directly with Collins during this process, but she held out hope Collins would not let her pro-choice constituents down. There were warning signs, however, that Collins might be leaning Kavanaugh's way. Her relaxed, friendly body language captured by the cameras after her courtesy meeting with Kavanaugh, which ran a full two hours, sparked concern. Collins proclaimed the meeting "excellent," another bad sign for pro-choice forces. Under pressure from the media and Democrats, the Republicans agreed to an FBI follow-up investigation into Ford's allegations. However, they then severely limited its scope. The FBI did not bother, for example, even to interview Kavanaugh or another complainant and a credible witness who alleged Kavanaugh had engaged in inappropriate sexual conduct during his time at Yale. Collins nevertheless accepted the sham FBI investigation as confirmation of his innocence. She credulously told reporters in early October, "It appears to be a very thorough investigation." It was anything but.

Delivering a hammer blow to Hogue and her fellow activists, Collins not only announced she would vote with her party but delivered an interminable speech on the Senate floor in which she said she believed Blasey Ford but that the Senate couldn't "punish" Kavanaugh based on one accuser. Of course, this was not a criminal trial; it was a job interview in which the issue was the character of someone being offered a lifetime tenure. A legitimate doubt regarding a lifetime appointment should weigh *against* his confirmation. Even more galling, Collins claimed against all evidence to the contrary that Kavanaugh would uphold *Roe*. The fury from progressives reflected both the importance of the seat and their personal sense of betrayal. They vowed to find a candidate to beat her in 2020. While any other Republican could have defected and denied Kavanaugh his majority, Collins, in the eyes of pro-choice activists, was the decisive vote. She was supposed to be pro-choice, supposed to be an ally of women's rights. Her vote therefore was particularly stinging, a political and personal blow to millions of women.

After Collins's long speech—which went "on and on and on"

Hogue glumly recalled later—she sent everyone in the NARAL office home. The intense battle of the past few weeks was over, leaving her tired to the bone. She went home, emotionally and physically exhausted. She woke up the next morning, a Saturday, in an empty house. Her kids' grandmother had taken them to the beach; Hogue's husband was traveling on business. "It was as dark a moment as I'd ever experienced," she recalled. "It was the biggest professional and personal failure of my life." For years she had promised women that if they came forward with their personal stories, they would have an impact. Now she felt as if she had been selling a bill of goods. Women *had* come forward to share their most painful experiences, but it made no difference. Moreover, the right to legal and safe abortions was now in jeopardy for women from states that would surely make abortions illegal explicitly or all but impossible with severe restrictions to access.

She dragged herself out of bed. NARAL and other groups had planned a rally at the Supreme Court for later in the day to "bear witness" to the final vote. When she arrived, she was stunned by the hundreds and hundreds of people, mostly women, who showed up. "I was just blown away," she recalled. The fight for this seat on the Court was over and yet these people had all turned out. "It totally changed me. It profoundly changed me," Hogue recalled. "It told me that even in the face of a devastating loss we had built something resilient."

Republican politicians and pundits insisted the Kavanaugh ordeal was a boon to Republicans who had painted him as a victim of a left-wing plot, another instance in their minds in which a White man was suffering at the hands of liberal elites. Republicans were adamant that they finally found the way to get their base as engaged as the Democratic voters, who were ready to unleash two years of anger at Trump. The court nomination fights certainly were catnip for the right. And no one could doubt that focus on the election shifted to the nomination battle at a critical time for Democrats' final sprint to the polls. That was not the whole story, however, and indeed it underestimated the degree to which the Kavanaugh fight had cemented women's opposition to Trump. The mainstream media, overwhelmingly male, had not fully appreciated women's building anger and thirst to put an end to Trump's agenda. With this blind spot most media commentators concluded the Kavanaugh incident likely was a net plus for Republicans. Republicans "won," in their telling.

I saw something different. The Kavanaugh hearings reminded millions of women less than a month before the election of their anger, their frustration, and their fear that the clock was turning back. The ongoing effects of Trump's election had bludgeoned them once more. The potential loss of opportunity, equality, and self-determination was terrifying for many women. For women old enough to remember a time when abortion was illegal, this was an especially demoralizing moment. Their ability to achieve economic, political, and social equality was more precarious than at any time in their lives. In particular, Blasey Ford's testimony unleashed an outpouring of outrage, pain, and catharsis for women victims of sexual assault. I too was enraged that Trump and his Republican allies had demeaned and then chosen to ignore a dignified, credible woman and more generally disparaged women whose trauma may have delayed reporting their own victimization. On social media, women voiced their anger; in person, protesters took to Capitol Hill and other gathering spots. Survivors and families of survivors met with senators and protested in Senate offices to express their fury that Blasey Ford could be treated, well, just like every Trump and Roy Moore accuser. Many women seethed in private.

Carol Catron and her throng of women in Chesterfield County were representative of many groups in which some if not most women had experienced a #MeToo incident in their work lives. For them it was "beyond infuriating" that a credibly alleged predator should be elected to the presidency and now another one elevated to the Supreme Court. The angrier they became the more they poured their energy into get-out-the-vote efforts. Katie Porter running in Orange County saw Republicans were more energized after the Kavanaugh confirmation, in part because the courts had become such a critical issue for their base. However, she could also see that for many women this was just one more collective blow at the hands of privileged men.

I certainly tucked away the experience and observed women's emotional torment and fury over not merely the loss of the fifth seat on the high court but the smearing of a female victim. The mainstream press seemed grossly ignorant of the impact on women voters. They were too susceptible to right-wing arguments that a court fight was always good for the Republicans. And they really did not grasp that when events transcend politics to matters of personal identity, they take on an outsized importance to those who perceive they have suffered a loss. Only two years later, another court fight revealed that their political antennae had not improved one iota.

CHAPTER 11

THE MIDTERM GAME CHANGER

Two years after the nightmarish election night of 2016, the women who had thrown themselves into a righteous political battle against Trump's agenda made their final preparations for the midterms. I nervously eyed the polls, trying to gauge whether the Kavanaugh fight had helped or hurt Democrats. After two years of covering the Resistance, I could only wait patiently with the rest of Americans to see whether voters would reward Trump by retaining Republican control of the Congress or erect a Democratic barrier to protect our democratic institutions.

Democrats in their 2018 midterm campaigns for House and Senate seats stuck to the game plan Pelosi had recommended: focus nationwide was on health care. Speaker Nancy Pelosi later recalled she intuitively knew "that's how we were going to win the House." She firmly believed Democrats could "create our own environment." Not only did she feel a proprietary devotion to the ACA but she had seen how Trump's attempt to rip it away had united Democrats and even angered some Republicans. "They saw the threat was there," as she put it. Democrats' pitch on economic security promised higher wages and lower health care costs. Democrats had held more than ten thousand town halls and events on the ACA, and the mass mobilization to retain the ACA convinced Pelosi they could win not only the fight to retain the ACA but also the fight for the House.

The candidates had been working to get their message out for over a year. For Katie Porter, the Orange County law professor-turned-candidate, the first hurdle in 2018 was the California Democratic state convention in February. While it was possible the party could decide to endorse one of the five or so candidates, Porter and her team figured the most likely outcome would be no endorsement, which would take 60 percent of the delegates.

What she did not expect was the sharp elbows of intraparty fights. David Min, who along with his wife taught at the Irvine School of Law with Porter, got 60 percent of the assembled delegates, just barely enough thanks to a single, late-appearing delegate. Porter and two other candidates decided to exercise an infrequently used rule that allowed candidates who lost the endorsement to collect three hundred signatures for the matter to be reconsidered on the floor. Min's supporters engaged in some heavy-handed tactics, both trying to block Porter's team from making their case and in running a bare-knuckle fight urging delegates not to let the nomination come to the floor. It was a struggle, but Porter got the required signatures, only to lose on a voice vote on the floor. As things would turn out, losing the endorsement was consistent with her "brand"—a tough outsider, not beholden to party or special interests.

At the time, however, Porter felt devastated and worried that the race might be over then and there. Her spirits were soon buoyed by Rep. Loretta Sanchez, the veteran Democratic congresswoman from Orange County, who told her to hang in there, to keep going. At that juncture in the race that small gesture boosted Porter's spirits.

Things were about to get much worse, however. A whisper campaign had surfaced in the early spring concerning Porter's experience with domestic violence. The "word" was that she had a "problem" because of her divorce. A supporter who donated up to the legal limit for Min's began tweeting "Katie 'Restraining Order' Porter," insinuating that she had a shady past, making the bogus restraining order sought by her husband that was eventually rejected by the court seem like a deep, dark secret that could sink her. Her staff spotted it, waited a few days, and then brought it to her. Porter was aghast, especially because her kids were old enough to access social media. She did not know if her opponent had instigated the attack or if this was a matter of an overzealous donor. In any event, "It caused a lot of pain to my kids," she confessed later. "It opened up things with my ex-husband that should have been stapled shut." (In the ultimate display of letting bygones be bygones she would endorse Min when he ran for state senate in 2020.)

The attack was wounding but Porter decided that she could not and would not drop out. If she—a law professor—allowed such an experience familiar to so many women derail her she would be conceding that women could be chased from politics. She decided to share her story with the left-leaning *Huffington Post*, describing in detail her ex-husband's mental and physical abuse. In the interview Porter's anguish at being targeted this way came through loud and clear. "To be made to feel like I've done anything wrong—I'm just outraged," Porter said. "I have a wonderful track record. I've worked really hard to fight for consumers. That's what I should be campaigning on." She continued, "I'm not going to let someone, anyone, say that because a woman's been a victim of domestic violence, because she stood up for her children's safety, she's disqualified. Who will run then?" In perhaps her most memorable line of the campaign, one that evidenced her authenticity and feistiness she said, "I mean, what part of Me Too isn't soaking in?"

At the time she was outraising and outpolling her top Democratic opponent. To give in now would mean that even the most capable female candidates could be derailed by this kind of attack. She reached out to the women at EMILY's List, who assured her they were all in for the race and were going to be there through the finish. In those interchanges—a woman candidate finding both financial and emotional support from a pro-choice women's powerhouse organization—one could see the full force of the women-based network. A candidate like Porter could overcome sexist attacks and survive without the traditional channels of support open to men because she had an alternate network of supportive women. It is a truism that women often enter politics with the help of personal relationships; they can only survive political battles with assistance from those relationships.

Under California's election system, Porter had to come in at least second in the "jungle-style" race in which the top two contenders regardless of party would move on to the November general election. Despite the roller-coaster campaign Porter did manage to place second and advance to the general election against incumbent Republican representative Mimi Walters. Porter remains grateful to Walters and respectful of her personally, given that she did not take the low road in the campaign nor try to make hay out of the divorce. Perhaps to Porter's benefit, Walters never seemed to fully appreciate the threat Porter posed. At one point in the campaign, after Walters had finished speaking at a local event, Porter went up to her, introduced herself with a smile. Walters registered little emotion, briskly turning away.

By the time Election Day came, Porter thought she *could* win but was far from certain. As the results came in on election night the margin was tiny, too tiny for the race to be called. Many of the voters she had reached out to—infrequent and new voters— voted by mail so their votes would take days to come in. Hanging in suspended animation, Porter followed her staff's advice to go out, thank her followers, and tell them it was just too close to call. Porter called this the "I don't know" speech.

That evening, however, the star was her son, aged twelve, who gave a stunning introduction for his mother. "Watching with her, the more I see about what's happening across the country, and especially what's coming out of the White House, the more I *really* understand why Mom felt like she had to run for Congress," he told the crowd. "If all you did was watch the ads on TV and the internet, you'd think the people of Irvine are always mad at each other, and especially at my Mom. But that isn't true." He recounted, "People stop their bikes on the street and tell us how much they appreciate what Mom is doing, how important it is. Even people we disagree with understand why this campaign is important." Citizen engagement plainly had changed Porter's life but also the lives of those around her.

A week passed and the race was not yet officially called. By then, she felt compelled to go to Washington, DC, to join the freshmen orientation already underway. As she sat in Statuary Hall for a welcome speech from presumptive speaker Nancy Pelosi, she heard a buzz. Her colleagues whispered, "Are you listening? Hey, congratulations!" Pelosi was the one to announce her victory, confirming her win and praising the record number of women in the 2018 class. It was a nontraditional end to a campaign by an unconventional candidate running a grassroots campaign with the help of legions of women donors, volunteers, and voters.

In Kentucky, McGrath beat the party's favorite, Lexington mayor Jim Gray in the primary. As soon as the race was called, congratulatory calls poured in from the DCCC, Nancy Pelosi, and Minority Whip Steny Hoyer, none of whom had lifted a finger to help her. McGrath recalled that "this was how politics was played." Those who previously thought she was not cut out to run now gathered around for congratulations and figurative high-fives. Nevertheless, hers was not a district in the top fifteen or even twenty-five of the seats identified as potential pickups. She learned that in these kind of races "the party doesn't help you much. You're on your own."

She had another disadvantage running in Kentucky. While she was pro-choice, accepting money from NARAL or EMILY's List would have been the kiss of death in the socially conservative state. She was running, as she liked to say, as "a complete outsider" so accepting money from an inside-the-Beltway group—a pro-choice group at that—also ran completely counter to the rationale of her campaign. From her vantage point, voters "hated both political parties," so her only shot was to run an anti-insider race.

She had her share of rookie mistakes. Coming out of the primary, her campaign coffers were empty. Her Republican opponent Andy Barr quickly went on the air with attack ads painting her as an out-of-touch left-winger. For two weeks the ads ran unopposed as McGrath scrambled for money and decided to tuck away her resources for the final stretch. Barr flooded the airwaves with ads filled with distortions of her record—falsely claiming, for example, she was coming to take away voters' Social Security. The ads regrettably proved effective. Even late in the campaign voters retained the ads' message that she was a carpetbagger and socialist.

Another mishap occurred during a fundraising event in New York. McGrath was taking heat from progressive donors who thought she was insufficiently supportive of gun safety legislation. She tried to explain to donors that "I am further left, I am more progressive, than anyone in the state of Kentucky" because she did not take NRA money. She warned that she nevertheless was not going to trample on Second Amendment rights. Barr obtained a recording of the statement but cut short her comment so as to characterize McGrath as copping to the allegation that she was further left than anyone in her state. Period. Barr's ads featuring that distortion blanketed the airwaves.

Debate negotiations went back and forth, with Barr wanting debates in only small, rural locales in a town hall setting. McGrath wanted a big TV audience. They finally agreed on a single debate. McGrath had done plenty of town halls by then, so she felt no need to "cram." She also knew Barr was arrogant and aggressive. In the debate, he continued to interrupt. At one point she let him finish his point, waited a beat, and then asked him bluntly, "Are you done?" For any woman interrupted and dismissed by men it was an "ah-ha" moment.

In the final days leading up to the election McGrath saw a canvasser in her neighborhood passing out her opponent's flyers. On one side of the flyer was a photo of a smiling Andy Barr, on the other a grainy image of McGrath, something akin to a screenshot from a bank robbery video. The young man obviously did not recognize her when she approached and asked for a flyer. She held up Barr's picture, "Do you know who this guy is?" The young man shook his head, no. Flipping the flyer she asked, "Do you know who this woman is?" He admitted he did not. So, what was he doing? Well, he was making nineteen dollars an hour to pass out these hit pieces while unpaid volunteers who knew exactly who she was and were emotionally invested in the race, passed out her literature. She was convinced from incidents like this and from the enthusiastic crowds she turned out on the trail that she had this thing in the bag.

On election night, her mother, husband, older child, and siblings and their spouses huddled in a hotel room in Richmond, Ky. awaiting the returns. The polls closed in part of her state at six p.m., the rest at seven p.m. The race remained close but as rural counties came in the margin for her opponent increased ever so slightly. The numbers from Franklin County were disappointing; McGrath's campaign manager looked worried. Before the race was called, she knew she had fallen short, albeit by a slim margin of 3 percent. Dazed and deflated she nevertheless went out to face the crowd. In her concession speech she gave a stirring call to action. "Do not give up on our country. Do not. We cannot surrender to this climate!"

It was a devasting loss for her personally, one that left her wondering what all the effort was for and pessimistic about an election process where the difference between winning and losing could be a few hundred thousand dollars to fund blatantly false attack ads.

"I was just so disappointed," she recalled. "I was sad. I was angry." She sat deflated and still on the couch with the tissue box on the day after the election when her campaign manager and chairman came to check in. They let on that they had told the press she had not ruled out running for governor. Governor? Running again, let alone for governor, was not something she wanted to think about. She, however, acknowledged that it was theoretically right to leave a door open.

Her race demonstrated that even with a dynamic, well-credentialed woman, running as a Democrat in a deep red state still carries a significant handicap. McGrath might have done better than past Republicans and any male candidate in 2018, but even in the best of years for Democrats and for women, not all races are winnable.

Some seats were certainly more gettable for Democrats. In Virginia, Spanberger's race in the Virginia Seventh Congressional District was one of the toughest in the cycle. David Brat, a Tea Party Republican who'd dislodged then majority leader Eric Cantor in 2014, held the seat. The race tested her thesis, her hope really, that America was not irretrievably lost. She refused to accept the conclusion of many left-wing pundits that Republican districts were filled with racist yahoos who could not be reasoned with or that Democrats had been permanently branded as out-of-touch elites. In June she had crushed retired Marine colonel Dan Ward in the Democratic primary with over 70 percent of the vote. She outworked her opponent, showing up at over a hundred meet-and-greet events in the primary, according to the *Richmond Times-Dispatch*. Even though politics was a second career, she proved to be a far more effective communicator than her opponent, who graciously backed her as soon as the primary ended.

The general election would be an uphill fight for her. Trump won the district by six points in 2016; a Democrat had not represented the district since 1971. While Spanberger never went ahead in the polls, she never doubted she would win. Perhaps the confidence came from the knowledge her opponent was arrogant and dismissive of her campaign. Perhaps she sensed an overwhelming desire among ordinary voters to cast an anti-Trump vote.

The decisive moment for the race came in her first and only debate with Brat on October 15. She wanted five debates, he wanted three. They had only one. She knew Brat would try to tie her to more progressive Democrats, so she was ready to distinguish herself from the national party. She would not, she had pledged, vote for Pelosi for speaker. She was ready to spell out her views on taxes, spending, and the rest. Throughout the debate Brat essentially ignored Spanberger's answers and referred again and again to Pelosi and liberal Democrats' position on issues. Brat accused her of harboring left-wing views and mixed up her position on health care with her Democratic primary opponent who had supported a single-payer health care plan. At a certain point she was able to mentally step back, spot her primary opponent sitting in the audience, and exchange a knowing glance. "No, you're the single-payer guy, not me," she thought. All she could think of in response to Brat's childish mischaracterizations was: "You've got to be kidding."

The audience also sensed he was not really addressing the woman on the stage; at times audience members laughed at his robotic attacks. By the time the candidates reached their closing remarks, she had had enough. She had no zingers ready, but she was well prepared to articulate her own moderate positions. She quickly rebutted Brat's accusation about Democrats not being in favor of growth, chided Republicans for racking up the debt, and ridiculed his comment that he found foreign policy "mind-numbing."

She then unspooled one of the most memorable rhetorical blasts of the 2018 campaign. She said plainly, "I am not Nancy Pelosi. I am not Barack Obama." She continued, "I am a woman who grew up in Henrico County, who grew up in this community, who was taught service, hard work, and a commitment to the belief that the American people can be anything and we will lead the way in this world, and that's who I am." She declared herself to be fiscally responsible and in favor of a public option, not a single-payer health care plan. She then wrapped up: "I want to serve this community; it's the community that made me who I am, and I ask for your vote on November the sixth. Abigail Spanberger is my name."

The audience exploded with applause. She left the stage knowing she had done well, but not anticipating her forceful closing was about to go viral. Soon enough, her closing comments were all over social media, serving as a rallying cry for women candidates and triggering a final burst of donations and momentum. Brat refused to have any more debates; he had experienced quite enough of Spanberger's rhetorical zeal.

Spanberger waited for her district to be counted on election night. She remained optimistic judging simply by the reaction of crowds at her events and observing the Republican voters who were now on board with her campaign. She could see early in the evening that the vote counts from key precincts looked solid. Her heart sank when McGrath's race was called early for the Republican. Her spirits rebounded when Democrat Jennifer Wexton's race in Virginia's Tenth District was called quickly, representing a pickup of a previously Republican-held seat. She was heartened that Wexton's race was called so early, meaning the margin of victory was large.

Looking at her numbers, there was still a chunk of votes outstanding, but her staff calculated based on the outstanding votes that she had won. They encouraged her to go out to meet her supporters. Nevertheless, she fretted that she did not yet have that blue check next to her name on the TV crawls showing she had won. She finally relented and walked out to meet the crowd. As soon as she headed out the blue check appeared on the screen. Yes, she had in fact won a red district, one held by a Tea Party firebrand. In doing so, she confirmed her first impression of the incumbent David Brat: that there was no secret sauce to politics.

For the women in the LWCC who had traveled to be there and

await the results with Spanberger it was a moment of unbridled joy as they jumped and hugged. The hours they had spent carrying signs, door-knocking, even cleaning the campaign office had come to something. And in that moment of pure satisfaction and joy, the despair and demoralization felt on election night two years earlier seemed to evaporate. They had not intended to become full-time political activists but that is precisely the identity they'd taken on. "As horrible as it was," Catron recalled of the Trump election, "it also created opportunities. This whole country needed a wake-up call."

On election night, the extent of Democratic wins was not yet apparent when most of the country went to bed. California, which allows mail-in ballots, had a raft of uncalled races that would not be settled for days. Other races around the country were too close to call. When the votes were all counted, the number of Democrats' House victories was jaw-dropping, the largest gains since the first post-Watergate election. Democrats flipped forty-two seats, enough to take over the House majority.

Two years of women activism and a raft of new female first-time candidates played a critical role in Democrats' triumphant victory. Many like Spanberger and Porter were first-time candidates propelled into politics by Trump's victory. Candidates like these were imbued with a sense of public service, and many brought to office a wealth of experience in the foreign policy, military, and intelligence communities.

While media-savvy progressive women such as Rep. Alexandria Ocasio-Cortez from New York beat more moderate Democrats in some primary races, it was moderate candidates, including first-time women candidates, who conquered the suburbs and flipped seats from red to blue. The gender composition of these winning candidates was striking. The Center for American Women and Politics at Rutgers found that "Women candidates won the majority of U.S. House seats that flipped from Republican to Democrat in election 2018. More than one-third of women of color elected to the U.S. House for the first time in 2018 won in majority-White districts." The center also concluded, "The rise in the number of women donors and their concentration of support for Democratic women candidates created more equitable financial conditions between women and men in 2018."

Along with Spanberger, a cadre of moderate Democratic women won races in competitive seats. Elaine Luria, a former Navy commander who had been responsible for a combat-ready force of four hundred sailors, won in Virginia's Second District. Elissa Slotkin, another veteran of the CIA, flipped a Republican seat in Michigan. Mikie Sherrill, who had served as a Navy pilot and then flag aide to the deputy commander in chief of the US Atlantic Fleet, won a formerly Republican seat in New Jersey's Eleventh District, and Chrissy Houlahan, an Air Force veteran, knocked off a Republican in Pennsylvania's Sixth District.

Democrats also won with the most diverse field of candidates in history. "There will be a record total of 43 women of color in the House," the Center reported. "Of the women of color selected, 22 (22D) are Black women, 12 (11D, 1R) are Latinas, 6 (6D) are Asian/Pacific Islander women, 2 (2D) are Native American women, and 1 (1D) is a Middle Eastern/North African woman." That beat the previous high of 34 women of color. "The number of non-incumbent women of color elected in 2018 is also a record high; 13 (13D) new women of color will enter the 116th Congress, up from a previous record of 6 (first set in 2012)."

Money was certainly a factor and EMILY's List did its part. In 2018 it bundled $12.8 million for its candidates while its independent expenditure arm spent an all-time high of $46 million. In a single cycle EMILY's List raised $110 million. However, it was not just the money. The recruitment, training, and encouragement they provided to thousands of women candidates made the difference in race after race, in seats no one thought winnable. Gillibrand's PAC Off the Sidelines endorsed and raised $7 million for some of the 2018 class superstar-candidates including Katie Porter, Amy

McGrath, Mikie Sherrill, and Chrissy Houlahan. Gillibrand became a political powerhouse in her own right by helping to boost a flock of women candidates. It remained an open question as she mulled a presidential run whether she would cash in on these political IOUs.

Certainly not all capable women in the Resistance won in 2018. In Georgia, the Democratic candidate for governor, Stacey Abrams, failed in her attempt to become the first African American woman governor—of any state. She lost by only thirty thousand votes, which she attributed to her opponent secretary of state Brian Kemp's efforts to suppress the African American vote. She pointed to a variety of techniques from a familiar Republican handbook, including purging voter roles, limiting polling places in African American neighborhoods, and disqualifying absentee ballots when the signature did not match the voting card on file. She was hardly surprised by the voter suppression efforts. She had watched Georgia elections for years with dismal results for Democrats. The key, she learned, was not to persuade Republicans to vote for Democrats, but to get more Democrats registered. In her mind, with time, energy, and resources Georgia could turn blue maybe even by 2020— as states like Virginia and Colorado recently had done. It was a matter of getting the electorate to look more like Georgia.

To that end she had founded the New Georgia Project in 2014 aiming to engage and register "infrequent voters," including low-income, nonwhite, and young voters. Her 2018 loss was heartbreaking for her many supporters but she saw the election as even more reason to double down on voter outreach. The electorate was moving in the right direction, just not as fast as she would have liked. She also set out to mount legal challenges to voter suppression measures through a group named Fair Vote Action. She firmly believed this was not a matter of finding the perfect moderate, inoffensive Democrat to woo White voters in a conservative state but changing the electorate to include more nonwhites and young voters so Democratic candidates had a bigger base of support.

As successful as Democratic women were, the 2018 midterms were a debacle for Republican women. The Center for American Women and Politics reported, "The gains for women in election 2018 were concentrated among Democratic women; at every level of office, the number of Republican women officeholders declined." Only thirteen Republican women would be in the next Congress, a low in the last quarter century and a net decrease of ten seats. A single Republican woman would join the freshman class. Starting from a smaller base of women in Congress, just a few losses put Republican women even further behind their Democratic counterparts. The gap between Democratic women and Republican women in the House and Senate was nothing short of embarrassing. A total of 106 Democratic women and just 20 Republican women would join the Congress in 2019. Prominent Republican women registered their concern publicly.

The smaller number of GOP women on the ballot and the lack of financial support were profoundly disturbing to many Republican women. Jennifer Pierotti Lim (who had cofounded Republican Women for Hillary, now renamed Republican Women for Progress) recalled, "It was a real low point. Very, very few women won." Worse, Republicans still did not seem to care about the small number of elected women. In a poll of six hundred Republican primary voters taken in December 2018, 71 percent said they were not concerned about the few women in elected office. Republican women were only marginally more concerned (35 percent) than men (24 percent) about the lack of women. The pipeline from state and local offices also had narrowed. Republican women badly lagged their Democratic counterparts in state legislatures. After 2018, Democrats made up 68 percent of the women in state legislatures, a five-point bump and more evidence of Republican women's travails.

The time for silence had ended for Republican women who had lamented the lack of party support over the years. Lim said, "It was a wakeup call for a lot of folks. It just wasn't a wake-up call for the party." The party leadership didn't want to play "identity politics," as they called efforts to recruit more women. There was a widely reported dustup between New York Rep. Elise Stefanik and GOP officials, who rejected her plea for a concerted focus on electing more women. *Roll Call* reported, "Rep. Tom Emmer, the newly elected NRCC chairman, isn't interested in changing that policy. 'If that's what Elise wants to do, then that's her call, her right. But I think that's a mistake.'" On one hand, Emmer was defending a long-standing NRCC policy not to intervene in primaries, but his stance meant GOP women's numbers would remain low. In that case, Stefanik would marshal her own forces to help elect Republican women. If the party itself wouldn't help then her Elevate PAC would fundraise, recruit, and support women. Julie Conway, head of the Value in Electing Women (VIEW) PAC—one of the critical organizations for funding, supporting, training, and advising Republican women—recalled, "You need to get more women in the primaries to get an inclusive House." And if the Republican Party was going to succeed, Conway said, the party "needs to look like America."

Republican women who had labored as pollsters and consultants recognized the urgency of increasing the number of women candidates at all levels. Rising media star and pollster Kristen Soltis Anderson told the *New York Times*, "On the left, groups have recognized that women often have more hurdles to overcome on the road to political office. Democrats have, for decades, built infrastructure to support women candidates in overcoming those hurdles. Republicans have let the chips fall where they may." The former Republican senator from New Hampshire Kelly Ayotte also told the *Times*, "I know that we need to up our game on the Republican end."

Spurred by these defeats, some Republican women activists vowed to do better. "It was very much the year of the women on the left. If they can do it, so can we," Olivia Perez-Cubas, a Republican activist and organizer later told *Vox*. Her organization Winning for Women dedicated to electing more Republican women would need to walk a fine line—recruit women but avoid the Republican aversion to "identity politics." They had to find candidates young working women could identify with—but not defy Republicans orthodoxy on abortion. It would be an uphill but not impossible climb.

Meghan Milloy, the cofounder of Republicans for Progress, looked at the dismal state of women in the GOP. For the 2018 campaign her group raised about $1 million and backed moderate Democratic women in eleven districts. Nine of them won. In order to promote reasonable anti-Trump women, she believed they had to clear out the "worst of the grifty White, male Republicans." In other districts her group backed moderate Republican women, such as Susan Brooks in Indiana's Fifth and Ann Wagner in Missouri's Second Congressional District. Surveying the losses in the 2018 election, she took note of Republican women such as Jenifer Sarver, an outspoken anti-Trump candidate who was wiped out in the primary. "Trump was still a polarizing figure," she recalled. The task ahead was to find Republican women free from the Trump taint, encourage them to run, and help raise their visibility.

Susan Brooks added her voice to those speaking up after the election, expressing her dismay at the paltry number of Republican women in the House. She told *USA Today*, "I've been saying this ever since I've been here. The women in the Republican Party have not been supported financially and have not had the fundraising success that many of our male counterparts have."

Looking at the overall midterm results, the shift in the electorate between 2016 when Republicans won the White House and both houses and 2020 when they were swept out of the House majority was remarkable. On a national basis, House Democrats in 2018 won women by nineteen points (losing men by only four), tied with Republicans among White women, won White college graduates by eight points, and won college-educated White women by twenty points. In 2016, Trump won suburban voters by four points; in 2018 Democrats pulled even (49 to 49 percent). Analysts were divided on whether Democrats had converted Republicans or merely turned out more of their own voters.

Democrats had changed some Trump voters from 2016 into Democratic midterm voters, according to research by the Democratic voter-targeting firm Catalist. It found that the party's big gains in the 2018 congressional election were fueled not only by unusually high turnout among voters sympathetic to the party, but also by larger-than-expected defections from the GOP among voters who had backed Trump two years earlier. Other studies of House races showed a somewhat different picture. Unlike Catalist, Pew found turnout among groups favoring Democrats, not party switching, was more critical. Pew Research determined that turnout among millennials doubled from 2014 to 2018. "Hispanics and Asians each saw their turnout rates increase to about 40%. . . . Blacks, Hispanics and Asians accounted for a record 25.0% of voters, up from 21.7% in 2014," the researchers found. "Whites continue to make up the vast majority of voters (72.8%) and their overall numbers continue to grow. However, as a share of U.S. voters, the 3.5 percentage point drop among White voters since 2014 is one of the largest declines between midterms in decades." Clinton's 2016 voters turned out in higher numbers and gave more support to Democrats in 2018 than 2016 Republicans did for their 2018 candidates. Pew found party switching was minimal: 7 percent of Republican Trump voters defected while only 4 percent of Democrats did.

There was an important caveat to all these studies: Republicans shed voters after 2016, so by 2018 they would show up in polling as independents or Democrats. In 2020, Gallup showed that over the course of the entire Trump presidency Republican affiliation was down 8 percent, Democratic affiliation was up 5 percent. Some of those Never Trumpers, especially women, were helping to shrink the pool of available Republican voters. Republicans who stayed might be rabid Trump fans, but there were fewer of them than when the Trump presidency began. Vox was among the media outlets pointing to evidence of Republican defections. It noted that "across the country as a whole, about 49 percent of White women voted for Democrats in House races, while another 49 percent voted for Republicans, according to exit polling by CNN." In 2016, just 43 percent of White women voted for House Democrats while 55 percent backed Republicans. "Half of White women is hardly a landslide," *Vox* observed, "but the shift contributed to a history-making night for Democrats, who scored the highest margin of victory ever among women voters in a midterm election, with 59 percent of women across the country voting for Democrats in the House."

Whether party switchers were a big or small reason for victory in 2018, Democrats successfully engaged voters in a way Republicans could not. There was little doubt about the "Trump Effect," as described by a 2017 survey conducted by Jennifer Lawless and Richard Fox of two thousand potential candidates. The research found that "negative feelings toward Trump were strong among Democratic women, and that those feelings appeared to spur heightened political participation. For example, Democratic women who were appalled or depressed by Trump's election were two times as likely as respondents who did not share those reactions to communicate about politics via social media, sign a letter or petition, donate to a candidate or cause, attend the Women's March or other rally, and join a political interest group in the six months after the 2016 election." More men than women continued to show interest in becoming candidates but among those who considered running for office "more than 25% of Democratic women had first thought about it in the six months after Election Day 2016."

The Center for American Women and Politics likewise found that "many women said negative emotions—such as anger, urgency, or fear—motivated their decisions to run in 2018. In many cases, and particularly among Democratic women who were responsible for the surge in women running, those negative emotions were cued by the current President, as well as the broader agenda of the Republican Party." That was certainly true of the women whose races I studied. Katie Porter was among the most candid. While Clinton's loss in 2016 was devastating, she told me bluntly, "Hillary Clinton losing made me powerful." And it was true of the women who supported first-time candidates. By 2018, as Carol Catron put it, many women felt that it was "horrifying that he should be president." She emphasized, "You don't take babies away from parents. You don't spread conspiracy theories from the Oval Office."

As in 1992, women in 2018 demonstrated that they run for many different reasons than do men. The Center for American Women and Politics' study showed that women tended to be "influenced by the beliefs and reactions, both real and perceived, of other people and to involve considerations of how candidacy and officeholding would affect the lives of others with whom the potential candidate has close relationships." For that reason, a network of supportive women was critical to the decision of hundreds of women to enter electoral politics. Without new relationships forged in the aftermath of the 2016 debacle, many likely never would have run.

There were plenty of lesson to be drawn for both parties from the 2018 returns. Democratic women could win in large numbers even in red districts. Democrats could persuade Trump voters to switch *and* raise turnout in their own base. Democratic women fired up by Trump's victory got into politics and won. And Republican women needed to organize, recruit, train, and fundraise for women candidates or see their representation in the party continue to slide. The question for both sides was whether 2020 would represent a return to the 2016 model of Republican dominance or a shift away from Republicans, driven in large part by women.

CHAPTER 12

PELOSI TAKES CHARGE AMID A RED STATE BACKLASH

A historic milestone was reached in January 2019, albeit one that did not command coverage commensurate with its importance. Nancy Pelosi, the consummate legislator and keen political strategist, reclaimed the House speakership and prepared to torment Trump. Pelosi seized the speaker's gavel for a second time in her career, the only speaker in the modern era since Sam Rayburn to serve nonconsecutive stints in the third highest office in the country. She was the architect of her party's House victory, who insisted health care be the focus of the 2018 campaign, actively playing down talk of impeachment. She would recall that Democrats "made their own environment," recognizing that Trump's effort to take away the ACA had unified Democrats because it threatened the economic survival of millions of Americans. "Higher wages, lower health care costs" was the sort of bread-and-butter Democratic platform that had lifted them to victory in so many elections.

Pelosi also understood that in the conservative districts Democrats hoped to flip from red to blue, a San Francisco liberal speaker did not appeal to moderate and conservative voters. When several of the Democratic challengers (including some women) pledged not to vote for her for speaker she took it in stride. "I think if they had to do that to win the election, I'm all for winning," she said at a *Politico* event in Washington. "I'm OK. Just win, baby," she said cheerfully. "I think many of them are saying we need . . . new leadership, yeah. I don't take offense at that." Pelosi once again was the most powerful woman politician in America, one who achieved her position by endlessly consulting, stroking, praising, and simply listening to her members.

Pelosi was fully aware how different the class of 2018 was from the 1992 class, which at that time had a record number of women. The women in the 1992 class by and large had been in politics already, usually as mayors, state representatives, or county officials. Unlike Pelosi who had her children first and then entered elective politics, many women in the 2018 class were young and had young children; a substantial number had never held any elected office before. Some certainly recruited themselves to run, but Pelosi also encouraged younger women, overcoming their objections that they could not manage a career and kids or that they lacked the background to run. In an interview with CNN's Dana Bash after the midterms, she explained, "I want more young women in Congress who are in the course of raising their children, because it's important for women in that situation to see someone who shares their experience at the table." She made the case: "Being a mom, what are you? You're a diplomat, interpersonal relationships. You're a chef. You're a chauffeur. You're a problem solver. You're a nurse. You're a health care provider. You have so much, and that's just with the children, not to mention the other aspects of family."

Pelosi readily acknowledged years later that she was "in complete awe" of these women. She confessed that when she was raising her kids, she "didn't have time to wash my face," let alone run for office. Her message to women seeking to enter politics was simple. "You are uniquely who you are. Nobody can make your contribution," she would say. If you have a vision or passion for something, know your subject and know your "why"—the reason for seeking political office—she would tell them.

When it came time to vote for speaker, candidates like Spanberger had to let her know they had pledged not to vote for her. In conservative districts where women had flipped seats from red to blue, they were obliged to keep their promises to constituents not to vote for Pelosi. Spanberger was all too aware when she had made the pledge that the speaker, if she prevailed, would have the power to deprive her of committee assignments or allow votes that would be problematic for her and other moderates. Pelosi did not react angrily when Spanberger told her she had to stick to her pledge not to vote for her for speaker. She was relieved that Pelosi carried no grudge, and in fact Pelosi took great pains again and again over the next two years to protect Spanberger and other freshmen moderates, even at the expense of her vocal left flank in the House. Spanberger remained a great admirer of Pelosi and would enthusiastically vote to retain her as speaker in 2021.

Pelosi understood the new crop of women would need to acquire leadership experience and some element of national security expertise. Having served on the intelligence committee for years, she knew how critical national security expertise was to women's advancement in the House and beyond. "I want women to have authority on issues beyond what people might pigeonhole them into," she recalled. Unlike 1992, when male leadership was stingy with committee and subcommittee chairmanships, she made sure certain freshmen got plum assignments; eighteen of the freshmen were selected as subcommittee chairmen, ten of them women. Rep. Debra Haaland of New Mexico got the subcommittee on National Parks, Forests and Public Lands on the Natural Resources Committee, the perfect training ground for the future secretary of the interior. Rep. Elaine Luria of Virginia headed up the Veterans Affairs Committee's subcommittee on Disability Assistance and Memorial Affair; Spanberger headed the Agriculture Committee's

Conservation and Forestry. Not a single woman was granted a sub-committee chair in Pelosi's freshman year. Pelosi used her power to make certain history would not repeat itself.

There would be no greater delight for those in the Resistance than watching Pelosi taunt and outfox Trump, be it in forcing him to back down on the government shutdown, on impeachment, or on hot-button issues like guns and health care. Her iconic poses—strutting from the White House with sunglasses affixed or looming over Trump in a Cabinet room confrontation—never failed to lift my spirits. She did not plan on viral moments. She wore the orange coat to a meeting with Trump because it was cold and the coat was clean, she joked. She had not intended for her disgusted response to Trump's State of the Union—tearing up the speech on the dais—to catch fire. "It was a pack of lies," she insisted and worse, he had politicized the chamber.

Like so many other political junkies, I looked forward to her Thursday press conferences where for thirty minutes or so she would show how a woman can inhabit and delight in her own position of power. When attention was on the presidential race and one calamity after another—from impeachment acquittal to government purges to assaults on the courts—she remained an island of confidence and purpose. She provided solace for distressed voters with virtuoso performances, clucking over her committee chairmen like a mother hen, joking with the press, and reminding us that Trump, not us, was the crazy one. She effortlessly would deliver one indictment after another against her Republican foes. "Can you imagine not including food in a relief package?" she asked incredulously during the fight over a stimulus bill in the summer of 2020. She was a mother and an Italian American, she wisecracked, so food was really important to her. She purposefully called women reporters for questions. Resplendent in bright colors (with coordinated masks after COVID-19 struck), she commanded the stage like few politicians, male or female. She reminded us that power is not inconsistent with elegance and fashion, and women need not imitate the male politicians' drab wardrobe.

She assumed and wielded her power unapologetically. When she had the upper hand in negotiations, as she increasingly did during the coronavirus pandemic, she held her ground and seemed to appear on every cable news show to make her case: The Republicans are for the fat cats; Democrats for caring for the children, the little guy, the unemployed. It was political messaging at a virtuoso level. She stood as a reminder that powerful women can succeed and dominate the political stage.

This was a woman who maternally protected her most vulnerable members from both Trump *and* the far left, who mourned when one of their own died and celebrated when one married and never forgot to praise her committee chairmen to the hilt. This was a model of leadership that could not be more different from Trump's. Her power rested in her ability to read the landscape and recognize the individual needs of her members. "Our strength comes from our unity," she liked to say, but their unity had to be nurtured and carefully preserved. If members felt heard and part of the decision-making process, it would be to Pelosi's benefit. In a December 2018 meeting to discuss the government shutdown Trump had precipitated, Trump suggested Pelosi was in a political bind. She firmly instructed him, "Mr. President, please don't characterize the strength that I bring to this meeting as the leader of the House Democrats, who just won a big victory."

From the outside it often seemed that Pelosi had Trump pegged because he acted like a child throwing a temper tantrum, something the mother of five and grandmother of nine had plenty of experience with. She was convinced her ability to manage him stemmed from something else, however. "I think he knows that I was onto him," she explained. She knew he was lying, faking his way through the job—and he knew that *she* knew. She was not about to humor or flatter him. And any intuitive politician who viewed him close up could see there was something terribly wrong with him. She later would wisecrack, "I practice medicine on the side without the benefit of a diploma as a mother and a grandmother." Trump and his acolytes did not speak with the authority that comes from truth and facts; she did and was ready to marshal her evidence on any issue confronting her. She never hesitated to call out his lies, rebuke his nonsensical attacks, and condemn his nasty rhetoric. When he lashed out at foes, she reminded us, he was simply projecting his own inadequacies. When he trampled on the separation of powers, she calmly explained that he had no conception of the Constitution. When Trump celebrated his impeachment acquittal, Pelosi said simply that impeachment—the action by the House—remains forever. He would always be the third president impeached by the House of Representatives.

While Pelosi took charge inside the Beltway, she was powerless to stop a conservative backlash in the South and Midwest. Conservatives may have suffered a major defeat at the polls in Congress, but they merely shifted their agenda to a different venue: the states. Congress might be able to thwart Trump's agenda, but reactionary forces were very much intact in large swaths of the country where Republicans remained firmly in control of state and local governments. One component of the Make America Great Again message—the promise of return to a hierarchical order when White men ruled the country—was to cut short and reverse part of the feminist revolution of the 1970s. Before Trump, it seemed impossible to imagine the end of forty-five years of legal abortion. Now, Republicans had the political pieces in place to take the country back to the days before access to safe abortions; to a society that disallowed women control over their lives. And sure enough, a horror show unfolded not just in the southern states but in the midwestern states as well, where with lightning speed state legislatures passed radical measures to effectively outlaw abortion.

Throughout the Kavanaugh fight, Hogue had warned that the right's intent was not merely to fiddle with *Roe, Casey,* and the string of cases that followed, but to tear them up and *recriminalize* abortion. The anti-abortion forces scoffed that this was all hysteria—even though they had given Kavanaugh and every other right-wing judge on the list a stamp of approval and had vowed for decades to reverse *Roe*. She was not swayed by their protestations. Hogue was practiced enough in observing the pro-life side's salesmanship to disbelieve their promise not to seek a wholesale repudiation of *Roe*. She knew in her bones that this was the moment the right wing had pined for over decades. They had seeded the lower courts with judges hostile toward abortion and elevated a majority of conservatives to the Supreme Court for whom precedent seemed to be no obstacle. Hogue's prediction quickly proved to be entirely accurate. Any satisfaction she felt in correctly calling out anti-abortion activists' deception did not lessen the blow as she saw her worst nightmare play out in state after state.

With Kavanaugh on the Supreme Court, anti-abortion advocates were convinced they had the five votes they needed on the Supreme Court to shred nearly forty-five years of precedent on abortion. In recent years they had pursued a successful strategy that nibbled around the edges of Supreme Court precedent, making it harder for abortion clinics to operate in states and more onerous for women to obtain abortions. Now it was a whole different ball game. Anti-abortion activists believed that they could craft one or more cases to force the Supreme Court to reconsider whether the Constitution guaranteed women *any* right to abortion. The more radical the restriction in a state law, the broader a ruling they might hope to achieve.

A maneuver executed with military precision spanned multiple states, which swiftly passed the harshest anti-abortion legislation possible. The Guttmacher Institute, a pro-choice research and advocacy group, recounted: "This surge in abortion bans [was] a distinct departure from the strategy deployed by abortion opponents for decades, which was to adopt incremental abortion restrictions with the cumulative impact of denying care to patients and forcing clinics to close. This approach had led to passage of laws that were less likely to be challenged in the courts than outright bans." Now the aim was to pass legislation clearly at odds with current Supreme Court precedent, thereby pushing cases up to the high court where conservatives could reverse case law that had preserved women's rights to legal, safe abortions.

Hogue fully expected anti-abortion activists to push for outright abortion bans in some of the poorest states in the country, where low-income women and particularly women of color would bear the brunt of legislation passed in state houses that had few women members. Hogue and NARAL were ready and waiting for the fight but their tools were limited. Hogue anticipated Georgia would be a major battleground given that Republican governor Jeff Kemp had run on a platform of rolling back abortion. Sure enough, the Republican legislature introduced a bill to ban abortions after six weeks, when many women do not even know they are pregnant. Georgia at least was one of the few places in the South where NARAL had the support to wage a fight *during* the legislative process, holding rallies and blanketing the airwaves with its message and the voices of women's health care advocates. Thousands turned out at the Georgia state house to protest passage of the anti-abortion bill. Film producers and workers who provided ample revenue to the state threatened to pull out of Georgia. The Atlanta City Council voted on a symbolic resolution condemning the bill. The measure restricting abortion finally passed on the second try, after the bill had to be pulled once for lack of votes, by a narrow margin. It was a lesson that political organization and pressure campaigns alone would not protect the right to choose; it would be necessary to pick up more seats in state legislatures to stem the tide of these bills.

The day after the Georgia legislature passed the ban, NARAL along with Planned Parenthood Southeast announced a campaign fund, the Reclaim Georgia Fund, designed to challenge lawmakers who voted for the ban. (Similar funds were started in other states.) "Consequences are critical," Hogue said. "We don't have the luxury of writing off states."

Stacey Abrams and Black organizations such as SisterSong did the hard work of organizing opposition to the ban and joined in a lawsuit successfully blocking it. After the court victory, Monica Simpson, executive director of SisterSong put out a written statement: "As a reproductive justice organization based in Georgia for over 20 years, SisterSong is committed to centering and amplifying the needs of those communities historically pushed to the margins. This win is tremendous, and it . . . also makes a very bold statement." She continued, "No one should have to live in a world where their body and reproductive decision-making is controlled by the state. And we will continue to work to make sure that is never a reality in Georgia or anywhere else." That organizing effort Abrams and other Black groups undertook, which included outreach to infrequent voters, would pay dividends in the 2020 election.

In its political operation and legal fight, pro-choice forces put lawmakers on notice immediately that their vote will cost them politically. Hogue believed it was possible to make gains in the state house in future election cycles. The real prize would be the governorship in 2022.

Georgia was the exception rather than the rule, however. In most cases abortion bans were passed with little organized opposition. In contrast to Georgia, Alabama pro-choice forces did not have a fundraising reserve, a developed strategy, or an information campaign ready to go. It was simply impossible in many of these states to create opposition to extreme abortion legislation from whole cloth in time to stymie conservative legislatures. Abortion bans spread like wildfire even outside the Deep South, in states such as Ohio and Missouri. The sheer speed of the legislative measures had NARAL and others at a disadvantage. Since there was no apparatus in many of these states to rally public opinion or pressure lawmakers, Hogue decided to go national with a show of strength that might supercharge local activists, engage the media, and prompt lawmakers to think twice before passing draconian anti-abortion laws. On May 21, Stop the Ban protests organized by dozens of groups including NARAL, Planned Parenthood, MoveOn.org, Indivisible, All* Above All, and the Center for Reproductive Rights were held in every state, over four hundred events in total. Hogue told an NPR reporter, "We are seeing the same level of energy, possibly more, because some people didn't believe even with Justice Kavanaugh on the bench that *Roe* was threatened." She added, "But these laws show that it absolutely is, that there is a goal coming out of these states with a national anti-choice movement to criminalize abortion and punish women."

Democratic presidential candidates including South Bend, Indiana, mayor Pete Buttigieg and Senators Amy Klobuchar, Bernie Sanders, Cory Booker, and Kirsten Gillibrand all appeared at the DC rally. Hogue spoke defiantly: "We stand together to call out these anti-choice politicians who talk so much about life and yet ignore the lives of half the population," she said. "*You* matter. *We* matter." In cities across the country, progressive activists, many of whom had engaged in the ACA fight, came out in force. In Chicago, scores of women in red *Handmaid* costumes poured into the streets. In Michigan, the *Detroit Free Press* reported on a mass gathering in Ann Arbor, one of twenty in the state, quoting former Planned Parenthood president Cecile Richards. "This has lit a fire all across the United States," Richards declared. "And this is a fire that is going to burn a pathway all the way to the White House next year." As in other locations, crowds chanted and signs bore the slogan "My Body, My Choice."

The day after the Stop the Ban marches, Hogue put out a statement. "Yesterday was the beginning of a new day in this country. Women and our allies all across the country made it clear that these demeaning and dangerous abortion bans sweeping the nation will forever be remembered as a tipping point," she said. "The unprecedented outpouring of activism should send a clear message to those seeking to roll back our fundamental freedoms: if you continue to use our fundamental freedoms as a political weapon, expect an army of women ready to make you pay the price."

In all, twelve states would enact some sort of restrictions, with nine passing outright bans, according to the Guttmacher Institute. Some prohibited abortion after six weeks, others after eight. Two states banned a common abortion technique used after fourteen weeks. Some laws aimed to transform the fight into an issue of disability rights by banning abortion because of a positive test for Down syndrome or other genetic condition. In addition, Kentucky and Missouri banned abortion based on the race or predicted sex of the fetus. So-called trigger bans to outlaw abortion under state law if the Supreme Court dismantled federal abortion rights were passed in Arkansas, Kentucky, Missouri, and Tennessee, making for a total of eight states with such laws on the books.

Working with the litigators at the ACLU and Center for Reproductive Rights, pro-choice groups struggled to inform women that the bans were not yet in effect. They hopscotched the country filing suits to strike down the bans and to stay legislation that clearly violated Supreme Court precedent. That preserved the status quo for women in affected states, but the laws' mere passage served anti-abortion forces' interests. Even if not enacted, the new laws created confusion and trauma for many women, leaving them uncertain if they could still access clinics and doctors.

The Guttmacher Institute tallied up the damage to pro-choice forces: "State legislatures across the South, Midwest and the Plains enacted 58 abortion restrictions, 26 of which would ban all, most or some abortions." Less remarked upon were some pro-choice successes in blue states where *Roe v. Wade* was concretized in state law. Guttmacher reported that "more proactive legislation, including measures on sex education and contraception access, was enacted in the first six months of 2019 than abortion restrictions and bans." States primarily in the West and Northeast "enacted 93 proactive provisions, including 29 that protect abortion rights, 23 to decrease maternal mortality, 11 that increase access to contraceptive services and 15 that improve sex education."

On one hand, the state bans were a reminder that the 2016 election, which ushered in Trump and a phalanx of conservative lower federal court judges and two right-wing Supreme Court justices, would have consequences for decades to come. It was also a reminder that progressives could not focus entirely at the federal level. Their organization and activism need to bulk up in the heartland. However, the bans also provoked a rush of fundraising and organizing, a rise in public approval for *Roe* and a rallying cry for 2020. By 2020 support for *Roe* in battleground states topped 70 percent. The larger Resistance movement could see that another four years of Trump would mean lasting damage to women's rights. The fierce reaction to the bans demonstrated once more that in the Trump era, the Resistance would not shy away from critical fights in which women would be front and center, even those that they would not win in the short term.

The strong pushback against abortion laws was also meant to influence judges, who read the news and watched TV like everyone else. Hogue and her forces wanted them to understand that abortion restrictions or outright bans would set off a firestorm. If that transpired, the public's ire would be directed at the courts, specifically the Supreme Court, which was already suffering from a crisis of credibility after hyper-politicized confirmation hearings and years of rulings in which appointees voted lockstep to defend the political positions of the president who appointed them. The usually mild-mannered Chief Justice John Roberts had publicly rebutted Trump's accusation that there were "Obama judges," rejecting the idea that the Court was simply another manifestation of partisan politics—conservatives on one end and liberals on the other. Hogue hoped his concern for the Supreme Court's institutional integrity would restrain him in future cases.

When an abortion case from Louisiana reached the Supreme Court, Hogue and pro-choice activists steeled themselves for the worst. At issue was a law identical to one in Texas that required abortion clinics to have someone on staff with admitting privileges at a nearby hospital. Such laws were designed to burden and drive clinics out of business with no benefit to women's health. The Texas law was narrowly struck down by a 5 to 4 majority. Four conservative justices including the chief justice had written in dissent to uphold the Texas law. Now with the addition of Kavanaugh there were presumably five justices on the Court who could either narrowly or broadly undo abortion precedent. As the term ended in June 2020 amid the coronavirus pandemic, activists on both sides nervously waited for the decision. Hogue and her colleagues were surprised, if not shocked, when Chief Justice John Roberts sided with the four liberal justices to strike down the Louisiana ban. Roberts went so far as to cite the Texas precedent, one in which he had joined in the dissent. Just as Hogue hoped, Roberts, it seemed to many trained observers, was seeking to protect the Court from a public backlash and from accusations—heightened during the Kavanaugh hearings—that the Court was a puppet of the right wing. Roberts's vote to strike down the Louisiana law suggested he had no stomach for provoking a public revolt against the Court.

Perhaps the onslaught of protests and vocal opposition of pro-choice activists had at some level conveyed to Roberts just how cataclysmic the loss of abortion access would be for women, especially poor women and women of color. Pro-choice forces had made clear that the reaction to a decision to uphold the Louisiana bill would be precisely the political imbroglio Roberts wanted to avoid. On the day of the decision, Hogue was relieved more than exuberant. This was a reprieve for pro-choice forces, not a final victory. The loss of another liberal justice might well provide the right with the opening to obtain an insurmountable 6 to 3 majority on hot-button social issues. That would come quicker than Hogue and her opponents imagined.

As the country experienced the brunt of the coronavirus pandemic in 2020, Hogue would comment on the sheer hypocrisy of the right wing, which advertised itself as guardians of the sanctity of life but pushed for prematurely reopening the economy despite the risk of widespread death and refused to be inconvenienced by wearing a mask. It seemed that the right too often treated life as sacred up to the moment of birth; when the issue was no longer about controlling women's bodies and lives, they felt perfectly comfortable prioritizing the economy and Republicans' political advantage over human life. Like many Americans, Hogue feared the country and women could not endure four more years of Trump.

PART TWO

WOMEN REMAKE POLITICS

CHAPTER 13

CAN WOMEN RUN BOTH ENDS OF PENNSYLVANIA AVENUE?

With Pelosi reinstalled in the speakership another "first" played out in the fall of 2018: Multiple women began seeking the presidential nomination of a major national party. Even before the midterm election, the *New York Times* highlighted Senators Elizabeth Warren from Massachusetts, Kirsten Gillibrand from New York, and freshman Californian Kamala Harris as potential presidential candidates. "Three prominent female Democrats all but openly began running for president . . . taking their most active steps yet to challenge President Trump and claim leadership of a movement of moderate and liberal women that has come to define their party during the 2018 elections," the paper reported. CNBC upped the number of potential women candidates to four, adding Klobuchar, in the story just weeks after the midterm: "A historic number of women were elected in 2018—these four are expected to run for president in 2020." By January 9, 2017, the *Washington Post* ran a story with the headline "11 Democratic Women Who Could Run for President in 2020, Ranked."

There was every reason to put the four senators—Warren, Klobuchar, Harris, and Gillibrand—at the top of the "women to run" list. Warren had made a name for herself first as a law professor and then author and advocate on bankruptcy. Contrary to the conservative myth, she documented that bankruptcy was rarely the result of profligate spending, but more often the result of an unexpected event like a mammoth health care bill. She came to the attention of President Obama, who charged her with setting up the new Consumer Financial Protection Bureau. The Senate refused to confirm her so she opted to run for the Senate herself in 2012, beating moderate incumbent Scott Brown. She soon won the hearts of progressives nationwide with her quick wit, policy acumen, and commitment to fight for working Americans. For the sake of party unity, she decided not to run against Clinton in 2016 despite the encouragement of many progressives. Now she was determined to show a full-throated progressive could win and beat out aging socialist Bernie Sanders, who had lost in the primary to Clinton in 2016.

When I wrote a piece for the *Washington Post* raising questions about some of Warren's economic views in an interview she gave with CNBC's John Harwood in July 2018, she took the initiative to answer in writing—personally and at length. This was obviously written by her, not an aide deployed to put out platitudes. Her willingness to engage with an outspoken critic impressed me immensely. I might not agree with her views, but she was precisely the sort of creative, civil, and intellectually honest politician I appreciated.

Closer to my own policy views, Klobuchar was a hard-nosed moderate. She prided herself on getting more bills passed than any other senator and often reached across the aisle to make deals with Republicans on agriculture and other issues that interested red state Republicans. She was also a sensible defender of American leadership in the world, something I found too often lacking in Democrats with national ambitions. I knew, however, she had a reputation for losing her cool and cycling through staff in the Senate, but were not a lot of male politicians equally tough to work for?

Gillibrand, to my mind, had made a calculated political move when she went from moderate congresswoman from upstate New York to liberal senator who replaced Hillary Clinton after she left to take the job as Obama's secretary of state. Policy transformations for political gain are hardly new in politics, but hers seemed particularly blatant and jarring. Going from Second Amendment defender to gun control advocate was a bit much and raised questions about her authenticity. Nevertheless, she had launched a one-woman crusade to root out sexual assault in the military, an issue which few lawmakers wanted to take on for fear of appearing anti-military. Every year since 2013 she had introduced and fought tenaciously for the Military Justice Improvement Act, designed to take sexual harassment and assault claims out of the hands of supervisors and give responsibility to independent prosecutors. Year after year she would present the cringe-worthy statistics on the number of women assaulted, ask tough questions in hearings, and find support from veterans and other outside groups. Invariably the military brass would object to taking disciplinary matters out of the chain of command, and the bill would fail. Nevertheless, she was educating the public long before #MeToo became a familiar phrase. Despite her advocacy for this and other issues affecting women, I was not at all sure Democrats needed to run another New York liberal.

At the start of the presidential season, Harris was less familiar to most voters outside California. To introduce herself to the country, she came out with a pre-campaign book, *The Truths We Hold*. I had been forced to read dozens of these prerace autobiographies, and most were dreadful. This one was different, however. The life story of an African American and Asian American daughter of immigrants who chose a career as a prosecutor, not a common path for progressives, was intriguing. Her single mother, who was one of the few women of color at the time working as a medical researcher, was her greatest inspiration. Harris would often quote her mother "all of 5 foot 2." When she or her sister Maya would come complain about something, her mother, hands on hips would reply, "Well, Kamala, what are you going to do about it?" She spent summers visiting her mother's family in India, but she explained in her book and on social media, "My mother was very intentional about raising my sister, Maya, and me as strong, Black women. She coupled her teachings of civic duty and fearlessness with actions, which included taking us on Thursday nights to Rainbow Sign, a Black cultural center near our home." She was a proud alumna of the jewel in the Historic Black Colleges and Universities system, Howard University.

More than her biography, however, the book conveyed her buoyant personality. My colleague at the *Post* Jonathan Capehart interviewed her at Howard University as part of her book roll-out. The combination of legal acumen, self-effacing humor, and emotional connectivity was striking. Few politicians had the "it" factor—Bill Clinton and Ronald Reagan being two—but she certainly did. While less experienced and well known than the other women senators climbing into the race, she seemed, to my eye, to be uniquely talented.

Less than four years after Clinton's devastating loss it was now *assumed* women would run for the presidency. The success of women candidates in 2018 played a part. Moreover, Clinton's run, although unsuccessful, had gone a long way in normalizing at least the *presence* of women in presidential races. It was on one level, remarkable that Democratic insiders, the media, and the public at large no longer considered *if* there would be a woman presidential candidate, but which ones would enter the race. The preannouncement stage of a presidential election can be critical, especially for women who must establish their credibility as serious contenders. Simply being considered presidential material means a candidate's name appears in hundreds if not thousands of news articles and her picture sits side by side with male candidates on hundreds of hours of news coverage about the race.

Just two years earlier at the Women's March, Democratic Senators Kirsten Gillibrand and Kamala Harris had appeared on the stage, facing a sea of pink hats. Now, at the start of the preseason of the 2020 presidential race, it was certainly no coincidence that both were included in the field of likely presidential contenders. EMILY's List, which helped the march organizers make a show of support from women inside the halls of power, recruited them precisely because they were dynamic, pro-choice progressives, well known to those who followed politics albeit not yet household names for those who were occasional political watchers.

By the early spring of 2019 four female senators—Gillibrand, Harris, Klobuchar, and Warren—plus spiritual guru Marianne Williamson and Democratic congresswoman Tulsi Gabbard from Hawaii had announced their presidential runs. The four female senators' preparation, experience, and accomplishments assembled over decades often dwarfed those of their male counterparts. Stacey Abrams told me in an interview, "We often tell ourselves we have to be experts in everything before we run. However, there is an entire class of [male] politicians who wake up one day, had a good hair day, and decide they should be in charge of the world." The self-imposed, extremely high level of credentials may hinder some women from making a leap of faith and running for president, but the corollary is that those who did run were among the most experienced and resilient campaigners. And surely, many women felt, however naively, one of them could convince the primary electorate that she was the best person to go up against Trump.

Had Clinton won in 2016, none of these women would have sought to challenge her in a primary. With Trump, however, they had every reason to run. If she needed any more motivation to seek higher office, Trump's election certainly spurred on Gillibrand. She later told me, "I do think he inspired a lot of women to get off the sidelines." She was not sure she would have made the decision to run had Trump not been elected. After initially disclaiming interest in running for president, she reversed herself and declared her candidacy in January 2019. She explained to me that as one of the most visible advocates of women's issues, someone who had taken on sexual assault in the military and in Congress, she felt obliged to take him on. "He's tearing the country apart, tearing the fabric of this country apart," she observed. "A lot of women are anxious. There's a lot of anxiety, a lot of fear." Unlike the three other women senators, Gillibrand made a point of leaning into her gender, stressing issues like abortion, women in the military, and childcare. She also made no pretense of being an "outsider." Having worked as a lawyer for a white-shoe law firm defending tobacco companies and then served in Congress since 2006, she presented herself as a tough-as-nails political pro.

With a field of more than two dozen candidates with no dominant candidate, all vying to go up against Trump, someone with as little as 15 to 20 percent might win a primary and seize momentum. That suggested an experienced albeit less well-known senator like Klobuchar had as good a shot as anyone. It was not only Trump's presence in the race, but the potential a woman might be the one to oust him that inspired many to support her and the other women. As she liked to say to crowds, "We know a woman can beat Trump because Nancy Pelosi does it every day." The crowd invariably burst into applause and laughter. That said, the climb to the nomination turned out to be much steeper for the women candidates.

The sheer number of women in the race meant this would be dramatically different from 2016. For the first time in history no woman had to bear the burden of being "the" woman candidate. The Center for Women and Politics reported: "At the presidential level, six women entered the Democratic primary contest by February 2019. This not only tripled the record high for major party women presidential candidates in any one cycle, but also made stark the differences among women." Unlike 2016, when a solitary woman inspired strong reactions both positive and negative, the presidential race in 2020 included female candidates with different ideologies, backgrounds, styles, and "motivating factors." Warren was a strong progressive who advocated "big, structural change."

She viewed big business as often predatory and too many politicians as downright corrupt. She was going to deploy her full array of policy proposals—which gave her the catch-phrase "I've got a plan for that!"—to help level the playing field for the ordinary American. On foreign policy, she called for an end to "forever wars" and argued that there was a whole lot of waste in the Pentagon. She was nothing like Klobuchar, who stressed her electability and moderation.

In contrast to the progressive New Englander, Klobuchar argued that she was from the "heartland," precisely where Clinton had lost the 2016 race. If Democrats wanted to carry the Upper Midwest, she argued, there would be no better choice than a Democrat who won even in Republican districts. She was not pushing for single-payer health care like Warren and Sanders, but for incremental reforms that would not put off more moderate voters. Moreover, she had a track record of delivering results. In February 2019, a Vanderbilt University study found that she was the most productive Democratic senator. "Sen. Klobuchar put forward 69 pieces of legislation in the 115th Congress, eight of which passed the Senate and four of which became law (compared to an average of 42 bills, 2 passing the Senate, and less than one becoming law among other minority-party Senators)," the report found. "Her proposals ranged across numerous policy areas, finding their way to nearly every standing committee in the Senate. Her legislative accomplishments include laws designed to improve telecommunications call quality in rural areas, to fight human trafficking, and to add protections against sexual harassment to the Congressional Accountability Act of 1995."

In contrast to those two women, Harris had been in the Senate only two years and had yet to amass a major list of legislative accomplishments. What she did have was executive experience supervising five thousand lawyers as California's attorney general, a deep appreciation for systemic racism, and a prosecutor's zeal for skewering Trump. She liked to say, "I know a predator when I see one."

In an interview with *The 19th* magazine, Harris later recalled that rather than view the other women as competitors to be vanquished, she luxuriated in the experience of presenting a diverse range of female candidates. Joe Biden was not expected to have the same views or style as, say, Pete Buttigieg. There was no single prototypical male candidate that each was measured against. Now the voters could enjoy a variety of women candidates, each to be considered individually—just as they had always treated male contenders. Part of the process of normalizing women in the highest ranks of politics would begin by understanding that their gender may not be their most distinctive feature, although all faced the challenge to recast the picture in voters' minds of what a president should look and sound like.

The four leading female presidential contenders shared some superficial similarities to Clinton. All four were lawyers who ran from the Senate. Unlike several male candidates in the 2020 field who had little or no public experience, these four had built their résumés over decades, moving from law to public service. Each had developed an area of expertise—Warren on financial regulation, Harris on criminal justice, Gillibrand on equal pay and sexual assault, and Klobuchar on prescription drugs and rural issues.

Given the suspicions about a woman as commander in chief all four had been careful to include foreign policy as part of their portfolios just as Clinton had and as Nancy Pelosi always had advised women. This would be particularly helpful as they faced off against Trump, who had claimed "bone spurs" kept him out of the Vietnam War. David Wasserman, analyst for the *Cook Political Report* told Reuters in 2018, "The top traits for Trump's nightmare opponent would be a young, charismatic woman with a national security background." Gillibrand and Warren served on the Senate Armed Services Committee, Harris on Intelligence and Judiciary, and Klobuchar on Judiciary. Klobuchar had over the years also cultivated a relationship with Sen. John McCain, traveling overseas with him to acquire invaluable experience. After his death,

Klobuchar reminisced, "He just had this amazing ability to teach people, younger senators, first of all how to work together at home, but also how to work on the world stage. And he passed that torch on to so many of us." In short, these women had developed exquisite résumés that would, they hoped, remove any doubt as to their readiness to lead especially in the realm of national security.

In contrast to these meticulously prepared women, a fleet of male White candidates, many lightly credentialed, threw their hats into the ring. Beto O'Rourke, who had lost the Texas Senate race to incumbent Sen. Ted Cruz, was immediately touted as a top contender after his defeat, but Stacey Abrams, an African American woman, was not after her loss in Georgia. An ex-congressman from Maryland, John Delaney, with six years in the House thought he was more than ready to run as did little-known Ohio congressman Tim Ryan and a virtually unknown mayor from South Bend, Indiana, Pete Buttigieg. While women senators were still agonizing over whether to run, by November 2018 the virtually unknown ex-congressman Delaney had already visited all ninety-nine Iowa counties and was preparing to open thirty campaign offices. Supreme confidence in their own abilities was in no short supply for these largely unknown men.

It was a sad commentary on the state of American politics, but perhaps unsurprising after electing a know-nothing real estate mogul with no public sector experience, that so many lightly qualified men were treated as serious candidates. The *Columbus Dispatch* in March 2019 noted the trend, which many in the media and policy circles deplored. "It used to be you needed an impressive resume and an appealing message to become president of the United States. But during the past two decades, American voters have turned away from candidates with extensive backgrounds in government and opted for new models such as Donald Trump in 2016, who pledged to 'drain the swamp' in Washington, or Barack Obama in 2008, who said the time had come 'to turn the page.'" It was perhaps to be expected that after a candidate with no experience—or policy knowledge, for that matter—won the presidency so many candidates and voters alike would think experience was not necessarily a bonus.

Moreover, as Tom Nichols documented in his bestseller, *The Death of Expertise: The Campaign Against Established Knowledge and Why It Matters*, the trend toward contempt for expertise extends well beyond politics. "Narcissism and know-nothingism are not afflictions found only among a few disgruntled high-school dropouts in the heartland," he explained. "They are endemic across the country, exacerbated over the past half-century by affluence, technology, a permanent youth culture—and, above all, politics: academic postmodernism and fashionable relativism on the left, and the anti-intellectualism of certain evangelical strains and a long history of populist skullduggery on the right."

Among the most certain of their own competence in an arena in which they have zero experience are the superrich. That was quite evident in the Democratic primary. Entrepreneur Andrew Yang and two billionaire businessmen, Tom Steyer and Mike Bloomberg, one who had never held public office and the other who had never run outside New York City, all piled into the race. They seemed unbothered by their lack of high-level public service; they felt no need to justify why they wanted to run for president. Their "vision" was justification enough to run for president, and their competence, they insisted, could be gleaned from experience outside federal or executive office. With the exception of Buttigieg, the press and pundit class rarely questioned the legitimacy of male candidates who lacked a deep well of public experience. NBC News, for example, declared that Yang "has no political experience and has never held elected office, but voters describe him as intelligent and data-driven and believe that he will be able to seriously conduct himself on the world stage." It would be hard to imagine any woman getting away with such a dearth of political experience.

At times, I was exasperated by the disparity between what it took for a woman to be a credible contender and what was sufficient for a man. I would not infrequently shoot off an email to a female friend or colleague. *Imagine if a female mayor of South Bend decided she was presidential material.* Frankly, it would have been laughable. My frustration with unbalanced media coverage that betrayed a blatant double standard—swooning over the uncredentialed O'Rourke while dissecting specific cases supervised by Klobuchar and Harris as prosecutors—periodically boiled over. "The women who run are still going to be, I think, more scrutinized about their appearance," Debbie Walsh, director of the Center for American Women and Politics at Rutgers University told the *New York Times* in early 2019. "I would love to think that they won't get the kind of comments that Hillary Clinton got about, 'Why is she yelling at me?' 'Why doesn't she smile more?' I'd love to think that that's all gone now, but I don't believe that to be true."

The intensity of the scrutiny, the harshness of the reviews, and the fixation on the trivial (Klobuchar's bangs were blown by the air-conditioning at a debate!) seemed simultaneously blatant and ordinary, as if that simply came with the territory for women candidates. A critical mass of women in the field did not mean that the public and media treatment of similarly situated male and female candidates would be equal.

When Warren was a law professor she had indicated, based on family anecdotes, that she had Native American ancestry. She received no hiring preference or other benefit from identifying as such. Nevertheless, Trump took to derogatorily referring to her as "Pocahontas." In October 2018 she took a DNA test showing she had negligible Native American ancestry. Trump mocked her even more intensely. The press covered the story incessantly, arguing that this showed her inability to withstand Trump's barbs. *Politico* declared, "Warren stumbles with 'Native American' rollout." Although its own polling showed a large percentage of voters did not care, it continued to hype the story well into 2019. "Warren confronts question of whether DNA test was a misfire," it pronounced in January 2019. In August, it was still harping, with a story,

"Native American critics still wary of Warren despite apology tour." Warren had made an unforced error, and she had irritated some segment of Native American voters. However, the coverage of this incident—as opposed to Sanders's heart attack in the fall of 2019 or Beto O'Rourke's self-absorbed video of his visit to the dentist—was entirely disproportionate to its importance to voters or its impact on her competitiveness in polling against Trump.

Charlotte Atler of *Time* expressed the dilemma for women candidates: "When a woman runs for President of the United States, it's like she wraps herself in a giant roll of clear Scotch tape: everything sticks to her, and she can't move." She continued, "In American politics, a woman's gender acts as both an invisible adherent and a tight constraint: it's harder to shake off mistakes, harder to pivot, harder to throw punches and harder to avoid them. Sexism is transparent, easy to look through if you don't want to see it, which makes it possible to pretend it isn't there at all."

Certainly, obscure Hawaii congresswoman Tulsi Gabbard and flaky New Age guru Marianne Williamson showed unqualified women could run for president too, but whether voters demand higher credentials or whether women *think* voters demand more, the serious women candidates were among the most accomplished and the most organized presidential candidates to run in 2020—or any recent presidential contest.

Female candidates in the presidential race not only seemed to insist on a higher level of credentials for themselves but felt compelled to display unusual grit and create high drama. The contrast between female and male candidates was at times jarring. For a woman politician, toughness is critical. Unlike a man who is assumed to possess some intrinsic strength, a woman's stamina must be demonstrated. In 2016, Trump had turned Clinton's case of the ordinary flu into grounds for hyperbolic speculation that she was at death's door. In the early stages of the 2020 presidential cycle, it seemed women presidential candidates needed Herculean efforts to get attention. Klobuchar kicked off her campaign literally in a snowstorm in Minnesota, the white flakes covering her hair and camel hair coat. (Her hair stylist had touched up her roots with a common spray-on product; as the snow fell, she began to panic that the spray would get wet and run down Klobuchar's face. Fortunately, it did not.) Klobuchar and her team used the campaign rollout in a snowstorm as a metaphor for her midwestern toughness. When Trump taunted her as a "snow woman," she retorted, "I'd like to see how his hair would fare in a blizzard."

Warren had her own feat of endurance. She decided that after campaign events she would stay to sign autographs and take a "selfie" with everyone who asked. As her crowds increased in size, her selfie lines and the hours it took to work through them expanded. Even her dog Bailey got his own line. For a Washington Square rally in New York City, she spent four hours getting through the line. By January 2020, she hit her hundred thousandth selfie.

Harris used other means to add drama and heft to her announcement. She pulled off the largest rollout event of the campaign, with a crowd estimated at over twenty thousand in Oakland, California. This signaled she had remarkable appeal, far in excess of many of her male competitors. Had the media been paying closer attention, they might have noticed that while the relatively unknown men drew respectable crowds, the voters were turning out in droves for Harris, right from the start. Despite her splashy entry she nevertheless lacked the media attention in the early going that was lavished on O'Rourke, who entered the race to great fanfare and 24/7 coverage. Despite the intensity and size of Harris's crowds, she did not receive the same breathless coverage. O'Rourke's rollout on the cover of *Vanity Fair* seemed to be an unabashed display of male privilege. His declaration that he was "born to do this" neatly encapsulated male candidates' unwarranted self-regard. It is hard to imagine a woman candidate making the same declaration—or the public accepting such a declaration of confidence. O'Rourke's practice of jumping onto chairs, tables, and bar tops was cast as Kennedy-esque by some commentators; it would have been ludicrous for a woman to do the same thing. I watched his rollout slack-jawed, truly amazed that someone so lacking in gravitas was that confident in his own political prowess.

The four women senators' achievements, determination, and organizational strength gave millions of women a sliver of hope that a woman might end the Trump presidency. Unlike Clinton, none of them had to combat an aura of scandal and none had been married to an impeached president. None had been the target of the right wing for decades. All were experienced campaigners; all had a record of achievement. This really could be the year, a moment of political karma and payback for Trump, I thought. What a comeback story, from defeat to victory for a woman presidential candidate.

In retrospect my optimism that this time a woman would win the nomination and the presidency failed to account for the terror Democratic voters felt over the prospect of another woman losing to Trump. While the prospect of a woman beating Trump was enticing, I felt the nagging suspicion early in the race that even if the female candidates' achievements and crowds dwarfed those of their male rivals, the coverage and the playing field simply were never level.

In early 2019, whether at the debates, in large arenas, or on the campaign trail, Harris displayed charisma, a force of personality not unlike Bill Clinton. It came across on TV and onstage in big venues, but also in more intimate settings. In a small gathering she could make each person feel as if—of all the people in the room— she is speaking only to you. One-on-one, her face lights up, her gaze fixes on you, never scanning the room for someone more important, and conveys an unusual degree of interest and empathy in your life. At an early campaign appearance in New Hampshire I asked her husband, Doug Emhoff, if she always had this ability to connect with total strangers. He smiled, and said, "Always." She was the same on camera as she was walking down the street or sitting in a restaurant outside the media's glare, he said amiably. (I could only imagine how many of their dinners out were interrupted by a parade of strangers, each getting a few minutes of her undivided attention.) In my mind, none of the other contenders in the field came close to her in the "it" factor.

Nevertheless, the media seemed to shrug over her exceptional ability to connect emotionally with voters or her successive "firsts" for a woman of color as chief prosecutor and California senator. Instead, they swooned over an unflappable wunderkind, Pete Buttigieg, whose verbal dexterity seemed to dazzle the press. *The Hill* cooed: "He is arguably the most articulate. . . . Policy aside, it's hard not to be impressed with any and every interview he's done to this point in terms of the presentation, whatever argument he's attempting to make."

Buttigieg's achievements—seven languages! classical pianist!— *were* impressive, but perhaps more to college-educated journalists than average voters. He was smart and well-traveled like them; he was able to hold forth on virtually any topic like them. He was tech savvy like them. He was the polite honor student every parent adored, the overachieving and highly credentialed millennial who most closely tracked the profile of the people covering him. Not without reason, the still overwhelmingly White and male cable TV anchors and hosts were unstinting in their praise of him. In a huge field, it sometimes seemed as if the media had room to marvel at just one standout newcomer, even if he was far back in the polls for months. In one week in April 2019, *FiveThirtyEight* tabulated 366 media mentions of Buttigieg, outpaced only by Sanders. At the time, Buttigieg was in the low single digits in national polling. That sort of coverage suggested the media was more mesmerized by a thirty-seven-year-old gay mayor who was certain he was qualified to run, if only because he could bring a new generation of leadership to the country, than a fifty-five-year-old Black and Asian American woman, a statewide officeholder who had broken barriers—as San Francisco district attorney, state attorney general, and senator—with the credentials to be president. To his credit, Buttigieg made himself the most accessible candidate, willing to go on virtually any cable channel and take any interview. His savvy communications director Lis Smith told me multiple times, unlike some other campaigns, she felt confident sending him "everywhere." Her flood-the-zone strategy to give the media a steady diet of her boss, more than any other factor, helped him soar from near total unknown to a top-tier contender.

The disparity in coverage in favor of relatively unknown men went beyond the amount of time they devoted to them. Collectively, the women in the field presented a dizzying array of detailed plans on everything from racial injustice to day care to housing. Klobuchar had proposals on issues including infrastructure, prescription drug costs, and trade. Warren put out plans on childcare, housing, racial equality, government corruption, climate change, student loans, corporate responsibility, and more. She had the most policy plans that were also the most *detailed*.

The press still needled her: Where was her full-blown health care plan? When Warren finally came up with a multipage funding scheme for Medicare for All the press and pundits dissected its assumptions and figures. That was entirely appropriate—if only the same standard was applied to Sanders and the other male candidates. The press, in interviews and debates, insisted she spell out the details of her health care plan, while candidates like O'Rourke and Yang were not quizzed about their comparatively undetailed agendas. Neera Tanden told NBC News, "The fact that Warren paid a penalty for laying out the specifics of her Medicare for All plan and that Senator Sanders has never paid such a penalty is a sign of the challenges women face at this moment in politics."

Meanwhile, Harris was dinged as light on policy because she "only" had proposals to increase teachers' pay, hold corporations accountable for pay discrimination, provide a monthly payment of $3,000 to the struggling middle class, and sign an executive order to protect Dreamers. Harris too was rapped on the knuckles for fuzziness in her health care plan. But did Yang even have a plan? Rep. Julián Castro? The same microscope was not deployed in equal measure to evaluate the raft of male candidates who stood next to Harris at the debates. Before the Nevada caucus Klobuchar was raked over the coals for not coming up with the name of the president of Mexico, although she was obviously informed on foreign policy. By contrast, no one thought to ask Yang how he would get up to speed on thousands of issues on which he had no relevant experience.

The more policy papers the women generated, the more scrutiny they got; meanwhile among the men only Joe Biden seemed to have made an effort to generate anything close to the policy specificity the women senators had come up with. To his credit, early in the race, he presented a health care plan and a green energy plan. Sanders, meanwhile, literally told interviewers that no one really knew how much his single-payer health care scheme would cost. In a *60 Minutes* interview, he said his health care plan alone might cost $30 million. And the rest? "Well, I can't—you know, I can't rattle off to you every nickel and every dime," he said. "But we have accounted for—you—you talked about Medicare for All. We have options out there that will pay for it." I could only imagine how that could be received from a female candidate. Nevertheless, in nearly a dozen debates moderators never effectively confronted Sanders's disdain for detail and his fantastical plan to spend three times the amount we spend for the entire federal government just on Medicare for All. It seemed Warren and her female colleagues were running a race with an entirely different set of rules while bluster was enough for Sanders to get by.

Sometimes the gender pressure was more nuanced. The Barbara Lee Family Foundation's 2012 election study found that if a woman touted her accomplishments voters wanted her to include "personal elements, like why an issue is a particular passion, or how constituents have been positively impacted by the achievement." Women often feel compelled to arm themselves with an "origin" story, a justification for going into politics. To explain her interest in politics, Klobuchar frequently cited her experience when she was forced to leave the hospital just after giving birth while her newborn daughter had to stay behind for treatment for a birth defect. Warren had a tale of her upbringing on "the ragged edge of the middle class." Men had no need to supply a personal justification for running; they had something to say. Billionaire Tom Steyer, for example, simply claimed, "The only way we can make change happen is from the outside." What more need be said? The media never bothered to point out that he was seeking to run against "outsider" Trump who showed business experience is no replacement for that of holding public office.

Women presidential candidates also faced a unique challenge in fundraising in 2020. For progressive women's groups and other women politicians, the large number of female candidates was a blessing, but it also meant they were not going to play favorites. EMILY's List saw Warren, Klobuchar, Gillibrand, and Harris all as allies and friends of progressive women. Therefore, as long as more than one remained in the race none would get its endorsement and backing.

Likewise, other women politicians in the Senate, House, and state offices declined to pick a favorite among the four, some waiting months before choosing a candidate. Someone like Katie Porter with both a mentor (Warren) and the senator from her state (Harris) in the race decided to lay low for a time. It was not until the fall of 2019 that Porter felt she had given both Harris and Warren time to make their case. With Harris languishing in the polls and Warren putting together the kind of grassroots movement Porter thought essential, she enthusiastically endorsed Warren. The circle was complete; the woman who had helped launched Porter's candidacy now was the recipient of an endorsement from Porter, one of the stars of the 2018 class.

As this critical mass of women candidates vied for money and support, they faced a new phenomenon, the rise of self-funded male billionaires with virtually unlimited assets to buy name recognition. To make matters worse, the DNC put even greater emphasis on fundraising prowess by instituting a threshold number of donors to qualify for each debate in 2019, in an effort to narrow the field. Billionaire Tom Steyer, who'd never held public office and made his money running a hedge fund, used his fortune to swamp the airwaves and social media with ads and solicitations for donations, thereby enabling him to qualify for the debates. Former New York mayor Michael Bloomberg could bypass the debates altogether throughout 2019 and flood Super Tuesday states with TV ads. Meanwhile, candidates like Warren struggled to conserve money for a final push in New Hampshire, thereby diminishing available funds for states like Nevada and South Carolina. Warren addressed the problem with a commitment to small-dollar donations while other women had to take valuable time away from campaigning to raise money at big donor events. Warren had vowed not to take PAC money, an unwise display of ethical purity, in my mind. It made no sense for her to operate with one set of rules, while others raised money by whatever means they could devise.

Certainly not all male candidates in the race were wealthy, let alone billionaires. But campaign rules that allow billionaires to self-fund disadvantage female candidates. There simply are not as many women as men among America's superrich. In *Forbes*' 2019 list of the four hundred richest Americans, only fifty-six were women, just over 14 percent of the list. Among just the run-of-the-mill millionaires, men still predominate. "Almost 8,000 men earned at least US$5 million in 2016 and more than 400,000 earned half-a-million dollars or more in wage income," one study found. "About six times as many men vs women earned an income of US$500,000 or more in 2016 but this is down from 10 times as many in 2009." Fewer women can self-finance and fewer have connections to the superrich through social or business circles.

As 2020 unfolded, the male advantages of extreme wealth and presumed competency and strength came to the fore, as did, to my surprise, the media's role in shaping a narrative inherently hostile toward a woman nominee.

CHAPTER 14

THE ELECTABILITY/
LIKABILITY TRAP

Of all the challenges confronting the female presidential candidates, their biggest was the same one that had vexed Hillary Clinton and her contemporaries for decades. In the early 1970s, an incumbent Democratic congressman from Brooklyn criticized his upstart challenger Elizabeth Holtzman for statements he characterized as "irrational," and he went on to say that she was "as irritating as a hangnail." Attacks like this would cause the *New York Times* to pose the question in a headline: "On Aggression in Politics: Are Women Judged by a Double Standard?" The unsurprising answer was: of course. Marjorie Bell Chambers, head of the National Advisory Committee for Women, told the *Times*, "Women are supposed to be genteel, soft spoken, passive, dainty—all those things that most of us aren't under any circumstances! But you'd better follow the traditional pattern if you want to be acceptable." First Lady Nancy Reagan was a "Dragon Lady," painted as the conniving power behind the throne. Hillary Clinton was attacked as shrill, unlikable, and cold. The names change but the pattern is familiar. As the first African American female Senator Carol Moseley Braun said in an interview in 2016, "It is really the very,

very fine line of being a shrew on one hand and a puppet on the other that any woman in public life has to walk."

Each woman in the 2020 presidential race had to climb an "electability" mountain far steeper than the male candidates faced, all while preserving their "likability," a concern that did not seem to afflict the men, no matter how grouchy, ornery, or short-tempered they appeared.

The Barbara Lee Family Foundation's 2012 election study made clear that women must be both qualified and likable. "Like it or not, likeability is a non-negotiable quality voters seek in women officeholders and candidates. At the same time, it's an intangible quality," the study noted. "Voters have difficulty clearly defining what it means to come across as likable. When it comes to articulating what attracts them to a candidate or officeholder, voters have an 'I know it when I see it' mindset."

"Electable" for Democrats in the age of Trump meant in part that their standard-bearer could not get bossed around, intimidated, or thrown off guard by the bully in the White House. The Democratic nominee would need to dish it out as easily as Trump did, show the toughness expected of a potential commander in chief, and display the cross-examination skills to interrogate and vanquish Trump on the debate stage. But electability represented a unique challenge for women in 2020 when the overwhelming desire for Democratic primary voters was to oust Trump. The stakes were unbelievably high, and many Democrats felt they could not "risk" another defeat—meaning not another loss like the one they experienced in 2016 with Clinton. Many Democrats interpreted the 2016 results as evidence of the inherent difficulty of electing a woman rather than evidence of voters' rejection of the status quo politics Clinton seemed to represent.

Members of underrepresented groups find their status often becomes *the* defining feature of their election campaign, and they in turn become the model for their group. Clinton's gender was front and center in 2016, a function of her history as a feminist trailblazer, her expressed determination to shatter the glass ceiling, and her matchup against a notorious womanizer and misogynist. Political insiders, the media, and ordinary voters jumped to the conclusion, one never seriously questioned, that Clinton's gender was at the very least part of the reason for the 2016 upset.

Male Republicans had lost to President Obama in 2008 and 2012. No one seriously recommended Republicans stop running White men because Sen. John McCain and then Mitt Romney lost. Their losses were attributable to specific shortcomings, gaffes, or conditions outside their control (e.g., the 2008 financial meltdown). Not with Clinton. Columnists such as Peter Beinart at *The Atlantic* ("Hillary Clinton's candidacy has provoked a wave of misogyny— one that may roil American life for years to come") and Carl Bialik at *FiveThirtyEight* ("How Unconscious Sexism Could Help Explain Trump's Win") as well as academic studies ("Him, Not Her: Why Working-class White Men Reluctant about Trump Still Made Him President of the United States") postulated that America simply was not ready for a woman president.

To make matters worse, the favored media analysis of the Democratic Party's travails reinforced the narrative concerning electability. Democrats as a party were losing ground, according to scores of political pundits because they had lost working-class, non-college-educated White males. The Associated Press intoned, "After the 2016 loss, Democrats know they need White male voters." The *Washington Post* explained, "How Trump won: The revenge of working-class Whites." The *New York Times* told us, "Why Trump Won: Working-Class Whites." The *Columbia Journalism Review* took stock of the conventional wisdom:

Virtually all national outlets have run some version, and likely multiple versions, of a story taking the temperature of Trump country, be it a hard-on-its-luck coal town in Appalachia or a hollowed-out manufacturing hub in the upper Midwest.

Regional newspapers have more recently jumped on the bandwagon as well. The pieces focus heavily on the White working class, a group portrayed as struggling to come to grips with its dimming economic fortunes and diminished social dominance in a multicultural and post-industrial America.

The review also noted that satire of the "dispatch from a diner" coverage began to pop up and "become a well-worn Twitter meme."

If only Democrats could win over those White guys the party would return to its victorious ways. This line of thinking was powerful but flawed. In fact, had Clinton turned out African Americans in higher numbers in cities or won over more White women voters or more college-educated voters she also could have made up the difference of 78,000 votes in Michigan, Pennsylvania, and Wisconsin. If James Comey had not weighed in eleven days before the election, she might have won. Gender per se might have been *a* factor, but it is impossible to make the case it was *the* difference between winning and losing in a race that tight. Moreover, two years later a slew of women won races in the midterms in red and purple areas. Wasn't that a powerful example of the viability of women? Somehow the impressive wins of women candidates seemed entirely forgotten just months later. The only race that seemed to define electability in 2020 was 2016, and that was inextricably attached to gender.

I wrote column after column explaining there were many routes to 270 electoral votes, going through Arizona, Texas, Georgia, and Florida—all diverse states—or maximizing urban votes in the Upper Midwest (e.g., Detroit, Cleveland). I pointed out that women in the suburbs, voting in many cases for other women, had delivered the House for Democrats in 2018. I seemed to be hollering into the wind. The dominant analysis remained: Men were safer and hence more electable; women had a gender hurdle to overcome so the risk of loss was higher. Walter Shapiro writing for the *New Republic* joked, "So to borrow a simile . . . Joe Biden is the Democrats' safety school."

Susan Carroll of the Center for American Women and Politics noted that in this political cycle when electability was Democrats' overriding concern, anything that "diverged from the White, male norm" was considered to be too risky. Not only Clinton's loss but the "whole history of the presidency" seemed to point in the direction of a "traditional" candidate, which meant White and male. There likely never could have been a female candidate with Sanders's attributes. "Try to imagine a female Bernie Sanders," Susan Carroll of the Center observed. "You just can't."

It was not only pundits who expressed the view in the 2020 election cycle that voters could vote either for a woman or for a safer, more electable man; Democratic women themselves adopted this mindset. Again and again, women voters and women veteran Democratic operatives whom I spoke to throughout the campaign, would suggest the election was "too important to screw up." They could not afford to "gamble" on a woman. I heard this from former Clinton associates, from Democratic women at rallies, and from Democratic women in suburbia, the very same voters who had elected women candidates in the suburbs in 2018 by large margins. Women themselves had internalized the message that women were risky. Early polling based heavily on name recognition showed two men, former vice president Joe Biden and Sen. Bernie Sanders, leading the field and beating Trump by the largest margins in head-to-head contests. That reinforced the perception that White men were more electable.

With the widespread assumption already fixed that they were less electable, the female contenders could afford little margin for error. They dared not appear frivolous or too serious, too daring or overly cautious. Nothing short of perfection on their part and the meltdown of the male contenders would shake the belief that Democrats' best chance for ousting Trump rested with a White male. If primary voters deviated from the norm of selecting a White male candidate the country would face a greater chance of the unthinkable, four more years of Trump.

If White women came up short on electability according to conventional wisdom, then women of color were going to be *really* high-risk propositions regardless of talent, qualifications, or organizational strength. Kamala Harris was familiar with the knock that voters were not ready for someone like her. In every race, starting with her runs for district attorney and continuing to her campaigns for state attorney general and senator, she heard voters would not accept a woman, especially a woman of color. In a mocking tone Harris would reiterate the admonitions she received from political commentators, insiders, and donors: *Wait your turn. Don't be so nakedly ambitious* (the latter a slam rarely made against male candidates). She was acutely aware of the ambivalence toward women candidates.

On the trail she liked to tell a story recounting her experience as a surrogate for President Obama in 2008. Door-knocking in Iowa, an exquisitely attired, well-coiffed elderly African American woman opened the door a crack, leaving on the chain lock. Harris explained who she was. The woman responded, "Oh, they're not going to let him win." Harris was dumbstruck but retained the lesson that if your dreams had been dashed, if your political idols (Shirley Chisholm, Jesse Jackson) had been blocked from power, you don't want to have your heart broken once again. Nevertheless, the woman did turn out at the next day's caucuses, which Obama won. Getting voters past their fear of disappointment remained a central task for Harris.

"Let's talk about women and ambition, shall we?" Harris told me in an interview in New Hampshire in early 2019. She understood that fully accepting a woman of color as the presidential nominee meant overcoming a host of expectations about how women should behave in public confrontations with men. Convincing voters that ambition was entirely appropriate if not essential for a woman of color—just as it was for a White male—would not be easy. She remained adamant, however, that voters understood "we have so much more in common than what separates us." In retrospect, it was not surprising she had this early insight about aversion to ambitious, aggressive women of color; she had dealt with it her entire career. The only difference now was the size of the stage and the political stakes.

On May 5, 2019, Harris delivered her most direct rebuttal to the electability argument. "There has been a conversation by pundits about 'electability' and 'who can speak to the Midwest.'" Harris told ten thousand people at an NAACP dinner in Detroit. "But when they say that, they usually put the Midwest in a simplistic box and a narrow narrative. And too often their definition of the Midwest leaves people out." She argued that "the conversation too often suggests certain voters will only vote for certain candidates regardless of whether their ideas will lift up all our families. It's shortsighted. It's wrong. And voters deserve better." The speech was powerful but did not dampen skepticism about the electability of anyone but a White male. For months thereafter Harris talked frankly about how the "first" of any underrepresented group must convince voters to accept someone as a viable candidate who did not match their image of what a president looked and sounded like. In essence, Harris was demanding voters cast aside concerns that both race and gender would be drags on her chances in the general election, no easy task.

Harris faced another issue, in part but not exclusively driven by gender. Before her election to the Senate in 2016 she had spent her entire career as a prosecutor, first as San Francisco's district attorney and then as California's attorney general. Prosecutorial experience is a common way for women to establish their "toughness." That would normally be the perfect frame for Harris. However, her record as a prosecutor fell under scrutiny by some in the Democratic Party, evidencing the shift in thinking about criminal justice reform, even before the murder of George Floyd ignited nationwide protesters in 2020. A track record of locking up hardened criminals used to be a plus for those entering politics; now contributing to mass incarceration was seen as a negative. Harris took flak from progressives, from the press, and even from desperate also-ran contenders like Tulsi Gabbard for being insufficiently progressive as a prosecutor. For weeks she chose to talk relatively little about her prosecutorial experience. Self-censorship proved to be unhelpful. Voters and the press wanted her to talk more about herself. As the campaign went on, Harris came to realize that it did no good to steer clear of her biography. She began to tout her accomplishments as California's attorney general. She boasted she had started the first mandatory antibias training for police and a program to reintegrate ex-felons back into society. She recounted her success in taking on the banks during the housing collapse and fighting international drug cartels. By the late spring she had introduced a new meme: She knew all about predators—and Trump met the profile.

She also began to reveal how she thought of her job as a prosecutor. She wrote for *Essence* magazine, "I went into the system to change it." She recalled her work as a young prosecutor specializing in sexual assault cases. "I spent a lot of time in Oakland's Highland General Hospital talking with rape victims—young girls, elderly women and kids who'd been abused by people they trusted and loved. At the time, the hospital was drab, with no life in it, and musty," she recounted. "Beyond the process of talking to them about what had happened and asking them to open up about painful moments, I looked around and thought, 'A person who is already traumatized shouldn't have to spend hours in a place like this.' So, I took action. I got a few friends together, formed a volunteer auxiliary group through the Alameda County prosecutor's office and we painted and installed artwork to ensure that a room that sees survivors of indescribable trauma doesn't reflect that horrific experience." The more she talked about her work as a prosecutor, the more she revealed her deep well of empathy. That in turn helped her with the flip side of "electability," namely likability.

On the likability score, women candidates also face disadvantages. Male candidates have a variety of accepted activities to show they are just one of the guys. They duck hunt. They grab a beer with shift workers. Women do not yet have widely accepted tropes of their own, and when they adopt ones used by men they often are criticized for it. If a male candidate drops in for a beer at a local bar, he is authentic; if a woman does, she is trying too hard. If a man tears up, he is empathetic; if a woman does, she is weak. Shopping? Too frivolous! When O'Rourke posted a video of getting a haircut on social media, *Washington Post* columnist Karen Tumulty wrote, "Among campaign stunts, hopping into a barber chair ranks among the most orthodox and time-tested . . . [but] would any of the half-dozen female contenders survive putting her salon cut-and-blowout on social media? Or God forbid, letting anyone see her get her nails done?" As she aptly described the dilemma, "Though more women are running for office than ever before, there remains a huge relatability gap between the sexes. When female candidates do some of the very things that are deemed to make their male counterparts more likeable, they find themselves the objects of scorn and suspicion instead."

The likability critique had reared its head in the 2008 election when none other than candidate Barack Obama dubbed Clinton "likable enough." Clinton's loss in 2016 was attributable to a range of factors, but her high unfavorable personal ratings were often cited as a significant factor. Among voters who disliked both candidates, a large majority went for Trump even though his unfavorability rating of 61 percent, according to Gallup, was the highest in history and nine points higher than Clinton's unfavorability score. Many voters seemed irrationally resentful and put off by her. Was this attributable to her gender or was there something specific to Clinton's track record and personality? It was hard to divine whether gender per se was the problem or whether Clinton provoked resentment, either because of her perceived ethical failings or simply because decades of anti-Clinton right-wing attacks had taken their toll. Clinton was not on the ballot in 2020, but the ghost of likability reappeared almost immediately. The media narrative that women in particular had to avoid Clinton's likability deficit became a dominating feature in campaign coverage. A right-wing columnist for the *New York Post* insisted, "No, it's not sexist to call Elizabeth Warren 'unlikable.'" Actually, that is precisely what it was. Boston.com showed a tad more self-awareness with a headline, "Is the Media's Elizabeth Warren Coverage Repeating the Same Mistakes of 2016?"

Physical appearance and dress were a less prominent part of the coverage of women candidates (if only because there were more of them), but it did pop up from time to time. When, for example, Harris went shopping with the media gaggle to support local merchants in South Carolina her purchase, a colorful sequined jacket, was scrutinized. Right-wing pundits like Brit Hume groused reporters were "helping pick out clothes and then putting out glowing tweets about it." NBC's Kasie Hunt responded, "Nobody seemed to have a problem when the candidate was Scott Walker and the activity was motorcycle riding. Or Mitt Romney riding jet skis on vacation. Or skeet shooting with Lindsey Graham." She added, "I'm all for female candidates expanding the list of campaign activities." Finding an acceptable activity for a female candidate to show her common touch turned out to be uncommonly difficult.

The likability issue attached itself to Warren in early coverage of the race. Her toughness became "abrasiveness" and her intellectual strengths were converted into a criticism of her "schoolmarmish" style. On December 18, 2018, *Politico* ran a story devoted entirely to Warren's likability. The conversation continued for weeks. Even women reporters and pundits commented on Warren's supposed likability deficit, demonstrating once again that women are not immune from gender stereotyping. On December 31, another *Politico* column flogged the likability issue. In early January 2019, NBC.com and other outlets joined the discussion about likability. On January 14, *Vanity Fair* went back to the same theme. Virtually every national outlet, whether TV or print, harped on the subject.

Warren's style of campaigning tended to fuel the likability debate. Her determination to have a plan for everything—tackling the electability issue by showing how prepared and smart she was—at times made it difficult to connect with non-college-educated voters. Her wonkiness, intellectual firepower, and ability to put others (often men) in their place may have won over a certain segment of the chattering class, but she also might have been off-putting to many ordinary voters. A televised town hall illustrated this phenomenon. She was asked how she would respond to someone objecting to gay marriage on religious grounds, she retorted, "Well, I'm going to assume it's a guy who said that, and I'm going to say, 'Then just marry one woman. I'm cool with that.'" As the laughter died down, she added, "assuming you can find one [a wife]." It was clever but condescending.

Klobuchar's likability problem surfaced at the start of her campaign. Klobuchar's finesse in the Kavanaugh hearings and her status as the single most productive member of the Senate added to her résumé, but she was soon assaulted with a series of stories making her out to be the proverbial boss from hell. She was angry, insulting, erratic, and mean according to unnamed sources. She threw things at aides, used a comb as a fork to eat salad on an airplane and let employees have it when they were late. The *New York Times* finger-wagged, "She was known to throw office objects in frustration, including binders and phones, in the direction of aides, they said. Low-level employees were asked to perform duties they described as demeaning, like washing her dishes or other cleaning—a possible violation of Senate ethics rules, according to veterans of the chamber." *Vanity Fair* sounded appalled about "an alleged incident in which most of the staff had been running late to the office, prompting Klobuchar to leave tardy slips on their desks." The horror of it all.

The debate about these stories and how to evaluate a tough

woman boss became part of Klobuchar's story in the opening weeks of her presidential run. There were virtually no such
tales about any of her male competitors, which either meant over
a dozen male presidential candidates were angelic bosses or that
more attention was paid to a woman candidate who displayed these
behaviors. Klobuchar did not attempt to deny the reports, a recognition that there were too many accounts out there—and too
much turnover in her office—to dismiss them out of hand. Instead
she settled on a response that conceded she was tough on her staff,
maybe too tough at times, but she was equally if not harder on herself. Even though no new information was uncovered, essentially
the same reports were told and retold in the early weeks of 2019.
With her announcement in the Minnesota blizzard she began to
pivot to a different image—one of resilience and toughness, someone not about to whine or complain. As the campaign continued,
it was that image of the gritty gal from the heartland that began to
define her.

By contrast the most unlikable candidate in the race was never
cornered for being curt, rude, and dismissive. Sanders made being
a "grumpy old man" seem like a virtue. The ongoing concern for
women candidates has traditionally centered on coming across as
"strident," "shrill," or "bossy," qualities that practically never applied to a candidate like Sen. Bernie Sanders whose high-decibel
delivery prompted many voters and journalists to ponder, "Why is
he screaming?"

Part of Sanders's brand was his *aversion* to being nice, warm,
and fuzzy. Indeed, Sanders had readily admitted to his gruff personality. Back in 1990 Sanders even conceded, "Some people say I
am very hard to work with. They say I can be a real son of a bitch.
They say I can be nasty [that] I don't know how to get along with
people. Well, maybe there's some truth to it." Such candor, even
relish in being a jerk, was not an option for a woman candidate, as
Klobuchar found out. Only after Klobuchar was out of the race and
Super Tuesday was in the rearview mirror did the *New York Times*

finally run a story on Sanders, skewering him for his unlikable personal qualities. The *Times* intoned: "People who have known Mr. Sanders for years say that, if anything, he is more intense and can be insensitive to people who encounter his moods—in other words, even more Bernie than Bernie." That is an odd way to describe a figure who is moody, angry, disdainful, and stubborn. ("He has a history of angry outbursts, especially when he believes people are not working hard enough or are exposing him to political risk.") The description of his conduct and lack of remorse were strikingly different from Klobuchar's apologetic approach: "Mr. Sanders denies that he has ever been an abusive boss, but allows that he can be difficult to work with, and has attributed his impatience to his own sense that he is falling short of his own high expectations."

"Look, I don't tolerate [expletive] terribly well," Sanders told the *New York Times* editorial board in December. "I'm not good at backslapping. I'm not good at pleasantries. If you have your birthday, I'm not going to call you up to congratulate you, so you'll love me and you'll write nice things about me."

And yet Sanders's likability was a nonissue throughout the campaign. The only explanation for the double standard is gender.

CHAPTER 15

THE DEBATES

The Democratic presidential debates began at the end of June 2019 and concluded in March 2020. The field was so large that the June and July debates were spread over consecutive nights with the participants chosen randomly. Together with the nine more events held between September 2019 and March 2020, the debates served to highlight specific issues and to help narrow the field while providing some of the most memorable moments in the Democratic primary campaign.

Just ahead of the first round of debates in Miami, Florida, in late June 2019, the issue of child separation, a compelling one for women, came to the fore. Laurie Woodward Garcia, the immigration activist from South Florida, traveled to Homestead, Florida, which had become ground zero in the child separation fight. With the Democratic candidates nearby for the debate she and other activists attended a rally for Sen. Elizabeth Warren, carrying signs "Don't Look Away." A Warren aide spotted them and said the senator wanted to speak with them privately. They made their pitch directly to her that Homestead was a human rights disaster that required national attention. On June 25, Warren announced at a town hall, "I'm going to Homestead." She told the audience, "We have to shut down that facility and shut it down now!" This was among Woodward Garcia's proudest moments. It was, she recalled, the rare issue that could penetrate the fog of news and move everyday people to plunge into the rough and tumble of national politics. And they had gotten the attention of a presidential contender.

The top women candidates faced an ongoing challenge at the Democratic presidential debates that their male competitors did not. The four female senators fully understood that in the context of a debate, voters have less tolerance for women's anger and aggression, which might consist of nothing more than interrupting other speakers as men regularly do. Women must project a command of the issues and the confidence to take on opponents but without invoking the sexist labels that they are "bossy" or "strident." At all costs they had to avoid the impression of being angry, an insult often thrown at Clinton in 2016. The men had their own challenges when it came to confronting the women on the debate stage. A male candidate's sharp response, finger-pointing, or invasion of a female opponent's personal space could work against him. Facing women on the stage, a male candidate could not afford to be condescending, let alone menacing. Buttigieg kept this clearly in mind during debate preparation thanks to his sharp campaign team, which included many strong female voices. Communications director and senior adviser Lis Smith told members of the campaign who played the roles of Warren and Klobuchar in practice sessions to take no prisoners, spare no feelings. Buttigieg's female-heavy team had the collective experience and insight to warn their candidate not to sound sarcastic, dismissive, or disrespectful. He generally followed their advice, which helped maintain his polite and even-keel image.

The stakes were high for the first debate, although the candidates did not appear onstage on the same night. One cannot but wonder what would have happened if, say, Warren and not Harris had appeared onstage the same night as Biden. For many candidates this was their first introduction to a national audience. Harris had always told her staff she was in the race to win it, not to audition for vice president and not to raise her profile. She was dead serious about winning and fully cognizant of the need to stand out in a huge field. She came galloping out of the gates in that first debate. Harris's team knew that Biden's comments regarding his ability to work decades ago in the Senate with segregationists, made days before the first debate in June, would come up. It is debate prep 101 to anticipate questions about recent news items. Another Biden opponent, Sen. Cory Booker of New Jersey, had already publicly criticized Biden for his cheery recollections of working with people who opposed civil rights legislation, the very laws that made Booker's and Harris's careers possible. Harris was determined not to shy away from the issue nor give her opponent a pass.

In the debate Harris turned to face Biden. "It was hurtful to hear you talk about the reputations of two United States senators who built their reputations and career on the segregation of race in this country," she said. She then took the conversation in a slightly new direction. "You also worked with [those segregationist senators] to oppose busing," Harris told Biden. "And there was a little girl in California who was part of the second class to integrate her public schools and she was bused to school every day. And that little girl was me." Biden insisted, "I did not oppose busing in America. What I opposed is busing ordered by the Department of Education. That's what I opposed." Biden seemed caught off guard while Harris got initial credit for a "take no prisoners" style of campaign—in other words, campaigning as any man would without worrying about competitors' hurt feelings.

During the debate, Harris's team was ready to post a picture of the elementary school-aged Harris on social media. She and her team were surprised Biden did not seem to have a well-prepared response. She also did not anticipate, however, that it would become *the* major story coming out of the first debate. She certainly did not expect it to linger, to get dredged up again in the second debate, and then during the vice president selection process to become an albatross around her neck. While the debate is remembered almost

solely for that Biden-Harris interchange, her overall debate performance that night may have been her best of the entire campaign,
the kind of in-the-zone debate campaigns pray their candidates can
deliver. Her answers were strong and crisp, and she came across as
fresh, knowledgeable, and energetic. CNN proclaimed, "Kamala
Harris shines in commanding Democratic debate performance."
NBC reported that Indivisible conducted a quick poll of its members: Harris was chosen as the most impressive by 65 percent. Her
poise, command of her material, and controlled attack on Biden
told me she was a unique talent. She arguably did not turn in a
performance that effective until the vice presidential debate in October 2020.

In the July 2019 debate, Harris's performance was less sure-
footed, in part, because she had taken on the aura of a front-runner
whom moderators and opponents felt compelled to knock down.
To a degree her polish, charisma, stunning first debate performance
and background in the most populous state put her prematurely in
the top tier of candidates. She was, after all, a first-term senator,
but her sudden rise made her an inviting target for her opponents.
When the busing topic came up again Biden was prepared and able
to point out that neither Biden nor Harris favored mandatory, fed-
erally imposed busing. The media criticism mounted as reporters
pointed out there was actually little difference in the two candidates' position on busing. The public's sympathy for Harris seemed
to fade. *FiveThirtyEight*'s Nate Silver observed, "In particular,
[her poll numbers] show further downward movement for Kamala
Harris, who had already lost much of her bounce following the first
debate." *Vox* declared her one of the "losers" in the debate, dinging
her for sounding too defensive. Her margin for error seemed to be
nonexistent. On one hand she was expected to beat back attacks
from her competitors, but if she became too aggressive, she would
fall prey to the stereotype of the "angry, Black woman" that was
thrown at Michelle Obama in 2008.

The press made much of the dustup but in Harris's mind it did not change their relationship, which had developed years earlier during her close alliance and friendship with Biden's son Beau, who died of brain cancer in 2015. Harris spoke fondly of Beau throughout the campaign, often recalling how they had worked together during the housing crisis. On the fourth anniversary of his death, Harris tweeted that she was thinking of the entire Biden family. "Beau was my friend. We were AGs together, and you couldn't find a person who cared more deeply for his family, the nation he served, and the state of Delaware. Four years after his passing, I still miss him." Biden tweeted back his heartfelt appreciation. The press might want to cast them as frenemies; for Harris, Biden remained someone she respected and personally liked. They continued to cross paths throughout the summer and fall. The warm relationship continued, despite the media coverage. The two candidates certainly thought the incident was behind them, never imagining it would once more be front-page news a year later.

As the debates continued through 2019, Hogue and other pro-choice activists were dismayed that despite the presence of women candidates and moderators, abortion was barely discussed. It would not be enough for her and her members for candidates simply to check the box as "pro-choice." In social media and at NARAL's fall annual held in Washington, DC, Hogue publicly urged moderators to ask questions about abortion rights—and encouraged candidates to raise the topic even if they were not asked. Sure enough, in the October debate Harris, initiated the conversation. "This is the sixth debate we have had in this presidential cycle and not nearly one word, with all of these discussions about health care, on women's access to reproductive health care, which is under full-on attack," Harris said. "People need to keep their hands off of women's bodies and let women make the decisions about their own lives." Hogue was pleased. Harris got kudos from women's rights activists, but it did nothing to lift her in the polls, most likely because all of the contenders were pro-choice.

By December over half the field was gone and the survivors

were gathered on the same single stage. Here gender differences became a flash point. The candidates were asked at the end of the debate what they would either apologize for or what, in the holiday spirit, they would give as a gift. One could not have written a more exasperating script: The males on the stage bestowed presents. Andrew Yang joked, "I would love to give each of you a copy of my book." Buttigieg chimed in, "I should probably send my book around more, too." Steyer offered a cloying answer: "The gift that I would like to give everyone on this stage, which was the original question, is the gift of teamwork." The women candidates apologized for their anger. Warren said, "I will ask for forgiveness. I know that sometimes I get really worked up, and sometimes I get a little hot. I don't really mean to." In a similar vein, Klobuchar told the audience, "Well, I would ask for forgiveness any time any of you get mad at me. I can be blunt. But I am doing this because I think it is so important to pick the right candidate here. I do."

The *Washington Post* reported on the debate, quoting Amanda Hunter, a spokeswoman for the Barbara Lee Family Foundation: "In a campaign that has emphasized policy differences, generational divides and geographical values, this single question illustrated another dimension—what many see as a double standard in the ways men and women are expected to behave. It's an ingrained gender stereotype that men don't have to apologize for being labeled angry." She added: "Many of the women watching the debate could relate to feeling that pressure."

Were we stuck in a political environment when presidential-caliber women feel compelled to apologize for their anger? I thought back to a conversation with Harris almost a year before. "Let's talk about women and ambition, shall we?" she had asked rhetorically. She understood from the earliest days of the campaign that the anger, ambition, and ego ("I alone can fix it") men commonly exhibit in political campaigns had to be tempered if not hidden by women.

Wearing the cloak of authority, inhabiting one's ambition, and being comfortable with expressions of righteous anger did not come naturally even to women at the highest level in our political culture. And if they did not fully demonstrate those emotions, they would remain permanently in the business of second-guessing and fine-tuning their tone so as not to give offense—and not convey weakness. They could have used a pep talk from Pelosi who liked to say, "You don't have to apologize to anybody for anything. You're here." She would counsel women, "Your spontaneity is your authenticity."

At the end of 2019, the outcome of the race was far from clear. The field was smaller, but no clear leader emerged. I could afford only a few days off at the holidays with the first primary just weeks away, but the campaign intruded in a new and troubling way. On New Year's Eve day 2019, a pair of FBI agents came to my front door. At the time I lived in an area of Northern Virginia where many neighbors work in high-level government positions requiring security clearances, so I therefore assumed they were there to ask routine questions about a neighbor. No, this was about *me*. A tinge of panic swept over me, but I remained outwardly calm. They showed me a printout from a radical right-wing website suggesting I needed to pay a price for my appearances on MSNBC and my writing. The agents said it was probably nothing, but they had a "duty to warn." Was there evidence the person was going to act? Had the person made other threats? No. But the FBI officers would put in an alert with the local police, which hardly inspired much confidence. I had become accustomed to the usual hate emails, comments, and tweets, but the FBI's appearance entirely unnerved me. There was nothing I could really do about the threat, even if it were real, and my sense of helplessness turned to frustration. Why bother to warn me about something out of my control? Fortunately, nothing came of this, and the FBI never returned. My antennae remained on high alert and I took to forwarding threatening messages to the *Washington Post*'s security personnel. It was a troubling reminder that social media is infused with hostility, especially toward women.

The gender issue spilled out again at the January 14, 2020, debate.

CNN had reported that at a private dinner Sanders said to Warren that he did not think a woman could win the presidency. Warren's camp confirmed the remark, Sanders's denied it. CNN's debate moderators asked about the story. Sanders indignantly replied, "Well, as a matter of fact, I didn't say it. And I don't want to waste a whole lot of time on this, because this is what Donald Trump and maybe some of the media want. Anybody knows me knows that it's incomprehensible that I would think that a woman cannot be president of the United States." He continued, "Hillary Clinton won the popular vote by three million votes. How could anybody in a million years not believe that a woman could become president of the United States?" Was he sure he never said something like that? He insisted, "That is correct." The moderators then pivoted to Warren. What did she tell Sanders when he said a woman could not win?

WARREN: I disagreed. Bernie is my friend, and I am not here to try to fight with Bernie. But, look, this question about whether or not a woman can be president has been raised, and it's time for us to attack it head-on.

And I think the best way to talk about who can win is by looking at people's winning record. So, can a woman beat Donald Trump?

Look at the men on this stage. Collectively, they have lost 10 elections.

(LAUGHTER)

The only people on this stage who have won every single election that they've been in are the women . . .

(APPLAUSE)

. . . Amy and me.

KLOBUCHAR: So true.

Oddly, the CNN moderators did not follow up to ask Warren if she believed Sanders was lying or to ask Sanders why Warren would make up or imagine such a story. Immediately after the debate Warren approached Sanders and declined to shake his outstretched hand. An awkward conversation picked up on microphones followed:

WARREN: I think you called me a liar on national TV.

SANDERS: What?

WARREN: I think you called me a liar on national TV.

SANDERS: You know, let's not do it right now. If you want to have that discussion, we'll have that discussion.

WARREN: Anytime.

SANDERS: You called me a liar . . . You told me—all right, let's not do it now.

The conversation in the media about this clash was gender-driven as well. Many male commentators—some who had written the same stories doubting Warren's "likability"—sounded incredulous that Sanders would say such a thing. For women journalists and political watchers who had been hearing the very same concern about women's electability both from men and women throughout the campaign, Warren's version of the conversation sounded entirely believable. While Warren rhetorically may have scored debating points with some voters, the exchange did not work to her benefit. Warren's poll numbers had been in decline since October, but this episode seemed to trap her in a gender-driven narrative. Rather than rallying women to her cause, she had managed to incense Sanders's loud, vitriolic social media followers. *BuzzFeed* reported, "Bernie Sanders supporters are bombarding Elizabeth Warren's social media accounts with snake emojis, memes, and GIFs in a ramp-up of the tension that's been brewing between the two campaigns over the past week." *GQ* also observed that some Sanders supporters were simply underscoring their reputation "as cyberbullies who can lean on misogynist tropes."

In the debate before the February 3 New Hampshire primary Warren seemed unusually subdued and absent from the conversation for long stretches. By the eve of the New Hampshire primary, in her last appearance in Portsmouth at a packed church, she seemed just a little wistful as she tentatively prepared her supporters for a disappointing result while vowing to plow forward. Polls did not look promising. She sounded tired. Even if she did not win in her neighboring state she would soldier on. In reality, another poor performance coupled with a shortage of funds (forcing her to borrow $3 million and kick in $400,000 of her own to keep her campaign afloat) left her on the verge of elimination. Her supporters objected that the media had virtually erased her from coverage, even leaving her out of a *Wall Street Journal*/NBC News poll in mid-February, which matched up top contenders against Trump.

At the February 19 debate Warren, on the verge of elimination and with nothing to lose, let it rip. She acknowledged to an MSNBC reporter before the debate that women get slammed for being too reticent but also too aggressive. She would get flack either way. She could not afford to be irrelevant, so she lit into billionaire candidate Mike Bloomberg. She slammed him on everything from use of nondisclosure agreements to silence former women who claimed gender discrimination or sexual harassment while employed by Bloomberg's company, to his dumping hundreds of millions of dollars into the race. She lit into him for the stop-and-frisk plan he defended as mayor of New York that disproportionately targeted Blacks. Her withering blows pierced the billionaire's aura of competence and invincibility. She won plaudits from the press and from her supporters. CNN's Van Jones bluntly said, "Elizabeth Warren destroyed Bloomberg." *Politico* declared Warren "hits Bloomberg while he's down."

However, when it came to Sanders, she never seemed willing to take him on with gusto. She would chide him for not releasing his medical record in interviews, but once they were face-to-face Warren avoided going after her rival for lack of transparency or for supporting unelectable positions.

Her attacks however were not limited to Bloomberg and Sanders. She seemed, at times, to be indiscriminately attacking everyone onstage, mocking Buttigieg's and Klobuchar's health care plans and tormenting Biden for saying something nice about Mitch McConnell. When I dashed off a tweet arguing that scattershot attacks did not make for a "good look" and could seem "angry" and "mean," her supporters, as well as other progressives, including Rep. Alexandria Ocasio-Cortez, descended on me on social media, accusing me of stereotypical sexist thinking. In the spur of the moment, I had used language that often is deployed *selectively* against women; the complainants did not care that I used the same terms to critique other candidates or had pummeled Bloomberg for his performance. Moreover, the bottom line was that her tactics did not help her in the polls.

I was relieved when Warren's staff deployed humor to needle me rather than a full-fledged assault on my feminist credentials. I joked after the debate on Twitter that she should send a cease and desist letter to Bloomberg who had released a doctored video falsely suggesting he had left Warren and other rivals tongue-tied. Maya Rupert, a Warren aide, wisecracked they would have done so but they did not want to seem "mean and angry." The score was settled. I commended her restraint. We moved on.

Warren increasingly became the punching bag for a social media phenomenon, the so-called Bernie Bros. Sanders had developed an almost cultlike following, predominantly White and male, who would peruse social media, slamming critics and doubters. Their language was often rude, vulgar, demeaning, and threatening.

While Sanders pleaded ignorance when they attacked critics, his paid staff also adopted search-and-destroy tactics that were not altogether different from Trump's.

Warren felt the wrath of the Bernie Bros many times as Sanders's online allies pilloried her. *Vox* called this group the "dirtbag left": "Its leading voices believe very deeply that biting mockery—including, yes, insults targeting your opponents' physical appearance—are a vital tool for holding the powerful accountable. . . . What makes their political style distinctive is its embrace of harsh, often cruel, humor as a deliberate political tactic." The targets were often media figures whom the Sanders crowd felt failed to appreciate their candidate and were too soft on his opponents. Asian American NBC commentator Kurt Bardella explained, "The attacks against Warren come from the same corners of social media that disparage Democrats (like myself) . . . for having the audacity to question or scrutinize their chosen leader. People of color and women who dare to disagree with Sanders' political assertions have often borne the brunt of this abuse." As I did, Bardella found some similarity between the Trump and Sanders online mobs: "Disturbingly, there are times where you really can't distinguish between the tone and tactics of Trump's #MAGA nation and Sanders' Bros. We don't want to give political cyberbullies undue attention. Indeed, racism and sexism from the cult of Trump is pretty much expected at this point; after all, they are taking cues from their leader. But in the case of Sanders supporters and anyone claiming to be a 'progressive,' this type of toxicity should not be tolerated."

In Warren's case, the attacks were not limited to social media. For example, a script from the Sanders camp in January 2020 circulated in campaign circles, demeaning Warren as an "elite" candidate. The Sanders camp sheepishly pulled back the script. In another incident, a White male at a town hall challenged Warren as to why she was insisting a candidate needed a majority of delegates rather than just a plurality (that would benefit Sanders who was ahead on delegates at the time). She told him sternly that Sanders had flip-flopped since 2016 when he had tried to appeal to superdelegates even when Clinton had a *majority* of the delegates. The man suggested this was not true. She would not stand for the gaslighting routine. She firmly corrected him and pointed out everyone knew the rules and should play by them. Warren arguably "won" that encounter, but the Bernie Bros were unrelenting.

To my chagrin I also found myself directly targeted by Sanders's nasty staffers. Sanders had a mild heart attack but returned to the race. Nevertheless, his refusal to release his full medical records became an issue. Let it all out—the medical records, the tax records, everything for every candidate—I argued. Sanders's press secretary Briahna Joy Gray appeared on CNN, called me out by name, and accused me of leading a smear campaign, even suggesting it was akin to the birther attacks on Obama. The deluge hit; emails and tweets poured in. The venom, misogyny, and vulgarity were unlike anything I had experienced from any candidate, with the possible exception of Trump's MAGA crowd. Some were overtly anti-Semitic (although Sanders is Jewish); others used violent imagery and welcomed my demise.

Matters became even more intense the same week when Trump tweeted my name, dubbing me the "wacko conservative" and pointing to a typo in a tweet (this from the same man who made "covfefe" famous). Now the MAGA crowd's noxious messages rained down as well. Like the ones from Sanders's Bernie Bros, these missives were also threatening, anti-Semitic, violent, and almost always misogynistic. I now fully understood that even in a presidential race with multiple women remaining in competition—with candidates vying for the women's vote and unbending in their defense of women's rights—social media remained a space for bullies and blowhards to try to shout me and other women down. That the rhetorical abuse came not only from Trump's followers but from the camp of a Democratic contender—who at that point was a front-runner—was as maddening as it was dispiriting. Had Clinton and female presidential candidates who followed her accomplished anything or was this arena a place where an outspoken woman still could be intimidated without recourse?

On one hand, I took all the attacks as a badge of honor, telling myself that these assaults and threats implicitly confirmed my wide reach in the political debate. Friends and colleagues gave me literal and emoji high-fives, but the sheer volume of negative attacks and the aggression displayed in them was unnerving. That week vividly confirmed for me that the political culture created by populist candidates on both the right and the left could be abusive, angry, and often anti-woman.

Most every female journalist receives some sort of abuse, and rarely do social media companies respond to complaints. In 2018, Amnesty International conducted an extensive study of the prevalence of online harassment, concluding that "for many women, Twitter is a platform where violence and abuse against them flourishes, often with little accountability. As a company, Twitter is failing in its responsibility to respect women's rights online by inadequately investigating and responding to reports of violence and abuse in a transparent manner." The problem persisted. "Facebook Criticised After Women Complain of Inaction over Abuse," the *Guardian* reported in 2019. The Women's Media Center, the Global Fund for Women, and the Anti-Defamation League have all surveyed and reported on online hate speech and bullying, which often fall disproportionately on women. It is not the exclusive province of one party nor did it begin with Trump. However, as with the rise of hate crimes during the Trump era, the online climate became more toxic, mean, and aggressive. I tried to put it all aside, continue full steam ahead with columns, but the weight of the harassment and venomous threats at times rattled me.

The debates were certainly a mixed blessing for the top women in the race. Despite the conflicting demands put on them, they provided a forum to show their wit, their tenacity, and their policy smarts, especially for Warren and Klobuchar.

Klobuchar, at least, came to the decision her opponents' lack of preparation was fair game. She regularly denigrated Buttigieg's experience. At the November debate Andrea Mitchell questioned Klobuchar on her comments on experience:

MITCHELL: Senator Klobuchar, you've said this of Mayor Buttigieg, quote, "Of the women on the stage, do I think that we would be standing on that stage if we had the experience he had? No, I don't. Maybe we're held to a different standard." Senator, what did you mean by that?

KLOBUCHAR: First of all, I've made very clear I think that Pete is qualified to be up on this stage, and I am honored to be standing next to him. But what I said was true. Women are held to a higher standard. Otherwise, we could play a game called name your favorite woman president, which we can't do, because it has all been men.

   (APPLAUSE)

   And including all vice presidents being men. And I think any working woman out there, any woman that's at home knows exactly what I mean. We have to work harder, and that's a fact.

The two continued to scuffle at the December debate. Buttigieg said his experience with immigration "isn't theoretical . . . [and] not something I formed in committee rooms in Washington." Klobuchar pounced. After recounting some of the accomplishments of the senators onstage, she told him, "So while you can dismiss committee hearings, I think this experience works." After some back-and-forth she tore into Buttigieg's preparation:

I know you ran to be chair of the Democratic National Committee. That's not something that I wanted to do. I want to be president of the United States. And the point is, we should have someone heading up this ticket that has actually won and been able to show that they can gather the support that you talk about of moderate Republicans and independents, as well as a fired-up Democratic base, and not just done it once, I have done it three times.

I think winning matters. I think a track record of getting things done matters. And I also think showing our party that we can actually bring people with us, have a wider tent, have a bigger coalition, and, yes, longer coattails, that matters.

In these exchanges, Klobuchar demonstrated that aggression can pay off, and dinging a male opponent for lack of preparation can be effective.

It was thrilling and affirming to see the women candidates duke it out as equals with their male opponents. But, as they faded from contention, there was understandable dismay from many women who had hoped to avenge Clinton's loss. What more could these women do? How much more expertise did they need to demonstrate to convince voters they were presidential-caliber competitors?

The questions suggested a catch-22 in presidential politics that had plagued Clinton and now the 2020 contenders. Women at this level in politics got there by working extra hard, making few errors, knowing their material inside and out, in many cases, better than male peers. These were the proverbial A students. Yet as women candidates fell by the wayside, we collectively saw once again that presidential politics is not an SAT exam nor a merit-based contest. If high-wattage brainpower and mastery of policy were the critical difference between winning and losing in presidential politics, we likely would have had, for example, George H. W. Bush and not Ronald Reagan as the Republican nominee in 1980, and certainly Hillary Clinton, not Trump, as the presidential winner in 2016. The very ways in which women have excelled in politics, we learned again in 2020, were not necessarily the metric by which voters selected their choice at the presidential level. Charisma, emotional connectivity, and relentless, repetitive messaging can be far more critical in presidential contests where voters are deciding who they want in their living rooms and on their screens for four years.

At a critical time before the first primary contests a new impediment popped up for the senators still in the race: They would have to leave the campaign trail to sit through Trump's impeachment trial.

IMPEACHMENT

The first impeachment and trial of Donald J. Trump will absorb future historians and legal scholars for decades. From the point of view of women and politics, however, it had a dual impact: It dramatically raised the profile of several Democratic women in the House, and it complicated the 2020 presidential contest.

In March 2019, Special Counsel Robert Mueller released his report looking into Russian interference in the 2016 U.S. election. While Mueller did not find evidence that rose to the level of a criminal conspiracy, he did find evidence of cooperation between Russian officials and members of the Trump team, including campaign manager Paul Manafort, deputy campaign manager Rick Gates, and Trump confidant Roger Stone. Moreover, the report documented nearly a dozen categories of activities for which there was ample proof Trump had obstructed justice. Warren, a former law school professor, read through the entire report, all 448 pages. In a written statement, Warren declared, "To ignore a President's repeated efforts to obstruct an investigation into his own disloyal behavior would inflict great and lasting damage on this country, and it would suggest that both the current and future Presidents would be free to abuse their power in similar ways." She called for his impeachment, the first presidential candidate to do so. Although Mueller did not conclude Trump had committed a crime, he made clear Congress had the obligation to move forward as it saw fit. Warren quoted from the report, "Congress has authority to prohibit a President's corrupt use of his authority in order to protect the integrity of the administration of justice." Warren explained that "the correct process for exercising that authority is impeachment."

Warren's studious review of the report and quick call for impeachment were very much "on brand" for her. Her intellectual prowess and her willingness to lead rather than follow the crowd endeared her to progressives. With an ongoing string of zingers, she distinguished herself on the topic of impeachment. "If he were anyone other than president of the United States, he would be in handcuffs and indicted," she told the hosts of *The View* in May. In addition to TV appearances, she found plenty of ways to highlight her stance on impeachment. In May, she rebutted Majority Leader Mitch McConnell's assertion that the report meant it was "case closed" on the Russia investigation. On the Senate floor, Warren declared, "Wishing won't make it so." She made clear she had read late into the night on the day it was released and "into the next morning." She continued, "There is no political inconvenience exception to the Constitution." Congress must act, she said. "Since the majority leader has pronounced his judgement here on the Senate floor, I'd like to spend some time reminding him of exactly what the report said." She then proceeded to read sections of the report into the congressional record.

In essence, she was providing a minicourse in constitutional law to the country, at least to those willing to listen. While I feared impeachment would be unsuccessful and allow Trump to claim vindication once the Republican-led Senate failed to remove him, Warren once more impressed me. This was the sort of defiant, smart leadership many Democrats were looking for. Indivisible's Leah Greenberg criticized more timid Democrats, telling the Associated Press, "What we're seeing is, some Democrats would prefer to keep the topic focused on places where they're most comfortable and some Democrats would prefer to play pundits on this."

MSNBC reporter Jonathan Allen commented, "It was a rare moment in a crowded and unsettled primary: A seized opportunity for a candidate to cut through the campaign trail cacophony and define the terms of a debate that will rage throughout the contest." As he saw it, "She sided with that base of core party supporters, defined its cause in moral terms and hollered the message from the mountaintop. That's classic Warren." Sure enough, Warren's polling rose steadily during the summer.

Many House Democrats, most critically Pelosi, resisted the call to impeach. It did not poll well with voters. Democrats had won in 2018 talking about health care so why change to a controversial topic? Pelosi was all too aware that her freshmen members who won in swing districts would face trouble back home if voters perceived they went to DC just to remove the president. Not all the freshmen were so cautious, however.

For some freshmen House women, the decision whether to support impeachment was easy. Katie Porter had avoided talking about the issue in the campaign, explaining that she needed to see the facts. Once she digested the Mueller report she could tell her constituents she recognized "obstruction of justice" and "substantial evidence" when she saw it. In her eyes, Trump had committed impeachable acts so it was a simple decision to support impeachment. Her district, however, was more conservative than she was, and she had won her seat with the votes of plenty of Republicans, many of whom opposed impeachment. She felt compelled to explain her decision in a short video in June 2019. "I didn't come to Congress to impeach the president," Porter said. "But when faced with a crisis of this magnitude, I cannot with a clean conscience ignore my duty to defend the Constitution." Impeachment was still not popular with the public, however. At one point she heard a fellow House member make a snide aside. "Well, [Porter] will need to retire. She's for impeachment." It was a Democrat, no less. In the fall, the rest of the Democratic caucus would move toward her position on impeachment.

The political landscape on impeachment changed radically in September. House Intelligence chairman Adam Schiff of California, a cautious moderate who had not come out for impeachment, learned there was a whistleblower complaint that had not been forwarded to the House and Senate Intelligence Committees in violation of existing law. He pressured for its release, and the story became front-page news as attention focused on a call between Trump and the president of Ukraine, a US ally that was in a hot war with Russia. Trump convinced himself the call was "perfect"—when in fact it was self-incriminating—and released a rough transcript documenting the conversation between himself and Ukrainian president Volodymyr Zelensky on July 25.

In that conversation Trump appeared to condition US aid appropriated by Congress for Ukraine on Ukrainian officials coming up with and disclosing dirt on former vice president Joe Biden. Zelensky pressed Trump to release aid vital to defend Ukraine in its war with Russia. Trump instantly responded, "I would like you to do us a favor though because our country has been through a lot and Ukraine knows a lot about it." The phrase "do us a favor though" was plainly an effort to link Ukrainian aid to something else. The "favor" was "find[ing] out what happened with this whole situation with Ukraine, they say CrowdStrike . . . I guess you have one of your wealthy people . . . The [DNC] server, they say Ukraine has it." This was a reference to ludicrous Russian propaganda generated to divert blame for interfering with the 2016 election to Ukraine. The notion that the server was in Ukraine was pure fabrication. Trump also directed Zelensky to talk to his personal lawyer, Rudy Giuliani, not a government official. He then clarified exactly what he wanted: "The other thing, there's a lot of talk about Biden's son, that Biden stopped the prosecution, and a lot of people want to find out about that so whatever you can do with the Attorney General would be great. Biden went around bragging that he stopped the prosecution so if you can look into it . . . It sounds horrible to me." Here was the president demanding a foreign leader turn up—or make up—dirt on an opponent in exchange for aid Congress had already appropriated to fight a mutual adversary, Russia. He was selling out our own national security interests for his own political advantage in the 2020 election.

Trump's plot to get anti-Biden information confirmed that, of all the Democratic presidential candidates, Biden was the one whom Trump feared the most. An experienced and moderate insider would be harder than the others to paint as a "crazy socialist." Moreover, he had appeal with both African Americans and working-class Whites. The attempt to smear Biden was the biggest backhanded compliment Trump could give him.

After the whistleblower complaint documenting troubling conduct inside the administration, Trump started threatening to reveal the whistleblower's identity, suggesting he was a traitor. Still, it was far from certain that Pelosi would greenlight impeachment.

The Ukraine development shifted the thinking of a group of critical House freshmen women. Spanberger, the CIA veteran elected in 2018 from Virginia, was part of a large group of a class of rookie lawmakers with military or intelligence backgrounds. Five of these were women, who came to be known as the "Five Badasses," had crushed their GOP opponents in 2018. Mikie Sherrill (D) from the New Jersey Eleventh won by 15.6 percent; Elissa Slotkin (D) from the Michigan Eighth won by 10.5 points; Chrissy Houlahan from the Pennsylvania Sixth won by 8.5 percent; and Spanberger won by over 8 points in a district Trump won by 5. Finally, in the Virginia Second, Elaine Luria won by 5.6 points. During the 2018 campaign these women had seen one another at Democratic Party events and fundraisers, encouraged one another, and developed friendships. Those relationships blossomed when they arrived in Congress. These self-confident, articulate women engaged in a running conversation on Signal (an encryption app) about everything from votes to office personnel, and eventually, to impeachment. Representing swing districts where impeachment was unpopular, these women had little reason to support it based on the Mueller investigation, the results of which were complicated and obscured by White House spin. When Ukraine came along, their exchanges intensified. They sensed things had changed, and the threat to national security Trump posed was too serious to ignore. If they acted in unison, they would have far more impact on Americans trying to understand what was going on.

They looked at the Ukraine scandal differently than the Mueller inquiry. Here, they had Trump's own words in black and white seeking to bend US foreign policy for his personal gain. They realized they could not remain true to their oaths if they remained silent. For women who had served in the CIA or the military, Trump's willingness to subvert US national security for political advantage struck at the heart of their reasons for running for office and to their ethics of public service. Spanberger thought Trump's language in threatening the then anonymous whistleblower was "shocking" and "unpresidential." Her colleagues agreed.

Mikie Sherrill had grown up with the legacy of her grandfather, whose plane had been shot down over Normandy in World War II. She had served as a Navy helicopter pilot and as a Russia policy officer. Sherrill did not think coming out for impeachment was about how *she* felt. This was about bringing the country along. In ten, twenty, or fifty years she wanted to look back and see that she had done what was right for the country. As a former prosecutor she knew she could gain a conviction for obstruction outlined in the Mueller report. That however was not the question. She viewed Trump's actions regarding Ukraine as a "direct attack" on democracy, impossible to swallow for a woman who "had served all over the world . . . and understood how critical our alliances are." The only thing standing between Russia and a complete invasion of Ukraine was US military aid, which Trump was ready to withhold, not for some national security objective, but to fulfill his personal agenda. Here was the commander in chief egging a foreign government to investigate a US citizen. She concluded, "This cannot go unchallenged." Moreover, if Trump had decided to seek foreign interference in the current election, Americans could not rely on a compromised vote to banish a lawless president.

The five women watched with horror as democracy itself seemed imperiled by a president willing to wield the powers of the federal government for his own uses. They reached the same conclusion: Now was the time to make their voices heard. Sherrill and the others thought a news conference would be too much of a "circus" and instead favored an op-ed to convey their reasoning and the gravity of the situation. They jointly compiled a draft, with each contributing sections of the argument. A round-robin of edits ensued.

Along with Democratic freshmen representatives Gil Cisneros of California and Jason Crow of Colorado they produced an op-ed for the *Washington Post*. They sent the op-ed off and then arranged a call to Pelosi, to make sure she heard it from them before the op-ed published. Not knowing what to expect, they looped in everyone for a conference call with the speaker. They explained their reasoning. She was agreeable and even encouraging. She told them that their voices really mattered. The five women were a perfect illustration of Pelosi's adage that women should develop national security experience, as Pelosi did in her years on the Intelligence Committee. The Five Badasses were demonstrating just how powerful they could be by wielding national security expertise. Pelosi had resisted the call for impeachment in part to protect her moderate members in at-risk seats. Now they had let her know not to hold things up on their account.

In the op-ed, the five freshmen told their fellow Americans, "We have devoted our lives to the service and security of our country, and throughout our careers, we have sworn oaths to defend the Constitution of the United States many times over. Now, we join as a unified group to uphold that oath as we enter uncharted waters and face unprecedented allegations against President Trump." Their piece continued: "The president of the United States may have used his position to pressure a foreign country into investigating a political opponent, and he sought to use U.S. taxpayer dollars as leverage to do it." They argued that the facts were "stunning" and that "flagrant disregard for the law cannot stand." They added that it was essential to find out if Trump had used foreign assistance for his own private benefit. They concluded, "If these allegations are true, we believe these actions represent an impeachable offense." No single action did more to encourage Pelosi and House leadership to move forward on impeachment.

The House conducted impeachment hearings under the auspices of Intelligence Committee chairmen Rep. Adam Schiff. The contrast between the parties could not have been starker. Democrats generally stuck to the facts, drawing out information from a list of witnesses that helped educate voters about Trump's conduct, why it was so objectionable and why impeachment was the appropriate remedy. A panel of legal experts opined on whether Trump had engaged in impeachable conduct. Stanford Law professor Pamela Karlan explained, "The framers of our Constitution realized that elections alone could not guarantee that the United States would remain a republic. One of the key reasons for including an impeachment power was the risk that unscrupulous officials might try to rig the election process." That was precisely what had occurred here. She and Harvard Law professor Noah Feldman agreed this was impeachable conduct. "President Trump's conduct described in the testimony and evidence clearly constitutes an impeachable high crime and misdemeanor under the Constitution," Feldman argued. "According to the testimony and to the publicly released memorandum of the July 25, 2019, telephone call between the two presidents, President Trump abused his office by soliciting the president of Ukraine to investigate his political rivals in order to gain personal political advantage, including in the 2020 presidential election. This act on its own qualifies as an impeachable high crime and misdemeanor." The House Judiciary Committee voted out two articles of impeachment on a party line vote, twenty-three to seventeen. The full House voted to impeach, with only two Democrats voting no on one or both articles. No Republican voted to impeach.

The action then shifted to the trial in the Senate for which Pelosi named the first three female impeachment managers in history. Her selection was purposeful. While another speaker might simply have selected committee chairmen as managers, Pelosi was willing to dive into the well of talent and put some previously unknown women in the national spotlight. With that in mind she looked to put a group together with diverse skills that complemented one another.

Pelosi immediately thought of Rep. Zoe Lofgren of California. This would be Lofgren's third impeachment, having been an aide to the Democrats during Watergate and a House member during Bill Clinton's impeachment. Lofgren had refrained from supporting impeachment until the Ukraine transcript was released. She proved to be a valuable resource and steady hand to her colleagues.

Pelosi also heeded the advice of one of her daughters, who had experience as a district attorney. Nothing, she had told her mother, compares to the experience of standing up in court before a jury to make your case. Pelosi therefore turned to someone she had known for years and who fit that description, Rep. Sylvia Garcia of Texas. She would be the first Hispanic and the first Texan to serve as an impeachment manager. The *Texas Tribune* reported, she was a "virtual unknown in national politics, a quiet freshman not noted for flash or self-promotion, one who hasn't logged hundreds of hours on cable news shows like others on the impeachment team." She was the epitome of the overachieving, nose-to-the-grindstone lawmaker who learned to find allies on both sides of the aisle. Her training as a municipal court judge certainly helped her prepare for her role as an impeachment manager, but without the woman speaker she might not have wound up in the limelight. "When it came time to pick the impeachment managers Pelosi cast her eye toward Garcia not just because of her political record, but because the two were already close, a relationship that developed years before Garcia ever took federal office," the *Texas Tribune* surmised. Pelosi once more proved that she could identify and boost talented and prepared women.

Pelosi also selected Rep. Val Demings of Florida, who became the first African American female impeachment manager. In addition to her time on the House Permanent Select Committee on Intelligence and the Judiciary Committee, she had an impressive record as chief of police of Orlando, Florida. She embodied the American Dream, the youngest daughter of a family of six had once tagged along with her mother who cleaned rich southern Whites' homes for a living. She became the first in her family to go to college, then launched a career in law enforcement, and ultimately won a House seat in 2016. The country witnessed a fervent and sincere defender of the rule of law. In clear, uncompromising tones she launched her initial set of remarks on the opening day of the trial. "The first article of impeachment charges the president with using the power of his office to solicit and pressure Ukraine to announce investigations that everyone in this chamber knows to be bogus," said Demings. "The president didn't even care if an investigation was actually conducted, just that it was announced. Why? Because this was for his own personal and political benefit." As to the charge of obstructing Congress, she declared, "He did so by ordering his entire administration—every office, every agency, every official—to defy every subpoena served in the House impeachment inquiry. No president in history has ever done anything like this. Many presidents have expressly acknowledged that they couldn't do anything like this." Her own background added to her credibility. "President Trump did not take these extreme steps to hide evidence of his innocence, or to protect the institution of the presidency," added Demings. "As a career law enforcement officer, I have never seen anyone take such extreme steps to hide evidence allegedly proving his innocence. And I do not find that here today. The president is engaged in this cover-up because he is guilty, and he knows it."

To no one's surprise, Republicans were not about to remove Trump. Despite a wealth of evidence that Trump had violated his oath, Sen. Mitt Romney of Utah was the only Republican to vote to convict and remove Trump. Romney declared, "The people will judge us for how well and faithfully we fulfilled our duty. The grave question the Constitution tasks senators to answer is whether the President committed an act so extreme and egregious that it rises to the level of a 'high crime and misdemeanor.' Yes, he did." He included a brief review of the evidence, concluding, "My vote will likely be in the minority in the Senate. But irrespective of these things, with my vote, I will tell my children and their children that I did my duty to the best of my ability, believing that my country expected it of me. I will only be one name among many, no more or less, to future generations of Americans who look at the record of this trial. They will note merely that I was among the senators who determined that what the President did was wrong, grievously wrong." He added, "We're all footnotes at best in the annals of history. But in the most powerful nation on earth, the nation conceived in liberty and justice, that is distinction enough for any citizen."

I was moved to tears. Here was at least one Republican who took his oath seriously. If the rest of the Senate Republicans had snubbed their noses at the facts and shirked their responsibilities, Romney defied the tribalism that had driven Republicans to embrace and enable a lawless president. He remained an example that decency, courage, and intellectual honesty were not yet extinct in his party.

After acquittal, Demings passionately defended her role. "Was it worth it? Every day it has been worth it," she told NPR. She continued, "The House managers were the defenders of the Constitution. And just like when I was a law enforcement officer, when I saw someone breaking the law, I did not stop and think about, well, my goodness, what will the judge do? What will the jury do down the road? I did my job to stop that threat and then go to court and plead my case."

While the impeachment process raised the visibility of these women, it also disrupted the presidential primary schedule. For the candidates trapped on the Senate floor for the trial—Sanders, Klobuchar, and Warren—it meant missed time on the ground in Iowa. Sanders was already surging in the polls and had the advantage of a prior run and a strong operation in the state. His absence from the trail was not fatal, but the momentum of other candidates slowed as the impeachment thoroughly dominated the news. While the impeachment trial was not the sole cause of Warren's disappointing fourth and Klobuchar's fifth place finishes in Iowa, it contributed to their inauspicious start to the primary season.

The impeachment trial had one positive impact for Klobuchar. Forced off the trail and required to sit on the Senate for hours on end, she finally had time to think clearly and methodically about the race. What was the great divide between Trump and the Democrats? How could she boil down the contrast to its essence? The key, she decided, was empathy. Trump had none of it; Democrats actually cared about the lives of ordinary Americans. She turned this over in her mind and went back to an anecdote about FDR's funeral train. Just days before the New Hampshire debate she tried it out on the debate stage. She began: "There's an old story of Franklin Delano Roosevelt, and when he died, his body was put on a train and went up across America and there was a guy standing by those tracks along with so many Americans, and he had his hat on his chest and he was sobbing and a reporter said, Sir, did you know the president?" With a hint of excitement in her voice Klobuchar continued, "And the guy says, no, I didn't know the president, but he knew me. He knew me." It was a powerful moment.

Klobuchar pivoted to Trump. "I will tell you this, there is a complete lack of empathy in this guy in the White House right now. I will bring that to you." She went on to assure voters, "If you have trouble stretching your paycheck to pay for that rent. I know you and I will fight for you. If you have trouble deciding if you're going to pay for your childcare or your long-term care, I know you and I will fight for you. If you have trouble figuring out if you're going to fill your refrigerator or fill your prescription drug, I know you and I will fight for you." It was a high note on an outstanding debate performance, one that gave her momentum going into New Hampshire where she scored her best result of the race, third place. It was not in sharing dazzling policy, but in making an emotional connection with voters that Klobuchar, however briefly, found her voice and enjoyed a presidential-level viral moment.

In the days leading up to the Senate trial Harris made regular TV appearances. Her legal background and knack for boiling down complicated issues into language accessible to ordinary Americans was on full display. Along with frequent TV interviews, she cut her own videos for Twitter commenting on the trial. Having attained a large following and raised her profile, she wisely displayed her strengths on the national stage. She had gained stature, what the press calls "gravitas," during her year on the presidential campaign trail. When she spoke, she sounded like more than just another senator.

As the trial came to an end, Harris delivered a powerful speech on the Senate floor to explain her vote. She argued, "Donald Trump will want the American people to feel cynical. He will want us not to care. He will want us to think that he is all powerful, and we have no power." However, she vowed, "We're not going to let him get away with that." She added, "We're not going to give him what he wants. Because the true power and potential of the United States of America resides not with the president, but with the people. All the people." She would have plenty of opportunities to share that message later in 2020.

CHAPTER 17

AND THEN THERE
WERE NONE

The debates helped narrow the field of candidates from an un-
wieldy two dozen to a handful by the end of 2019. Failing to
meet the threshold for the debates—a combination of minimum
polling results and number of donors—forced candidates from the
race. Gillibrand was the first woman to go.

Among the women in the race, Gillibrand's early exit was the
least surprising. She had been unable to raise money, establish a
distinct persona in a crowded race, or create a viral moment on the
debate stage. She also had carried two unique burdens throughout
the race. The first was what some called the "ghost of Al Franken."
She had played a leading role in ousting the popular progressive
Minnesota senator when allegations of sexual misconduct surfaced.
That left a bad taste in the mouths of some progressives who saw
Democrats as too eager to throw their own members overboard.
Second, she had annoyed the Clinton network when in a November
2017 interview with the *New York Times* she opined that President
Bill Clinton should have stepped down when the Monica Lewin-
sky scandal broke. "Yes, I think that is the appropriate response,"
she said. "Things have changed today, and I think under those

circumstances there should be a very different reaction." Philippe Reines, a longtime senior adviser to Hillary Clinton, blasted her on Twitter. "Over 20 yrs you took the Clintons' endorsements, money, and seat. Hypocrite," he growled. "Interesting strategy for 2020 primaries. Best of luck." She was too forward leaning in the case of Franken, for some in the party, and insufficiently defensive of the Clintons for others.

Gillibrand also had decided to run as the most overtly feminist candidate, stressing issues like pay equity, childcare, and abortion rights. When abortion bans were introduced in southern state legislatures, she was first out of the gate with a very tough statement on defending access to abortion rights. It is impossible to say whether it was her feminist focus or more mundane problems (for example, lack of a clear rationale for her candidacy or distinctive biography) that determined her fate.

By contrast, the withdrawal of Harris, one of the most promising candidates who had displayed flashes of brilliance, caught even her competitors by surprise. Harris's departure at the end of 2019 was emotionally gut-wrenching for women who had admired her panache, her joyful style of campaigning, and her passionate articulation of social justice issues. Of all the candidates, male or female, she displayed the most charisma, natural talent, and ability to understand the challenges facing girls, women, and nonwhite Americans.

Her campaign message was sometimes fuzzy and her stance on health care hard to pin down, but perhaps the margin of error for her was tiny to nonexistent. After a disappointing drop in the polls over the summer, Harris hit her stride once again at the Liberty and Justice Celebration dinner in Iowa, an annual fundraising affair to benefit the state Democratic Party, when she fully embraced her criminal justice experience. In a moving refrain she ticked through the issues, after each one reminding them that "justice was on the ballot": "Economic justice," "health care justice," and "reproductive justice." It would not be enough to reverse her slump in the polls and in fundraising, although any observer could see what a unique talent she was.

She seemed the most relatable of all the candidates. She spoke to a generation of women—regardless of color—who were the "firsts" in their jobs. While she had a distinctive heritage, she shared the universal experiences of a minority or immigrant child raised with high expectations, straddling multiple cultures. She was self-possessed, and self-defined. Her departure felt like a personal defeat for those whose lives bore some resemblance to hers.

The drop-off in fundraising, though, was too much to overcome and it was the primary factor that drove her from the race. The battle for money was fierce, and many Democratic donors simply assumed she was a front-runner with enough to continue for the long haul. Money problems plagued the campaign for weeks, though, causing cuts to the New Hampshire operation. Those close to her knew it was only a matter of time before she would be forced to decide if she really wanted to put the campaign as much as $10 million in debt.

She entered the race to win, not to prepare for a vice presidential run nor to elevate her platform. If she did not have the resources and did not have a realistic path to victory, she was not going to press on and keep asking people to fork over their hard-earned money. She recalled, "I *hated* getting out. It was the worst. I am not a quitter." She was convinced that her campaign could really go all the way. "But I ran out of money," she said. "I had to be honest, I couldn't go out there to ask for money [with no hope of success]." She felt the weight of the decision. "There is a burden when someone's expectations are riding on us." At the time she had no thought of a VP race. After her announcement, she traveled to campaign offices around the country to thank her staff and volunteers, a demonstration of the graciousness that many admired.

While money was the precipitating factor, pundits after her departure advanced various theories as to why she had not been able to go the distance. Press reports hinted at campaign intrigue, and postulated infighting as a cause of her demise, but there is rarely a failed campaign in which "infighting" is not part of the story-line. All campaigns have infighting; the accounts of the losers get told in the press. There also were legitimate criticisms of her campaign such as the fuzziness of her health care stance. She had stunning debate performances but also mediocre ones. In addition, she never made a dent in the support Biden enjoyed among African American voters who pragmatically sought a "safe" candidate and someone with whom they had developed a uniquely close relationship as Obama's right-hand man. Try as she might and despite numerous visits to South Carolina, Harris could not dislodge this critical group of voters. By contrast, her strong appeal with college-educated women would have given her a leg up in most races. In this one, however, competition for these voters was fierce.

Above all else, however, the electability demon plagued her campaign. She would take her staff through an exercise. "Close your eyes. Now four words: the boy next door," she would say. "What comes into your mind? You immediately have an image in your mind. You've attributed a life experience and certain characteristics from those four words." She would then ask her staff, "What are those four words for me?" There was no ready-made image that instantaneously conveyed a whole set of attributes and cemented an aura of credibility. She was different, outside the familiar mode of presidential candidates, and for voters and donors obsessed with electability, different meant risky—and risky meant the potential for four more years of Trump. The pressure that fell on the African America female contender with the best chance in history to run for president could not be ignored. Shirley Chisholm was the first African American to make a serious run for the presidency, but Harris was the most viable Black woman to run for the Democratic nomination. She felt it; her staff felt it. She candidly told her communications team they had a higher burden to explain who she was.

Those who had worked on other campaigns describe the scrutiny as "outsized." She suffered at times from ridiculous expectations. In late February 2019 *Politico* ran a piece arguing, "She's connecting with audiences—sometimes to a fault." Connecting *too much* to voters? This is the dilemma of candidates who are barrier breakers: They cannot have a bad day and are forced to meet mythical levels of perfection. Inevitably they fail to strike exactly the right balance to satisfy critics. In an interview a reporter from a respected publication asked that since so many of her family members went to elite schools, why did she choose Howard? She was taken aback by a supposedly well-educated and sophisticated person not seeming to grasp that Howard was the Harvard of the HBCUs (or as some alumni liked to say, Harvard was the Howard of the Ivy League). If a political reporter did not understand who she was, what her life story entailed, how much harder, she concluded, would it be for voters with busy lives to take time to figure out exactly who she was.

With Harris's departure from the campaign, the debates and the race became less diverse. Only two viable women remained when the voting began in Iowa, Warren and Klobuchar. Klobuchar entered the race believing she had a 5 to 10 percent chance of winning. If the Democratic Party wanted another Obama—a "wow" candidate—the hardworking, unflashy candidate would be out of luck. Her success depended on the perception that she was a solid, electable moderate—but also on the collapse of Biden, which evaporated with his win in South Carolina. As candidates dropped from the race and the debate stage through the summer and fall of 2019, Klobuchar continued to grind away, albeit without the benefit of a huge network of donors. Her effective debate performance days before the New Hampshire primary generated momentum to land her in third place. I spoke to her backstage after her triumphant speech to her supporters and a national TV audience. Sipping from a water bottle and glistening from the hot TV lights she was clearly energized by the win. And yet the tension was evident. With her staff looking on, she did not tout their hard work or compliment their strategy. Instead, she pointedly noted that *she* had been the one to insist her campaign advisers spend real money in New Hampshire, an implicit criticism of her staff. She had her best showing to date, a strong third-place finish, but ahead lay states with higher percentages of nonwhite voters whom she had yet to win over. I wondered whether this was her high point and what path, if any, she had going forward.

Klobuchar was savvy enough to realize her chances were indeed narrowing. She knew she had money troubles and her appeal with nonwhite voters was limited. A tranche of campaign money, over $18 million, flooded into her campaign coffers after New Hampshire, too late to create a nationwide media presence. Her moment of triumph in New Hampshire quickly faded when she stumbled in Nevada, forgetting the name of the Mexican president and bickering back and forth on the debate stage with Buttigieg, who, as a lightly credentialed male competitor, plainly irritated her.

The results in Nevada cut off her New Hampshire momentum. As she described it, the caucus system there was essentially a "black box" where voters seemed to decide it was to be a two-person race between Biden and Sanders, to the detriment of her and Buttigieg.

Meanwhile, I had growing concerns about the direction of the race as Sanders virtually tied in Iowa and won victories in New Hampshire and Nevada. I started to worry, agonize really, that Democrats might pick the one candidate Trump could beat. Sanders already identified himself as a socialist so Trump would have no trouble making this a choice between himself and a "Marxist," rather than a referendum on Trump's pitiful performance as president. Trump openly rooted for Sanders, as he did in a tweet in February. "It is happening again to Crazy Bernie, just like last time, only far more obvious," he said in an oblique reference to the Sanders's camp argument that the DNC had favored Clinton in 2016. "They are taking the Democrat Nomination away from him, and there's very little he can do. A Rigged System!" Trump's effort to lend a hand to Sanders so he could draw a weak opponent was evident to most of the media. "Every corpuscle of Trumpworld appears dedicated to propping up Sanders," wrote *The Atlantic*'s Peter Nicholas. "One obvious tip-off that Trump is trying to promote Sanders's candidacy: He's relatively sparing in his insults."

Sanders's weakness as a candidate was one thing Trump and many sober-minded Democrats could agree upon. After three years of pushing back against Trump, the Resistance would be an utter failure if Sanders was the nominee and Trump reelected. Like many other observers anxious to oust Trump, I realized that to have a chance of defeating Trump the party would have to coalesce quickly around a single not-Sanders candidate, Biden being the most viable. As much as I admired the women candidates and got to personally like several of them and their teams, I knew this was a ruthless process of elimination. If the remaining women candidates could not prove their mettle, they would have to leave the race to make way for someone who could defeat Trump.

I was hardly alone in fearing the Democratic primary electorate would blow it by nominating Sanders. Never Trump operatives and conservative pundits who had underestimated Trump's march to victory in 2016 felt as if they had seen this horror film before. Even more vociferously than some establishment Democrats—who also knew nominating Sanders would be a disaster but feared offending him—Never Trumpers wrote frantic warnings to try steering Democrats away from making the same mistake Republicans did in 2016 (i.e., splitting up the vote among mainstream candidates, allowing the most extreme populist to win). These included Sarah Longwell, Tim Miller (a columnist at *The Bulwark* and a former Jeb Bush adviser), Republican operative Rick Wilson, Bill Kristol, and the author Tom Nichols.

After Klobuchar's poor showing in Nevada, it was clear she had no real path to the nomination. Moreover, if she and other moderates like Buttigieg stayed in the race, they would divide up the not-Sanders vote and allow the unelectable Sanders to sail to the nomination. Unless she and some of the remaining moderate candidates cleared out, Sanders would have the upper hand. About a year earlier I had sat down with Klobuchar after her appearance at the New Hampshire state convention, at a time few thought she still would be in the race in the fall of 2019, let alone make it all the way to Super Tuesday. At the time, her tenacity and midwestern pragmatism could be considered attractive to primary voters looking for a middle-of-the-road Democrat in the mold of Bill Clinton. I therefore covered her closely, even when she toiled in the low single-digits in the polls. She was ideologically perhaps closest to my own views and embodied the sort of problem-solving attitude I look for in politicians. Despite my admiration for Klobuchar and rooting interest in a woman candidate, I became convinced that she—like Buttigieg, Warren, Steyer, and Bloomberg—could not win and, if she remained in the race, would prevent the consolidation of the field around a more viable contender. Conflicted and gloomy in the latter part of February, I recognized the longer Klobuchar stayed in the greater the likelihood Sanders might prevail. Given the choice, in my mind, between maximizing the chance for a woman president and maximizing the chance to rid the country of Trump, I easily favored the latter. If the future of the country, of women's rights, and of our democracy meant consolidating around one of the male front-runners then so be it.

In South Carolina for the primary, I wrote a piece urging Klobuchar, Steyer, Buttigieg, and Bloomberg to get out of the race so as not to enable a Sanders win. They all should move on, I argued. I took no joy in urging Klobuchar to leave the race, having seen her mature as a candidate. I admired her feistiness and sympathized with her frustration over the attention less qualified men received. I watched her improve over the course of the campaign. Hoping she could become the nominee, however, was not a sufficient reason to encourage her—or the others—to stay in the race and divide up moderate votes that Biden needed to win.

Klobuchar was apparently thinking along the same lines. After Nevada and South Carolina, she weighed whether to stay in the race. Her staff said she could win her home state of Minnesota on Super Tuesday. She had a huge crowd in Oklahoma City, an encouraging sign that she still had support outside progressive strongholds. She had qualified for the next debate. However, she could see that "the polls were not getting dramatically better." Staff and family wanted her to go on, hopeful that something would happen. But as she thought through her options, she asked herself, "If I win Minnesota how will I have advanced the ball?" She ruminated over whether remaining in the race would serve the cause of Trump or her party. Her husband, who was in Maine, was taken aback when she told him it was over. "But I just convinced this lobster fisherman from Maine to vote for you!" he exclaimed.

At an event to commemorate Bloody Sunday beginning at the Edmund Pettus Bridge, civil rights hero Rep. John Lewis, Klobuchar, and most of the remaining contenders attended the symbolic walk where fifty-five years ago Lewis and others were beaten by police. Usually stoic and unflappable, Buttigieg, who was on the verge of his own announcement, was emotional. The combination of a campaign end and the intensity of the commemoration served as a catharsis for Klobuchar as well. She decided to pull out and began to call the other candidates. Her supporters and staff still asked about planned events in Utah and elsewhere, as if they had not fully processed the campaign's end. When she spoke with Sanders she began to cry. Biden's upcoming events in Houston and Dallas to her seemed like "karma." Why not end with a big bang in Texas of all places? An appearance in a hot, large room seemed like a perfect bookend to a campaign started in a blizzard. On March 1, before Klobuchar's own announcement in Texas, Buttigieg told a South Bend crowd he was getting out and endorsing Biden. He, Beto O'Rourke (who dropped out months earlier), and Klobuchar could show the party was rallying around Biden.

As Klobuchar waited backstage in Texas on March 2 to make her announcement a notary hustled in to have her sign a document to release her delegates, just moments before her appearance. She also spoke to Biden about Minnesota. Although he was polling at only about 10 percent in her home state, she told Biden if she looked straight into the camera and asked Minnesotans to vote for Biden, it would work. He told her, "Go for it." She took to the stage, her voice cracking as she announced, "Today I am ending my campaign and endorsing Joe Biden for president." She was emotional because she knew her staff, family, volunteers, and supporters around the country were all watching. "I knew they had all been working to the end," she recounted. As difficult as it was, her and Buttigieg's departures made it more likely that the party would rally to Biden and have a fighting chance against Trump. Both of them were realists who could see their poll numbers dropping. Both wanted to avoid the reputation as spoilers and were convinced Sanders was not the most electable candidate. Separately they came to the same selfless realization: *It is not about me. Do what is right for the country.*

As the Democratic campaign headed to Super Sunday, a nonpolitical story was receiving more attention. The COVID-19 virus, which had started in China, was crippling Europe. It was obvious to informed Americans it was only a matter of time before outbreaks occurred here. Watching Biden work the rope line, Klobuchar fretted whether that was the best thing for the soon-to-be nominee to be doing. She did not realize that big campaign events would soon become a thing of the past. The next few hours were dizzying for her. She cut a radio ad with Biden right after the rally in Texas and then hopped on a plane to arrive in New York at 3:30 a.m. to do the network morning shows. It had all come together and to an end in the best way possible, she concluded. This was the right thing to do, and her endorsement helped lift Biden to an unexpected victory in Minnesota on Super Tuesday.

As I had, Never Trump Republican Sarah Longwell watched Sanders's wins in early contests and worried his nomination would make a Democratic victory in November impossible. She leapt into action. She noticed that Trump followers had tried to make mischief by showing up to vote in Democratic primaries for Sanders, especially in South Carolina, thereby helping the person they thought would be the weakest opponent for Trump. Well, Longwell figured why couldn't disaffected Republicans be encouraged to vote in the primaries to pick someone they *could* vote for in November?

Longwell wrote in the *New York Times*: "Through our organization Center Action Now, my colleague Tim Miller and I have engaged these voters through a phone and text get-out-the-vote operation. We don't advocate any candidate, but we do educate disaffected Republicans and right-leaning independents about their ability to vote in the Democratic primary in open-primary states like Virginia and Texas." Longwell had the capability to reach "soft" Republican voters because she had painstakingly created a voting list of hundreds of thousands, later culled to a target list of self-identified Republicans who either did not vote for Trump in 2016 or who did and then figured out he was a menace. Her audience was Republicans who would acknowledge Trump was terrible but could be goaded into rallying behind him if they felt the media was beating up on him or the Democrats were conducting an impeachment witch hunt. Many of the voters were women, but they did not want to necessarily make a gender statement. (To the contrary, those who wanted Trump out would make comments in Longwell's focus groups such as: "I would *even* consider voting for a woman.") Longwell converted her operation into a text and call center urging unhappy Republicans to vote in Democratic primaries. They had done some preliminary work during the early primaries, but in advance of Super Tuesday Longwell went into high gear to hit those states and the ones with primary contests the following week (e.g., Michigan, Missouri).

Her efforts focused on Northern Virginia and Texas suburbs, where Biden crushed Sanders and turnout did go through the roof. It is impossible to attribute her actions to specific votes in favor of Biden, but her gut told her there were plenty of Republicans out there who had finally had enough of Trump. Here was the nucleus of something—maybe a group that could be expanded for the sole purpose of ousting Trump in the fall, maybe the beginning of a new ideological coalition. She was convinced that while there was virtually no evidence of defections from Trump among Republicans *inside* the Beltway, out in the country something was changing.

By Super Tuesday, Warren was the last woman standing. She had been in a polling free fall since autumn, taking fourth place in Iowa and New Hampshire, a third in Nevada, and a dismal fifth place in South Carolina. After a weak showing on Super Tuesday (including a third place in her home state) she took Wednesday off from the trail. On Thursday, she announced she would leave the race.

Warren was the A student, the consummate debater who simply could not get ahead of the critics, the press scrutiny, and the fanaticism of Sanders's base. Warren had made her share of errors. The DNA test to prove her Native American heritage was a debacle, her attempt to evade questions about her health care plan's spending followed by rolling out a gargantuan tax proposal was unwise, and her refusal to take on Sanders in the debates were strategically flawed. She had not been my favorite candidate, although I admired her intellectual heft and doggedness and felt she had been treated far more harshly than Sanders. Her exit left me despondent despite my conviction that the party's best chance to beat Trump now rested with Biden. I was not alone.

Democratic women pained by the failure of every woman candidate in the field took to social media in droves to express their angst. The very same mainstream media outlets that had contributed to the framing of electability meanwhile ran incredulous stories: *Is there really sexism? Was it gender?* There was little question in Warren's mind or in the minds of many women that gender played some role in her and every other woman's defeat, resulting in another election cycle in which the dream of a woman president would be deferred. Nevertheless, the New York *Daily News* declared, "No, Elizabeth Warren's loss isn't about sexism." An opinion piece for the *Detroit News* asserted "No, Elizabeth Warren is not a victim of sexism." The libertarian outlet *Reason* proclaimed, "Sexism Didn't Kill the Warren Campaign. The Warren Campaign Killed the Warren Campaign." The *Washington Examiner* insisted, "Sexism isn't to blame for Elizabeth Warren's Super Tuesday nightmare." At times, I was convinced the political reporters and pundits were among the least self-aware people on the planet.

Warren's announcement in front of a swarm of reporters outside her home was heartbreaking for her supporters. After briefly stating that she would end her campaign she took questions:

Question: And I wonder what your message would be to the women and girls who feel like we're left with two White men to decide between?

Warren: I know one of the hardest parts of this is all those pinky promises and all those little girls who are going to have to wait four more years. That's going to be hard.

Asked about her experience voting for herself, she seemed vulnerable and so very sad. "I stood at that voting booth, and I looked down and I saw my name on the ballot. And I thought, 'Wow, kiddo, you're not in Oklahoma anymore.'" She continued, "I had gotten a long email from my nephew and how proud his dad, my brother, is, and how they all had their plans to vote, and had met other people. It is these long ties for that moment standing in the booth. I miss my mom and my daddy." Watching the online stream on my computer, I choked up, realizing how very personal the journey had been for her—and for many women.

Then came her answer on whether gender played a part: "Gender in this race, you know, that is the trap question for every woman. If you say, 'Yeah, there was sexism in this race,' everyone says, 'Whiner!' And if you say, 'No, there was no sexism,' about a bazillion women think, 'What planet do you live on?'" She added,

"And, thinking about all those pinky promises. You know, I take those pinky promises seriously. So those were the things I needed to think through, and how we make all those pieces work, at least as best we can, for everyone." She had aptly summed up the gender catch-22 that still ensnared women candidates.

Her decision not to endorse Sanders was unsurprising. Biden's star was now rising so it made little sense to waste political capital on Sanders. Moreover, it was clear to many in Warren's camp that Sanders had lied about telling her a woman could not win. His Bernie Bros had pilloried her on social media. Who could blame her for not turning the other cheek?

In an interview with MSNBC's Rachel Maddow following her decision to suspend her campaign, Warren talked frankly about the Bernie Bros onslaught during the campaign. "It's not just about me," Warren said about the social media attacks. "I think that's a real problem with this online bullying and sort of organized nastiness. . . . I'm talking about some really ugly stuff that went on." While politics has become riddled with such behavior, she said it was a particular problem with Sanders's supporters. "It is. It just is," she told Maddow. She was unsparing. "They didn't just disagree," she said of the Sanders forces in Nevada who attacked women union leaders. "They actually published the phone numbers and home addresses of the two women, immigrant women, and really put them in fear for their families. . . . These are tough women who run labor organizing campaigns . . . and yet said for the first time because of this onslaught of online threats that they felt really under attack, and that wasn't the first time it happened." She described how his supporters referred to her using a snake emoji and called her a "traitor." She insisted politicians take responsibility for their supporters who "do really threatening and dangerous things." It was telling that only when the race was over, did she really speak her mind about Sanders's campaign. Perhaps she had lacked the killer instinct to take Sanders down when it mattered; maybe she had made a strategic decision that attacking him would turn off progressives. Whatever the motive, one wonders what would have happened if she had spoken this candidly about Sanders during the race.

Biden, who proved critics predictions of defeat wrong, now was on the verge of victory. The fear that Democrats would pick an unelectable extremist was behind us. And still, I was crestfallen that a woman yet again had been denied the chance to reach the highest rung of political power. It certainly was demoralizing for many Democratic women who would have to go through another presidential cycle without hope of a woman president. Fortunately, the ticket was not yet complete.

CHAPTER 18

FORGING A FEMINIST TICKET

At the start of the 2020 presidential cycle, Hogue at NARAL and Schriock at EMILY's List had high hopes that one of the four overqualified women senators would snag the presidential nomination. That did not happen, but women's groups nevertheless played a role in keeping the eventual winner in the race. In June 2019, the Biden campaign stumbled when his team created confusion over whether he still supported the Hyde Amendment, which allows federal funds to be used for abortions only in the cases of rape, incest, or a threat to the woman's life. At a campaign event Biden answered to a shouted question that, yes, he did still stand by his position. A spokesperson initially said he had not heard the question, suggesting he might have dropped support for the Hyde Amendment. Back at his headquarters aides pushed for him to shift his stance. Progressives furiously called in to register their concern. Hogue and other pro-choice activists called to speak with Biden's senior advisers. Repeal of the Hyde Amendment had always been a threshold position for NARAL and other groups given its impact on poor women, especially women of color who depended on public health care coverage. The Biden team had a choice: Adjust

Biden's prior position or stick with it and run the risk that women's groups would speak out publicly to denounce his position, effectively blowing up his campaign.

The day after Hogue spoke with the campaign team, the Biden camp soon "clarified" his position. He no longer wanted to keep the Hyde Amendment in place given that millions of women now received their health care through the ACA or Medicaid, which under the Hyde Amendment might cut off access to abortions. Hogue put out a gracious statement: "We're glad that Joe Biden listened to the voices of millions of women and further clarified his position on the Hyde Amendment. Let's be clear, the Hyde Amendment discriminates against all women but particularly poor women and women of color." The statement added, "We're pleased that Joe Biden has joined the rest of the 2020 Democratic field in coalescing around the Party's core values—support for abortion rights, and the basic truth that reproductive freedom is fundamental to the pursuit of equality and economic security in this country."

The *New York Times* made an oblique reference to the roll pro-choice activists played. "As abortion rights groups expressed their displeasure publicly, officials at organizations such as Planned Parenthood and NARAL Pro-Choice America—as well as senior Biden campaign staff members—were privately lobbying him to change his stance." Hogue chose not to highlight her own role. "The salience of the issues has been obvious over the last 48 hours, but I think that's only going to grow," she told the *Times.*

Biden's campaign had come within a hairbreadth of self-immolation. The women's rights community had put its foot down and won. Had Biden not moved on the issue, his campaign would have been dead long before he got to South Carolina the following year, where African Americans brought his campaign back to life.

Part of the reason for the savvy shift was the composition of his staff. Biden's campaign had more women in senior positions than any in presidential history. Anita Dunn had temporarily assumed management of the campaign. Kate Bedingfield held down the deputy campaign manager and communications spot. Among other top aides were Symone Sanders and Biden's sister Valerie Biden Owens and his wife Jill, both of whom had been involved in his campaigns over the decades. In March 2020, Jen O'Malley Dillon assumed the post of campaign manager. In contrast to the O'Rourke campaign that had a "good ol' boy vibe" and fewer women, the Biden team had a much different sensibility. The team could not turn Biden into something he was not, but the plethora of women voices certainly provided a sounding board for messaging to women and emphasis on the issues women voters cared most about.

Biden's overall message and policy proposals also were heavily directed to and influenced by women. Both Warren's campaign and Neera Tanden's think tank CAP had put forward extensive proposals to rebuild the social safety net. Tanden came out with a proposal for a "Social Contract for the 21st century," complete with proposals for childcare, elder care, paid sick leave, and extended Obamacare benefits. Multiple aspects of her proposal for a "caring economy" just weeks later showed up in Biden's elaborate economic revival plan. In May 2020, Rep. Rosa DeLauro of Connecticut and Health, Education, Labor, and Pensions Committee ranking member Sen. Patty Murray of Washington introduced a CAP-inspired proposal for childcare support providing that no family should pay more than 7 percent of household income on childcare; on July 21, Biden delivered a speech in Delaware proposing a plan that followed that guideline.

Even with an agenda attentive to the needs of women and a campaign featuring so many high-powered women, the failure to nominate a woman for president still stung for millions of women. For the second presidential cycle, no woman, no matter her qualifications or talents or political bent, would make it to the presidency. A palpable sense of disappointment and exasperation rose among women activists and progressive groups who dreaded a return to the pattern of all-male, all-White tickets. The Democratic Party, which had traditionally relied on women voters and especially women of color, could not risk a backlash nor give Trump ammunition to tell women that Democrats really did not care about them. Within days of Warren's departure from the race, the drumbeat began in Democratic circles, echoed in the media: Biden needed to pick a woman. It was not just women and progressives who pushed for a woman on the ticket; donors and establishment Democrats conceded that Biden could benefit from increased "excitement." Frustration begat news coverage, which congealed into "conventional wisdom" that a male VP pick would be a disappointment.

The question then was not really whether he was going to pick a woman running mate—that was always where Biden was headed and what party activists increasingly pushed for—but whether he should explicitly pledge to pick a woman, and if so, when. During the debate preparation Ronald Klain (Biden's former chief of staff), Anita Dunn, and Biden discussed the idea. O'Malley Dillon, who had just joined the campaign, had some discussions with him as well. Limiting his selection process to women would be an unusual move. It would constrain Biden's options for his running mate, something campaigns rarely like to do. The announcement might steal some of Biden's thunder when he did reveal his final pick. However, Biden seized on the idea of making the announcement early, given that he was almost certain to pick a woman when the time came. His aides reiterated he had felt for some time that "in this day and age" an all-male ticket was not the right thing for the Democratic Party. With the field just then down to two men— Warren had dropped out days before—it seemed like the right time to finally say it. As long as a woman was in the race, talking about a female VP would have been "condescending," as one top adviser put it. Once no female was left to compete for the top of the ticket the time was ripe to make Biden's private inclination into a public commitment.

The announcement could end grumbling within the party over the elimination of women from the field and likely catch Sanders off guard. In the debate, Biden made his commitment; Sanders hedged as to whether he would name a woman, as the Biden team thought he might. The motive for the announcement was not to give the Biden camp a surefire story coming out of the debate, as some surmised. At this point Biden was confident of his position in the race and eager to provide a contrast between his own center-left views and Sanders's socialist outlook. Biden's commitment nevertheless became the lead story from the last debate, engendering widespread praise.

Watching the debate alone, Klobuchar threw a pillow up in the air. "Well, that makes it less exciting!" she declared to no one in particular about the early reveal. In retrospect, however, she recognized it was a smart move, effectively closing off flavor-of-the-month contenders (e.g., New York governor Andrew Cuomo) later in the selection process. Moreover, as his team anticipated, Biden's bold announcement did win plaudits from Democratic women who warmed to the idea of a woman-only veepstakes.

Behind the scenes an excruciatingly meticulous and thorough vetting process got underway. Four cochairs, former Connecticut Senator Christopher J. Dodd, Los Angeles mayor Eric Garcetti, former Biden adviser Cynthia Hogan, and Rep. Lisa Blunt Rochester from Delaware headed the effort. The *Post* reported that they "logged more than 120 hours meeting with party activists, interest groups and other stakeholders with designs on who could best serve the party and country." They narrowed the field from about two dozen to eleven, interviewing each contender. Teams of lawyers scoured their records for every imaginable controversy, abiding by the rule that is the first law of VP selection: The pick should do no harm.

Coverage of the vice presidential search left the impression that current events pushed one or another candidate forward. As the coronavirus pandemic raged through America, exposing Trump's utter inability to lead, Democratic governors including Michigan's Gretchen Whitmer rose in prominence in media accounts. She got a lift when Trump publicly attacked her as "that woman from Michigan," a slam she adopted with gusto. She appeared on late-night TV with the expression emblazoned on a T-shirt. New Mexico governor Michelle Lujan Grisham also received mention in the stories about the VP search both as a Latina and as a competent chief executive of her state. The pandemic, followed by the economic collapse in the spring of 2020, seemed to make experience, expertise, and sound judgment a priority. Stacey Abrams, who had not held executive office and who had not run on the national stage, would be at a disadvantage, but she clearly remained in contention. Her aggressive, public pursuit of the VP role drew criticism, suggesting that ambitious women, especially women of color, were still expected to be demure when it came to their career aspirations. Other women, including the eventual pick, understood how the game was played and studiously avoided a public pressure campaign.

The media narrative of shifting front-runners was illusory. Biden had made a commitment to withhold judgment until the process was complete. Coverage of who was up and who was down rarely resembled the internal decision-making process. Despite public statements from advisers whom the press assumed had Biden's ear, he and his wife were the only voices that really counted, and they were determined to go through the full vetting process.

Even before the brutal murder of George Floyd in Minnesota the debate over whether Biden needed to pick a woman of color had been robust. African American women have long been the most reliable Democratic voters. African American women had been critical in saving Biden's campaign, responding to Rep. James Clyburn's call to rally to the former vice president in the South Carolina primary. At first, Clyburn publicly suggested that while a woman was essential, he preferred that woman be a woman of color, although that wasn't critical.

Floyd's murder and the mainstreaming of the Black Lives Matter movement sent Trump back to the racist well, tweeting out a 1960s slogan "When the looting starts, the shooting starts," further inflaming the situation. The use of tear gas and rubber bullets to clear peaceful protesters from Lafayette Square drew scathing bi-partisan criticism. By early June multiple US cities were awash in demonstrations, with sporadic, opportunistic incidents of looting and violence. The Floyd killing accelerated the momentum for an African American pick. Clyburn publicly declared that the "tim-ing" might not be there for Klobuchar, whose record as a prosecu-tor was already a point of contention with African Americans. By June 18 it seemed obvious that Biden would likely pick a woman of color. Klobuchar called Biden to take her name out of consideration on the grounds an African American woman should be picked, a clever move. Her deference to women of color might help to start repairing her own relationship with the African American commu-nity that had frayed during the campaign and post-campaign pe-riod. Her call also had the effect of undercutting Warren, a White woman still under serious consideration. The Biden campaign's praise for Klobuchar and lack of pushback on picking a woman of color was telling.

In a July interview from his home in Delaware, Biden made clear that four Black women were under consideration for his vice pres-ident, but he declined to promise his final pick would come from that group. Soon after, Grisham took herself out of the running.

Given Biden's comments and the racial unrest buffeting the country, Americans got to know a group of qualified and im-pressive African American contenders. The focus on racial bias in policing and the protests around the country worked to Harris's benefit. She already possessed many of the qualities Biden was looking for. She had a close relationship with the Biden family by virtue of her friendship with Biden's late son Beau, who had served as his state's attorney general at the same time Harris had held the job in California. Harris also had debated many times on the national stage and been vetted by the media, both advantages for the VP pick. While Harris's presidential campaign may have lacked policy focus, her rhetorical skills and deep reservoir of empathy had never been in doubt. Someone who had worked with law enforcement for most of her adult life could add weight to the indictment of police tactics, the implicit bias rampant in police departments, and the flawed policy choices that led to mass incarceration that devastated the African American community. The former attorney general could not credibly be accused of being soft on crime. In a country starved for bridge-builders she looked like she could help lead the country to higher ground. With civil rights credentials *and* experience as a former prosecutor she would check many boxes for Biden.

This transformation—from a presidential race in which a woman was too risky and a woman of color even riskier to a vice presidential search where an African American woman was considered political gold—was rich with irony. Suddenly the very same qualities that made someone like Harris an *unsafe* choice as president now commended her as a vice presidential pick. She could turn out the base. She could have credibility on racial justice without ceding the law-and-order issue to Republicans. Why had these same qualities not allowed her to be seen as a "safe" presidential candidate just months before? It was apparent to anyone who cared to observe that "electability" and "risky" were totally artificial constructs having little to nothing to do with the actual prospects for election.

Harris reminded her colleagues and the public at large in the early days of the COVID pandemic that African Americans were getting sick and dying at much higher rates than Whites. She introduced legislation to at least gather data so the inequality in health outcomes could be addressed. She further helped her cause with Democratic activists when she went to the streets with Black Lives Matter protesters outside the White House on May 30. Instead of speaking *to* the protesters she joined them *as* a protester. Harris posted a video on Twitter showing her standing among peaceful protesters chanting "Hands up. Don't shoot." She tweeted, "People are in pain. We must listen." Her spokesman underscored that she was "advocating for people to be heard."

A day later the Trump administration deployed tear gas on peaceful protesters in Lafayette Square to make way for a presidential photo op, Bible in hand, at a church across from the White House. Two days later, Harris appeared at a press conference to condemn the gassing of peaceful protesters in Lafayette Square. She also implored the country to look beyond single incidents of police violence. "It is time that we say that bad cops are bad for good cops. It is time that we say that one should not be subjected to the indignity of being told to get on your knees and put your hands behind your head, simply because you are walking while Black. And it happens every day in America." She continued, "There's not a Black man I know, be he a relative, a friend, or a coworker, or colleague, who has not been the subject of some form of racial discrimination at the hands of law enforcement, not one I know." She was in her element as a former prosecutor able to speak with law enforcement credentials but also with her finger on the pulse of the African American community.

A week after Trump gassed peaceful protesters in Lafayette, she went before the cameras in support of a comprehensive criminal justice package she and her colleagues had put together. Together with Sen. Cory Booker of New Jersey she introduced a far-reaching police reform bill that included a ban on choke holds, a curb on qualified immunity (the legal doctrine that prevented people harmed by excessive force to sue police), new monies for training police, and transparency for police officers' disciplinary records. She spoke passionately. "America's sidewalks are stained with Black blood. In the wake of George Floyd and Breonna Taylor's murders, we must ask ourselves: how many more times must our families and our communities be put through the trauma of an unarmed Black man or woman's killing at the hands of the very police who are sworn to protect and serve them?" She also reminded Americans that "it's 30 years after [the Los Angeles beating of] Rodney King, and the chants and the marches and the songs are about the same issue that we were marching for back when my parents did in the 60s and when we did after Rodney King 30 years ago. So, now's the time to act." Her rhetoric was more passionate, her demeanor more sober than the country had seen during the campaign.

She spoke passionately later in June on the Senate floor in favor of an anti-lynching bill. "The pain experienced not only by [George Floyd], that human being and his family and his children, but the pain of the people of America witnessing what we have witnessed since the founding of this country, which is that Black lives have not been taken seriously as being fully human and deserving of dignity."

Appearing with Booker, Rep. Karen Bass (the head of the Congressional Black Caucus), and other colleagues the following week, she told the press that the bill was held up by a single Republican, Sen. Rand Paul of Kentucky. Pivoting to police violence, she explained, "We're here because Black Americans want to stop being killed." Yes, there has been progress, but she repeated, "In the year of our Lord 2020 we could not get an anti-lynching bill passed in the United States Senate." Speaking slowly with a heavy heart, she explained that police reform is in the "interests of all Americans." Criminal justice was just one piece of the problem in addressing racial injustice. Invoking her experience as a prosecutor she urged a national standard for use of force, independent investigations for police misconduct, and federal investigations of any "pattern or practice" of discriminatory treatment. She also widened the lens to the topic of "safe communities," which require jobs, schools, and access to capital and credit.

Later that week she wrote a compelling column on racial justice in *Cosmopolitan*. "We cannot let up in the fight for equality, fairness, and justice. Even when, if not especially when, it is hard or uncomfortable to talk about," she declared. "Together, united, as one country we can be a force for change." She concluded, "The time for outrage is now. The time for solidarity is now. The time for action is now. The time for change is now." Her week reached a crescendo on the day of George Floyd's funeral when she stood on the Senate floor to excoriate Sen. Rand Paul for blocking a vote on an anti-lynching bill. She declared there was no rationale for Paul's actions other than "cruel and deliberate obstruction on a day of mourning." Her raw pain coupled with stunning eloquence was bracing.

She appeared to many Americans as the most prominent voice on racial justice. She was familiar enough to many voters who perked up when she spoke, and she was addressing issues in her wheelhouse—public safety and race. In her mind, she was one of several voices along with Senator Booker. "I knew I had to speak out," she said. But in the public's view this may have been the moment when Harris elevated herself over other contenders, displaying her telltale empathy but, moreover, exhibiting why a woman of color should be at the top of Biden's list. Over the summer she sought out and conferred with progressives and racial justice advocates. *Politico* reported in early June, "Harris spent the campaign and months since working to burnish her image on criminal justice issues and contending that her decades in the field, which were viewed as a liability, instead provides her with unmatched perspective into how to achieve systemic change."

She made frequent appearances on cable TV shows to talk about Floyd's death, the president's utter tone deafness, and the urgency of police reform. In a meaningful way her campaign had come full circle. During the campaign Harris had described her decision to become a prosecutor as motivated by her desire to bring about change from the inside. Unless progressives and people of color entered the halls of power, especially in the criminal justice realm, they would remain advocates without the power to enact their agenda, she'd argued. Now she seemed to be in precisely the position she had envisioned—on the inside with the experience and credibility to advance a progressive agenda on criminal justice reform.

Harris, however, was not the only African American contender for Biden's vice president. With the national response to police brutality, the rise of Black Lives Matter, and the sporadic violence in major cities, Americans were introduced to a phalanx of capable and dynamic African American women mayors—Keisha Lance Bottoms of Atlanta, Lori Lightfoot of Chicago, and Muriel Bowser of Washington, DC. They combined a tough message condemning looting with expressions of support for the protesters' message. They joined the people on the streets for days of protests and marches. They decried the president's attempt to militarize policing and denounced examples of unjustified use of force in confrontations with protesters. Bowser and others came to the logical conclusion: Rather than create conflict, the police should hold back and let peaceful protests play out. Bowser not only raised objections to use of federal forces in her city but ordered a "Black Lives Matter" mural painted on Sixteenth Street NW and renamed the stretch of street leading up to the White House "Black Lives Matter Plaza."

These women's empathetic governance stood in strong contrast to Trump's attempt to suppress protesters with violence. Tough-love mayors who comforted and consoled their residents managed to project the power of female leadership. A generation of Black women mayors, at a seminal moment in a time for race relations, dispelled any notion that toughness and caring were mutually exclusive. Their style of leadership—seeing, hearing, and making common cause with protesters—proved to be more effective than force. In turn, their performance and inclusion in the veepstakes increased these women's status and visibility. Bottoms in particular became a familiar face on cable TV talk shows and was singled out at Rep. John Lewis's funeral for her leadership during a time of racial unrest.

Former Orlando police chief Rep. Val Demings, who had gained visibility during the impeachment, also became a media favorite during this time. She went from a total unknown outside of her district before the impeachment trial to a rising star in the Democratic Party. By the spring, she was part of the buzz for vice president. In an interview with the *Washington Post*'s Jonathan Capehart, she said such talk was an "honor." When George Floyd was murdered, setting off peaceful protests but also isolated instances of opportunistic violence, the congresswoman was a steady voice urging calm but also reform. Demings could speak both to the need for racial justice and police reform but also to the unacceptability of violence. In interview after interview she struck the right balance between empathy and tough love, between fervent support for reform and determination that the movement not be hijacked by violent elements.

If not this election cycle, these African American women proved they were fully prepared to ascend to higher offices. In addition to newcomers to the national stage, other African American women with years of experience in politics and policy got their turn in the spotlight. Susan Rice, a close colleague of Biden's in the Obama administration when she served as ambassador to the United Nations and then national security adviser, certainly had the foreign policy credentials to put her in the top tier of Biden's VP choices. When Biden spoke publicly about being "simpatico" with his eventual pick, many suspected Rice would be a finalist in the selection process. There were obvious downsides to her as VP, however. She had never run for public office and had never debated on a national stage. Moreover, during the Benghazi furor her reliance during Sunday talk show appearances on what turned out to be inaccurate talking points earned her the enmity of the right. (For that reason, she had dropped from consideration to replace Hillary Clinton as Obama's secretary of state, a post subject to Senate confirmation.)

Another African American, Rep. Karen Bass of California, also got her share of attention. The former speaker of the California assembly and leader of the Congressional Black Caucus was well-liked among her peers and had sterling progressive credentials. However, reports surfaced of her trips to Cuba, her sympathetic words following Fidel Castro's death (which would be a bitter pill for the Cuban exile population in Florida), and a speech to Scientologists in which she praised the group. The vetting process was "working" in the sense that potentially embarrassing material on a potential candidate surfaced.

Press reports, mostly incorrect, speculated as to who the finalists might be. Many progressive pundits and commentators publicly pushed for an African American vice president. Tiffany Cross, a prominent African American commentator, remarked in an interview with *Forbes* that Biden would be helped by "having Black women validators at the local and national levels. And, again, having a Black woman on the ticket who can energize this voting base and speak to this key constituency would be the most logical start."

The week before Biden announced his pick, anti-Harris sniping broke out in public. *Politico* featured a quote from former Senator Chris Dodd that he did not trust Harris because she had attacked Biden in the debates. While he was nominally the head of the search committee, he did not speak for Biden. Nevertheless, the story went viral. George H. W. Bush could call Ronald Reagan's supply-side tax plans "voodoo economics" during the 1980 primary, but a woman, especially a woman of color, was expected to be docile and contrite in a debate. The campaign was hesitant to react to each of the VP selection stories, finding it unwise to rebut every inaccuracy. But the cacophony of voices debating Harris's loyalty provoked Biden's campaign manager Jen O'Malley Dillon to tweet in defense of Harris. She declared, "Ambitious women make history, change the world, and win. Our campaign is full of ambitious women going all out for Joe Biden. He will make this decision, and this is clear: whoever he chooses from the very qualified options to help him win & unite the country, she'll be one too." The pushback not only reflected her own views but also was designed to give Biden some "space" to make his decision.

I pressed the campaign for a more specific response denouncing Dodd's comment. I probed as to whether this reflected Biden's thinking about women and ambition. The campaign initially declined to go any further or to specifically slap down Dodd. As I was writing a piece ridiculing Dodd's mindset, seemingly out of the blue I received a statement from the former senator praising Harris and edging away from the reported comment. The Biden camp had plainly sent him crawling back to attempt to distance himself from the remarks.

The news accounts and whisper campaign continued. Another older, White man long out of office, former Pennsylvania governor Ed Rendell, hissed, "Kamala can rub some people the wrong way." A more misogynistic statement embodying the trope of a sweet, nonconfrontational woman would be hard to come by. As the stories continued, my anger intensified. I warned in tweets and columns that this kind of talk threatened to turn a historic milestone into evidence of deep misogyny.

Harris obliquely referred to the controversy at an event for African American women. CNN reported on her remarks:

> There will be a resistance to your ambition, there will be people who say to you, "you are out of your lane." They are burdened by only having the capacity to see what has always been instead of what can be. But don't you let that burden you. . . . You know how many times I've been told it can't be done? "Nobody like you has done it before. They're not ready for you." And I could not listen.

The "ambition" issue was hardly new. When it reared its head in the VP process, it was immediately familiar to her. In fact, after she left the race she had become increasingly candid about it. As Zoom replaced in-person events, she recalled, "I would much more explicitly bring it up." She would tell audiences, "Raise your daughters to be ambitious."

Many female voices shared my frustration with the misogynistic chatter. Michelle Ruiz wrote in a piece for *Vogue*: "Political ambition is tantamount to striving for power, and when it comes from women, it makes people deeply uncomfortable. . . . To *try* is to offend the increasingly delicate status quo of White-male rule and the evident fragility of Biden's inner circle. The truth is: Every woman on their short list is powered by ambition." An exasperated Rebecca Traister spoke for many when she wrote, "Biden has permitted his League of Mediocre White Men to run around dinging up a group of trailblazing female politicians, most of them Black, all of whom have plied paths unimaginably more challenging than any taken by these men. *This* has been the vice-presidential selection process of Joe Biden's 2020 campaign, and it should leave us all hot with anger."

In Harris's corner was an informal online army of supporters, including a high percentage of women and using the hashtag #KHive, derived from the moniker for Beyoncé fans, the BeyHive. The group operated independently of the campaign but with the full encouragement of Harris. Loosely formed in 2017, the KHive grew during the campaign to tens of thousands of Harris supporters, generating online content, fundraising, and responding to attacks on Harris. As the onslaught against Harris intensified so did the pushback from the KHive. They denounced the comments from Rendell and Dodd. They slammed reporting that regurgitated the sexist and racist stereotypes circulating online. The KHive was evidence of women's increased activism in presidential politics. It was also an example of robust, even heated advocacy, without the sort of personalized attacks, threats, and vulgar language we had seen from the Bernie Bros and pro-Trump forces.

The tone of the public discussion became so disconcerting that on the Friday before the selection announcement a group of progressive women leaders, including Hogue and Schriock, released an open letter to news executives, anchors, editors, and journalists warning against perpetuation of "stereotypes and tropes about qualifications, leadership, looks, relationships and experience," noting they are especially damaging to women of color. They enumerated a list of objectionable memes including reporting "on a woman's ambition as though the very nature of seeking political office, or any higher job for that matter is not a mission of ambition" and harping on "whether a woman is liked (a subjective metric at best) as though it is news when the 'likeability' of men is never considered a legitimate news story." They also cautioned against promulgating chatter "about who is legitimately American" (that one proved prescient when a day after the pick Trump was speculating that she might not be eligible to run). The letter reminded us that whether intentional or not news coverage had a major role in perpetuating misogynistic attitudes toward women.

Progressive journalist and commentator Joan Walsh expressed the exhaustion and frustration of many women. She wrote, "By the end of the vetting period, it seemed the 11th commandment of women's politics, 100 years after we won the vote, was 'Thou shalt never be just right.'" In a similar vein Connie Shultz, the Pulitzer Prize–winning columnist, wrote, "I've been angry for some time now. . . . I've been angry because I'm to-the-bone tired of this movie. I'm tired of the decades—my whole lifetime—of waiting and waiting and waiting. I'm tired of these degrading notions of what a woman can and cannot do and how too many women still believe them."

The days before the announcement were excruciatingly tense. Some handicappers—based on nothing but hunches—felt certain Biden would cave to the old White voices in the party and pick someone other than Harris. Others expressed confidence he would recognize Harris was the most dynamic contender, someone with national security credentials and experience running for president on the national stage. The Harris campaign called me the weekend before the pick to confirm they would make time for an interview, which I had been requesting for weeks. I did not know if this meant she was *out* of the running or if they simply had not heard yet from Biden. (It turned out to be the latter.) This aggravated my anxiety that she was to be punished for her "ambition," for debating like the contest was for keeps. I fretted Biden would wind up reinforcing an awful stereotype just as he was making history.

Harris recounted later that she was "very Zen" about the process. Biden would make a decision in "some smokeless room" as to who would help him win. She had from the start of her own presidential campaign understood at all costs Trump had to go. "My purpose in getting in the race in that sense remained true." She neither expected nor wrote off the possibility of getting the nod.

On Monday and Tuesday, rumors flew on social media and offline. A *Post* colleague who lived in Harris's building in DC tried to track her every move. No Secret Service, no unusual activity. On Tuesday, a list of names who would not be the pick trickled out, creating a pseudo-mystery as to who would be left standing. The Biden campaign then made it official, announcing first on social media that Harris was his choice. "You make a lot of important decisions as president. But the first one is who you select to be your Vice President. I've decided that Kamala Harris is the best person to help me take this fight to Donald Trump and Mike Pence and then to lead this nation starting in January 2021," he said in an email to supporters. "I need someone working alongside me who is smart, tough, and ready to lead. Kamala is that person." He acknowledged that she had a deep reservoir of empathy. "I need someone who understands the pain that so many people in our nation are suffering," Biden wrote. "Whether they've lost their job, their business, a loved one to this virus."

The team had pulled off a flawless announcement with no leaks. (Harris would not leave her apartment until the next day.) I was relieved and, yes, joyful for the first time in the entire 2020 cycle. Here was a woman—of color, no less—who did not fit male stereotypes of the submissive female.

Harris told me she had not focused on the irony that diversity, once a burden, was now viewed as an asset. She looked at the decision from a different angle. She believed that while she and Biden had diametrically different experiences, they had a lot in common and could complement one another. Within an hour what she would later jokingly refer to as a "SWAT team" rushed into the apartment, arms full of binders and schedules. That night, she and her husband had to pack. She left the apartment, heading for Delaware the next day.

Her pick raised the possibility that a woman might get to the presidency by way of the vice presidency. The road that had started in Oakland and seemingly ended in December 2019 was now leading to the White House for a woman Trump dubbed "nasty." It was a rebuke to Trump and his vicious brand of White supremacy and misogyny. This was a turning of the table, a karmic moment I could celebrate wholeheartedly.

After her nomination was announced the Barbara Lee Family Foundation put out a statement identifying many of the stereotypes that Harris had or would encounter. "While men are assumed to be qualified, women candidates have to prove over and over they are up to the job. . . . Women candidates pay a higher price for 'going negative,' even though all candidates must show how they differ from their opponents."

The slam against ambitious women would not disappear overnight. "I don't think I slayed that dragon," she conceded. However, she offered, "More people will be aware of this frame of reference," and hopefully put it aside.

CHAPTER 19

THE PITCH TO WOMEN

In a fundraising explosion for the Biden camp, $48 million poured into the campaign in the forty-eight hours following Harris's selection. The ticket's poll numbers continued to climb. The media reviews of her performance at the rollout were overwhelmingly positive. An ambitious woman had not just made history but exceeded expectations. Biden for the second time in his career had broken barriers. As President Obama's vice president, Biden had blurted out his support for gay marriage in an interview, thereby pushing the president and the rest of the party to move forward on the issue. Now, he had elevated a barrier-breaking woman of color, setting up a historic election.

The race settled into a battle between candidates aimed at two distinct sections of America and espousing two dramatically different conceptions of America. Just as he did in 2016, Trump played to mostly White, male, rural, and non-college-educated voters while Biden attracted primarily nonwhite, female, urban, suburban, and college-educated voters. One ticket was all White and played to its White base's resentments. The other was eclectic (including Harris's Jewish husband) and projected an inclusive vision of American democracy. One party's leader was openly misogynistic, the other promised to appoint women to his Cabinet and advanced an agenda tailor-made for women.

Beyond White voters, Trump's team also focused on Latino voters in Florida, raising the specter of "socialism" with Cuban Americans whose anti-Castro sentiments he could manipulate. Biden's team, meanwhile, targeted discrete communities of color who could make a difference in swing states. In Arizona, local organizing had been underway for months to reach Native Americans. Meanwhile, in Georgia, Stacey Abrams's formidable operation continued to register and engage with irregular voters. Georgia Democrats also took note of the increase in Asian American and Pacific Islander (AAPI) voters in the Atlanta greater metropolitan area. Abrams reached out to these voters in 2018—doing Korean language interviews, for example—and won 77 percent of these voters. The Democratic Congressional Campaign Committee aided efforts to turn out AAPI voters with a major investment in multilingual organizers while local groups such as the Asian American Advocacy Fund did their own outreach. Trump's racism toward AAPI with his "Wuhan flu" references also worked to solidify these voters' traditional Democratic leanings.

Despite Republicans' ongoing difficulty attracting women voters, Trump and his Republican cohorts seemed unable to conceal their hostility to women each time they opened their mouths. In a widely disparaged tweet in late July, Trump tried scaring "suburban housewives" with the prospect that a horde of "low income" (i.e., nonwhite) Americans would invade their neighborhoods. Trump shamelessly revealed his low opinion of these women, whom he thought he could petrify with the prospect of integration. Trump knew his support among suburban women was eroding but he had no clue how to appeal to them. His blatant fearmongering and crude racism only repelled them further.

Trump was not the sole Republican official inclined to insult women. The loudest voices in the Republican Party tended to be the most hateful toward women, women of color especially. Shortly after Harris's pick right-wing talk-show host Rush Limbaugh (to whom Trump had awarded the Presidential Medal of Freedom) referenced a sportscaster who had been fired for a Facebook post. Limbaugh declared, "[He] posted an image that read 'Joe and the Hoe,' h-o-e. Now, what do you think that's about, Joe and the Hoe?" He then quoted a story from the right-wing *American Spectator*, "It is no secret but public knowledge that Kamala Harris slept her way up into California political life by being a very public escort and mattress [sic] for California Democrat kingmaker Willie Brown." Limbaugh continued his on-air reading of the piece, "So, we have two different stories here that are trading off the known fact that she was Willie Brown's mattress [sic], and that he has written about it and that he has talked about how it propelled her, that he ended up being one of her mentors."

It was not public knowledge nor true that Harris "slept her way" to the top. While she had a brief relationship with Brown decades earlier, no one following California politics doubted that Harris earned her way up through the ranks and onto the national stage. The suggestion that she and, by implication, other women use sex to succeed was as egregious as it was expected from the increasingly misogynist right. Trump's GOP was a party that neither respected nor understood the lives of many American women. The Republican Party previously had pushed for laws limiting women's rights to make their own choices about reproductive health and celebrated "traditional marriage," but Trump had ventured where no Republican presidential candidate had ever gone. Trump's vulgar, nasty, and demeaning language toward women as a way of endearing himself to his White, non-college-educated, and mostly male base was unprecedented, not to mention self-destructive. Trump knew precisely how to play to the fears and resentments of aggrieved White men, especially in a race in which Harris provided unnerving evidence that they no longer dominated all the levers of power. The result, however, was to further alienate women voters, a majority of the electorate.

Other elected Republicans deployed abusive language toward women as well. In late July, Rep. Ted Yoho of Texas, among the wackier members of the right-wing Freedom Caucus and a "birther" conspiracy-monger, verbally accosted Rep. Alexandria Ocasio-Cortez just outside the Capitol. She later described the incident: "I was minding my own business, walking up the steps, and Representative Yoho put his finger in my face, he called me disgusting, he called me crazy, he called me out of my mind. And he called me dangerous." She entered the building, cast a vote, and walked back out. She recounted that "there were reporters in the front of the Capitol, and in front of reporters, Representative Yoho called me, and I quote, 'a fucking bitch.' These are the words Representative Yoho levied against a congresswoman."

AOC took to the House floor, with the support of her female colleagues, to denounce Yoho and voice her outrage over the all-too-common experience of women being bullied by male colleagues. By using such vulgar language, Yoho, "gave permission to use that language against his wife, his daughters, women in his community, and I am here to stand up to say that is not acceptable." In a calm and deliberate voice, she dismissed the myth that a married man and a father of daughters could not possibly behave like a thug. "What I believe is that having a daughter does not make a man decent. Having a wife does not make a decent man," she said. "Treating people with dignity and respect makes a decent man. And when a decent man messes up, as we all are bound to do, he tries his best and does apologize. Not to save face, not to win a vote. He apologizes genuinely to repair and acknowledge the harm done so that we can all move on." She continued, "I want to thank him for showing the world that you can be a powerful man and accost women. You can have daughters and accost women without remorse. You can be married and accost women. You can take photos and project an image to the world of being a family man and accost women without remorse and with a sense of impunity." Speaking for millions of women who had faced putdowns and harassment, she reiterated, "It happens every day in this country. It happened here on the steps of our nation's Capitol. It happens when individuals who hold the highest office in this land admit, admit to hurting women, and using this language against all of us." Yoho would only apologize for the "abrupt manner of the conversation." That did not come close to admitting his vulgar attack nor expressing remorse for his insults. AOC's grace, defiance, and determination not to allow misogynistic conduct to go unanswered were widely praised, even by some conservative women ordinarily critical of her politics.

After the incident, Pelosi spoke with NBC's Andrea Mitchell, comparing Yoho to Trump, who deploys "bigotry, fearmongering, condescension and distortion." Pelosi continued, "Weren't we proud of Congresswoman Ocasio-Cortez? As a grandmother of two young granddaughters and a mother of four, during the course—I just want to say, you go, Congresswoman," said Pelosi. "You go, Congresswoman." Mitchell asked if having so many women in Congress helped AOC make her point. "Of course," Pelosi answered. "Well, you know, what was clear from what she said is that what happened that day was [Yoho's] problem and continues to be his problem. She's not taking any insult from him in terms of any diminishment of competence that she has as to who she is. We couldn't have been prouder." A critical mass of women could not only defend a single victim but reset the standard for acceptable conduct in the House.

Not all women were necessarily hearing or reacting to this message in the same way. For professional White women and certainly for women of color who had encountered put-downs and bias in the workplace, these incidents struck a chord. However, for White women without a college education and buried deep within the Fox News bubble, this coverage of AOC fed into their narrative that she was a radical leftist and a social media showboater. Although she had no position on Biden's campaign team and had backed his opponent Bernie Sanders in the primaries, Republicans still splashed her image over anti-Biden ads, with the voice-over ominously warning, "The radical left has taken over Joe Biden and the Democratic Party. Don't let them take over America."

In contrast to Republicans' continued barrage of misogynistic attacks, Democrats not only courted but relied upon the organizing heft of those women voters most devoted to the Democratic Party: African American Women. As Megan Botel wrote for *USA Today*, "Being the 'backbone' of American democracy, identity activists say is rooted in a history of racial oppression and gendered disenfranchisement, comes at a cost." Throughout the civil rights movement and up through the #MeToo movement Black women were front and center in advocating for progressive causes and candidates. In the Trump era, their work began even before the Black Lives Matter protests galvanized women of color.

Since March 2020, a coalition called the Black Voters Matter Fund had been hard at work to elect a Democratic ticket. Botel noted it had "partnered with more than 600 grassroots organizations to get-out-the-vote among the Black community in swing states and vulnerable counties, providing supplies, funding and strategic guidance." Other groups such as Woke Vote founded by DeJuana Thompson organized in major cities, making a ten-city swing through the country to engage voters. She the People also helped to mobilize women of color. Its founder Aimee Allison told the *Guardian*, "You have a group of voters of Black women who are the most effective organizers on the ground because they are trusted voices and are working in organizations year round. They don't come in six weeks before and kind of rent out a storefront, they're actually invested in, long-term, empowering the community through civic and political action."

African American women organizing for Biden did not limit their focus to urban areas. Over the last decades, the suburbs surrounding major American cities like Philadelphia, Phoenix, Charlotte, and Atlanta have become more diverse. African American women not only boosted registration and turnout in big cities; they helped Biden increase his support in, for example, the Philadelphia suburbs.

Ron Brownstein spotted the suburban trend and its implications for 2020. "President Donald Trump's racially charged warnings to suburban voters about crime and housing face a fundamental headwind: the suburbs themselves are much more racially diverse than even two decades ago," he wrote. "In contrast to the stereotype of homogeneous communities of White families behind white picket fences, in many of the largest suburban counties around America Whites now compose only about half or less of the population." Brownstein concluded that while Trump might find some suburbanites willing to buy the portrait of him "as a human wall protecting them from chaos and disorder in the cities," the suburbs were nothing like the electorate Richard Nixon faced "when making similar arguments half a century ago."

With grassroots Democrats plowing forward to turn out every possible Biden voter, the sprint to the presidential election started in earnest in August with the Democratic National Convention. The pandemic forced the Democrats to create something out of whole cloth, a virtual convention. For decades, presidential conventions featured the same basic elements: four days of speeches—some too long, many from little-known figures, and an occasional opportunity for a rising star to break out; tedious meetings to decide on the party's policy platform; and high-dollar donor parties. In a large convention hall with an immense stage, the national convention organizers filled the void left by an absence of real news with pageantry. The media and public had grown accustomed to the sight of thousands of delegates, many sporting funny hats and strewn with buttons from years of convention-going, holding signs appropriate for each speaker or segment of the program ("We're with Her!" "Save the ACA!"). The TV audience would listen to the lengthy roll call during which each delegation's leader would stand next to a post bearing the state's name and, after a long warm-up touting the state's features, declare the number of votes for the chosen candidate. None of that was doable in the coronavirus-plagued election year. Democrats, fully cognizant of the challenges, started months earlier to map out a convention unlike any other. For that task they hired a seasoned operative Stephanie Cutter, a veteran of the Obama White House and cofounder of the marketing firm Precision Strategies.

The Biden campaign team, from campaign manager Jen O'Malley Dillon on down, remained acutely aware that women would be the deciding factor in the race. That meant the convention had to fire up women voters and stress issues essential to them. The diversity of the women speakers and the plethora of women participants in videos—from African American elevator operator Jacquelyn Brittany, who embraced Biden in a viral video, to a Latina daughter of a COVID-19 victim mourning the loss of a father who took no comfort in Trump's lack of urgency—reflected how critical women of color were to Biden's coalition. In addition, the convention designers aimed to keep in the fold the sort of women, many suburban and college-educated, who had abandoned the GOP in 2018. Democrats were eager to reassure them that they had a permanent home in the Democratic Party.

One could not help but notice the extent to which female staff and speakers shaped the extravaganza for and about women. While the presidential candidate certainly remained the top attraction, the emphasis on his decency, empathy, and devotion to family highlighted qualities especially appealing to women—and of course entirely absent in the incumbent. The hosts of each of the four nights were women. Women speakers including Hillary Clinton, Dr. Jill Biden, Michelle Obama, Amy Klobuchar, Nancy Pelosi, and the others who were on Biden's short list for vice president dominated the program. Dr. Biden spoke from a classroom to commiserate with parents anxious about sending their kids back to school in a pandemic. She expertly delivered the broad-based message to all parents suffering through the ordeal of virtual learning. The Democrats could feature so many women because so many of them had run for and won office, and ascended to national prominence.

The convention emphasized moderation not revolution, competence not ideological purity. The formula was simple: Remind women alienated from the GOP of Trump's obnoxious know-nothingism that turned them off from the GOP in 2018. Hit Trump for failing to confront the COVID-19 pandemic that had killed 170,000 Americans by August. Offer the Biden-Harris ticket as an island of stability, competence, and decency. In short, the convention planners aimed to produce lively entertainment to establish an unbreakable bond with women voters of all backgrounds who would be the difference between winning and losing. Traditionally, convention managers seek to keep the party's base pumped up and convert other winnable voters; they need to make certain that they do not communicate only to the already committed voters. And as much as political junkies like me enjoyed the convention festivities and distraction from COVID, I wondered if Democrats were reaching swing voters in swing states cynical about politics who would decide the election.

Media expectations were low for a purely virtual event. The very same media analysts who for years had ridiculed conventions as contrived and boring now predicted it would be impossible to re-create the excitement of a big crowd and live events. Cutter and her staff had the brilliant insight not to mimic a live convention but to reimagine the convention. The result was a remarkably engaging eight hours of political entertainment over four nights featuring crisp speeches and some poignant appearances of regular Americans speaking about their COVID experiences, police shootings, or other events that had rocked their lives. Glossy videos highlighting the biographies of the nominees and explaining the policies at the heart of the Democratic agenda popped up throughout the evenings. Cutter and her team transformed the roll call of the states into a travelogue around the country with video from each delegation's home state or territory. The endearing tribute to America's physical and demographic diversity proved to be a whimsical and patriotic break from the gloom that had engulfed the country. Viewers who had not been able to travel for months could at least enjoy a virtual swing around the country.

Cutter and her team had to walk a fine line. She wanted to unify and engage the party with progressive superstars like Elizabeth Warren, Nancy Pelosi, and Michelle Obama, but these figures might not thrill reluctant Trump voters from 2016 nervous about voting for a party more progressive than they were. Given Trump and the Republicans' expertise in tarring progressives as anti-police and anti-capitalism, Cutter had to be conscious that the message they delivered did not turn off the working-class White voters Biden was trying to win back. College-educated voters might thrill to abstract issues like "the fate of democracy," but other voters might not see the direct relevance to their own lives.

Media, politically engaged voters, and even some viewers looking for entertainment in the COVID era after exhausting their Netflix queues found it compelling television. Some spectators and political groups hosted virtual viewing parties. Rather than traveling to the convention in Milwaukee as I had for conventions of both parties over the years, I watched from home like other Americans. I searched for evidence that the Biden team had managed to rev up its base without putting off moderates. There did seem to be something for everyone. Women infuriated by Trump's obnoxious and mean behavior might appreciate the discussion of character as the critical factor in choosing a president. A parade of Republican politicians who could not bring themselves to vote for Trump explained why their love of country and concern for democracy prompted them to back Biden; progressives like Warren and Sanders assured their supporters that Biden was a vehicle for obtaining their policy goals. Despite the competing and conflicting demands, Cutter struck the right tone and delivered high ratings.

The convention was also the first time many voters heard Harris speak at length. The vice president nominee's convention speech is among the top two or three most critical moments in a campaign. In this case, a lush video about women's suffrage and political activism, appropriate for the hundredth anniversary of the passage of the Nineteenth Amendment, set the stage for Harris's speech. "She was called an instigator, a rule breaker, a rabble-rouser," the narration began over a montage of women activists, past and present. "And she is called the agitator, the pushy one, the one with attitude." This was a direct rebuke to the Republicans' misogyny and to Trump's characterization of suburban women as "housewives." The film provided an energizing tribute to the generations of women who laid the groundwork for Harris and her peers and certainly reflected the degree to which the Democratic Party shifted from a party merely supported *by* women to one *run* in large part by women.

Harris, facing a room without delegates, would not have the energy of a crowd to buoy her. The sort of lines designed to generate applause would not work since no one would be applauding. Only socially distanced members of the press sat before her. To make matters even more tricky, she also had the unenviable task of following President Obama, who gave one of the most memorable speeches of his career. He extolled the Democratic ticket's virtues and warned that "this president and those in power—those who benefit from keeping things the way they are—they are counting on your cynicism." He warned, "They know they can't win you over with their policies. So, they're hoping to make it as hard as possible for you to vote, and to convince you that your vote doesn't matter." He told millions watching at home, "You can give our democracy new meaning. You can take it to a better place. You're the missing ingredient—the ones who will decide whether or not America becomes the country that fully lives up to its creed." A less adept VP nominee's speech might have seemed anticlimactic after that. Harris, by now a practiced speaker on the national stage, projected confidence as she strode to the podium. Many women disappointed by the lack of a female presidential nominee could now reframe Harris's unsuccessful presidential race as a necessary warm-up to her historic debut. Her presence confirmed that women could embrace their own ambition openly and without apology. She was self-assured and radiant in her delivery despite the weird setting.

"That I am here tonight is a testament to the dedication of generations before me," Harris began. "Women and men who believed so fiercely in the promise of equality, liberty, and justice for all." She acknowledged the hundredth anniversary of women's suffrage. "Yet so many of the Black women who helped secure that victory were still prohibited from voting, long after its ratification. But they were undeterred." In words that captured the historic fight for women's rights but also her own life story, she declared, "Without fanfare or recognition, they organized, testified, rallied, marched, and fought—not just for their vote, but for a seat at the table. These women and the generations that followed worked to make democracy and opportunity real in the lives of all of us who followed. They paved the way for the trailblazing leadership of Barack Obama and Hillary Clinton. And these women inspired us to pick up the torch and fight on."

Harris told the country about her immigrant mother who had raised her sister and Kamala as a single parent and her Jamaican father. She also spoke about her career as a prosecutor, which had proved to be a two-edged sword in the primary. "I know a predator when I see one," she said unsubtly referring to Trump. She took another stab at Trump. "The constant chaos leaves us adrift," she said. "The incompetence makes us feel afraid. The callousness makes us feel alone." However, the bulk of the speech was about her biography and her testament to Biden's character. It was both an utterly unprecedented speech by virtue of her identity and yet one entirely in keeping with the sort of convention speech expected of a nominee for vice president.

She had earned her place in history, not by playing to the stereotype of helpmate but by leaning into the profile of a competent, strong, and bold politician, one with a multiracial background in a blended family of her own. Like many Americans, she had multiple roles (prosecutor, immigrant daughter, stepmother) with no single racial or ethnic identity. That might have made it hard to instantly categorize her but it allowed a wide variety of voters to relate to her in some way.

While the campaign carefully managed Harris's rollout leading up to the convention, on her own out on the general election campaign trail she soon became a voter favorite and fundraising juggernaut. Her confident jog down the airplane steps in her Chuck Taylor sneakers became an internet meme. In early September she arrived at a Philadelphia fundraiser expecting the well-appointed women to be dressed in heels. To her delight, they all wore brand new Chucks purchased for the occasion.

Harris found receptive audiences of women, some of whom could see their lives reflected in Harris's life and some who were simply fed up with Trump's mishandling of the pandemic as well as his racism and sexism. Harris found it easy to empathize with women whose lives had become chaotic due to Trump's incompetence. If still employed, mothers now had to work and manage "virtual" learning for their kids. If a woman had elderly parents, she now faced physical separation from them and constant anxiety about their health. Some of the independent and Republican women who had disliked Clinton more than Trump no longer could rationalize supporting him. Presented with an empathetic, competent, and decent alternative, they could comfortably make the leap to the Democrats. That was the pitch, at any rate, for O'Malley Dillon and her team. Harris, together with Biden, ran one of the most disciplined races in memory, a fundraising behemoth with an optimistic Build Back Better message. That certainly contrasted with Trump's incoherent and hateful campaign, one so badly managed it blew through $1 billion in 2020 and got outspent down the stretch.

The Republican National Convention could not have been more

different from the Democrats' technologically sophisticated show. Instead of a slick TV program, the Republicans commandeered the White House in a stunning departure from tradition. No administration of either party had ever tried to convert the seat of government into a crass political prop. For one thing, the affair seemed to be a massive violation of the Hatch Act, which prohibits government employees from campaigning and using government facilities for campaign purposes. Instead of a party policy platform, Republicans put out a loyalty oath. The "platform" committed the party "to enthusiastically support the President's America-first agenda." The party might as well have said, "Whatever Trump says is fine."

Instead of a slew of prominent women lawmakers who had risen in the party, the Trump team relied heavily on Trump relatives like Melania, Ivanka, Tiffany, and his sons' significant others. At times it seemed the only women willing to tout him were those who stood to inherit something. This was the party of the 1950s, where women's position depended on their relationship to men in power. Instead of a calm, problem-solving outlook, the program featured screaming, unhinged voices playing strictly to the base. A clip of Kimberly Guilfoyle, Donald Trump Jr.'s girlfriend and former Fox News personality, shouting her way through her speech became an internet meme that ruthlessly mocked her.

Bizarrely, Republicans made little mention of the pandemic, which Trump still hoped to will out of existence. To anyone outside Trump's cult of true believers his refusal even to acknowledge the death toll seemed bizarre and uncaring. Biden got an unintentional boost for his message that Trump had accepted defeat in the war against the pandemic. Outside of Trump's army of MAGA supporters, voters saw someone hopelessly out of touch with and indifferent to a country's suffering. A senior Biden adviser told me, "COVID is the way through this election. It's a referendum on him."

The plethora of lies, norm-breaking, and law-defying antics was infuriating to the Biden team, like it was to many Americans.

However, as frustrating as the Republican convention was to watch, Biden campaign's direction was clear: Do not get distracted by Trump's schtick. Let him be the candidate of chaos. Let Melania Trump try to convince women her angry and condescending husband cared about them. Let Trump's kids offer rote defenses of their father without a single personal memory evincing good character. Let Trump vilify Biden as a wild socialist. As soon as the theatrics were over, the Biden campaign felt confident its ticket could steer the electorate back to the real world, cast aside Trump's preposterous claims, and drive home Trump's abject unfitness for office. The campaign leaders had confidence women voters would not forgive Trump for his serial failures. They knew the shout-a-thon convention replete with painting Trump as a victim of the "Russia hoax" and Biden as senile would not go over well with women voters who already viewed Trump as lacking a presidential temperament. The Biden team remained optimistic that, if anything, Trump's convention would drive women from a party dominated by a racist, mean-spirited bully. And, as they predicted, Trump's audience was smaller than Biden's, and he received virtually no bump in the polls customary after a president's nominating convention.

The dueling realities from tribal camps was evident in the reactions to the two conventions. Biden supporters saw the Republican affair as part of a loud, crass freak show that was selling lies and bigotry; Trump followers got entertainment and emotional catharsis, an outlet for anger and resentment. They enjoyed watching Trump stick it to elites and find scapegoats for their problems. As with so much else in American politics, nothing in either of the conventions seemed to change many voters' minds. If nothing else had, perhaps the debates would move voters one way or the other.

CHAPTER 20

RACE TO THE FINISH

Entering the final stretch of the 2020 race, Democrats redoubled their work to build a broad coalition and attract women from the Republican Party. An empathetic and reasonable ticket promised competent government responses to the COVID pandemic and economic downturn. By contrast, Trump doubled and tripled down on fearmongering and conspiracies. Trump highlighted the very few incidents of violence during the BLM marches, but illogically made the case that this amounted to "Biden's America." He praised right-wing groups seeking out conflict with BLM protesters and fanned the flames of White resentment as he vilified Democrats' efforts at police reform. Trump seized on nonelected progressive activists' call to "defund the police"—a slogan Biden disowned. Trump nevertheless highlighted the slogan to frighten wavering White voters and paint down-ballot Democrat as weak on lawbreakers. Biden chose a compassionate, rational response to chaos, the type of measured reaction that ex-Republicans, suburban women, and college-educated Whites would appreciate. Biden's polling numbers remained strong, with leads in the high single digits or even in double digits, convincing me and political insiders that Biden was holding his own by a comfortable margin.

Never Trumper Sarah Longwell was not content to leave the

outcome of the race to general election trends. In over fifty two-hour sessions during the Trump years Longwell likely learned more about soft Trump voters than any pollster or consultant. She began by talking to men and women, college- and non-college-educated. In the six months before the 2020 election she narrowed her focus to women who'd voted for Trump in 2016 but were now undecided. It was her own experience in the Republican Party that gave her the perspective to elicit revealing answers from Republicans and Republican-leaning independents.

Even if the voters whose views these women represented amounted to only a few percentage points in national polls, in close state contests they could be the difference between winning and losing. Longwell's findings mirrored public polling that showed the pandemic dragged down Trump's approval rating. Up until the coronavirus hit, women were conflicted. They disliked Trump's personality and knew he was a liar, but they loathed the mainstream media and grew defensive when they attacked Trump. They may have thought Trump was a rotten person, but they liked the economic results. When the pandemic hit, Longwell saw a sea change among these voters. Longwell heard "a lot of pain" from women who freely shared their experiences. Many were trapped in their homes, laid off or with reduced hours, they struggled to help their kids with remote learning. Some had lost a parent to COVID. Now politics was intensely personal. They knew mask-wearing was responsible. They knew this was a deadly disease, and they saw Trump as grossly incompetent, indifferent, and irresponsible. Still they seemed reluctant to make the jump to the Biden-Harris ticket. It was clear that Trump's messaging that Biden would be controlled by socialists, no matter how silly, gave these women pause.

Republican women in Longwell's focus groups appeared to reach another inflection point when the Black Lives Matter marches went to the streets to protest a Minnesota police officer's killing of George Floyd. For the first time, Longwell heard Christian, pro-life women say that their understanding of what it means to be "pro-life" was shifting. It meant more than abortion, they told her; it meant looking out for others who were at risk and vulnerable. Longwell saw in some women a wholesale "revisiting of their values."

Longwell knew from her experience in focus groups and her campaign activities that many Republicans still needed "permission" to vote for Biden. A validator to encourage them to break with their Republican tribe could make the difference between retreating to the GOP or embracing Biden. She believed that more than candidate appeals and endorsements from other politicians, voters paid attention to people like themselves. Longwell understood that the best way to wean Republicans off Trump was to hear from ordinary Republicans who had voted for Trump but now regretted it. She aimed to convince them through actual Republicans' testimonials that Trump could not represent them, their interests, or their values.

Under the banner Republican Voters Against Trump (RVAT), she enlisted ordinary Republicans to film short videos explaining why they could not vote for Trump again. Because they were real people, using ordinary computer or phone cameras, the videos struck viewers as more authentic than campaign ads. By the end of the race, she produced nearly a thousand of these messages from ex-Trump voters.

Longwell's RVAT ads went viral, garnering millions of hits. On the RVAT website and across multiple social media platforms, hundreds of Republicans and former Republicans told their stories. There was Justin, a retired Army Ranger who fled the party because of Trump. "I did five deployments in service of this nation . . . I've been in countries that have had authoritarian regimes," he said. "If Trump is not defeated the United States, as we know it, will never be the same." Thomas said he began having doubts when Trump lied about the size of his inaugural crowd and then about the path of Hurricane Dorian. "Doesn't it bother you that he lies incessantly?" He added, "If they put a circus monkey up with a little hat," he would vote for the monkey against Trump. Many of those giving testimonials bemoaned that Republicans had given up everything they believed in to blindly follow Trump. Danika from Texas voted for Trump to get conservative judges, but she explained in her video that judges were not enough. "We need somebody who is going to help heal this country," she declared. Longwell received the highest compliment when Democratic convention producers used some of her RVAT videos.

Longwell's crowning achievement may have been a video, followed by an ad, featuring a former Trump official, Miles Taylor, former chief of staff for the secretary of Homeland Security. He told viewers, "What we saw, week in and week out, and for me, two and a half years in that administration, was terrifying. The president wanted to exploit the Department of Homeland Security for his own political purposes and to fuel his own agenda." Taylor later revealed that he was the Trump staffer who penned the "Anonymous" op-ed in the *New York Times* in which he attempted to warn the country about Trump's unfitness. Another former Homeland Security employee Elizabeth Neuman also cut an ad, explaining that she was a pro-life Christian who nevertheless would vote for Biden. Then came Olivia Troye, a former Pence aide, who attested to Trump's utter lack of concern about victims of COVID-19.

Longwell also constructed other highly praised ads. Never Trump Republican and MSNBC host Nicolle Wallace called one of them the best she had seen all cycle. The ad featured Sen. Lindsey Graham, who had turned into a fierce Trump apologist, excoriating Trump during the 2016 primary election. "If you want to make America great again, tell Donald Trump to go to hell!" Graham said back then. He then praised Biden to the hilt. "He is as good a man as God ever created," Graham intoned. It received over eight million hits and played in the South and North Carolina TV markets.

A virtuous cycle developed in which anti-Trump Republican politicians and anti-Trump voters boosted one another. After the slew of RVAT ads, a parade of Republicans—ex-congressmen, Ohio ex-governor John Kasich, Michigan ex-governor Rick Snyder, former senators, former national security officials, and law enforcement figures—soon lined up behind Biden. They, in turn, spurred more voters to feel empowered to break with Trump. Still more Republican politicians and ex-officials went public with their decision to vote for Biden.

In a year like no other, the presidential race still had a couple more dramatic twists. On September 18, 2020, Justice Ruth Bader Ginsburg passed away. The legendary justice was not merely a legal or even a political hero for progressives. She essentially made the careers of women of my generation possible. She opened doors in the workplace and academia, removed a host of discriminatory laws from the books, and helped make pregnancy discrimination illegal. She was a role model for immigrants, for women, for Jews, and for lawyers. Elegant and tenacious she was a fixture in feminism for five decades, a trailblazer who created gender discrimination law out of whole cloth. In her later years she issued blockbuster dissents as the Court leaned increasingly right. She was a petite eighty-year-old judge when she became more than a jurist but a cultural icon. The "Notorious RBG" moniker delighted her.

Like many women, I felt crushed by her passing. It was one more blow in a year of blows, one especially painful death in a year with so much death. News of her passing intruded into the Jewish New Year that began on Friday night. In virtual synagogue services rabbis and congregants discussed and mourned her passing over the weekend following her death. Spontaneous rallies and vigils erupted not just in Washington, DC, but in other cities. And over $40 million in donations poured into Democratic coffers. The spontaneous vigils and torrent of public grief were proof of her profound influence on Americans.

On the Saturday after her death, after livestreaming Rosh Hashanah services, I went down to the Supreme Court building to see for myself. Mothers stood with daughters and granddaughters to view the mound of flowers, notes, and memorabilia piled high around the barriers outside the Court. The visitors—young and old, tourists and DC residents, Black and White, came by foot and bike. They amply reflected the diversity of America, of the ever expanding "we" in "we the people" that Ginsburg had worked to include within the Constitution's protections. Her death was not simply a political and legal shock but a personal tragedy for many Americans who looked to her for inspiration.

For Kamala Harris, Ginsburg's death was a "gut punch." She waited until Saturday to go to the Court, trying to minimize the commotion. She mused on a "a life well lived" by the diminutive justice. "She never asked permission," Harris observed later. "I don't think there is any question of women being inspired and feeling an immense loss." As she looked around, seeing generations of women out to honor Ginsburg she became more convinced that women felt a bond with and an obligation to Ginsburg. Observing the scene, she concluded, "It will motivate women to vote and to fight." Harris noted, "Ginsburg was a serious person," and hoped her passing would remind the country of the seriousness of the moment.

In the days that followed, polls showed slight movement in Democrats' direction. The *FiveThirtyEight* average hovered in the range of a 10 percent lead for Biden. CNN showed Biden with a twelve-point lead in October, Quinnipiac had him up by ten.

Women's grief over Ginsburg's passing quickly turned to anger. Republicans who had denied Judge Merrick Garland a hearing when Justice Antonin Scalia passed away in February 2016 because it was an election year now insisted on ramming through Trump's pick to replace Ginsburg—after presidential and congressional voting was already well underway. Republicans pulled yet another political norm-busting power grab to achieve their aims. Consistency, fairness, and comity were for Democrats. "Heads we win, tails you lose" seemed to be their guiding principle. On the Tuesday after Ginsburg's death, in what became known as a super-spreader COVID event, Trump introduced Judge Amy Co-ney Barrett in the Rose Garden. She was the former clerk for the late Justice Antonin Scalia, a judge on the Seventh Circuit, a vehement opponent of abortion, and a self-described "originalist" who believed the Founders' intentions and only their intentions determined legal outcomes.

As was true so many times in the Trump era, Republicans bet that their base's knee-jerk reaction to a court fight would benefit the right. However, Barrett's nomination, literally before Ginsburg's body was even in the ground, also managed to anger millions of women for whom Ginsburg was an icon. They were furious Trump—elected by a minority of voters and credibly accused by about twenty women of sexual harassment or assault—would try to jam in one last right-wing judge to replace one of the great progressive women in American history. Women in Longwell's focus groups sensed it was unfair and rash to move so quickly to rush through a nominee. Partisans on both sides were convinced this could be a decisive issue. As things would turn out, among 60 percent of the electorate for whom the Supreme Court was the most important or an important issue, Biden won 52 percent, Trump 46 percent.

In the ensuing confirmation fight, Democrats recognized it would likely be futile to appeal to Republican senators to delay the confirmation vote until after the election. To their credit, however, Democrats realized this was a teachable moment and a potential campaign gift to their candidates. The hearing would not block Barrett's confirmation, but it might inflict damage on Republicans. Democrats would lose another seat on the Court but perhaps gain a Senate majority.

Like most analysts and pollsters, Democrats imagined they had an excellent shot at winning back the Senate. They set out to use the hearings to show how the Senate Republicans lacked in humanity and principle, setting the stage for a Democratic Senate majority. With a Senate majority Democrats hoped to tackle everything from expanding the Supreme Court, thereby diluting conservatives' influence, to granting statehood to DC and Puerto Rico. With a large enough mandate, they dreamed of protecting the ACA from legal assaults, concretizing abortion rights in a federal statute, and passing a bill in defense of all marriages, including gay marriages.

In the hearings, Democrats focused relentlessly on the Affordable Care Act, making the case that a vote for Barrett was a vote to eradicate health care coverage for tens of millions of Americans. The rush to put her on the Court, Democrats argued, was designed to allow her to take part in an ACA case to be heard in early November. That suit, brought by red state governors and backed by House and Senate Republicans, aimed to invalidate the entire ACA and thereby deprive voters of health care coverage in the middle of a pandemic.

As they had two years earlier in the Kavanaugh hearings, both Harris and Klobuchar put on an impressive tutorial in witness interrogation. Harris devoted her opening remarks to the danger of Republicans repealing the ACA so as to underscore one of the Democratic ticket's most critical issues. She also went after Barrett's myopic views on voting. Under Harris's grilling, Barrett made the dubious assertion that she could not say if voting discrimination exists. Barrett came across as clueless. In response to Klobuchar's questioning, Barrett gave the equally unbelievable answer that she did not know if Trump wanted justices to repeal the Affordable Care Act. In response to these and other Democratic senators, Barrett sounded out of touch, indifferent to the consequences of her brand of jurisprudence, and unwilling to acknowledge her biases. Biden would go on to win 63 percent of voters for whom health care was the most important issue, although they made up only 11 percent of the electorate. Barrett was confirmed on a party-line vote. Harris and progressives got out their desired message that Republicans would take away their health care, but Republican activists got what they needed as well: the gratitude of White evangelicals.

If Democrats had unrealistic expectations that Barrett could help sink Republican senators, Republicans were equally unrealistic about what Barrett could do for them in the short and long term. If they were counting on her to resolve election disputes, they badly failed to anticipate that virtually all claims of fraud would be summarily thrown out by the lower courts. If Republicans banked on her striking down the ACA, they might have done well to examine how weak the Republican case was and how little appeal the radical remedy—invalidating the entire statute—would have for Barrett and other conservative justices.

Moreover, the right's notion that conservatives would now control the Court for a generation was overly ambitious. Justices Clarence Thomas and Samuel Alito were seventy years old and Chief Justice John Roberts sixty-five at the time. No justice—liberal or conservative—is immortal. Occasionally, justices deliver surprises as Justice Neil Gorsuch showed in a decision finding sexual orientation is protected under Title VII of the 1964 Civil Rights Act. Justices do not always act in ways "their side" prefers. Whatever temporary victory Trump and McConnell might secure on the Court would be of little use if Republicans lost the White House and the Senate for the foreseeable future.

Starting weeks before Election Day, Trump ramped up his efforts to discredit the election. If he lost, he insisted, it was because it was "rigged." He urged states to ignore some ballots and falsely insisted mail-in ballots would be rife with fraud. Polls at the end of September showed Biden-Harris with a large national advantage, healthy leads in swing states, and nearly tied in states such as Georgia, Texas, and Ohio that Trump should have wrapped up months earlier. Few suspected, though, that the polls could be even more inaccurate than they were in 2016. Had Americans known that the margins would be small in so many critical states, their anxiety might have been even higher about the peaceful transfer of power.

One last shoe dropped less than forty-eight hours before the first general election debate. A *New York Times* blockbuster story reported what many Americans already knew: Trump was a world-class failure at business and paid less to the federal government in taxes than the average American worker. He was not a business colossus but a huckster and a financial loser. For Trump loyalists, however, this was more "fake news" and an effort to undermine their hero. Aside from the debates, no story seemed sufficiently powerful to change the election dynamic.

The presidential debate on September 29 gave Trump an opening to prove he could be rational and disciplined. Instead, he delivered an obnoxious, bullying, and unhinged performance. It was Trump's best chance to reassure moderates, independents, women, and suburban voters he was not the madman the media portrayed. Instead, the president amply demonstrated how crazed he was. Implored to condemn a White supremacist group, he declined. Instead, he ominously declared, "The Proud Boys. Stand back and stand by. But I'll tell you what, I'll tell you what, somebody's got to do something about Antifa and the left, because this is not a right-wing problem."

Media and voters dubbed the performance "embarrassing" and a low point for democracy. His refusal to condemn violent racists received blistering condemnation. Republican insiders saw whatever chance they had to shift the trajectory of the race evaporating. Trump's first debate performance sealed the choice of many women in Longwell's focus groups—for Biden. They told her they were horrified by his rudeness and frustrated they could not hear what Biden had to say. They were especially offended that Trump interrupted Biden when he praised his dead son Beau to ridicule his other son Hunter who had once had a drug problem. "Awful," "terrible," and "embarrassing" were some of their reactions to Trump's attempt to sow chaos. His manic performance went down poorly with many viewers, especially women who knew someone who had a drug problem in their family or community.

Shortly after the debate, the White House revealed Trump had tested positive for COVID-19, which indicated that he had not been tested regularly and that Barrett's ceremony at the White House had been a super-spreader event. It did not take long for news outlets to recognize Trump probably had the virus when he had appeared for the debate, potentially putting others at the venue at risk. In fact, some advisers who helped him prepare for the debate contracted the virus. Trump's blatant disregard for others' health and his own delusions of invincibility reinforced the perception he was reckless, selfish, and starved for attention. Rather than use his illness to convey empathy for others or increase his vigilance in mask-wearing, he highlighted his frightening narcissism. He forced a Secret Service detail to drive him around the block to wave at supporters, returned from the hospital early, and removed his mask at an *Evita*-like balcony scene before entering the White House. He insisted on going into the Oval Office when still communicable. COVID-19 infections spread through the White House staff. All this was stunning even for observers who intellectually understood his narcissism blinds him to others' well-being. Trump had succeeded only in highlighting his irrationality and malicious rule-breaking, the very qualities that had turned off many voters since 2016.

While Trump's deranged behavior continued, Harris faced her final test of the campaign at the vice presidential debate on October 7. Pence interrupted, hogged time, spoke condescendingly, and consistently evaded answering the questions. Harris put on an impressive display and reminded me how far she had come in just a few years on the national stage. Her answers were crisp and on message, delivered straight to the camera. This was the performance of a warm and dynamic politician but also one who had worked furiously to prepare for the event, meticulously studying both Biden's positions and Pence's favorite ploys. When Pence derided her record as a prosecutor, she struck back. "I will not sit here and be lectured by the Vice President on what it means to enforce the laws of our country. I'm the only one on this stage who has personally prosecuted everything from child sexual assaults to homicide," she declared. "I'm the only one on the stage who has prosecuted the big banks for taking advantage of American families. I am the only one on this stage who prosecuted for-profit colleges for taking advantage of our veterans." She also reminded the audience that the "President of the United States took the debate stage in front of 70 million Americans and refused to condemn White supremacists."

More than any specific answer, her authoritative voice, restraint, and poise in the face of Pence's bullying won her the night. She would not to be pushed around by a domineering man. When interrupted for the umpteenth time she delivered the perfect retort. "Mr. Vice President," she said sternly, "I am speaking." As he persisted, she told him, "If you don't mind letting me finish . . . [Pence continues to interrupt] We can then have a conversation. Okay?" I was among the many Americans who purchased an "I am speaking, Mr. Vice President" T-shirt the next day.

A few pundits let on that men might not have grasped how offensive Pence had been. *Huffington Post*'s Sam Stein was honest enough to tweet that "the male friends I have thought Pence did, on the whole, way better than the female friends I have. Worth understanding the lens through which you are viewing this stuff isn't universal." On CNN, when Gloria Borger tried to explain why Pence's interruptions were off-putting to women, Rick Santorum interrupted her—and got bashed on social media for doing so. GOP pollster Frank Luntz insisted Harris had been "abrasive and condescending." Women meanwhile took to Twitter to express their disgust over Pence's conduct. A female scholar at a center-left think tank tweeted that "every woman I know watching this debate knows that Kamala is performing a Herculean feat of being strong, courteous, funny, likable, straightforward, competent, and true to herself all while being interrupted, called a liar, & exposed to COVID." The tweet concluded, "You're a damn superhero." For several days, women professionals, especially academics, weighed in to share stories of male colleagues constantly interrupting them. Some journalists plainly had not grasped the extent to which the Republican ticket offended and infuriated women.

A post-debate CNN poll showed Harris convincingly won the

debate (59 to 38 percent) and boosted her own favorability rating by seven points. Among women, she won the debate by a 69 to 30 percent margin, yet another sign that Republicans were sending women fleeing into the arms of the Democratic ticket. Other polls reflected the same anti-Pence reaction. I savored the historic nature of the moment. Here a Black woman stood up to a bullying White man with grace, wit, and fact-based arguments—and came out victorious. Vindicating the wisdom of Biden's selection and comfortable with her own power, Harris definitively answered the question about how an accomplished woman deals with questions about ambition: She clobbers her opponents—with a smile on her face.

The next morning Trump sounded increasingly unhinged as he refused to accept the next debate's virtual format, which was designed to protect others from infection. He lashed out at Harris, calling her everything from a "monster" to a "communist." He resorted to the trite misogynistic phrase, dubbing her "totally unlikeable." The rage he expressed was nothing new, but it suggested the Republicans' furor at the prospect of a woman, especially a woman of color, challenging their power had only increased since 2016.

As the election drew closer, polls showed many suburban women voters were ready to abandon Trump. The *Post* reported in mid-September, "White women helped Democratic candidates win midterm elections. Those gains were driven mostly by college-educated women, but since then women of all backgrounds have been moving in Biden's direction." The conventional wisdom was that Trump's craziness, his racist appeals, erratic response to COVID-19, and volcanic personality had sent *all* kinds of women running into the embrace of a congenial, steady, and rational Democratic ticket.

However, news reports reflecting sunny expectations for all women shifting to Biden were not geographically well balanced. They also put undue reliance on early voting, which was heavily tilted toward Democrats. These sorts of reports often centered in northern suburbs that Trump had won in 2016. The Associated Press reported in late October on a surge of suburban women in Michigan for whom "the past four years have meant frustration, anger and activism—a political awakening that powered women's marches, the #MeToo movement and the victories of record numbers of female candidates in 2018." The report continued, "That energy has helped create the widest gender gap—the political divide between men and women—in recent history. And it has started to show up in early voting as women are casting their ballots earlier than men. In Michigan, women have cast nearly 56 percent of the early vote so far, and 68 percent of those were Democrats."

Likewise, the *Philadelphia Inquirer* informed us, "Trump won half of the votes cast by White women in Pennsylvania in 2016, according to exit polls, helping him narrowly win the state. But with Election Day just two weeks away and voting already underway, polls suggest those voters are abandoning the president in droves." Citing a poll finding only 37 percent of women backed Trump, the report concluded, "If that big shift holds, it could help deliver Pennsylvania—and the White House—to Democratic candidate Joe Biden."

On the eve of the election many Democrats and Never Trumpers were convinced we were reaching the end of Trump and a repudiation of Trumpism. That was only partially right.

CHAPTER 21

HOW IT HAPPENED

Harris was certain that Trump's election in 2016 had been an inflection point for women. His victory was all the more galling because he never had the majority of the country behind him. "It was not as though he won [the popular vote]," Harris observed. And it was Hillary Clinton whom he beat, a bogeywoman for the right but a trailblazer, the quintessential overqualified woman. Part of the impetus for women's dramatic involvement in politics over the previous four years certainly came from Clinton's defeat. "She might have lost," Harris noted. "But she was not going to be the last."

In the days before the election, the mainstream media sometimes sounded like anthropologist Margaret Mead reporting on news of a previously unknown tribe. In this case, the media traveled deep into suburbia to discover the wave of women-driven activism. *Atlantic* magazine in late October figured out that women were "expressing their outrage by voting in high-stakes national elections . . . And all of this activism has the potential to shape American politics in a much more significant way than their biennial votes." And yet for nearly four years this phenomenon seemed to be the best kept secret in the mainstream media. "Many of these women live in the suburbs of major cities, places that have traditionally been Republican but are rapidly turning blue as college-educated White women grow more and more repulsed by Trump and as neighborhoods become more and more diverse," *The Atlantic* found out. The story went on to explain, "Some are former Republicans, while others were simply inactive Democrats . . . These so-called Resistance groups are always somewhere between 75 and 100 percent women, and they generally operate independently of national bodies. Many of the women in these groups are middle- and upper-middle-class, well educated, and used to running or working on teams and planning big events. The level of organization this work requires . . . is already something they're good at." If more in the mainstream media had been paying closer attention none of this would have been news.

Going into Election Day the polls buoyed my spirits and gave me inordinate confidence that Republicans were going to be thrashed. However, things did not go as swimmingly as the media and virtually every Democratic insider expected. As the returns inched forward on election night the horror of 2016 gripped me again. The polls once more had underestimated the strength of the Republicans; moreover, because Republicans blocked processing of votes before Election Day in critical Democratic states those returns did not get fully counted for days afterward. Early returns favored Trump. Tuesday night I felt a sinking sensation as once more Florida fell to Republicans, as did Texas. *This could not be happening.* In a state of mild panic, I reached out to Wisconsin political guru and fellow Never Trumper Charlie Sykes. Could Biden win Wisconsin, one of the key states Trump had won in 2016? Without Wisconsin, he would have to win a more Republican state such as Ohio. His emphatic answer: yes. At that point I could go to sleep, albeit for only a few hours.

By Wednesday morning, the dark cloud began to lift. Biden was declared the winner in Wisconsin, as Sykes had predicted, and Michigan, Pennsylvania, Nevada, Arizona, and even Georgia followed. Once the election map was filled out the magnitude of the Biden-Harris win was apparent. This was as emphatic a win as was possible in a sharply divided country. On Twitter I dubbed it a "landslidey" win.

• • •

AFTER TV NETWORKS called the race on the evening of November 7, Harris and Biden delivered victory remarks in Wilmington, Delaware. Resplendent in a White pantsuit symbolic of the suffragettes, Harris strode to the podium. She thanked the country, the poll workers, and the voters. "And to the woman most responsible for my presence here today—my mother, Shyamala Gopalan Harris, who is always in our hearts," she recalled. "When she came here from India at the age of 19, maybe she didn't quite imagine this moment. But she believed so deeply in an America where a moment like this is possible." Fully cognizant of the significance of the moment she declared, "So, I'm thinking about her and about the generations of women—Black Women. Asian, White, Latina, and Native American women throughout our nation's history who have paved the way for this moment tonight. Women who fought and sacrificed so much for equality, liberty, and justice for all, including the Black women, who are too often overlooked, but so often prove that they are the backbone of our democracy." She told the crowd that she would not be on the stage but for the women "who worked to secure and protect the right to vote for over a century: 100 years ago with the 19th Amendment, 55 years ago with the Voting Rights Act, and now, in 2020, with a new generation of women in our country who cast their ballots and continued the fight for their fundamental right to vote and be heard."

I relished the moment, realizing that for four years, millions of Americans had dedicated themselves to jettisoning Trump from the White House. They'd succeeded and also made history with Harris's ascension. Harris gave full credit to Biden for the "audacity to break one of the most substantial barriers that exists in our country and select a woman as his Vice President." As she had so many times on the trail, she proclaimed that "while I may be the first woman in this office, I won't be the last." Bringing tears to my eyes and certainly to those of parents of daughters, she observed that "every little girl watching tonight sees that this is a country of possibilities." I could not help but recognize that she—like so many

other past winners—now projected a sense of gravitas and seriousness that no candidate can quite achieve during a race. Her cadence
was slower, and she seemed more settled and commanding at the
lectern. She was already inhabiting the role, and thereby normalizing a woman in that office. Blue America was in a joyous mood,
as people poured out onto the streets to dance and cheer, relieved
finally to be done with Trump, if not Trumpism.

Harris's success did not come effortlessly. On the presidential
ticket groups like EMILY's List had Harris's back. Its memo before
the general election recounted that the organization had "joined
with UltraViolet, Higher Heights, Color of Change, and a number of other allies on a campaign to educate the media and voters
on racist and sexist coverage and disinformation." The memo continued, "We have also joined with BlackPAC, PACRONYM, and
Planned Parenthood Action Fund in a $10 million campaign, with
a $5.5 million investment from EMILY's List, to lift awareness of
Senator Harris's record and defend her against attacks."

THE BIDEN-HARRIS WIN was historic. They accumulated 306 electoral votes by recapturing the Upper Midwest states and breaking
through in two Sunbelt states that had not voted for a Democrat
for president since the Bill Clinton era. More than eighty million
Americans voted for them, also a record surpassing Obama's 2012
total by about fifteen million votes. Biden's margin over Trump in
the popular vote was larger than Barack Obama's victory in 2012
and George W. Bush's in 2004; the ticket reached the highest percentage for a nonincumbent challenger since FDR.

By Saturday it was official: Biden and Harris were declared the
winners. I was nothing short of ecstatic. A great weight had been
lifted, a horrid period in American history was coming to an end.
Moreover, women had broken a critical glass ceiling. The Center
for Women and Politics noted the milestone. "This is an enor-
mously significant moment in the story of women's participation

in American politics and in the history of our country. That it happens during the centennial of the 19th Amendment, which expanded some women's political participation while women like Kamala Harris remained excluded, is all the more symbolic," a written statement declared. "At this pivotal moment in history, she is the face of the future of the Democratic Party. Her win puts to rest the question of the electability of women to high office—a question that haunted both the women and people of color who ran for the Democratic nomination this cycle. To women and girls of all walks of life, of every political persuasion, Harris's ascension to the vice presidency broadens the horizons of the possible."

However, the results immediately following Election Day—agonizingly close in many states and lacking crown jewels like Florida and Texas—did not amount to an unequivocal repudiation of Trump and his ideology. My feeling of disappointment stemmed in part from another polling debacle that had raised expectations and from the sequence of voting returns reported on election night.

In the election's immediate aftermath many Democrats felt both relieved and unsatisfied. The work of building a coalition to defeat Trump had succeeded. And yet, the victory did not amount to a wholesale rejection of Trumpism and its anti-democratic, deeply racists viewpoint. As I did in 2016, I had to wrestle with the uncomfortable realization that tens of millions of Americans, about seventy-four million in 2020, supported Trump, many *because* he was irrational, angry, racist, and xenophobic. Millions of others could tolerate his racism, lying, and anti-democratic rhetoric for the sake of a tax cut. I ruminated as to why, despite a pandemic, an economic recession, and four years of unhinged and authoritarian rantings, so many Americans nevertheless voted for Trump. The answer was unsatisfying: The country did not cease being tribalistic in four years. Demographic change and shifts in voting patterns happen gradually, around the edges. This was not a country capable of delivering a decisive ten-point winning margin. The pull of Trumpism and the fidelity of tens of millions of Americans to right-wing populism remained. The need to vent their racial resentment of nonwhites was not vanishing. And the power of right-wing media to create an alternate reality was substantial. Pollsters did not assess just how large the Republican turnout, which broke all records, would be.

As a result, Democrats did not come close to obliterating the Republican Party. The country was shifting but gradually. In 2016, the electorate was 71 percent White, it dropped to 67 percent in 2020 according to network exit polls. The suburbs that had gone narrowly for Trump in 2016 now tipped to Biden. The share of "none of the above" religiously unaffiliated voters grew from 15 to 22 percent, voting overwhelmingly Democratic. Catholics who had voted for Trump by four points in 2016 favored Biden in network exit polling by five. Biden also narrowed the deficit with White Catholics. However, Trump did marginally better in urban areas, picking up some support among voters in Detroit, Philadelphia, and elsewhere.

Dueling exit polls muddled the postelection analysis. A massive AP VoteCast survey of 110,000 voters provided one set of data; the traditional network exit polls under the auspices of Edison Research and the National Election Pool (NEP) provided another. The results were not identical and indeed diverged noticeably in several key categories. For the first few days after the election, NEP showed Trump winning college-educated White women by one point—a result that I knew could not possibly be correct and flummoxed academics sifting through the numbers. As the votes came in NEP's numbers were adjusted to mesh with actual vote totals.

Moreover, we must keep in mind that VoteCast and the NEP exit polls may be as far off the mark as the preelection polls had been. Their conflicting results and a growing lack of confidence in any polling left many political operatives, academics, and reporters exasperated. If a certain segment of Trump voters simply would not respond to preelection polls, there is no reason to think they would be any more willing to share their views with the VoteCast survey or the NEP exit pollsters. (As knotty a problem as this is for the press, the polling conundrum was even more dire for campaigns. If they could not rely on polling, how could they deploy resources, know where to send their candidates, and how to target groups of voters?) The final pronouncement on which groups of voters went for which candidate and by how much will not come until actual voter files are available and researchers at Pew and other entities can recalibrate the numbers. The shift may be as dramatic as we saw with the 2016 exits that had Trump winning White women 52 to 43, but which subsequent analysis revealed was only a 47 to 45 percent margin. Therefore, when we look for patterns in the vote, we should be mindful that what we see now may look different down the road. The available numbers suggest some significant shifts from 2016 and some areas of remarkable continuity:

	2016 EXITS	VOTECAST	2020 EXITS
Men	Trump 52—41	Trump 52—46	Trump 53—45
Women	Clinton 54—41	Biden 55—44	Biden 57—42
White Men	Trump 62—31	Trump 59—39	Trump 61—38
White Women	Trump 52—43	Trump 52—46	Trump 55—44
White College-Educated	Trump 48—45	Biden 52—46	Biden 51—48
White College-Educated Men	Trump 53—39	Trump 52—46	Trump 51—48
White College-Educated Women	Clinton 51—44	Biden 59—39	Biden 54—45
White Non-College-Educated Women	Trump 61—34	Trump 60—39	Trump 63—36
Latina Voters	Clinton 69—25	Biden 66—32	Biden 69—30
Black Women	Clinton 94—4	Biden 93—6	Biden 90—9
Non-College Graduates	Trump 51—44	Trump 51—47	Trump 50—48
Independent Women	Clinton 47—42	n/a	Biden 60—32
College Graduates	Clinton 52—42	Biden 56—42	Biden 55—43
Graduate Degree	Clinton 58—37	Biden 58—40	Biden 62—37
Suburban Voters	Trump 49—45	Biden 54—44	Biden 50—48
Suburban Men	n/a	Biden 49—48	Trump 54—44
Suburban Women	n/a	Biden 59—40	Biden 56—43

The overall gender gap for Biden was the largest in history, twelve points, with 57 percent of women and 45 percent of men supporting him. College-educated White women did shift to Democrats, dramatically in the VoteCast survey and to a lesser degree in NEP results. Biden gained very slightly with *non-college*-educated White women but still lost this group by double digits. College-educated White men still favored Trump but by a much smaller margin in 2016, a sign perhaps that misogyny did work against Clinton back in 2016. The shift of White women in national figures understates the critical role of women in the only venue that counts, the Electoral College.

Women voters were a large part of the suburban swing toward Biden, especially in the environs of Phoenix, Philadelphia, and Atlanta. Biden did reach suburban women winning by a huge margin of thirteen points in 2020 according to NEP and by nineteen in the VoteCast survey. All the scaremongering focused on "suburban housewives" seemed to have backfired on Trump. In addition, Independent women whom Clinton won by just five points went for *Biden by twenty-four points*. In short, college-educated White women, nonwhite women, suburban women, and Independent women broke heavily for Biden in a way they had not for Clinton.

In some states, such as Pennsylvania and Michigan, suburban voters were critical to Biden's victory. He did slightly worse than Clinton in a few major cities. In Pennsylvania, Biden did not quite match Clinton's numbers in Philadelphia (81 versus 83 percent) and did worse than Clinton statewide among Latinos. However, he did better than Clinton in the suburbs of Philadelphia (58 versus 55 percent) to deliver a win with a margin of nearly 70,000 votes (compared to Clinton's loss by about 44,000 votes). Likewise, in Michigan, Biden did worse in Wayne County, which includes Detroit (65 versus 73 percent) but more than made up for it in the suburbs on the way to a victory of more than 150,000 votes in a state Clinton lost by roughly 11,000 votes.

When we look at suburban women, we should not think this

means suburban *White* women. The suburbs have become more diverse and many of the "suburban housewives" are Latina, Black, or Asian American and Pacific Islander voters. In the suburban areas around Atlanta, for example, AAPI voters' turnout doubled, with Biden winning the lion's share. "The emergence in Georgia of Asian-American voters is a potential bright spot for a Democratic Party counting on demographic changes to bring political wins across the country," the *New York Times* reported. "Asian-Americans are the fastest-growing segment of eligible voters out of the major racial and ethnic groups in the country, according to the Pew Research Center; their numbers, nationally and in Gwinnett County, more than doubled between 2000 and 2020." Abrams's multiracial, multiethnic turnout operation had helped flip a state that was unwinnable for Democrats just four years earlier.

Data was mixed on so-called crossover voting. On one hand, 90 percent of self-identified voters of each party chose the presidential candidate of their own party. That, however, begs the question as to who still identified as Republican and, of course, whether the exit polls were accurate. A Republican woman in 2016 who voted for Trump might show up as an Independent or Democrat in 2020 if she reregistered or simply changed how she identified herself to pollsters. She had crossed over *before* she voted.

Never Trump groups like Republican Voters Against Trump likely had moved some 2016 Trump voters to Biden. For example, 8 percent of Trump voters in 2016 chose Biden while only 4 percent of Clinton voters chose Trump in 2020. RVAT's influence was evident in key swing states. In Michigan, 6 percent of Republicans voted for Biden, 10 percent did in Arizona, 7 percent in Wisconsin, and 8 percent in Pennsylvania.

Never Trumpers' efforts might also have moved Independents. Nationally, Biden improved with these voters by twelve points over Hillary Clinton's performance. Drilling down, in 2016, they split 52 to 36 percent for Trump over Clinton in Michigan; Biden won these voters by a 51 to 43 percent margin. In Arizona, Biden won

Independents by 52 to 39 percent (versus Trump's 47 to 44 percent advantage in 2016). Wisconsin independents flipped from 50 to 40 percent for Trump over Clinton to 55 to 41 percent for Biden over Trump; in Pennsylvania Independents switched from 48 to 41 percent for Trump to 51 to 43 percent for Biden.

Moreover, Trump underperformed compared to the GOP House candidate by about eighteen thousand votes (10 percent) in Nebraska's Second District, suggesting those were Republican voters who peeled off from Trump. In Pennsylvania counties where RVAT spent the most money, Trump underperformed GOP House candidates by about 74,000 votes (5 percent), likely Republican voters who stuck with their House member but not with Trump. In Wisconsin counties where RVAT also spent heavily House Republicans outpaced Trump by about 37,000 votes (7 percent), likely another batch of Republicans who dumped Trump.

It is indisputable that without the strong turnout and shift among suburban women of all races Biden would not have won the presidency. The difference between winning and losing was suburban women—many of whom were college-educated and some Never Trump Republican—in the critical states of Georgia, Pennsylvania, Arizona, and Michigan.

Nevertheless, in much of the South, in small towns and rural regions and among White evangelicals, women's attachment to Trump had not wavered significantly. Despite the best efforts of the Resistance, Biden made little or no headway with evangelical women, especially evangelical women in the South. If the data is accurate, Trump hung on to Florida with a margin of 59 to 40 percent among White women. He won White women by a margin of 62 to 38 percent in Texas. According to exit polls, White evangelical support for Trump was 86 percent in Texas where they made up 28 percent of voters; 85 percent in Georgia. which were 34 percent of the electorate; and 85 percent in North Carolina, where they amounted to 38 percent of voters.

White Trump supporters who may have acknowledged his

faults nevertheless bought into negative characterizations about Democrats, painted as elites, socialists, and anti-religion even if Biden objectively did not reflect any of those faults. It is hard to escape the conclusion that a racist demagogue can win over a significant segment of America. As Robert P. Jones argues, "The strong consensus is that fears about demographic and cultural change are a significantly stronger predictor of support for Trump among White working class and White evangelical voters. Even Trump's trademark slogan, 'Make American Great Again,' has been mostly understood through the lens of preserving and protecting a White Christian America from immigrants and African Americans who Trump portrayed as threatening forces 'invading' the country and increasing crime in White suburbs." This was not an economic phenomenon as evidenced by Trump's advantage among voters making over $100,000. Jones observes that "the theory in 2016 was that Trump's economic appeal was to those disaffected, struggling workers at the bottom of the income spectrum. And that's just not the pattern we see."

Immersed in the Fox News universe millions of Republican women remained deeply suspicious of elites and the mainstream news media. The right-wing media bubble cut off conservative women and men alike from data that contradicted their worldview. Jones observes, "Like Republicans, a significant proportion of White evangelicals (36 percent) say they most trust Fox News to give them accurate information about current events and politics." What is more, "White evangelicals who most trust Fox News are 25 percentage points more likely to approve of Trump's job performance. Only 38 percent of White evangelicals who most trust Fox News say they wish President Trump's speech and behavior were more like other presidents, compared to 65 percent of White evangelicals who most trust any other network." In sum, for evangelical White women, especially in red states, race and the Fox News bubble exerted much more influence than any other factor. They were no more amenable than their White male counterparts to rational appeals, to Resistance organizing, or to mainstream media coverage.

Given the Democrats' disappointments in Texas and Florida, pundits made much of the Latino vote in these states. Overall, according to network exit polling, Trump got 32 percent nationally of the Latino vote, up from 28 percent in 2016, and 30 percent of Latinas, up from 25 percent in 2016. In key states, he made headway with Latinas in Arizona (17 percent in 2016 versus 28 percent in 2020) but held even in Texas (28 percent) and actually declined in Florida (34 percent in 2016 versus 28 percent in 2020). In both Florida and Texas, if the exit polling is accurate, Trump won over 40 percent of males and females in the Latino community.

While those results suggested Democrats had a serious deficit with these voters, a massive polling effort by Latino Decisions showed a more nuanced result. It found just 27 percent of Latinos (23 percent of Latinas) voted for Trump, with even smaller numbers in key battleground states. The only group Trump carried was Cuban Americans (52 percent). He did well (40 percent) with voters whose families came from South America but garnered only 23 percent of Mexican Americans and 26 percent of Puerto Ricans. The pollsters also found, "Latino voters drove Biden's margin in key states like Arizona, Michigan, and Wisconsin." In short, Trump got a substantial chunk of Latino voters, but we cannot determine with certainty whether he improved over 2016.

Trump's use of incendiary ads exploiting Latino voters' aversion to socialism certainly played a part in his win in Florida. *Pro-Publica* reported that "a YouTube ad running 100,000 times in the days leading up to the election made the explosive—and false—claim that Venezuela's ruling clique was backing Democratic nominee Joe Biden." Fact-checkers thoroughly eviscerated the allegation and yet the vivid images of South American dictators coupled with the lie that they wanted Biden to win may have been effective. The *Miami Herald* reported that Trump's inflammatory appeal in the Miami-Dade area, home to a large Latino population "played out on several fronts, much of it in Spanish: in the traditional form of TV ads, mailers and rallies, as well as on the newer frontier of social media." Beyond the view of English-speaking mainstream media, "on Spanish-language talk-show radio and on social media, in particular, Trump's sometimes unofficial backers carried out what some critics have described as a brutal and relentless campaign of disinformation and distortion that often-promulgated conspiratorial memes to paint Biden and Democrats as dangerous radicals, and worse."

Trump's disinformation campaign painting Biden as a socialist, coupled with some Democrats' cries to abolish ICE, also found a receptive audience in the Rio Grande Valley of Texas. Casting Democrats as hostile toward law enforcement and supportive of "open borders" struck a chord in a region where the Border Patrol employed more than three thousand people, many of them Latino. Moderate Democrats chided more progressive Democrats for adopting the moniker of "democratic socialism," but in this election, with a moderate Democratic nominee, no one honestly thought the Democratic Party was synonymous with socialism. Only through deceitful advertising and snide messaging from Republicans like Sen. Marco Rubio of Florida—who absurdly proclaimed, "Not all Democrats are socialists, but all socialists are Democrats"—could Trump make headway with these voters.

Politicians and academics will be studying these results for years, but it bears repeating that "Latino" is a broad category encompassing very different groups of people, including recent immigrants from Cuba, Puerto Rico, and Mexico as well as first-generation Spanish-speakers and English-only speakers whose families have been in the US for generations. Parsing out whether Trump's Latino voters were more akin to non-Spanish-speaking Republicans is critical to understanding this portion of the electorate. Pollsters and campaigns in the future may need a more precise category for tracking this important group of voters.

Despite concerns about Latino voters in Texas and Florida,

there was some good news for Biden in other states. Women, including Latinas and Native Americans in Arizona, preferred Biden by nine points, leading to a historic win for Democrats. The *New York Times* reported that Biden got "more than 80 percent of the roughly 55,000 votes cast in the Arizona portion of the Navajo Nation—the country's largest tribe—and in the smaller Hopi Reservation, which shares precincts with the Navajo." The total vote from the reservations increased 13,500 over 2016, slightly more than Biden's 10,000 vote margin in the state. Motivated in part by the devastating effect of COVID on their communities, groups such as the Rural Arizona Project and Four Directions registered Native Americans and managed get-out-the-vote efforts. "It truly takes a village," Clara Pratte, who led national tribal engagements for the Biden campaign, told the Associated Press. "Could it have been done without a tribal vote? No."

While uncertainty may hinder analysis of other groups and Biden had made progress with college-educated White women, the backbone of the party remained African American women. They had been hard at work all year to register new voters and then getting them to vote, either by mail, in-person early voting, or on Election Day. In Georgia, African American turnout rose to 70 percent. Woke Vote had planned to reach out to 250,000 Black voters; instead, their organizers reached over a million. Taylor Crumpton wrote for the *Washington Post*, "As the Democratic Party's most loyal and dependable voting bloc, Black women were essential. From the 2016 presidential election to the Senate special election in Alabama in 2017 and the 2018 midterm elections, more than 90 percent of Black women voted for the Democratic candidate, and that's not even to mention all the work they did for voter registration and turnout." She added, "Black women are the country's most powerful political force. In times of political chaos and civic unrest, we need to remember the words of our foremothers, not turn to the nation's political parties." Without strong turnout for Biden among African American women in Michigan, Georgia,

Wisconsin, and other swing states Trump could have cobbled to-gether small margins to win the Electoral College. Women, many of whom were African American, plainly accounted for significant swings in key states—whether in the Philadelphia suburbs or in Maricopa County, Arizona, where Biden flipped Democrats' loss in 2016 by three points to a 50 to 48 percent win in 2020, adding about three hundred thousand votes to his total. Those turnout totals do not happen without years of political engagement.

Democrats extended their advantage among women in many subgroups in 2020, but this is not a one-election proposition. Presidential elections remind us America is a huge, complicated country in a constant state of demographic flux in which broad categories ("women," "Latinos") can be misleading. It is easy to say that Trump lost because of the pandemic or the economic collapse. However, he could well have won *despite* those factors if not for the growing number of college-educated White women who shifted to the Democrats, the change in suburban women's political preferences, and the enthusiastic turnout of *all* women. Some 57 percent of Biden's more than eighty million voters (the largest number of popular votes ever amassed by any candidate) were women.

There had been a shift at the margins in American politics, and in a close election that makes the difference between winning and losing. However, race, class, education, geography, and religion still drive passions in American politics—among both men and women. Democratic women will need to find a way to engage with non-college-educated White women and rural women. They need to better understand where they are succeeding with Latina voters and where they are not. Women may have saved America from the scourge of Trump, but their battle against Trumpism, amplified by right-wing media, will need to continue.

CHAPTER 22

CONGRESS IS A DIFFERENT STORY

The polls badly missed the mark on the Senate and House races, just as they had missed the margin of victory in the presidential contest. Trump won the second highest number of votes in history, which meant a huge turnout for him, especially in red states. These Republican voters came to the rescue of Republican candidates in the congressional contests. Republicans, especially Republican women, did exceptionally well in House races.

Before the January runoffs in Georgia, Republicans kept a 50 to 48 advantage in the Senate. While Democrats had hoped to pick up five to eight seats, they needed—and eventually got—two upset wins without Trump on the ballot just to achieve a fifty-fifty split. There were thousands of Maine voters who picked Sen. Susan Collins, who won by nine points, but not Trump, who lost by ten points in Maine. Texas Republican Senator John Cornyn, who won by ten points, outpaced Trump, who won the state by only six points. Senate contender John James lost by less than a hundred thousand voters, a much better showing than Trump (who lost by 150,000) in Michigan. These results may have been evidence of Never Trump voters who picked Biden but returned to their "home party" to vote for the Senate Republicans.

The toughest blow for many Democratic women activists was Susan Collins's win, the only instance in which a state that went for Biden chose a Republican Senate candidate. Given a pass by Republicans to oppose Amy Coney Barrett's confirmation and reminding voters of her opposition to Obamacare's repeal, she managed to preserve her image as an independent-minded moderate. It is noteworthy she did well in Maine's Second Congressional District where Trump campaigned regularly, boosting Republican turnout that benefited Collins. As one Democratic operative reminded me, a four-term incumbent in a small state knows a lot of voters personally; for them Trump was intolerable, but "Susan" was a familiar, moderate face.

For Amy McGrath, tribal politics in Kentucky—a deep red state that had benefited from the largesse of Majority Leader Mitch McConnell in his six terms in the Senate—spelled doom. She had a nearly impossible balancing act. She had to run against the majority leader who was instrumental in protecting Trump, delivering a big tax cut and appointing right-wing judges. However, with Trump's approval high in her state McGrath could not attack Trump directly. At times McGrath tried simply to paint McConnell as an out-of-touch insider. She got a break when McConnell led the charge to oppose funding for states and localities in the HEROES Act stimulus bill. He argued that this would simply "bail out" irresponsible blue states. In fact, virtually all states, including his own, were hurting from the COVID-19 pandemic. Shutdowns and layoffs reduced state revenue while states had huge outlays for health care. The result was a dire economic picture even for his own state. And yet, McGrath could not persuade voters to hold him directly responsible for stiffing his own constituents. McConnell won easily with a combination of attacks on "socialist" Democrats, emphasis on the judges he had gotten confirmed, and his association with Trump. In a deep red state that was enough for him to cruise to a comfortable win. McGrath, as she had in her 2016 House race, lost despite raising tens of millions of dollars.

Looking back on the race, some Democrats concluded the Kentucky race was not winnable, even with a talented Democrat like McGrath. Democrats will need to do some soul-searching about their propensity to spend wildly in red states in presidential years where GOP turnout is high and therefore their chance of victory is slight. Had they, for example, shifted some of the money sent to McGrath they might have had enough to win in more competitive states such as North Carolina.

In that state, Democrat Senate candidate Cal Cunningham came up shy of a victory, damaged by a sexting scandal in the closing days of the race and by Biden's inability to capture the state (as Obama did in 2008). North Carolina since the civil rights era had only voted twice for a Democrat for president (in 1976 and 2008). It may take a Stacey Abrams–type effort to register and turn out more African American voters before North Carolina turns blue.

Senate races in red states like Iowa, Montana, Alaska, and Texas—which Democrats had hoped to be competitive—turned into comfortable wins for incumbent Republicans. Trump carried those states at the top of the ticket and drove Republican turnout through the roof, leaving Democratic Senate challengers far behind.

Where Biden did well, however, Democratic Senate challengers won as well. In both Arizona and Colorado, Biden wins may have helped Mark Kelly and John Hickenlooper, respectively, throw out Republican incumbents. Then there was Georgia. Since neither incumbent Republican cleared 50 percent in the general election, Senators Kelly Loeffler and David Perdue headed to runoffs against Rev. Raphael Warnock and Jon Ossoff, respectively. Democrats were gloomy about their prospects, given that no Democratic senator had been elected there since the 1990s. However, Abrams's impressive political machine registered more than a hundred thousand voters *after* the general election, drove up rural Black turnout, and kept overall turnout at an unprecedented level, just under

90 percent of the general election. Warnock won by roughly two points, Ossoff by about one. Both won on the strength of women voters overall and Asian American voters—although both lost White women (college- and non-college-educated). Each narrowly lost the suburbs. In short, by keeping Democratic enthusiasm high, running up massive margins among African American and Asian women, and keeping it very close in the suburbs Abrams delivered the Senate to the Democrats. With Warnock and Ossoff, Democrats reached a fifty-fifty split, allowing Harris to cast tie-breaking votes. Abrams's contribution to the Democratic Party can be summed up in four words: *Minority* Leader Mitch McConnell.

Women candidates in 2020 excelled in House and Senate races. Along with Harris's historic election, voters increased the total number of women in Congress. A new record of 141 women were elected to serve in the 117th Congress (up from a previous high of 127). That included 105 Democrats and thirty-six Republicans (up from a previous high of thirty set in 2006) and fifty-one women of color, forty-six of whom were Democrats. In the House, twenty-six women nonincumbents won seats, seventeen of them Republican. One Republican female challenger, Cynthia Lummis, became the first woman senator from Wyoming.

Twenty-four women were set to serve in the Senate, sixteen Democrats including four women of color; with Harris's elevation to the vice presidency the number dropped to twenty-three. "Following the record-setting 2018 midterm elections, we've been cautiously optimistic that we were seeing the emergence of a new normal, rather than a onetime surge. With record levels of candidates and nominees in 2020, that optimism seems justified," the Center for American Women and Politics director Debbie Walsh said on the group's website. She added, "But successes like these don't just happen. They require the dedicated attention of parties, donors, activists, and voters, as is particularly evident from the expanded number of Republican women candidates this year. It takes hard work. And the work continues."

The superstar House Democratic freshmen women of 2018—Abigail Spanberger, Katie Porter, Mikie Sherrill, Elise Slotkin, and Elaine Luria—all won reelection, but some very narrowly. Spanberger's margin was about five thousand votes. Democratic women who had won in red districts in 2016 had to withstand the huge turnout of Trump voters; by hewing to the center during their freshman term and working assiduously to keep in touch with their voters back home, they hung on in a tough year for House Democrats.

Democrats had hoped to pick up five to ten House seats. Instead, Republicans picked up ten, leaving Democrats clinging to a narrow majority. The polls had been well off the mark, and both parties suffered. For example, Republicans and Democrats dumped money into Iowa, where Republicans easily won a Senate seat and batch of House races. Had Democrats known better they would have redirected those funds to House members in states that had a shot at victory. If Republicans had a better handle on the actual state of the races, they might have pulled out wins in two to three competitive districts, enough to flip control of the House.

The Republican women's wins were the culmination of two years of hard work by women, for women candidates. After the GOP rebuffed Elsie Stefanik's plea in 2018 to recruit women, she and other women's groups set to work. Stefanik successfully raised money for women candidates through her own Elevate PAC (E-PAC). Other women's groups acting independently of the Republican Party did the same, bringing in the lion's share of their money from outside the party.

House Republican women got off to a slow start in the cycle. In 2019, the *New York Times* reported, "Dr. Joan Perry, a newcomer whom Republicans regarded as a top recruit for 2020, was soundly defeated . . . by Dr. Greg Murphy, a state legislator, in a House Republican primary race in North Carolina that illustrated how steep the party's climb will be as it tries to build more gender diversity." Nevertheless, women pushed on, and could claim gains in 2020.

Julie Conway of VIEW PAC noted that in 2020 a slew of Republican women approached her and other Republican women's organizations, not waiting to be recruited. "I talked to more women wanting to run by March 2019 than in the entire 2017," she recalled. She credited both Democratic women's success in 2016 and Trump's 2016 victory as spurring women to run. Democratic women in 2016 showed their Republican counterparts that women were as competitive in House races as men. Trump showed you needed no special "pedigree"—years in public service, for example—to run. "A lot of Republican women said, 'We didn't have to wait our turn. This guy didn't,'" she explained. Getting in the race early provided them with an organizing and fundraising advantage in the primaries, something women who need to be prodded to run may miss. Republican women also benefited from a batch of open seats in which either the Democrat or the Republican retired.

Part of the credit for Republican women's wins went to WFW Action Fund, a super PAC to elect conservative women. Its website explained, "After the 2018 midterm elections, Republican women in the U.S. House of Representatives saw their ranks slashed to just 13, compared to over 80 Democratic women." It set a goal of electing twenty women in 2020, a figure it far surpassed. With the help of conservatives like former congresswoman Barbara Comstock and former New Hampshire Senator Kelly Ayotte, the group, according to OpenSecrets, raised and spent about $3 million in 2020. However, Republicans still had zero women of color in the Senate and only three in the House—a measure of the degree to which Republican voters remain overwhelmingly White.

Meghan Milloy's Republican Women for Progress also put out their list of "candidates to watch." They came up with three state and local candidates, sixteen candidates for the House and Cynthia Lummis of Wyoming in the Senate. In a media dispatch, they explained, "There are more Republican Women running for federal elected office in 2020 than in any previous year. This is an incredible accomplishment in and of itself, and RWFP applauds these candidates for their willingness to throw their hats into the ring—especially in such a tough cycle." They added, "The top of the ticket is perhaps the most polarizing presidential election in history, and many of these women are running in competitive districts, which could swing either way. They are part of a historic candidate class of Republican Women." Lummis won her Senate seat while ten of their House picks won, including women of color such as Young Kim in the California's Thirty-Ninth, Michelle Steel in California's Forty-Eighth, and Maria Elvira Salazar in Florida's Twenty-Seventh. Many of the winners, Milloy says, "were relatively young and mothers with young children." These candidates "really leaned into these demographics," which made them especially relatable to suburban women and working mothers.

Pleased with the results, Milloy nevertheless is cautious about the potential for women in the GOP. "It's too soon to say," she argues. Republican leaders may simply "check the box" and conclude they have taken care of the issue. They easily could return to an indifferent attitude when it comes to recruiting women. She also cautions that Republicans still have not "even come close" to the number of Democratic women in office. As for the freshmen Republicans, "A lot depends on how they perform."

Once the women proved successful in House races, Minority Leader Kevin McCarthy and other party officials were not shy about touting the results. Lim found that absurd. "It was definitely not the party's doing." McCarthy might have bragged about his support for women; Lim said, "The party did no such thing." Many Republican women who won got very little help from the party as they started out. Republican officials were even dismissive of some women.

Rosemary Becchi, for example, announced her run for Congress in New Jersey's Seventh District. New Jersey Republican National Committeeman Bill Palatucci tried to sabotage her race to help a male candidate, the state senate leader Tom Kean. Palatucci told Republicans not to give her money. Lim and Milloy weighed in publicly, releasing a statement to the press in her defense. "It's embarrassing for Palatucci and the rest of the party leadership that we can't even listen to our own advice on outreach to women," they said. "Changing demographics in the country and the GOP's continued active dismissal of women and minorities are incompatible with future success. If the party is going to compete in the future, we need more women like Rosemary in the halls of Congress—women with real world experience that actually want to work for the betterment of their constituents." Becchi was shunted off to run in New Jersey's Eleventh Congressional District following what her campaign manager described as "serious requests" from national, state, and local Republican leaders. She was essentially forced to run in a less favorable district. She lost. Tom Kean won in the New Jersey's Seventh.

Pushing women into harder-to-win districts was not a tactic unique to her. In Florida, Republican Vennia Francois, a first-generation American with immigrant parents from the Bahamas, found little party support in a multiperson primary in the Seventh Florida Congressional District. Instead, she was obliged to run in the heavily Democratic Tenth, where Val Demings easily defeated her.

Despite gains, "Republican women . . . face demographic challenges: there are simply fewer Republican women voters. Even if women run with the GOP, their minority status within the party makes it even harder to get elected," Abigail Fisher explained in the *American Political Review*. "Rather than focus on discovering the root cause of this demographic imbalance, E-PAC and WFW focus on propelling women forward within the existing male-dominated framework." She continued, "Part of the genius of WFW is its strategic choice only to support women who run on a platform of increased military spending and deregulatory economic policies." In other words, this is about getting more women to sell a traditional Republican message, one that intentionally avoids a focus on "women's issues." In general, Republican House candidates do not run as "feminists," Kelly Dittmar of the Center for American Women and Politics observed. They are conscious of the GOP's aversion to "identity politics," so they are much more likely to run on a standard Republican platform. If they do emphasize gender it is often in touting their roles as mothers or in asserting qualities traditionally associated with masculinity (e.g., toughness).

REPUBLICAN WOMEN'S VICTORIES, Dittmar observed, boiled down to "basic math." Republicans had more women on the ballot in 2020 so they could capitalize on a year that turned out to be unexpectedly strong for Republicans on the House level, especially in states Trump won. With more Republican women running, they were positioned to "capitalize on a better than expected year" for Republican House candidates. Of the seventeen seats won by non-incumbent Republican women, nine were flipped from blue to red, many of which in 2018 had flipped from red to blue. In other words, in the most competitive seats, women (Democrats in 2018 and Republicans in 2020) continue to play a critical role for their parties. More politically active women, more women candidates, more donations to women, and more women-driven organizations lead to more women officeholders on both sides of the aisle. From Julie Conway's perspective, Republican women in 2020 "had the right messengers with the right message in the right districts."

It is also noteworthy that Republicans won despite a money advantage for Democratic women. EMILY's List announced it had "raised $110 million and spent $112 million, including more than $48 million in independent expenditures . . . bundled $13 million for [Democratic] candidates and donated $6.85 million directly to their campaigns and allied parties. These are all record amounts that surpassed previous highs from 2018." In the Senate races, EMILY's List "spent heavily in Senate races and backed women in races in Kansas, Maine, Iowa with investments of $18.5 million in independent expenditures and bundling $5.1 million for our Senate candidates." (As results would show, however, some of that was misdirected at races that did not turn out to be particularly close.) Democratic women did not skimp on House races. "In addition to running $18.3 million in independent expenditure campaigns for 45 of our endorsed women, we bundled $7.5 million from our members for our House candidates." They recruited and backed diverse candidates, expanded staff, and innovated during a pandemic.

In sum, despite being outspent, Republican women ran in greater numbers, got in their races earlier, raised their own money, and competed in a cycle in which massive GOP turnout for Trump benefited them as well. One can expect many of these very same Republican women will be facing tough races in 2022, against many of the Democratic women they ran against in 2018 or 2020.

CHAPTER 23

2020 CHANGED POLITICS FOR WOMEN

The Trump era ended on a horrifying note. After the election, Trump and his Republican enablers, despite the clear outcome and absence of any significant evidence of fraud, took the opportunity to spread disinformation and whip their base into fits of rage. Even though allegations of fraud had been debunked in over sixty court cases, millions of Republicans including congressional leaders still insisted Trump had won and that the election had been "stolen." In furtherance of the Big Lie that the election was stolen, 126 Republican congressmen signed onto a Supreme Court brief in a suit brought by eighteen GOP state attorneys general seeking to throw out votes from states Biden had won, which just so happened to include ballots cast in primarily African American locales that had voted strongly Democratic. With no dissents, the Supreme Court summarily dismissed the lawsuit. Trump seethed that the Court was "incompetent."

Trump's continuing crusade to overturn the election and enrage his MAGA mob had ominous results on January 6, 2021, during what is normally pro-forma counting of the electoral votes. Over 140 Republican congressmen and eight senators objected to electoral votes from Arizona and/or Pennsylvania. The Trump-incited mob, including numerous Republican state officials, received a boost from Missouri Republican Senator Josh Hawley who cheered them on with a raised fist. The mob attacked the Capitol, killing five, injuring more, and inflicting trauma on those hiding from the roving mob. The "law-and-order" party ended the Trump presidency in a spasm of sedition and domestic violence. As the MAGA crowd, some wearing "Camp Auschwitz" T-shirts, displaying nooses, and carrying Confederate flags roamed the halls, the sinking realization set in: The Republican Party had been overrun by irrational, neofascist elements deploying the Big Lie and violence, as right-wing authoritarians around the world have done for decades. Nothing better underscored the ongoing divide in American politics—or the Resistance's inability to pierce the right-wing media bubble that played to White voters' fears.

And yet, just two weeks later, the inaugural committee transformed the scene of mayhem and violence at the Capitol. Albeit surrounded by tens of thousands of National Guard and police forces and cordoned off from visitors by fencing around an immense perimeter, the inauguration ceremony proceeded. I let out an audible gasp at the first sight of Harris, decked out in a bright purple dress and coat, climbing the steps to the Capitol for the swearing in, accompanied by her husband and the Bidens. The women and men who had felt crushed on election night 2016 now could revel in the triumph of democracy. Here, a woman of color, literally had arrived. Bright sunshine and a brisk wind replaced the cover of smoke that hung over the Capitol in the wake of the January 6 assault. The presence on the inaugural stage of Harris, escorted to her seat by Capitol Hill policeman African American Eugene Goodman, thrilled tens of millions of women (and men), provoking a burst of approval on social media and a flood of joyous tears. Her favorite instruction to young girls—walk with "chin up and shoulders back"—aptly described her regal presence on the stage as she took the oath administered by the first Latina

Supreme Court justice, Sonia Sotomayor. Nothing could have been a more forceful repudiation of the Trump era nor of the White supremacists who had terrorized the country at that very spot only a fortnight earlier. The role reversal—a supportive husband holding the Bible for his wife—confirmed that our collective image of who can lead had shifted.

Following the ceremony, Harris traveled to Arlington National Cemetery with Biden as well as three former presidents and their wives (the Clintons, the Bushes, and the Obamas) to pay respects to the Tomb of the Unknown Soldier. Harris's appearance at the White marble memorial alongside synchronized military guards challenged many viewers' preconceptions. The image in our mind's eye of two men (usually White) whom we had become accustomed to seeing over decades at such a solemn occasion was now changed. Here was a new depiction of civilian leadership—strong but feminine, professional but colorfully dressed. The full impact of her achievement was just beginning to dawn on Americans. She was deconstructing our expectations about how leaders should look and wield power.

I recalled the speech she had given so many times on the campaign trail to groups of young people. She would tell them that there will be times when they "are the only one in that room that looks like you." She would say: "Don't you ever let anybody make you feel alone. Because you must remember when you walk in that room, we are all in that room with you. And you are carrying our voice with you." And here she was with millions of women, standing for them at one of our most sacred national sites.

There was one more striking visual symbol in the series of inaugural rituals. Returning from Arlington Cemetery, Harris exited her limousine with her husband, stepchildren, and extended family for the final walk to the White House. Joined hand in hand, arm in arm, the Harris clan fell in behind their matriarch, the daughter of the Indian American immigrant mother and Black immigrant father.

She figuratively and literally marched her blended family—a

multiracial and multiethnic one at that—to the White House. It struck me that from that moment forward every appearance, every speech to the troops or visit with foreign heads of state, and every vote she would preside over in the Senate would redefine the image of a vice president and refashion our image of power. "Normal" for a vice president no longer meant White and male. Children watching the inauguration or studying the event years and decades from that day would never know a time when the vice president was the sole domain of White men. The power of that visual and what it foretold for women was thrilling. I texted and emailed with scores of women that day who had agonized over Trump's election and then spent years toiling away, seeking to oust him. Some were too emotional to put into words what they were feeling. Others were able to put their finger on it: pride. Pride in her and in their own role in creating that transformative moment.

Although a woman did not win the presidency in 2020, the race cemented a new reality in twenty-first century American politics: There likely would never again be a presidential race without multiple women nor a ticket on which two White men would be viewed as the norm. The public no longer found a woman presidential contender a curiosity. In the future, the *absence* of a woman in the primaries would likely strike voters as odd. Susan Carroll of the Center for American Women and Politics predicts the realistic potential for their own presidential run should also change the way women senators and governors think about their political prospects, compelling them to plan out their careers and lay the groundwork for future presidential runs.

IN CONTRAST TO 2016, the 2020 primary offered not only a critical mass of women, but diversity in their appearance, their views, and their messages. They were seen as unique individuals, finally, as male candidates had always been regarded. Some women from here on out would be serious contenders and others flaky; some would make women's empowerment and gender-specific issues the central focus of her campaign, while others would focus on concerns not specific to gender. To win the presidency, women candidates needed to become simply candidates, rather than "women candidates." In 2020, they took a big leap forward in that regard.

Klobuchar told me, "I take solace in that we had so many women there. We were different from each other. We debated each other." She believes, "The world had changed." There would not be a future presidential contest without women, she was convinced. "I never ran to 'put a woman in the job.' And I didn't here." But she did want to make a statement about women in presidential politics. Hence, her response to whether a woman could beat Trump ("Nancy Pelosi does it every day") was a way in which she felt she would "not be defined" by gender but still "take it on."

The critical mass of women who ran in 2020 proved that numbers make a difference in the rhetoric and substance of a presidential campaign.

Women in the presidential field emphasized different parts of the Democratic agenda because of their life experience and familiarity with the lives of other women. Among Harris's most intriguing policy initiatives during her presidential run was a subsidy to narrow the gap between teachers' pay and other workers. Teachers, who are primarily women, represent a large segment of the electorate and in many cases could be the frame for "the average middle-class American." The problem of higher mortality rates for African American women in childbirth played a role in her campaign as well, and to her staff's surprise often drew the reaction of African American men whose wives had had traumatic birthing experiences. Likewise, much of Warren's campaign centered on the needs of working-class women and their families—childcare, universal preschool, and college debt. Biden embraced those issues enthusiastically in the general election.

Male candidates often assume they can speak to and for all Americans, presenting their worldview as neutral and applicable to everyone equally. One high-ranking female campaign official told me that it is a fallacy held by many in the majority group (White men) who do not seem to understand that the perspectives and lived experiences of women can be fundamentally different from their own. It is only by having women on the stage and in the campaign offices that emphasis on different issues, an alternative way of political storytelling, and a more empathetic style of campaigning can emerge.

Most critically, with a woman vice president at the elbow of the commander in chief, the public's mindset as to what a president or vice president looks like will inevitably change as we began to see even on Inauguration Day. Once we have seen a woman as vice president it is less of a stretch to see her in the top job. The image in the public's mind of a chief executive likely will broaden to include women, just as it did to include an African American with the election of Barack Obama.

Harris is now well positioned to be a top contender for the presidential nominee in 2024 or 2028 and a transformational figure in Democratic and American politics. Most vice presidents get elevated and transformed by dint of the presidents they serve. Al Gore and Joe Biden swept previous weak presidential runs away when they joined the tickets and administrations of, respectively, Bill Clinton and Barack Obama. Vice presidents gain stature and become plausible commanders in chief and executives directing policy in an administration that recognizes their talents, as the Clinton and Obama administrations did. Indeed, Democrats have *never* denied the presidential nomination to a sitting or former vice president, further reason to think Harris will be the next in line.

Harris almost certainly will take on whatever legacy the Biden administration leaves as she cements her image as an advocate for Biden's reality-based, center-left brand of politics. Her fate will be tied to his, to the ability to reach out to red America while keeping progressives fired up. Her political future will depend on the administration's success in fighting COVID-19, reviving the economy, and accelerating the transition to green energy sources.

By virtue of her position as a vice president, Harris, if she chooses to run for president, will have the ability to short-circuit the endless cycle of questions and complaints. *Tough or too tough? Share more of yourself, but not that much!* The excess pressure on women to show their policy bona fides will be easier to bear if she can point to Biden-Harris accomplishments. As an emotive and charismatic figure, she can avoid the trap of women candidates who have too often been pushed into a one-dimensional and unemotional presentation that appealed primarily to the intellect and less to their emotional connection to voters.

Harris can help her political image by picking and choosing projects that allow her to cement her attachment to the base but also expand the reach to independents and Republicans. If she can assist in dimming the hostility and narrowing the tribal divisions of the Trump years, she has the ability to cement the wide center-right to center-left coalition that elevated Democrats in 2020. As a person of faith, she is well suited to champion partnerships between government and faith-based and secular private entities to address problems ranging from refugee resettlement to fighting hunger to mental health treatment to ending homelessness. She can strengthen her national security credentials and focus on the needs of military personnel in an administration that is inclined to advocate a sensible, moderate style of foreign policy engagement.

Nevertheless, in any future presidential race, Harris likely will not have the field to herself. Both men and women will no doubt compete for the job. She may be the Democrats' best chance once Biden leaves office to become the first woman president, but she may also make it that much easier for *other women* to break through as governors and private-sector CEOs once the presence of a woman at the highest rungs of our government is normalized.

In addition to a critical mass of presidential candidates, the elevation of the first woman vice president and big wins for Republican women in the House, other breakthroughs for women occurred in the 2020 election cycle. Women filled more critical roles in more presidential campaigns than ever before. Several factors boosted the number of women working on 2020 presidential campaigns. More women candidates meant more campaigns open to or specifically seeking women in top roles. In addition, the sheer size of the presidential field opened opportunities for women as well as non-white men. Simply speaking, there were not enough White males to fill all the available roles so talented women who might otherwise have been overlooked found campaign positions. Women who had long labored on campaigns for governor and senator, often the farm club for presidential campaigns, now had room to move up. On quite a few of the 2020 presidential campaigns women also dominated the ranks of volunteers, especially the most dedicated who trooped from state to state. Women who had gotten their feet wet in politics in the first two years of the Trump era now signed up in record numbers.

In late October 2019, Anita Dunn, a senior adviser to former vice president Joe Biden, appeared at a Citizen by CNN event in New York with four other women in senior positions for leading Democratic presidential campaigns: Nina Turner, national cochair for Sanders's campaign; Lis Smith, senior adviser to Pete Buttigieg's campaign; Lily Adams, communications director for Harris's campaign; and Kristen Orthman, communications director for Warren's campaign. CNN reported that this was "a show of force illustrating that the days of men running campaigns to elect other men are heading to the dustbin of history." In no past presidential cycle would there have been so many heavy-weight women from so many campaigns.

Jen O'Malley Dillon was initially campaign manager for Beto O'Rourke, and then shifted to Biden's team when O'Rourke stepped out of the race. Maya Rupert, Julián Castro's campaign manager later joined the Warren camp. Klobuchar, Harris (both in the primary and in the general election), Buttigieg, and Warren all hired women for their top communications job, the person who is often the face of the campaign.

The presence of so many women in so many campaigns made a difference in O'Malley Dillon's eyes. She had just had a baby at the start of the 2020 cycle, and until O'Rourke reached out to her at the annual South by Southwest conference in 2019, she had avoided committing to a campaign. She had not been on his team for his campaign's launch, which had received mixed reviews. O'Rourke was criticized for appearing with his silent wife in a video announcement and later for cracking that his wife was raising their three children "sometimes with his help." From Dillon's perspective his comments showed that the work of child-rearing was still not evenly divided between men and women. However, the negative reaction to his comments also showed her that public attitudes toward fathers had shifted. O'Rourke was a telegenic candidate, but Dillon knew this would be a "unique challenge," in part because the campaign manager from his failed Senate race remained on the team, often called "chief" by the staff. When she came over to the Biden camp, she sat atop a campaign with plenty of strong personalities but veteran campaign operatives who put a premium on collegiality.

In her experience, women in senior campaign roles before 2020 had a tougher time in rough-and-tumble high-level politics that often seems like a "boys club." She consciously realized she was "putting on airs of toughness" to establish her credibility in the male-dominated environment. When the guys went out drinking after work, she had to go home to her young child. By contrast, multiple senior women on presidential campaigns confirmed that campaigns with a woman campaign manager or with multiple women in high positions had a different "vibe" than the all-male clubs that dominated presidential campaigns for years. Perhaps as outsiders, women felt more comfortable breaking the mold, as Lis Smith did in sending Buttigieg to all sorts of nontraditional media. The ability to pipe up with suggestions without fear of ridicule prompted a more free-flowing, creative atmosphere.

A camaraderie developed among the senior women on different campaigns in 2020 based on mutual respect and the shared demands of splitting parenting duties and managing a national presidential campaign. Women at multiple campaigns felt comfortable calling one another, sometimes to get information, sometimes to ask for assistance, and sometimes to commiserate. Both the trauma of living in Trump times and the determination not to tear the eventual winning candidate apart contributed to a more cordial tone (at least until voting began) than previous campaigns. They also shared a bond in cracking the boys club in the first presidential race where a female candidate was not an oddity. Certainly, the party as a whole worked strenuously to avoid the bitter infighting and intraparty attacks that plagued the 2016 contest, but these women's lack of ego and happy warrior outlook were underappreciated assets in the effort to keep the party from splintering apart.

Perhaps no one better exemplified women's elevation to the top rungs of president than Karine Jean-Pierre, a prominent gay African American woman, a leading force in MoveOn.org, and a former adviser to President Obama. She had seen the 2016 election play out from the green room of MSNBC. Invited to speak about the expected winner, she never made it on air. The petite and feisty progressive had become an audience favorite as a panelist in the MSNBC lineup. As a Haitian American whose father drove a cab and mother was a health care worker, she understood how people with nothing came from impoverished countries to build a better life. Her parents would see their daughter go to college, get a master's degree from Columbia University, and go to work in the White House. In 2019, she released her memoir, *Moving Forward*, a deeply personal account of her experience as an immigrant, her struggle with her sexuality, and her battle to overcome mental illness.

During the primary she appeared with Harris in June 2019 as a moderator at MoveOn.org's Big Ideas Forum in San Francisco. As she was interviewing Harris, an animal rights protester leaped onto the stage and moved toward Harris. Jean-Pierre sprang to her feet and interposed herself between the protester and Harris, body blocking him from approaching Harris until security personnel could escort the protester off stage. Shortly before Harris's selection as VP was announced, Jean-Pierre was brought on board as chief of staff for the yet-to-be-named VP. When Harris joined the campaign, Jean-Pierre once more helped guide her through a historic announcement, a flawless debate performance, and a hugely successful introduction to the country. In case anyone doubted that 2020 marked a revolution in presidential politics the pairing of the first Asian American and first African American woman VP with a lesbian Haitian American chief of staff demonstrated that presidential politics was no longer the province of straight White men.

With women in top campaign posts came the potential for more women to be included in the winner's transition team and then in the highest ranks of the new administration. A majority of Biden's transition team, 52 percent, were women; 53 percent of the senior staff were as well. Biden's picks for top administration jobs included O'Malley Dillon as deputy chief of staff, Kate Bedingfield as communications director, Symone Sanders as chief spokeswoman for Harris, and Jean-Pierre as principal deputy White House press secretary. Among his first one hundred Cabinet and senior advisers, 61 percent were women. Women were nominated for critical Cabinet-level positions, including Janet Yellen as secretary of treasury, Neera Tanden as director of the Office of Management and Budget (although Republicans nixed her nomination with the hilarious excuse that her tweets were too spicy), Avril Haines as director of National Intelligence, Linda Thomas-Greenfield as ambassador to the United Nations, Deb Haaland as secretary of the Interior, and Cecilia Rouse as director of the Council of Economic Advisers. Filling top campaign posts with experienced women proved a critical launching pad for women for White House staff and other powerful positions. One would expect that women, not only on Biden's team but on other presidential campaigns, will parlay their experience into future campaigns and other desirable political slots.

Another "first" in the 2020 presidential cycle was the presence of a different sort of presidential support network—a woman's sorority. Harris at the start of her career, like many middle-class women in politics, lacked personal wealth, a network of CEOs, or even something as common for male politicians as a country club membership. She, however had cultivated a robust political and fundraising base in California. Moreover, she enjoyed a unique asset—something no other male presidential candidate could obtain. She was a member of the Alpha Kappa Alpha Sorority (AKA), from the founding Howard University chapter no less. AKA was established in 1908 and for over one hundred years has served as the critical connective tissue that to this day binds African American women of different generations, geographical regions, political persuasions, and professions. While many fraternities and sororities throw around terms like "service" and "sisterhood" or "brotherhood," AKA actually embodies the lifelong commitment to service and to mutual support.

Deborah Robinson, who graduated Harvard a few years before Harris, works as a lawyer in New York City but on a daily basis is in contact with multiple AKA alumnae, whether by Listserv, emails, texts, reunions, events, and phone calls. A sister ("soror" in the AKA lexicon) is diagnosed with breast cancer and multiple women fly into town to help her, monitoring her chemo schedule so as to provide extra support during the times she feels the worst. They serve as godmothers for their sorors' children; parents know and keep up with their daughters' sorors, extending the links across generations and great distances. The sorority itself is nonpartisan but whether it is a national presidential race or a local political contest in New Jersey, Robinson quite simply says, "We are there for each other."

AKA is not simply a college association but a critical aspect in African American communities in which African American women are still the "first" in many fields. As Robinson says, "I have been told more than once I'm not supposed to do things." In Harris's prior campaign runs, AKA sisters went to events, became donors, volunteered, and in many cases prayed for her. In the primary and later in the general election, the sight of African American women in AKA's green and pink colors became a common sight on the campaign trail.

In the fall of 2019 Harris often told crowds that in every race she won, people have said the public was not ready for someone like her or she was not electable. Harris liked to add that "the operative word is 'won,'" a reminder that the naysayers were proved wrong over and over again. "That message was not lost on us," Robinson says of her AKA sisters. Throughout the general election AKA groups remained active as donors, volunteers, and, when COVID conditions allowed, at public events.

AKA was not the only female network Harris could draw upon. KHive, the online group of mostly women Harris supporters, continued in force during the campaign. They raised money, beat back attacks on Harris on social media, organized their own virtual events, and provided an informal support system for both the Harris team and one another. The KHive may choose to stay active during her vice presidency, serving as a campaign in waiting for her own future presidential run.

Women in the media also enjoyed a first in 2020. On the media side of presidential politics, young women reporters have long been included in the ranks of "embeds"—reporters who follow a candidate day to day, regardless of the location. Some like Katy Tur, who covered Trump in 2016, became household names and went on to anchor slots. However, the coveted spots to moderate debates has long been the province of journalists at the top of news organizations—and those have been overwhelmingly men. Millions of people view the debates both in the primaries and in the general election so inclusion in that select circle conveys prestige on the moderators and increases their name recognition, most critical for women who want to rise to top anchor posts.

When women moderators first appeared in 1976, unbelievably, they were flanked by multiple men and *not permitted to ask questions.* In 2012, a petition demanded that a two-year drought in women moderators be addressed. CNN anchor Candy Crowley was selected to moderate a presidential debate between Romney and Obama. ABC News correspondent Martha Raddatz moderated the vice presidential debate. It was not until Gwen Ifill and Judy Woodruff moderated a *PBS NewsHour* debate in February 2016 between Clinton and Sen. Bernie Sanders that two women moderators appeared at the same Democratic presidential debate.

The DNC took a momentous step in the 2020 race, requiring all twelve sanctioned primary debates include at least one woman moderator. In the fall of 2019, MSNBC announced its moderators for the November debate would have an all-woman panel: Rachel Maddow, Andrea Mitchell, Kristen Welker, NBC News' White House correspondent, and Ashley Parker, a White House reporter for the *Washington Post.* The decision signified how far women had come in the top ranks of journalism and also reset expectations for future debates. It will no longer be surprising to see an all-female moderator panel; if anything, an exclusively male panel may seem odd.

The process of selecting and phrasing questions and scripting moderators is a group effort, involving dozens of network executives, writers, and producers. In the case of the *Washington Post*'s Ashley Parker, she received the assistance of her colleague Karen Tumulty as her producer for the event. Tumulty, herself a veteran of presidential debates, helped meticulously prepare Parker up to the day of the event, giving her practice asking questions over and over again until her delivery was perfect. Women had come so far as to have an older generation there to mentor a younger generation of journalists. "I began to realize what a powerful symbol this was during our preparation: We were in New York for a few weeks working together," Andrea Mitchell later told *Elle* magazine. "I'd been in similar settings before, but there was something unique about the collegiality and the supportiveness of this group. We all went with the mission of not making ourselves the story."

The resulting debate was fast-paced, substantive, and largely devoid of bickering. The questions, which included the topics of childcare, education, and others especially important to women, might have been asked eventually by male moderators in other debates. However, the critical mass of women network executives, producers, and ultimately moderator roles resulted in a wider range of issues than had been covered previously.

In the general election, NBC's Savannah Guthrie received widespread applause for handling a Trump town hall in which he appeared in lieu of a second debate. Critics had blasted NBC for giving Trump, who had ducked out of the second scheduled debate, a forum opposite Biden who previously was scheduled during the same time slot on ABC. However, Guthrie's persistent and tough questioning removed any doubt NBC was doing Trump any favors. In the final debate Welker, well-practiced from the primary debate, ran the event with a firm hand, moving Trump from one topic to another and preventing his nonstop interruptions that made the first presidential debate virtually unwatchable. The utility of the current debate format will be discussed in both parties going forward; if they continue or evolve into some other format, women will no doubt be on equal footing with men.

In sum, voters in 2020 did not select a woman for president, but they nevertheless placed one a heartbeat from the presidency, a woman drawn from a primary field with multiple women candidates. A plethora of senior campaign operatives (running both male and female candidates' operations) prepared a generation of women for high office and future top campaign jobs. At least on the Democratic side, women at the pinnacle of political power may be encouraged to follow their ambition and wield power on a playing field that has gradually leveled. There is little doubt that women on the Republican side will follow Carly Fiorina's example in 2016 and take the plunge in the 2024 primaries and beyond. No presidential election in history had seen greater strides for women.

CHAPTER 24

WOMEN CHANGE LAWS AND POLITICS

The Trump era marked a turning point for the #MeToo movement. The legal landscape shifted to respond to the raft of sexual assault and discrimination cases, offering protection for women in the workplace and removing obstacles to their advancement in politics and the rest of society.

In 2018, the Equal Employment Opportunity Commission announced that it had filed "7,609 sexual harassment charges—a 13.6 percent increase from FY 2017—and obtained $56.6 million in monetary benefits for victims of sexual harassment." In addition, the EEOC filed forty-one lawsuits alleging sexual harassment, more than a 50 percent increase over the prior year. "The EEOC recovered nearly $70 million for the victims of sexual harassment through administrative enforcement and litigation in FY 2018, up from $47.5 million in FY 2017." While these numbers dipped in 2019, the Biden administration is expected to pursue sexual harassment claims more rigorously.

The #MeToo movement also spawned new legislation at the state level. Writing for the American Bar Association, Erik Christiansen found, "Since 2017, as a reaction to the publicity surrounding these and other high-profile cases, 15 states have passed new laws protecting against sexual harassment in the workplace. New York, California, and Illinois have led the way with new laws focusing on mandatory sexual harassment training, softening the federal 'severe or pervasive' standard to make it easier to sue in state courts, and banning the nondisclosure agreements that predators have used to silence victims and protect their careers." Jurors, who are now sensitized to the #MeToo movement, are willing to render more generous verdicts to victims. Meanwhile, a growing list of states prohibit nondisclosure agreements that prevent victims from discussing facts about their suits and ban "pre-arbitration agreements, class action waivers, and jury trial waivers in sexual harassment cases."

Criminal law has also evolved. After a Stanford University student athlete received just six months (and serving only three in county jail) for a sexual assault, California passed new legislation mandating sentences be served in state prison. Texas increased sentences for groping in 2019 while New York extended the statute of limitations for some sexual assault claims. Meanwhile, an academic study in 2020 found that reports of sexual crimes increased by 10 percent, reflecting "a change in social norms or information." In the US "the movement also increased arrests for sexual crimes in the long run."

If the legal environment has changed, it follows that women in education, the workplace, and politics will face fewer barriers to achieve their goals. In the political realm, the forced resignation of a slew of alleged harassers and AOC's outspoken rebuke of her colleague make it less likely male colleagues will feel entitled to abuse their colleagues and staff.

In politics, however, what may matter most is a critical mass of women. Wins for Democratic House women in 2018 in concert with big wins for Republican House women in 2020 ensured that the number of women in Congress increased. Within the Republican Party, women still remain a sliver of the caucus. By contrast, Democrats' total number of seats shrank, while their contingent of women remained at eighty (including a woman speaker), making them a higher percentage of the caucus. With sixteen women in the Senate and a woman vice president, women can continue to exert influence in the Democratic Party. A woman speaker and a woman vice president will preside over the House and Senate, respectively. Undoubtedly, Democratic women will help determine the party's rhetoric, messaging, and issue-selection in significant and long-lasting ways.

Without women, the Democratic Party would not be the majority party. Women, as we saw in 2016, 2018, and 2020, are a greater percentage of the population and vote in greater numbers than men. When one party routinely can rely on support from 55 to 60 percent of women who make up over 50 percent of the electorate, it has a leg up in races for Congress, the presidency, and state races.

The numbers reveal Democrats' built-in demographic advantage. White men made up just 35 percent of the electorate in 2020, just 17 percent were White men without a college education. Compare that to White women (38 percent) and college-educated women of all races (33 percent) and you see how the numbers do not favor the Republicans. Combine Democrats' gender advantage with the shrinkage of the White electorate (which declined from 71 to 67 percent of the electorate between 2016 and 2020) and Democrats' support among Blacks and Latinos—especially Black women (93 percent) and Latina voters (66 percent)—and you see how Republicans, dependent on White, male, and largely non-college-educated voters, are running into a gender and racial cul-de-sac. Stacey Abrams has proven that if Democrats can register and engage the growing demographic of nonwhite voters they can flip previously red states.

As an indispensable part of the Democratic electorate and a substantial presence in elected offices, Democratic women can raise money, send women to Congress and state offices in greater numbers, and build new networks or expand on existing ones. Democrats in the Trump era also forged an army of politically activated women volunteers. Abigail Spanberger first ran in 2018 and won reelection in a conservative Virginia district in 2020. In looking back over the preceding four years, she could see that the mass networks of women volunteers formed in the aftermath of 2016 had survived COVID-19 and grown in size and sophistication. The endurance of engaged and women-dominated organizations backing female candidates promises that the gains of 2018 and 2020 will be long-lasting. Spanberger also thinks the women themselves have changed. Many women who had engaged as volunteers at food pantries, homeless shelters, or other causes in their community previously had not seen themselves as "political." Now, she says, they understood that "what they were doing *was* political." Women could clearly see how their activities connected to policy decisions made in DC. Owning their political identity and focusing on their obligations to fellow Americans have made them active citizens, the front-line defenders of democracy. Politics was no longer something other people did.

A Democratic majority in the House and Senate (thanks to Harris's tie-breaking vote) with a Democratic president will naturally produce far more progressive results than what we have seen in a unified Republican government. The degree to which Pelosi and Biden can attract GOP support in the Senate will in large part determine his legislative success. A centrist Democratic president, who could not have won without substantial support from women, may have the best shot at achieving progressive goals (certainly ones obtainable through executive orders). Nevertheless, the disproportionate influence of sparsely populated red state senators will pose an ongoing challenge for the Democratic agenda. In the Senate, Democrats will represent tens of millions more Americans although they do not control the body; this is a feature of our Constitution that gives even the least populated states two senators. That arrangement has become a significant partisan advantage for Republicans.

Moreover, a Democratic Party in which women are the pre-eminent force is likely to be different from a Democratic Party dominated by men. That is not a statement of intellectual or moral superiority but rather a recognition that women think differently about government and politics. A candidate like Biden, who wore decency and empathy on his sleeve, demonstrated the ability to attract women voters who might not agree with his positions on all issues. Despite those differences they still felt he was a decent person—someone who would not put children in cages, demean women reporters, or celebrate violence.

During the campaign, Democratic women and, in turn, the Democratic Party had begun to speak more frequently about politics, be it on child separation policy, guns, the environment, criminal justice, or dozens of other issues, as an expression of our values. In the Trump era, Democrats' political rhetoric increasingly focused on character and values, filling the vacuum resulting from the sell-out of White evangelical leaders who chose to blindly support a cruel, narcissistic president and his immoral policies, ranging from exclusion of refugees to child separation to support for murderous tyrants around the globe. Evangelicals gave up the moral high ground; women and the party they primarily supported rushed forward to seize it. With the right-wing descending into sedition and the bulk of Republicans sticking by a president who ignited the siege on the Capitol on January 6, Republicans cannot seriously maintain their claim to be the only "real Americans." They do not have bragging rights as the guardians of American patriotism and faith.

As a deeply religious person and regular churchgoer, Biden appealed to persons of faith (he won 60 percent of voters who were not White evangelicals or White born-again Christians) and those of no faith (a growing segment of the population) with the plea to fight for the "soul of the nation." More than any specific policy issue, he invoked appeals to unity, civility, and empathy. As Harris frequently said, "Character and decency are on the ballot." After

January 6, Americans understood that character and decency are tied to national security and preservation of our democracy.

In politics, talk of values, such as respect and inclusion, has come back in fashion. Biden displayed the rhetoric and value-laden goals of the Democratic Party in his victory speech on the Saturday after the election. "The purpose of our politics isn't total, unrelenting, unending warfare," Biden declared. "No. The purpose of our politics, the work of the nation, isn't to fan the flames of conflict— but to solve problems. To guarantee justice. To give everybody a fair shot. To improve the lives of our people." He spoke as he did so often about comforting and healing a bitterly divided nation. "We must put the anger—and the demonization—behind us. It's time for us to come together as a nation and heal," he said. He emphasized not specific policy but a different political ethos. "My responsibility as President will be to represent the whole nation. And I want you to know—that I will work as hard for those who voted against me as for those who voted for me. That's the job. It's called a duty of care. For all Americans."

By contrast, Republicans under Trump increasingly adopted moral nihilism, bullying, disinformation, and willful ignorance along with using voter suppression as their chosen means of retaining their grip on power. The Trump years exposed that Republicans' "pro-life" stance on abortion was a canard meant only to control the lives of women, not protect human lives. They were willing to risk infecting thousands of Americans with a deadly disease just to put Trump back on the campaign trail but not allow a desperate teenager or an overtaxed mother of multiple children to obtain a safe, legal abortion. They proffered concern about the sanctity of every life when abortion was the topic but remained indifferent to Trump's neglect of the pandemic and prioritization of economic growth over human beings' health and safety. And some of Trump's base were all too willing to descend into violence, egged on by grasping Republicans looking to curry favor with the MAGA mob.

A conservative movement and its chosen political party that had always prided themselves on upholding cultural standards of right and wrong, objective truth, personal responsibility and civic virtue undermined all that in the name of defending Trump supporters as the embodiment of "real America." Venting White grievances and "owning the liberals," whom they insisted had been insufficiently respectful toward their followers, became their primary aim. As conservative Peter Wehner wrote in 2019, "What the Republican Party is saying and signaling isn't simply that rationality and truth are *subordinate* to partisanship; it is that they have to be *obliterated* for the sake of partisanship and the survival of the Trump presidency." Nearly two years in advance of Trump's incitement of an attack on the Capitol, Wehner observed, "There is no limiting principle—almost nothing he can do—that will forfeit their support." In Trump's own terms: He could shoot someone on Fifth Avenue—or set off a riot that killed innocents—and still wouldn't lose his cult followers. It is hard to argue with Wehner's conclusion that the GOP under Trump "is a party built largely on lies, and it is now maintained by politicians and supporters who are willing to 'live within the lie,' to quote the great Czech dissident (and later president) Václav Havel." The lesson is not lost on Americans that living within the lie can result in incentivizing terrorists, endangering lives, and obliterating the sanctity of elections.

We saw plenty of signs that moral nihilism and willingness to accept lying has metastasized on the right to a frightening degree. Gallup found that in the Bill Clinton presidency 86 percent of Republicans thought it was important for the president to provide moral leadership; in 2018 that number dropped twenty-three points. Similarly, the PRRI surveys found that in 2011 only 30 percent of White evangelicals said a politician who commits a personal immoral act can still behave ethically and fulfill the duties of his or her job. In 2020 that number was at 68 percent. Jones observes, "They have exchanged a deontological ethic (measuring all candidates against a set of clearly-defined principles and values) for a consequentialist ethic (wherein the ends justify the means). Trump clearly fails the first test, but if Trump is a means to an ultimate end (e.g., preserving a White Christian America), that is all that matters." Nowhere was this more evident than in their plunge into conspiracies and refusal to accept Biden's victory. Rather than reel back their base in defense of objective reality and democracy, Republicans treated his defeat as another opportunity to infuriate, alienate, and convince millions of voters they were being robbed.

Republicans' shift to moral nihilism and refusal to uphold objective reality goes hand in hand with its evolution, accelerated during the Trump years, from a conservative party to one more akin to European right-wing nationalistic parties infused with White supremacy and misogyny. The White grievance party denies not only defeat in an election but basic truths about America. Rather than recognize actual discrimination against women and minorities, they paint themselves as oppressed, seek to exclude everyone but "real Americans" (defined as White and Christian), and refuse to tolerate let alone embrace an increasingly diverse country. That model is not rooted in American values and does not represent the sentiments of the country as a whole. Republicans try to play defense against irreversible demographic trends.

Republican men continue to insist they, not women or racial minorities, are the victims of discrimination. In 2018, PRRI found, "A majority (53%) of Republicans, compared to just 27% of Democrats, agree that discrimination against men is as big a problem as discrimination against women. Among Republicans, men (63%) are much more likely than women (44%) to express this sentiment." Evidencing the pervasive belief in male victimhood, PRRI's 2020 survey found: "Majorities of Republicans agree with both the statement that society punishes men just for acting like men (60% agree) and that society has become too soft and feminine (63% agree). Independents and Democrats are less likely to agree with either statement: 33% of independents and 24% of Democrats agree that society punishes men for being men, and 34% of independents and 23% of Democrats agree that society has become too feminine."

On race, Republicans' conviction that Whites are victimized by Blacks plays into their race-based fear of being dislodged from power. That, in turn, justifies their denial of real racism and staunch defense of the status quo. "Around eight in ten Republicans (79%), compared to 40% independents and 17% of Democrats, believe that killings of African Americans by police are isolated incidents," PRRI's 2020 survey found. "Republicans who trust Fox News most for television news (90%) are even more likely than Republicans as a whole to say that these are isolated incidents."

Even more alarming, Republicans increasingly reject the notion of America as a religiously and racially pluralistic society. As Pew's 2018 survey showed, Republicans are more inclined to see racial diversity as a negative. "Seven-in-ten Democrats and Democratic-leaning independents say growing diversity in the U.S. makes it a better place to live." However, the survey found that only 47 percent of Republicans see diversity as positive and "14% say it makes the country a worse place to live." The preference for Whites' domination came through loud and clear. "Republicans are more likely than Democrats to say that electing more individuals from underrepresented groups would have a negative impact: lesbian, gay, bisexual, and transgender people (40% vs. 12%), non-Christian religious groups (40% vs. 16%), non-religious people (40% vs. 14%), people from racial and ethnic minority groups (18% vs. 7%), or women (9% vs. 4%)." In 2020, the PRRI survey found just 13 percent of Republicans (versus 43 percent of independents and 53 percent of Democrats) prefer a religiously pluralistic America, while 43 percent of Republicans (as opposed to only 18 percent of independents and 16 percent of Democrats) say they "prefer the U.S. to be a nation primarily made up of people who follow the Christian faith." Moreover, "about half of Republicans (49%), compared to 35% of independents and 30% of Democrats, say the U.S. is a Christian nation."

In sum, the flight of more women from the Republican Party, its antipathy toward nonwhites and "elites" (college educated and/or urban Americans), and Trump's stoking of extreme and violent groups leave the Republican Party as a hotbed of White grievance and misogynistic resentment. Contempt for religious diversity and denial of racism are now hallmarks of the Republican identity. Republicans' defensive crouch leads them to a survivalist view of politics. Just about any means, even violence, to preserve White male dominance is justified to achieve that goal; self-delusion and outright lying are normalized. In finding a cult leader in Trump willing to play to their fears and prejudices, the GOP adopted the Machiavellian view that politics is about power; truth is relative. Decency and kindness are for suckers.

The GOP has a choice on whether it doubles down on its White male grievance mentality or heeds the call from the party's so-called autopsy report after the 2012 election to diversify the GOP and find a sane, inclusive message that is consistent with American values. The former forces the party to depend upon a declining White male demographic that is hostile to powerful women and unappealing outside a shrinking geographic area. It risks a long spell in the political wilderness as its paths to electoral victory narrow. Meanwhile, Republican women newly elected to Congress must decide whether to encourage their party to adopt a more inclusive and humane vision or to simply echo their White male peers' delusions and prejudices.

In evaluating the Trump era, we know women were central in the Resistance and played an indispensable role in holding on to democratic self-government. Without the gender gap in Biden's favor, Trump might have won another four years. Without active women, the Affordable Care Act would likely have fallen. Had Democrats not enjoyed overwhelming support among women they would not have won back the House in 2018, kept it in 2020, and taken the White House and Senate in 2020. However, if we learned anything from the debacle of 2016 and assault on the Capitol that followed Republicans' phony voter fraud claims, it is that democracy is a fragile thing. The mixed results in the 2020 election and Republicans' refusal to recognize the results of a democratic election affirm that Trumpism is not entirely behind us. By the same token it also would be foolish to imagine that women who worked to jettison Trump, elect a woman vice president, and revive the Democratic Party will be content to lay down their political arms and return to the sort of self-satisfied complacency that characterized the pre-Trump years. Having found their voice and inhabited powerful roles, women are unlikely to retreat. Trump taught us the unacceptable price of passivity.

ACKNOWLEDGMENTS

When I embarked upon the journey—and it was a journey—to write my first book, I imagined it would be a solitary exercise requiring long hours of isolation and lonely days and nights at the keyboard. Nothing could have been further from the truth. On every page, I can see the imprint of dozens of people who shared with me their time, insights, research, and personal stories. Academics, politicians, campaign advisers, pollsters, activists, and women who were newly engaged in politics generously provided the material you see in this book. Special thanks go to Speaker Nancy Pelosi, Vice President Kamala Harris, Neera Tanden, Stephanie Schriock, Ilyse Hogue, Sarah Longfellow, Rep. Abigail Spanberger, Rep. Katie Porter, and Sen. Amy Klobuchar (as well as their staffs, who succumbed to constant entreaties to clear time in their bosses' schedules for me). These women sat for extensive interviews and provided me with the granular detail necessary to explain this extraordinary moment in American history. Their accounts provide the core of the book; any errors or omissions are solely mine. Without the help of Jen O'Malley Dillon, Andrew Bates, Karine Jean-Pierre, Kate Bedingfield, Lily Adams, Ron Klain, and others who worked on the Biden and/or Harris campaign teams I would not have been able to understand how a campaign so heavily dominated by and geared toward women came together. Their consummate professionalism served as an example of poise, dignity, and good cheer under terribly stressful circumstances.

The book was not written for academics but the research and writings of scores of women scholars who have studied gender and politics informed and guided my work. Jennifer Lawless, Susan Carroll, Kelly Dittmar, Kathleen Jameson, Regina Lawrence, and Anna Greenberg were among those who freely shared their research and perspectives. They patiently answered a stream of questions as I tried to make sense of women's political journey in modern America. Robert P. Jones provided invaluable insight into White evangelicals and has had a profound impact on the way I view race and religion in the American experience.

I am blessed by the friendship and counsel of my *Washington Post* colleagues, most especially Karen Tumulty and Ruth Marcus, who answered questions that I was frankly too sheepish to ask others. It has been the honor of my life to be a part of the *Washington Post* editorial team where I am fortunate to work under the patient leadership of Fred Hiatt. I am continually inspired by the excellence and professionalism of our writers, editors, and digital staff.

I am also graced with wonderful colleagues at MSNBC— producers, hosts (especially Joy Reid, Jonathan Capehart, and Ali Velshi) and staff—who make me look and sound better than I normally do. They have allowed me to broaden my audience and solidify lasting relationships in the world of media and politics.

I am forever indebted to my agent Bridget Matzie who recognized, after several male literary agents did not, that there was a story to be told about women's political reawakening in the Trump era. She took a novice author through each step of the writing process, helping to keep me and the book on a steady course. Likewise, there would be no book without my editor at HarperCollins, Mauro DiPreta, who helped shape and reshape my story as it evolved during a time of political upheaval. Trying to make sense of once-in-a-lifetime events while writing a book in real time during a pandemic was challenging, to put it mildly; it would have been impossible without Mauro's calm hand and astute judgment. I am likewise indebted to Nainika Paul for her copious fact-checking and editorial help. Any errors that may remain are solely mine.

I am deeply grateful for an army of colleagues and fellow warriors in the battle to defend American democracy during a harrowing period in our history. They have been a constant source of interesting ideas, good humor, and encouragement. I was proud to be in the company of patriots including Mimi Rocah, Bill Kristol, Jerry Taylor, Charlie Sykes, Peter Wehner, Tim Miller, Joyce White Vance, George Conway, Neal Katyal, Larry Tribe, Norm Eisen, Rick Wilson, Harry Littman, Jill Wine-Banks, Ian Bassin, Evan McMillan, Mona Charen, Max Boot, Tom Nichols, Jennifer Taub, Peter Wehner, Julie Zebrak, Tiffany Cross, and the Republican Voters Against Trump team. You have inspired me to be a better writer and a better citizen. Without them and the brilliant humor of Sarah Cooper I would not have kept my sanity during the Trump years.

As I was rounding the bend on this book and the election, the country lost Supreme Court Justice Ruth Bader Ginsburg in September 2020. Never has a public figure's passing been so devastating to me on so many levels. As a Jewish woman lawyer and then judge and justice who balanced work and family while cultivating the arts, she could not have been a better role model for me and thousands if not millions of women. Her quiet voice, wit, steely determination, and incisive mind set a standard that few of us can attain. Without her trailblazing litigation that forced Americans to recognize gender discrimination existed and, moreover, to grasp that it denied both women and men equal protection under the law, doors would have remained shut and barriers still in place when I entered college and then law school. Every twenty-first-century woman stands on her shoulders. She—along with Nancy Pelosi—attained the highest rung in their respective branches of government and cleared the way for others to follow.

On a more personal level, I have been sustained over decades by the wisdom, humor, indulgence, empathy, and strength of a cadre of brilliant women—Beth Chilton, Carole Edelstein, Debra David, Lucy Zimmerman, and Sally Levinson. I am eternally grateful for their confidence in me, especially at times when I was adrift or overwhelmed by events. Such relationships make life worth living and encourage us to be the best version of ourselves.

I am fortunate to have parents who prized education and whose spirited debates at the dinner table over the decades encouraged me to think critically. They instilled in me a love of politics and history—and of newspapers. Throughout my childhood there was always at least one newspaper dropped on our driveway and left in the kitchen to peruse throughout the day. I learned from them to be an informed citizen and never, ever to miss an election.

Above all, without the love, support, and patience of my husband Jonathan and my sons Josh and Joe I would never have embarked on a second career in journalism, never made it to the *Post*, and never managed to write this book. They enthusiastically have read more of my columns and magazine articles and watched more of my TV appearances than any person should be forced to endure. My love for them is boundless.

AUTHOR'S NOTE

As for many other women, the Trump years have been an emotional roller coaster, at times heartening, at others frightful, and always chaotic. Political punditry, mine included, explored in real-time the worldwide rise of right-wing populism and the threats to Western democracies. Polls and anecdotal evidence suggested attachment to democracy was withering and appeals to illiberal, authoritarian governments were winning the day. However, I did not buy that narrative. When I looked around the country in 2017 and 2018, participatory democracy looked to be flourishing. Direct action in the streets, the birth of new political organizations, high voter turnout, and a spate of new candidates convinced me that the antibodies of democracy were surging. Rather than the end of democracy, I suspected the Trump era might provide the impetus for a new birth of active citizenship.

The more I examined the phenomenon the more I could see that women played a leading role in orchestrating this outpouring of civic enthusiasm. They were the foot soldiers, the organizers, the candidates, and the volunteers pulling their country back from the clutches of a racist, antidemocratic president and his enablers. Republican and Democratic women, White and Black, rural and urban, young and old were newly energized and helped enlist Americans who had been despondent on election night in 2016 into a vibrant political force. And yet, what was obvious to me—the centrality of women in the fight for American democracy—was often seriously underplayed or ignored in mainstream news coverage. We were undergoing a radical transformation of American politics driven by, for, and about women—but one would not know it from the day-to-day reporting in the media. It would be as if during the civil rights era the press failed to attribute the growth and success of the fight for equality to the work of African Americans. I was watching nothing less than a women's political revolution, but it remained underreported and undervalued.

The desire to tell the story of those women from all walks of life who undertook the battles for decency, democracy, the rule of law and racial justice was the inspiration for this book. Over the course of roughly eighteen months, I spent hundreds of hours interviewing women candidates and officials, participating in what amounted to a third women's revolution (following the suffragettes and the 1970s women's movement) as well as other newsmakers, academics, pollsters, think-tank scholars, and media figures who provided insight into events as they were unfolding. Comments that appear in quotations without citation to a secondary source come directly from those interviews. In other cases, remarks and observations are paraphrased. This book is not intended to be a comprehensive history of the Trump era. The individual women whose stories I tell are not demographically representative of American women, but rather serve as exemplars of certain types of women. They provide insight into their unique experiences. We are all informed and limited by our biases and life experiences, and I have tried to be candid about my own perspective and political inclinations. This book is the story of a discrete period told through the eyes of one journalist who was both an observer and participant in the women's uprising that freed America from the scourge of Trump.

SOURCES

Chapter 1

INTERVIEWS

Neera Tanden, interview by author, May 23, 2019

Ilyse Hogue, interviews by author, July 3, 2019, and September 3, 2019

Sarah Longwell, interviews by author, September 11, 2002, and April 2, 2000

Abigail Spanberger, interviews by author, May 21, 2019, and August 21, 2019

WORKS CITED

Cary, Mary Kate. "Ruth Bader Ginsburg's Experience Shows the Supreme Court Needs More Women." *U.S. News & World Report*, May 20, 2009. https://www.usnews.com/opinion/blogs/mary-kate-cary/2009/05/20/ruth-bader-ginsburgs-experience-shows-the-supreme-court-needs-more-women.

Clinton, Hillary Rodham. "Nancy Pelosi." *Time* 100. *Time*, April 2019. https://time.com/collection/100-most-influential-people-2019/5567750/nancy-pelosi-2/.

Collins, Eliza. "CNN Denies Trump's Demand to Donate $5 Million, Risking Debate Boycott." *Politico*, December 3, 2015. https://www.politico.com/story/2015/12/cnn-rejects-trump-debate-demands-216388.

Chapter 2

INTERVIEWS

Susan Carroll, interview by author, June 27, 2019

Palmieri interview. Palmieri, Jennifer, "Dear Madam President: An Open

Letter to the Women Who Will Run the World." Hachette Book Group (2018).

WORKS CITED

Bacon, Perry, Jr. "'An Enormous Deal': A Look at Hillary Clinton's Promise of a Cabinet Full of Women." NBCNews.com, May 2, 2016. https://www.nbcnews.com/politics/2016-election/enormous-deal-look-hillary-clinton-s-promise-cabinet-full-women-n564761.

Barbara Lee Family Foundation and Center for American Women and Politics. "Finding Gender in Election 2016: Lessons from Presidential Gender Watch." https://cawp.rutgers.edu/sites/default/files/resources/presidential_gender_gap_highlights.pdf.

Bowman, Bridget. "GOP Women's Group Looks to Be a Force in Future Elections." *Roll Call*, November 13, 2020. https://www.rollcall.com/2020/11/13/gop-womens-group-looks-to-be-a-force-in-future-elections/.

Carmon, Irin. "A 50/50 Cabinet? The Rest of the World Yawns." MSNBC.com, September 25, 2020. https://www.msnbc.com/msnbc/5050-cabinet-the-rest-the-world-yawns-msna839376.

Center for American Women and Politics. "Widows Who Succeeded Their Husbands in Congress." 2017. https://cawp.rutgers.edu/sites/default/files/resources/widows.pdf.

———. "Women in the US Congress 2016." January 5, 2017. https://cawp.rutgers.edu/women-us-congress-2016.

Clinton, Hillary Rodham. *What Happened*. London: Simon & Schuster UK, 2018.

CNN Money. "Fortune 500: Top Women CEOs." *May 3, 2010*. https://money.cnn.com/magazines/fortune/fortune500/2010/womenceos/.

Cox, Daniel, and Robert P. Jones. "Two-Thirds of Trump Supporters Say Nation Needs a Leader Willing to Break the Rules." Public Religion Research Institute, April 7, 2016. https://www.prri.org/research/prri-atlantic-poll-republican-democratic-primary-trump-supporters/.

Dittmar, Kelly. "Disrupting Masculine Dominance." In *Gender and Elections,* edited by Susan J. Carroll and Richard L. Fox, chapter 2. Cambridge: Cambridge University Press, 2018.

Dittmar, Kelly, Kira Sanbonmatsu, and Susan J. Carroll. *A Seat at the Table: Congresswomen's Perspectives on Why Their Presence Matters*. New York: Oxford University Press, 2018.

Duerst-Lahti, Georgia, and Madison Oakley. In *Gender and Elections,* edited by Susan J. Carroll and Richard L. Fox, 37–39. Cambridge: Cambridge University Press, 2018.

Eagleton Institute of Politics. Conversation with Hillary Rodham Clinton at Rutgers University, April 2018. https://www.youtube.com /watch?v=dmZIdq0eGR8.

Flaherty, Colleen. "Study Finds Gains in Faculty Diversity, But Not on the Tenure Track." *Inside Higher Ed*, August, 22, 2016. https://www .insidehighered.com/news/2016/08/22/study-finds-gains-faculty -diversity-not-tenure-trackglass-ceiling-female-attorneys-now-face-a -concrete-wall/?sh=5ec852838f39.

Graf, Nikki, Anna Brown, and Eileen Patten. "The Narrowing, But Persistent, Gender Gap in Pay." Pew Research Center, March 22, 2019. https://www .pewresearch.org/fact-tank/2019/03/22/gender-pay-gap-facts/.

Haub, C., and T. Kaneda (2015). *2014 World Population Data Sheet— Population Reference Bureau*. Prb.org. https://www.prb.org/2014 -world-population-data-sheet/.

Labor Review. https://www.bls.gov/opub/mlr/2002/05/art2full.pdf.

Marcus, Bonnie. "Forget the Glass Ceiling. Female Attorneys Now Face A Concrete Wall." *Forbes*, June 15, 2018. https://www.forbes.com/sites /bonniemarcus/2018/06/15/forget-the-glass-ceiling-female-attorneys -now-face-a-concrete-wall/?sh=38bbfb5c38f3.

OpenSecrets. "EMILY's List Outside Spending." opensecrets.org, April 2008. https://www.opensecrets.org/outsidespending/detail .php?cmte=C00193433&cycle=2008.

Palmieri, Jennifer. "Inside the Last Days of the Hillary Clinton Campaign." *Time*, March 21, 2018. https://time.com/5207773/jennifer-palmieri -hillary-clinton-campaign/.

Ross, Martha. "Hillary Clinton's Defeat Crushes Many Women's Hopes." *Mercury News*, November 10, 2016. https://www.mercurynews.com /2016/11/09/hillary-clintons-defeat-crushes-many-womens-hopes/.

Seelye, Katharine Q., and Claire Cain Miller. "Female Clinton Supporters Are Left Feeling Gutted." *New York Times*, November 11, 2016. https:// www.nytimes.com/2016/11/11/us/politics/female-clinton-supporters -are-left-feeling-gutted.html.

Stracqualursi, Veronica. "Hillary Clinton Cites Sexism in Criticism She Should Exit Political Stage." CNN.com, March 30, 2018. https://www .cnn.com/2018/03/30/politics/hillary-clinton-election-loss/index.html.

Swank, Eric. "Who Voted for Hillary Clinton?" *The 2016 US Presidential Election and the LGBTQ Community*, 2020, 23–44. doi:10.4324/9780429058639–3.

Toossi, Mitra. "A Century of Change: the U.S. Labor Force, 1950–2050." *Monthly Labor Review*, US Bureau of Labor Statistics, May 2002. https://www.bls.gov/opub/mlr/2002/article/century-of-change-the-us -labor-force-1950-2050.htm.

Toossi, Mitra, and Teresa L. Morisi. "Women in the Workforce Before, During, and After the Great Recession." *Spotlight on Statistics*, US Bureau of Labor Statistics, July 2017. https://www.bls.gov/spotlight /2017/women-in-the-workforce-before-during-and-after-the-great -recession/pdf/women-in-the-workforce-before-during-and-after-the -great-recession.pdf.

Traister, Rebecca. *Good and Mad: The Revolutionary Power of Women's Anger.* New York: Simon & Schuster, 2019.

US Census Bureau Public Information Office. "More Working Women Than Men Have College Degrees, Census Bureau Reports." May 19, 2016. https://www.census.gov/newsroom/releases/archives/education /cb11-72.html.

Wells, Jean A. "Women Workers in 1960: Geographical Differences." Women's Bureau, US Department of Labor, 1962. https://fraser .stlouisfed.org/files/docs/publications/women/b0284_dolwb_1962.pdf.

Wu, April Yanyuan, et al. "How Do Trends in Women's Labor Force Activity and Marriage Patterns Affect Social Security Replacement Rates?" *Social Security Bulletin*, vol. 73, vol. 4. https://www.ssa.gov /policy/docs/ssb/v73n4/v73n4p1.html#:~:text=The%20increase%20 in%20labor%20force,(Kreider%20and%20Ellis%202011).

Yeager, Holly. "Does EMILY's List Still Matter?" *American Prospect*, July 7, 2008. https://prospect.org/online-extras/emily-s-list-still -matter/.

Zarya, Valentina. "Female Founders Got 2% of Venture Capital Dollars in 2017." *Fortune*, January 31, 2018. https://fortune.com/2018/01/31 /female-founders-venture-capital-2017/.

Chapter 3

INTERVIEWS

Stephanie Schriock, interviews with author, June 7, 2019, and March 10, 2020

Leah Greenberg, interview with author, June 21, 2019

Carol Catron, interview with author

Susan Griffin, interview with author, November 5, 2019

Jennifer Levin, interview with author July 31, 2019

WORKS CITED

Center for American Progress. "The Path Forward: Economic and Democratic Renewal." 2016. https://cdn.americanprogress.org/content /uploads/2016/12/21082232/CAP_PathForward.pdf.

Chapter 4

INTERVIEWS

Kamala Harris, interview with author, February 7, 2019

Schriock, op. cit.

Sarah Schulz, interview with author, May 29, 2019

Carol Catron interview with author, November 22, 2019

WORKS CITED

Carlson, Kate. "400-Plus Rally in Midland Women's March." *Midland Daily News*, January 23, 2018. https://www.ourmidland.com/news /article/400-plus-rally-nbsp-in-Midland-Women-s-March-12513675 .php.

Chenoweth, Erica J. "Analysis: This is what we learned by counting the women's marches." *Washington Post*, April 18, 2019. https://www .washingtonpost.com/news/monkey-cage/wp/2017/02/07/this-is-what -we-learned-by-counting-the-womens-marches/.

Futter, Maddy, et al. "The W.O.M.A.N. Behind the Marches." *Update*, February 7, 2017. https://update.midlandps.org/index.php/2017/02/the -w-o-m-a-n-behind-the-marches/.

Hartocollis, Anemona, and Yamiche Alcindor. "Women's March Highlights as Huge Crowds Protest Trump: 'We're Not Going Away.'" *New York Times*, January 21, 2017. https://www.nytimes.com/2017/01/21/us /womens-march.html.

Kennett, John. "Sarah Schulz Considers Run for 98th House." *Midland Daily News*, January 25, 2018. https://www.ourmidland.com/news /article/Sarah-Schulz-considers-run-for-98th-House-12524334.php.

Rubin, Jennifer. "What a Difference a Day Makes: A Reprise of the March on Washington." *Washington Post*, August 28, 2020. https://www .washingtonpost.com/opinions/2020/08/28/what-difference-day-makes -reprise-march-washington/.

Scherer, Michael. "Trump Inauguration: David Brock Plots Revenge." *Time*, January 20, 2017. https://time.com/4641901/trump-inauguration -david-brock/.

Sedmak, Ryan. "Nancy Pelosi: 'We don't agonize, we organize.'" *Yahoo!News*, November 7, 2018. https://news.yahoo.com/nancy-pelosi -apos-don-t-134432278.html.

Wilcox, Allison. "WOMAN leader: We Want a Better America for Us All." *Midland Daily News*, November 4, 2020. https://www.ourmidland .com/opinion/voices/article/WOMAN-leader-We-want-a-better -America-for-us-all-15696842.php.

Chapter 5

INTERVIEWS

Tanden, op. cit.

Angel Padilla, interview with author, September 4, 2019

Susan Griffin, interview with author

Greenberg, op. cit.

WORKS CITED

CBS News. "Trump Travel Ban Sparks Protests at Airports Nationwide." January 29, 2017. https://www.cbsnews.com/news/donald-trump-travel-ban-sparks-protests-at-airports-nationwide-seattle-tacoma/.

Baker, Chris. "Syracuse's Leftist Tea Party: Meet the Protesters behind the 1,000-person Airport Rally." *Syracuse.com*, January 30, 2017. https://www.syracuse.com/news/2017/01/syracuses_left-leaning_tea_party_how_trump_energized_1000s_of_protesters.html.

Bangor Daily News. "Trump to Senate Republicans: Kill Obamacare Now, Replace Later." July 30, 2017. https://bangordailynews.com/2017/06/30/politics/trump-to-senate-republicans-kill-obamacare-now-replace-later/.

Beam, Adam. "Rural hospitals face uncertainty with health care proposals." Associate Press, July 19, 2017. https://apnews.com/article/af13117e66c447cbab04e6e5fc1b1116.

Calsyn, Maura. "The Senates ACA Repeal Bill Would Devastate Rural Communities." Center for American Progress, July 12, 2017. https://www.americanprogress.org/issues/healthcare/news/2017/07/12/435637/senates-aca-repeal-bill-devastate-rural-communities/.

de Vogue, Ariane, Eli Watkins, and Alanne Orjoux. "Judges Temporarily Block Part of Trump's Immigration Order, WH Stands by It." CNN.com, January 29, 2017. https://www.cnn.com/2017/01/28/politics/2-iraqis-file-lawsuit-after-being-detained-in-ny-due-to-travel-ban/index.html.

Dreyfuss, Ben. "A Federal Judge Just Issued a Stay against Donald Trump's 'Muslim Ban.'" *Mother Jones*, January 29, 2017. https://www.motherjones.com/politics/2017/01/muslim-ban-federal-court/.

Greenberg, Leah. "How Progressive Activists Turned the Table on Republicans to Help Save Obamacare." *Rolling Stone*, November 4, 2019. https://www.rollingstone.com/politics/politics-features/we-are-indivisible-excerpt-progressives-obamacare-affordable-care-act-907275/.

Jordan, Glenn. "Move to Repeal Affordable Care Act 'Just Inviting Chaos,' Maine Leaders Say." *Press Herald*, July 4, 2020. https://www

.pressherald.com/2020/07/04/defeat-of-obamacare-would-be
-catastrophic-for-many-in-maine-state-leaders-say/.

Knefel, John. "Inside the Huge JFK Airport Protest Over Trump's Muslim
Ban." *Rolling Stone*, June 25, 2018. https://www.rollingstone.com
/politics/politics-features/inside-the-huge-jfk-airport-protest-over
-trumps-muslim-ban-124190/.

Lutey, Tom. "As Health Care Battle Reignites, Daines and Tester Once
Again Are on Opposing Sides." *Montana Standard*, September 22, 2017.
https://mtstandard.com/news/state-and-regional/as-health-care-battle
-reignites-daines-and-tester-once-again/article_3b34c332–82c0–56d0
–80f1–11bf64c7d8c8.html.

Martinson, Erica. "Here's What Happens in Alaska with a Straight Repeal
of the Affordable Care Act." *Anchorage Daily News*, December 2, 2017.
https://www.adn.com/politics/2017/07/19/heres-what-happens-in
-alaska-with-a-straight-repeal-of-the-affordable-care-act/.

McCausland, Phil. "Sen. Collins Has 'Serious Reservations' Over GOP's
Obamacare Repeal." NBCNews.com, September 24, 2017. https://www
.nbcnews.com/politics/politics-news/sen-collins-has-serious
-reservations-over-gop-s-obamacare-repeal-n804261.

Newman, Andy. "Highlights: Reaction to Trump's Travel Ban." *New York
Times*, January 29, 2017. https://www.nytimes.com/2017/01/29
/nyregion/trump-travel-ban-protests-briefing.html.

Ramesh, Tarun, and Emily Gee. "Rural Hospital Closures Reduce Access
to Emergency Care." Center for American Progress, September 9, 2019.
https://www.americanprogress.org/issues/healthcare/reports
/2019/09/09/474001/rural-hospital-closures-reduce-access-emergency
-care/.

Scott, Dylan, and Sarah Kliff. "Why Obamacare Repeal Failed." *Vox*,
July 31, 2017. https://www.vox.com/policy-and-politics/2017/7/31
/16055960/why-obamacare-repeal-failed.

Seipel, Brooke. "ACLU Celebrates: 'I Hope Trump Enjoys Losing.'"
The Hill, January 28, 2017. https://thehill.com/blogs/blog-briefing
-room/news/316716-aclu-celebrates-victory-i-hope-trump-enjoys
-losing.

Sperance, Cameron. "Obamacare Repeal Could Cripple Rural Hospitals
and Lead to More Closures." *Forbes*, July 26, 2017. https://www.forbes
.com/sites/bisnow/2017/07/26/obamacare-repeal-could-cripple-rural
-hospitals-and-lead-to-more-closures/.

WGNO Web Desk. "#ResistTrumpTuesday Protest Returns to Sen.
Cassidys Office over Immigration Ban." WGNO, January 31, 2017.
https://wgno.com/news/local/resisttrumptuesday-protest-returns-to
-sen-cassidys-office-over-immigration-ban/.

Chapter 6

INTERVIEWS

Schriock, op. cit.

Griffin, op. cit.

WORKS CITED

"Alabama Senate Election Results." *Washington Post*, 2017. https://www
.washingtonpost.com/special-election-results/alabama/.

AL.com Editorial Board. "Our View: Voters Must Reject Moore; We
Endorse Jones." Al.com, November 19, 2017. https://www.al.com
/opinion/2017/11/our_view_alabama_voters_must_r.html.

Fausset, Richard. "For Alabama Women, Disgust, Fatigue and a Sense Moore
Could Win Anyway." *New York Times*, November 11, 2017. https://www
.nytimes.com/2017/11/10/us/alabama-women-roy-moore.html.

Johnson, Katanga, and Heather Timmons. "How Stacey Abrams paved the
way for a Democratic victory in 'New Georgia.'" Reuters, November 9,
2020. https://www.reuters.com/article/usa-election-georgia/how
-stacey-abrams-paved-the-way-for-a-democratic-victory-in-new
-georgia-idUSKBN27P197.

McCrummen, Stephanie, Beth Reinhard, and Alice Crites. "Woman says
Roy Moore initiated sexual encounter when she was 14, he was 32."
Washington Post, November 9, 2017. https://www.washingtonpost.com
/investigations/woman-says-roy-moore-initiated-sexual-encounter
-when-she-was-14-he-was-32/2017/11/09/1f495878-c293-11e7-afe9
-4f60b5a6c4a0_story.html.

Naylor, Brian. "'Black Votes Matter': African-Americans Propel Jones to
Alabama Win." NPR.org, December 13, 2017. https://www.npr.org
/2017/12/13/570531505/black-votes-matter-african-americans-propel
-jones-to-alabama-win.

Nilsen, Ella. "The Women, People of Color, and LGBTQ Candidates Who
Made History in the 2017 Election." *Vox*, November 8, 2017. https://
www.vox.com/policy-and-politics/2017/11/8/16622884/women
-minorities-lgbtq-candidates-made-history.

Nirappil, Fenit. "3 Democrats Who Never Held Office Vying to Be
Virginia's Lieutenant Governor." *Washington Post*, May 23, 2017.
https://www.washingtonpost.com/local/virginia-politics/3
-democrats-who-never-held-office-vying-to-be-virginias-lieutenant
-governor/2017/05/22/6b24b648-3b34-11e7-9e48-c4f199710b69_story
.html.

Przybyla, Heidi M. "It Wasn't Just a 'March': Six Months Later, Virginia
Women Run for Office." *USA Today*, July 18, 2017. https://www

.usatoday.com/story/news/politics/2017/07/18/wasnt-just-march-six
-months-later-virginia-women-run-office/484192001/.

Savransky, Rebecca. "DNC chair: Black Women Are the 'Backbone' of the
Democratic Party." *The Hill,* December 13, 2017. https://thehill
.com/homenews/campaign/364719-dnc-chair-black-women-are-the
-backbone-of-the-democratic-party.

Vazquez, Lucas. "Virginia's first Vietnamese-American legislator wants to
inspire others to run." NBC News, November 17, 2017. https://www
.nbcnews.com/news/asian-america/virginia-s-first-vietnamese
-american-legislator-wants-inspire-others-run-n821481.

Watson, Kathryn. "Trump at rally says country "can't afford" to lose a
Senate seat." CBS News, December 9, 2017. https://www.cbsnews.com
/news/trump-at-rally-says-country-cant-afford-to-lose-a-senate-seat/.

Weigel, David, and Lauren Tierney. "The Seven Political States of Texas."
Washington Post, October 4, 2020. https://www.washingtonpost.com
/graphics/2020/politics/texas-political-geography/.

Chapter 7

INTERVIEWS

Angie Maxwell, website of the Diane D. Blair Center of Southern Politics &
Society

Mindy Finn, interview with author May 22, 2019

Jennifer Lim, interview with author, May 17, 2019

Meghan Milloy, interview with author, August 16, 2019

INFORMED RESEARCH

Anna Greenberg, interview with author, May 13, 2019

Cooperman, interview with author, June 20, 2019

Kelly Dittmar, interview with author

Regina Lawrence, interview with author July 10, 2019

Robert P. Jones, interview with author, May 28, 2019

WORKS CITED

Abramowitz, Alan, and Ruy Teixeira. "The Decline of the White Working
Class and the Rise of a Mass Upper-Middle Class." *Political Science
Quarterly* 124, no. 3 (2009): 391–422. http://www.jstor.org/stable
/25655694.

Adler, K. "Why I, a Republican, Am Voting for Hillary Clinton." *Marie
Claire*, October 18, 2016. https://www.marieclaire.com/politics/news
/a23128/im-a-republican-voting-for-hillary-clinton/.

Agiesta, J. "Poll: Most see a Hillary Clinton victory and a fair count ahead." CNN, October 25, 2016. https://www.cnn.com/2016/10/25 /politics/hillary-clinton-2016-election-poll/index.html.

American Principles Project. "Tell WaPo: "Stop Calling Jennifer Rubin a Conservative." (n.d.) https://americanprinciplesproject.org/petitions /tell-wapo-stop-calling-jennifer-rubin-a-conservative/.

Black, Earl, and Merle Black. *The Rise of Southern Republicans*. Cambridge, MA: Belknap Press, 2004.

Charen, Mona. "Opinion: Beware Electing a Dangerous Narcissist." *Pocono Record*, March 24, 2016. https://www.poconorecord.com /article/20160324/opinion/160329745.

———. "I'm Glad I Got Booed at CPAC." *New York Times*, February 25, 2018. https://www.nytimes.com/2018/02/25/opinion/im-glad-i-got -booed-at-cpac.html.

Center for American Women and Politics. "Unfinished Business." (n.d.). Accessed January 28, 2021, from https://womenrun.rutgers.edu/why -how-women-run/.

Concha, J. "Conservatives to Washington Post: Jennifer Rubin Isn't One of Us; Hire Someone New." *The Hill*, October 4, 2018. https://thehill.com /homenews/media/409867-conservatives-to-washington-post-jennifer -rubin-isnt-one-of-us-hire-someone.

Conversation, The. "Paradox: Here's why White evangelical women love Donald Trump." Raw Story, December 17, 2020. https://www.rawstory .com/2019/02/strange-paradoxical-reasons-white-evangelical-women -love-donald-trump/?utm_source=fark&utm_medium=website&utm _content=link&ICID=ref_fark.

CNN 2016 exit polls. https://www.cnn.com/election/2016/results/exit-polls.

Crowley, M., et al. "Did Bill Kristol's Miscalculations Help Create Donald Trump?" *Politico*, July 2016. https://www.politico.com/magazine /story/2016/07/2016-bill-kristol-republicans-conservative-movement -donald-trump-politics-214025.

Gaddini, Katie. "Donald Trump: Why White evangelical women support him." The Conversation, 2020. https://theconversation.com/donald -trump-why-white-evangelical-women-support-him-112041.

Hansen, S. B. *The Politics of Sex: Public opinion, parties, and presidential elections*. New York: Routledge, 2014.

Jorgensen, Katrina. "A Trump Trainwreck is the only thing that will save the Republican Party." *The Guardian*, August 4, 2016. https://www .theguardian.com/commentisfree/2016/aug/04/donald-trump-2016 -election-loss-save-republican-party.

Kristol, Bill. Twitter, January 29, 2017. https://twitter.com/billkristol /status/825720952256348161?lang=en.

Lawless, J. L., and R. L. Fox. *Women, Men & US Politics: 10 Big Questions.* New York: W.W. Norton & Company, 2017.

Maxwell, Angie, and Todd Shields. *The Long Southern Strategy: How Chasing White Voters in the South Changed American Politics.* New York: Oxford University Press, 2019.

Moody, Chris. "Republican Women Organize to Support Clinton." CNN, July 3, 2016. https://www.cnn.com/2016/07/02/politics/republican -women-organize-to-support-clinton/index.html.

Nance, Penny Young. "Opinion: How evangelical women will vote in 2016." CNN, November 1, 2016. https://www.cnn.com/2016/11/01 /opinions/women-evangelicals-in-election-2016-nance-young/index .html.

Navarro, Ana. "Ana Navarro: I'm voting for Hillary Clinton—and Against Donald Trump." CNN, November 7, 2016. https://www.cnn .com/2016/11/07/opinions/navarro-republican-voting-for-clinton/index .html.

NPR. "Barbershop: Trump, Women and The Republican Party." *All Things Considered*, October 8, 2016. https://www.npr .org/2016/10/08/497200495/barbershop-trump-women-and-the -republican-party.

Republican National Committee. "Growth & Opportunity Report." 2013. https://online.wsj.com/public/resources/documents /RNCreport03182013.pdf.

Reuters. Business & Financial News, U.S & International Breaking News. (n.d.) from Lopez, Luciana, and Michelle Conlin. "Fed up with Washington, Trump's 'Deplorables' Shake up the Elite." Reuters. November 9, 2016. https://www.reuters.com/article /idUSKBN1341AB?edition-redirect=ca.

Scott, Eugene. "White Women Helped Elect Trump. Now He's Losing Their Support." *Washington Post*, April 28, 2019. https://www .washingtonpost.com/news/the-fix/wp/2018/01/22/white-women -helped-elect-trump-now-hes-losing-their-support/.

Serreze, Mary C. "William Kristol Talks 'Never Trump' Conservatism at Amherst College." MassLive.com, November 17, 2017. https://www .masslive.com/politics/2017/11/conservative_william_kristol_a.html.

Chapter 8

INTERVIEWS

Abigail Spanberger, interviews with author May 2, 2019, and August 21, 2019

Amy McGrath, interview with author, March 10, 2019, and October 10, 2019

Katie Porter, interviews with author, July 12, 2019, and August 28, 2018

INFORMED RESEARCH

Amanda Renteria, interview with author, June 6, 2019

WORKS CITED

Schneider, Elena. "'Something Has Actually Changed: Women, Minorities, First-Time Candidates Drive Democratic House Hopes." *Politico*, September 11, 2018. https://www.politico.com/story/2018/09/11/white -men-democratic-house-candidates-813717.

Chapter 9

INTERVIEWS

Randi Weingarten, interview with author, September 4, 2019

Schriock, op. cit.

Catron, op. cit.

Laurie Woodward Garcia, interview with author, November 4, 2019

Lane Murdock, interview with author

WORKS CITED

"The Condition of Education" (n.d.). https://nces.ed.gov/programs/coe /indicator_clr.asp.

Alter, Charlotte. "The School Shooting Generation Has Had Enough." *Time*, March 22, 2018. https://time.com/longform/never-again -movement/.

Brenan, Megan. "Support for Stricter U.S. Gun Laws at Lowest Level Since 2016." Gallup.com, January 14, 2021. https://news.gallup.com /poll/325004/support-stricter-gun-laws-lowest-level-2016.aspx.

Carranza, Rafael, et al. "Arizonans protest immigration policy at Families Belong Together marches." AzCentral.com, June 30, 2018. https://www .azcentral.com/story/news/politics/immigration/2018/06/30/family -separation-trump-immigration-protests-arizona/747184002/.

Cassidy, John. "What the Polls Show in the Run-Up to the Midterm Elections." *New Yorker*, November 2, 2018. https://www.newyorker .com/news/our-columnists/there-are-tight-races-everywhere-in-the -runup-to-the-midterm-elections.

CBS News.com Staff. "CBS Poll: The Gender Gap on Guns." CBS News, May 14, 2000. https://www.cbsnews.com/news/cbs-poll-the-gender -gap-on-guns/.

Connolly, Griffin. "Democrats' Final Midterm Pitch: Two Words—Health Care." *Roll Call*, November 11, 2018. https://www.rollcall.com /2018/11/06/democrats-final-midterm-pitch-two-words-health-care/.

Cunningham, Paige Winfield. "Analysis | The Health 202: Trump's Moves Haven't Yet Significantly Decreased the Number of People with Health Insurance." *Washington Post*, July 17, 2020. https://www.washingtonpost.com/news/powerpost/paloma /the-health-202/2018/05/22/the-health-202-trump-s-moves-haven -t-yet-significantly-decreased-the-number-of-people-with-health -insurance/5b03173d1b326b492dd07e04/.

Dittmar, Kelly, Kira Sanbonmatsu, and Susan J. Carroll. "Why Electing More Women to Congress Is a "Big Thing." Center for American Women and Politics, August 24, 2018. https://cawp.rutgers.edu /footnotes/why-electing-more-women-congress-%E2%80%9Cbig -thing%E2%80%9D.

Dodson, Tim. "Hundreds protest Trump immigration policies at 'Families Belong Together' rally in Richmond." *Richmond Times-Dispatch*, June 30, 2018. https://richmond.com/news/local /hundreds-protest-trump-immigration-policies-at-families-belong -together-rally-in-richmond/article_5a604312-d6f7-5f4e-8c16 -8bc80ff74c4e.html.

Falk, Mallory. "Across Southern New Mexico, Indivisible Groups Gear Up for Midterm Elections." https://www.krwg.org/post/across-southern -new-mexico-indivisible-groups-gear-midterm-elections.

Fielhouston. "PRESS ADVISORY: Houston Rallies to End Family Separation." July 29, 2018. https://fielhouston.org/2018/06/29/press -advisory-houston-rallies-to-end-family-separation/.

Indivisible Key Issues. https://indivisible.org/prioritizing-key-policy -issues.

Indivisible. "Families Belong Together Protests." June 18, 2018. http:// www.indivisibleoc.org/families-belong-together-protests/.

Jordan, Mary and Scott Clement. "Echoes of Vietnam: Millions of Americans Are Taking to the Streets." *Washington Post*, April 6, 2018. https://www.washingtonpost.com/news/national/wp/2018/04/06 /feature/in-reaction-to-trump-millions-of-americans-are-joining -protests-and-getting-political/.

King, Ledyard, and Korte, Gregory. "Trump Vows Tougher Background Checks, Mental Health Screens for Gun Buyers in Meeting with Students." *USA Today,* February 22, 2018. https://www.usatoday .com/story/news/politics/2018/02/21/president-trump-holds-listening -session-parents-students-prevent-school-massacres/358927002/.

Langer Research Associates. "Many See Societal Issues in CT Shootings; Most Back Ban on High-Capacity Clips." ABC News/Washington Post Poll, December 17, 2012. https://www.langerresearch.com/wp-content /uploads/1145a1GunControl.pdf.

Magnoli, Mike. "Miramar ICE office has hundreds of immigrants and protesters." CBS12, June 21, 2018. https://cbs12.com/news/local/miramar-ice-office-has-hundreds-of-immigrants-and-protesters.

Miller, Emily McFarlan, and Yonat Shimron. "Why Is Jeff Sessions Quoting Romans 13 and Why Is the Bible Verse So Often Invoked?" *USA Today*, June 16, 2018. https://www.usatoday.com/story/news/2018/06/16/jeff-sessions-bible-romans-13-trump-immigration-policy/707749002/.

Quinnipiac University. Poll Release Detail. July 18, 2021. https://poll.qu.edu/national/release-detail?ReleaseID=3687.

Reilly, Katie. "Exactly How Teachers Came to Be So Underpaid in America." *Time*, September 13, 2018. https://time.com/longform/teaching-in-america/.

Schochet, Leila. "Trump's Family Incarceration Policy Threatens Healthy Child Development." Center for American Progress, July 12, 2018. https://www.americanprogress.org/issues/early-childhood/reports/2018/07/12/453378/trumps-family-incarceration-policy-threatens-healthy-child-development/.

Stewart, Chelsea. "David Hogg Is Taking a Gap Year Before College & His Reason Is Kind of Perfect." Elite Daily, April 10, 2018. https://www.elitedaily.com/p/where-is-david-hogg-going-to-college-hes-taking-a-gap-year-8740348.

United States Department of Justice. "Attorney General Announces Zero-Tolerance Policy for Criminal Illegal Entry." April 6, 2018. https://www.justice.gov/opa/pr/attorney-general-announces-zero-tolerance-policy-criminal-illegal-entry.

Van Dam, Andrew. "Teacher Strikes Made 2018 the Biggest Year for Worker Protest in a Generation." *Washington Post*, February 14, 2019. https://www.washingtonpost.com/us-policy/2019/02/14/with-teachers-lead-more-workers-went-strike-than-any-year-since/.

Velasquez, J. J. "At 'Rally for Our Children,' Hundreds Call for End to Immigrant Family Separations at Border." *San Antonio Report*, June 1, 2018. https://sanantonioreport.org/at-rally-for-our-children-hundreds-call-for-end-to-immigrant-family-separations-at-border/.

Walters, Edgar. "Nancy Pelosi: Democrats should focus on health care, working families — not abolishing ICE." *Texas Tribune*, September 29, 2018. https://www.texastribune.org/2018/09/29/nancy-pelosi-democrats-should-focus-healthcare-working-families/.

Weingarten, Randi. "Electing to Improve People's Lives." American Federation of Teachers, November 18, 2018. https://www.aft.org/column/electing-improve-peoples-lives.

Chapter 10

INTERVIEWS

Hogue, op. cit.

Sen. Heidi Heitkamp, interview with author May 30, 2019

Catron, op. cit.

Porter, op. cit.

WORKS CITED

Diamond, Jeremy. "Trump Says It's 'A Very Scary Time for Young Men in America.'" CNN Politics, October 2, 2018. https://www.cnn .com/2018/10/02/politics/trump-scary-time-for-young-men-metoo /index.html.

Elliott, Phillip. "Here's the Real Reason Mitch McConnell Canceled August Recess." *Time*, June 5, 2018. https://time.com/5302138/congress -recess-august-mitch-mcconnell/.

Green, Emma. "Susan Collins Gambles with the Future of Roe v. Wade." *The Atlantic*, October 9, 2018. https://www.theatlantic.com/politics /archive/2018/10/susan-collins-brett-kavanaugh-roe-v-wade/572344/.

Ioannou, Filipa. "Kamala Harris goes viral grilling Kavanaugh on laws restricting the male body." *SFGate*, September 6, 2018. https://www .sfgate.com/politics/article/kamala-harris-kavanaugh-male-body-roe -abortion-13209859.php.

Lesniewski, Niels. "Mitch McConnell Sees Electoral Gains From Fight Over Brett Kavanaugh." *Roll Call*, October 6, 2018. https://www .rollcall.com/2018/10/06/mitch-mcconnell-sees-electoral-gains-from -fight-over-brett-kavanaugh/.

Malloy, Allie, Kate Sullivan, and Jeff Zeleny. "Trump Mocks Christine Blasey Ford's Testimony Tells People to 'Think of Your Son.'" CNN Politics, October 3, 2018. https://www.cnn.com/2018/10/02/politics /trump-mocks-christine-blasey-ford-kavanaugh-supreme-court/index .html.

Marcus, R. *Supreme Ambition: Brett Kavanaugh and the Conservative Takeover*. New York: Simon & Schuster, 2020.

Merica, Dana. "Kavanaugh gets combative with Democratic senator over questions about drinking." CNN Politics, September 28, 2018. https:// www.cnn.com/2018/09/27/politics/kavanaugh-klobuchar-questions -about-drinking/index.html.

Phillip, A., and D. Merica. "Kamala Harris rode the Kavanaugh wave once. Can she do it again?" September 17, 2019. https://www.cnn.com /2019/09/17/politics/kamala-harris-brett-kavanaugh/index.html.

Werner, Erica. "Some GOP senators concede Ford's credibility but point to lack of corroboration." *Washington Post*, September 27, 2018. https://richmond.com/news/local/government-politics/abigail-spanbergers-passion-for-languages-led-her-to-the-cia/article_d99787c8-8f5a-5e99-946c-be207565f62f.html.

Chapter 11

INTERVIEWS

Nancy Pelosi, interview with author

Porter, op. cit.

McGrath, op. cit.

Spanberger, op. cit.

Catron, op. cit.

Lim, op. cit.

Conway, op. cit.

WORKS CITED

Center for American Women and Politics. Press Release. July 28, 2020. https://cawp.rutgers.edu/sites/default/files/resources/press-release-update-end-of-filing_0.pdf.

——. Results: Women Candidates in the 2018 Elections.https://cawp.rutgers.edu/sites/default/files/resources/results_release_5bletterhead5d_1.pdf.

Chira, Susan. "Banner Year for Female Candidates Doesn't Extend to Republican Women." *New York Times*, November 15, 2018. https://www.nytimes.com/2018/11/15/us/politics/women-politics-republican.html.

CNN 2016 Exit Polls retrieved from https://www.cnn.com/election/2016/results/exit-polls.

Coppins, M. "Trump Cares About Only One Audience." *The Atlantic*, January 14, 2019. https://www.theatlantic.com/politics/archive/2019/01/trump-mocks-christine-blasey-ford-rally/580069/.

Fausset, Richard, Reid J. Epstein, and Rick Rojas. "'I Refuse Not to Be Heard': Georgia in Uproar Over Voting Meltdown." *New York Times*, June 9, 2020. https://www.nytimes.com/2020/06/09/us/politics/atlanta-voting-georgia-primary.html.

Gallup. "Party Affiliation." December 22, 2020. https://news.gallup.com/poll/15370/party-affiliation.aspx.

Galston, William A. "Why Did House Democrats Underperform Compared to Joe Biden?" Brookings Institution, December 21, 2020.

https://www.brookings.edu/blog/fixgov/2020/12/21/why-did-house
-democrats-underperform-compared-to-joe-biden/.

Ghitza, Yair. "Revisiting What Happened in the 2018 Election." *Medium*,
May 21, 2019. https://medium.com/@yghitza_48326/revisiting-what
-happened-in-the-2018-election-c532feb51c0.

Groppe, M. "'Year of the Woman'? Not for Republican women in the
House, where their ranks have plunged to a 25-year low." *USA Today*,
December 13, 2018. https://www.usatoday.com/story/news/politics
/2018/12/13/house-gop-women-shrinking-lowest-level-25-years
/2207124002/.

Holyk, G. (2016). Gender, Education Split Among White Voters Key to
2016 Election (POLL). https://abcnews.go.com/Politics/race-gender
-education-keys-2016-election-poll/story?id=41404170.

Kiefer, Francine. "How Republican Women Won a Record Number of Seats
in Congress." *Christian Science Monitor*, November 9, 2020. https://
www.csmonitor.com/USA/Politics/2020/1109/How-Republican
-women-won-a-record-number-of-seats-in-Congress.

Lawless, J. L., and R. L. Fox. *Women, Men & US Politics: 10 Big Questions*.
New York: W.W. Norton & Company, 2017.

Noe-Bustamante, Luis, Jens M. Krogstad, and Antonio Flores. "Historic
highs in 2018 voter turnout extended across racial and ethnic groups."
Pew Research Center, September 23, 2020. https://www.pewresearch
.org/fact-tank/2019/05/01/historic-highs-in-2018-voter-turnout
-extended-across-racial-and-ethnic-groups/.

North, A. "The midterm election shows white women are finally starting
to abandon Trump." *Vox*, November 7, 2018. https://www.vox.com
/policy-and-politics/2018/11/7/18064260/midterm-elections-turnout
-women-trump-exit-polls.

Pathé, Simone. "Elise Stefanik Wants to Play in Primaries to Help
Republican Women." *Roll Call*, December 4, 2018. https://www.rollcall
.com/2018/12/04/elise-stefanik-wants-to-play-in-primaries-to-help
-republican-women/.

Why Women Run. Center for American Women and Politics. Rutgers
University. August 8, 2019. https://cawp.rutgers.edu/bridge-report-1.

Wilson, P. Results of Spanberger vs. Ward in 7th District Dem primary.
Richmond Times-Dispatch, June 11, 2018. https://richmond.com/z-no
-digital/results-of-spanberger-vs-ward-in-7th-district-dem-primary
/article_d315b9e1-d801-5a37-91ab-b87a3e077f47.html.

Zhou, Li. "Why More Republican Women Are Running for the House
Than Ever Before." *Vox*, May 27, 2020. https://www.vox.com/21262150
/house-republican-women-candidates.

Chapter 12

INTERVIEWS

Pelosi, interview with author

Hogue, interview with author

WORKS CITED

Bash, D. "Nancy Pelosi: 'I want women to see that you do not get pushed around.'" CNN, November 13, 2018. https://www.cnn.com/2018/11/13 /politics/nancy-pelosi-badass-women-washington/index.html.

Bassett, L. "Katie Porter Survived Domestic Abuse, Only to Have It Used Against Her in Her Campaign." *Huffington Post*, May 11, 2018. https:// www.huffingtonpost.ca/entry/candidate-survived-domestic-abuse_n_5 af47e3ce4b0859d11d15299?ri18n=true.

Nash, E., L. Mohammed, O. Cappello, S. Naide, and Z. Ansari-Thomas. "State Policy Trends at Mid-Year 2019: States Race to Ban or Protect Abortion." November 11,2019. https://www.guttmacher.org/article/2019/07/state -policy-trends-mid-year-2019-states-race-ban-or-protect-abortion.

Stewart, Emily. "A leader in the fight to protect Roe v. Wade lays out the plan to stop Brett Kavanaugh." *Vox*, July 29, 2018. https://www .vox.com/policy-and-politics/2018/7/29/17625884/brett-kavanaugh -abortion-naral-ilyse-hogue.

Women Chairs of Subcommittees of Standing Committees in the U.S. House, 1947–Present. US House of Representatives: History, Art & Archives. (n.d.). https://history.house.gov/Exhibitions-and -Publications/WIC/Historical-Data/Women-Chairs-of-Subcommittees/.

Chapter 13

INTERVIEWS

Stacey Abrams, interview with author

Gillibrand, interview with the author

Klobuchar, interview with author

Harris campaigns, interview with author

WORKS CITED

Alter, Charlotte. "Other Countries Have Elected Women Leaders for Decades. Why Can't America?" *Time*, March 7, 2020. https://time.com /5798122/elizabeth-warren-woman-president-america/.

Astor, Maggie. "'A Woman, Just Not That Woman': How Sexism Plays Out on the Trail." *New York Times*, February 11, 2019. https://www .nytimes.com/2019/02/11/us/politics/sexism-double-standard-2020.html.

Becker, Amanda. "'Badass' National Security Women Offer Democrats a Trump Antidote." Reuters, December 5, 2018. https://www.reuters .com/article/us-usa-politics-women-idUSKBN1O419I.

Burns, Alexander, and Lisa Lerer. "In 2020, Democrats Expect a Female Front-Runner. Or Three." *New York Times*, October 19, 2018. https:// www.nytimes.com/2018/10/19/us/politics/democrats-women -president-2020.html.

Capehart, Jonathan. "Cape Up Live: Sen. Kamala Harris with Jonathan Capehart." *Washington Post*, July 9, 2020. https://www.washingtonpost .com/podcasts/post-live/cape-up-live-sen-kamala-harris-with-jonathan -capehart/.

Center for American Women and Politics. Unfinished Business from https://womenrun.rutgers.edu/why-how-women-run/.

Cillizza, Chris. "11 Democratic women who could run for president in 2020, ranked." *Washington Post*, January 9, 2017. https://www .washingtonpost.com/news/the-fix/wp/2017/01/09/11-democratic -women-who-could-run-for-president-in-2020-ranked/.

———. "Why is Donald Trump always defending Bernie Sanders?" CNN, February 18, 2020. https://www.cnn.com/2020/02/14/politics/trump -bernie-sanders-2020/index.html.

———. "Bernie Sanders' disastrous answer on '60 Minutes.'" CNN, February 25, 2020. Retrieved from https://www.cnn.com/2020/02/24 /politics/bernie-sanders-donald-trump-2020/index.html.

CNBC Digital Video: Senator Elizabeth Warren Sits Down with CNBC Editor at Large John Harwood. July 24, 2018. https://www.cnbc .com/2018/07/24/cnbc-digital-video-senator-elizabeth-warren-sits -down-with-cnbc-edito.html.

Concha, Joe. "Buttigieg Is the Media's 'It' Candidate." *The Hill*, April 4, 2019. https://thehill.com/opinion/campaign/437392-buttigieg-is-medias -internets-it-candidate.

Dugyala, R. Native American critics still wary of Warren despite apology tour. *Politico*, August 27, 2019. https://www.politico.com/story/2019 /08/27/native-american-critics-elizabeth-warren-1475903.

Entman, L. "Grassley, Klobuchar most effective senators of 115th Congress, according to study." myVU, February 28, 1970. //news .vanderbilt.edu/2019/02/28/grassley-klobuchar-most-effective-senators -of-115th-congress-according-to-study/.

Forbes 400 2020: The Richest People in America. (n.d.). https://www .forbes.com/forbes-400/.

Harris, Kamala. *The Truths We Hold: An American Journey*. London: Vintage, 2021.

Korecki, N. "John Delaney expands Iowa 2020 footprint." *Politico*,

November 17, 2018. https://www.politico.com/story/2018/11/16/john
-delaney-iowa-2020–1000484.

———. Warren confronts question of whether DNA test was a misfire.
Politico, January 5, 2019. https://www.politico.com/story/2019/01/05
/elizabeth-warren-native-american-ancestry-dna-test-1082570.

Nichols, Thomas M. *The Death of Expertise: The Campaign Against
Established Knowledge and Why It Matters*. New York: Oxford
University Press: 2019.

Newburger, Emma. "A historic number of women were elected in 2018
these four are expected to run for president in 2020." CNBC, November
26, 2018. https://www.cnbc.com/2018/11/21/four-women-expected-to
-run-for-president-in-2020.html.

Politics Is Personal: Keys to Likeability and Electability . . . (n.d.).
Retrieved from https://www.barbaraleefoundation.org/wp-content
/uploads/BLFF-Likeability-Memo-FINAL-1.pdf.

Pu, B., and J. Jester. "Andrew Yang isn't traditionally 'presidential.' Why his
supporters love it and how race may factor in." NBCNews, February 10,
2020. https://www.nbcnews.com/news/asian-america/andrew-yang
-isn-t-traditionally-presidential-why-his-supporters-love-n1134066.

Rubin, Jennifer. "Opinion: Elizabeth Warren Has Two Big Problems."
Washington Post, December 16, 2019. https://www.washingtonpost
.com/opinions/2019/12/16/warrens-two-troubles/.

Sarlin, B. "Why 'Medicare for All' wrecked Elizabeth Warren but not
Bernie Sanders." NBC News, March 5, 2020. https://www.nbcnews
.com/politics/2020-election/why-medicare-all-wrecked-elizabeth
-warren-not-bernie-sanders-n1150691.

Study: Klobuchar Most Effective Democratic Senator in Congress.
March 1, 2019. Retrieved from https://www.klobuchar.senate.gov
/public/index.cfm/2019/3/study-klobuchar-most-effective-democratic
-senator-in-congress.

Tanzi, Alexandre. "Women Millionaires Top Men on Average Wage
Earnings in U.S." Bloomberg.com. Bloomberg, July 27, 2019. https://
www.bloomberg.com/news/articles/2019-07-27/female-millionaires
-earned-more-than-men-in-the-u-s-on-average.

Torry, Jack. "Does experience matter anymore in US presidential
elections?" *Columbus Dispatch*, April 22, 2019. https://www.dispatch
.com/news/20190422/does-experience-matter-anymore-in-us
-presidential-elections.

Time, March 10, 2020. Twitter. https://twitter.com/TIME/status
/1237287747674570753.

Volden, C. "Cornyn Named One of Most Effective Lawmakers—Texas
Insider." February 27, 2019. https://thelawmakers.org/legislative

York Times, March 6, 2020. https://www.nytimes.com/2020/03/06/us/
politics/bernie-sanders-image.html.

Tumulty, Karen. "Opinion: Would a Female Presidential Candidate
Survive Putting Her Haircut on Social Media?" *Washington Post*,
May 16, 2019. https://www.washingtonpost.com/opinions/would-a
-female-presidential-candidate-survive-putting-her-haircut-on-social
-media/2019/05/16/2585d482–77eb-11e9-b7ae-390de4259661_story.html.

Vedantam, S. "Too Sweet, Or Too Shrill? The Double Bind for Women."
October 2016. Retrieved from https://www.wkyufm.org/post/too
-sweet-or-too-shrill-double-bind-women#stream/0.

Chapter 15

WORKS CITED

Alemany, J. "Analysis: Power Up: Women took center stage at Democratic
debate. And that was a good thing." *Washington Post*, July 17,
2020. https://www.washingtonpost.com/news/powerpost
/paloma/powerup/2019/11/21/powerup-women-took-center-stage
-at-democratic-debate-and-that-was-a-good-thing/5dd5ce5a602ff11
84c316741/.

Amnesty International. "Why Twitter is a toxic place for women." https://
www.amnesty.org/en/latest/research/2018/03/online-violence-against
-women-chapter-1/.

Bardella, Kurt. "Trump's MAGA supporters and Twitter Bernie Bros have
this ugly tactic in common." NBC News, January 19, 2020. https://
www.nbcnews.com/think/opinion/trump-s-maga-supporters-twitter
-bernie-bros-have-ugly-tactic-ncna1117901.

Bassett, Laura. "The #NeverWarren Attacks Are No Help to Bernie
Sanders Either." *GQ*, January 2020. https://www.gq.com/story/never
-warren-attacks-bernie-sanders.

Beauchamp, Zack. "The raging controversy over 'Bernie Bros' and the so-
called dirtbag left, explained." *Vox*, March 9, 2020. https://www
.vox.com/policy-and-politics/2020/3/9/21168312/bernie-bros-bernie
-sanders-chapo-trap-house-dirtbag-left.

Bowden, John. "Van Jones: Warren should get credit for having 'destroyed'
Bloomberg." *The Hill*, March 4, 2020. https://thehill.com/homenews
/campaign/485871-van-jones-warren-should-get-credit-for-having
-destroyed-bloomberg.

Brooks, Ryan. "Bernie Sanders' Very Online Fans Are Filling Elizabeth
Warren's Twitter Mentions with Snakes." *BuzzFeed News*, January 15,
2020. https://www.buzzfeednews.com/article/ryancbrooks/warren
-bernie-snake-twitter-2020.

Christopher, Tommy. "Bernie Sanders Spox Claims—Without Evidence—That Mike Bloomberg Has Had Multiple Heart Attacks." Mediaite, February 19, 2020. https://www.mediaite.com/news/bernie-sanders-spox-claims-without-evidence-that-mike-bloomberg-has-had-multiple-heart-attacks/.

Dylan Matthews, Z. "5 winners and 3 losers from the September 2019 Democratic presidential debate." *Vox*, September 13, 2019. https://www.vox.com/2020-presidential-election/2019/9/12/20863070/september-2019-democratic-presidential-debate-winner-losers.

First Democratic debate 2019: Live updates from Night Two. June 28, 2019. https://www.nbcnews.com/politics/2020-election/live-blog/first-democratic-debate-2019-live-updates-night-two-n1023321/ncrd1024306#liveBlogHeader.

Harris, Kamala. Twitter, May 30, 2019. https://twitter.com/kamalaharris/status/1134092540616069120?lang=en.

Lampen, C. "Of Course, a Woman Can Be President." The Cut, January 15, 2020. https://www.thecut.com/2020/01/elizabeth-warren-bernie-sanders-debate-woman-president.html.

Linskey, A. "The women asked for forgiveness. The men tried to sell their books: How a Democratic debate moment put a spotlight on gender." *Washington Post*, December 20, 2019. https://www.washingtonpost.com/politics/seek-forgiveness-or-give-a-gift-how-a-democratic-debate-moment-put-gender-in-the-spotlight/2019/12/20/6b77450c-22db-11ea-a153-dce4b94e4249_story.html.

McArdle, M. "Harris Demands Dem Candidates Address Abortion Rights During Debate." *National Review*, October 16, 2019. https://www.nationalreview.com/news/kamala-harris-demands-democratic-candidates-address-abortion-rights-during-debate/.

Moore, M. "Trump calls out Washington Post columnist Jennifer Rubin for 'Bloombefg' typo." *New York Post*, February 20, 2020. https://nypost.com/2020/02/20/trump-calls-out-washington-post-columnist-jennifer-rubin-for-bloombefg-typo/.

MSNBC Podcast Transcript: Running on Empty. October 28, 2020. https://www.msnbc.com/podcast/transcript-running-empty-n1245055.

Noor, P. "Facebook criticised after women complain of inaction over abuse." *The Guardian*, March 4, 2019. https://www.theguardian.com/technology/2019/mar/04/facebook-women-abuse-harassment-social-media-amnesty.

Paz, I. "Kamala Harris and Joe Biden Clash on Race and Busing." *New York Times*, June 28, 2019. https://www.nytimes.com/2019/06/27/us/politics/kamala-harris-joe-biden-busing.html.

Schouten, F. "Kamala Harris shines in commanding Democratic debate

performance." CNN, June 28, 2019. Retrieved from https://www
.cnn.com/2019/06/27/politics/kamala-harris-democratic-debate
-performance/index.html.

Silver, Nate. "Polls Since The Second Debate Show Kamala Harris
Slipping." *FiveThirtyEight*, August 7, 2019. https://fivethirtyeight.com
/features/polls-since-the-second-debate-show-kamala-harris-slipping/.

Ward, M. "Warren hits Bloomberg while he's down." *Politico*, February 20,
2020. https://www.politico.com/news/2020/02/20/elizabeth-warren
-attacks-bloomberg-debate-116362.

Chapter 16

INTERVIEWS

Spanberger, op. cit.

Mikie Sherrill, interview with author, November 29, 2019

Meghan Hatcher Mays, interview with author, November 5, 2019

Porter, op. cit.

Klobuchar, op. cit.

WORKS CITED

Allen, J. (n.d.). "On Impeachment, Warren Just Stole the Show from Her
Dodging Democratic Rivals." *Oregon Herald*. https://www
.oregonherald.com/bnews/story.cfm?id=1475.

Associated Press. "Warren calls for House to begin impeachment
proceedings." April 19, 2019. https://apnews.com/article
/46bf3ebf6a554c32b5b38b060db5b21d.

CNN. "Read Trump's phone conversation with Volodymyr Zelensky."
September 26, 2019. https://www.cnn.com/2019/09/25/politics/donald
-trump-ukraine-transcript-call/index.html.

Crow, J., and G. Cisneros. "Opinion: Seven freshman Democrats: These
allegations are a threat to all we have sworn to protect." *Washington
Post*, September 26, 2019. https://www.washingtonpost.com
/opinions/2019/09/24/seven-freshman-democrats-these-allegations-are
-threat-all-we-have-sworn-protect/.

Doubek, J., and M. Martin. "Val Demings Says House Impeachment
Managers 'Made Our Case.'" NPR, February 8, 2020. https://www
.npr.org/2020/02/08/803917385/val-demings-says-house-impeachment
-managers-made-our-case.

France-Presse, A. "Trump Would Be 'In Handcuffs' If Not President, Says
Democrat Warren." VOA News, May 2019. https://www.voanews.com
/usa/trump-would-be-handcuffs-if-not-president-says-democrat-warren.

Liptak, A. "Key Excerpts From Legal Scholars' Arguments on Impeachment." *New York Times*, December 4, 2019. https://www .nytimes.com/2019/12/04/us/politics/karlan-feldman-turley-gerhardt .html.

Livingston, Abby. "How U.S. Rep. Sylvia Garcia of Houston Landed in the Middle of Donald Trump's Impeachment." *Texas Tribune*, January 29, 2020. https://www.texastribune.org/2020/01/29/how-us-rep-sylvia -garcia-houston-landed-middle-impeachment/.

Phillips, A. "Analysis: 'The president is guilty': Mitt Romney's speech on his vote to convict Trump, annotated." *Washington Post*, February 5, 2020. https://www.washingtonpost.com/politics/2020/02/05 /mitt-romney-impeachment-speech-annotated/?utm_campaign=wp _main&utm_medium=social&utm_source=facebook&fbclid=IwAR2 -Ksg0c4E1OVR7umpLd6TkFuT5dmbHmeXKr4L3s_NhrWsOv2 _etkPxQq0.

Rubin, Jennifer. "Opinion: Klobuchar's friends tell a different story about her." *Washington Post*, February 12, 2020. https://www.washingtonpost .com/opinions/2020/02/11/klobuchars-friends-tell-different-story -about-her/.

Schor, E. "Impeach Trump? Most 2020 Democrats tiptoe past the question." APNews, May 27, 2019. https://apnews.com/article /16953d35ea6a489381fb67163fbd37f8.

Senator Harris' full statement on Trump's impeachment trial | Trump impeachment trial. PBS News Hour. https://www.youtube.com /watch?v=0U-yBNXYSOM.

Senator Warren Refutes Leader McConnell's "Case Closed" Conclusion; Urges Congress to Uphold Constitutional Oath: U.S. Senator Elizabeth Warren of Massachusetts. May 7, 2019. Retrieved from https://www .warren.senate.gov/newsroom/press-releases/senator-warren-refutes -leader-mcconnells-case-closed-conclusion-urges-congress-to-uphold -constitutional-oath.

Stevenson, Chris. "'I Would Like You to Do Us a Favor Though': The one sentence that could bring Trump down." *The Independent*, September 26, 2019. https://www.independent.co.uk/news/world/americas/us -politics/trump-ukraine-summary-impeachment-phone-call-transcript -zelensky-a9120521.html.

Chapter 17

INTERVIEWS
Klobuchar, op. cit.
Harris, op. cit.

WORKS CITED

Barbash, F. "Warren calls out Sanders for 'organized nastiness' and 'bullying' by his supporters." *Washington Post*, March 6, 2020. https://www.washingtonpost.com/nation/2020/03/06/warren-sanders-maddow-bullying/.

Cadelago, C., M. Severns, and M. Choi. "Kamala Harris' big question mark." *Politico*, February 28, 2019. https://www.politico.com/story/2019/02/28/kamala-harris-policies-1192919.

Chronicle Editorial Board. "Editorial: Harris runs out of money, and out of moments." *San Francisco Chronicle*, December 4, 2019. https://www.sfchronicle.com/opinion/editorials/article/Editorial-Harris-runs-out-of-money-and-out-of-14879703.php.

Edelman, A. "Elizabeth Warren reflects on sexism in 2020 campaign after exiting race." NBC News, March 5, 2020. https://www.nbcnews.com/politics/2020-election/elizabeth-warren-reflects-sexism-2020-campaign-after-exiting-race-n1150741.

Greenman, Josh. "No, Elizabeth Warren's loss isn't about sexism." *Daily News*, March 5, 2020. https://www.nydailynews.com/opinion/ny-oped-warren-sexism-20200305-hvmnaqzvynebvop3ceznl4v744-story.html.

Herzog, K. "Sexism Didn't Kill the Warren Campaign. The Warren Campaign Killed the Warren Campaign." March 6, 2020. https://reason.com/2020/03/06/sexism-didnt-kill-the-warren-campaign-the-warren-campaign-killed-the-warren-campaign/.

Longwell, S. "'Never Trump' Republicans Will Support Biden, Not Sanders." *New York Times*, March 9, 2020. https://www.nytimes.com/2020/03/09/opinion/joe-biden-never-trump.html.

Musumeci, N. "Gillibrand is a 'hypocrite' for saying Bill should've resigned: Ex-Clinton adviser." *New York Post*, November 17, 2017. https://nypost.com/2017/11/17/gillibrand-is-a-hypocrite-for-saying-bill-shouldve-resigned-ex-clinton-adviser/.

Nicholas, Peter. "Donald Trump, Bernie Bro." *The Atlantic*, February 28, 2020. https://www.theatlantic.com/politics/archive/2020/02/trump-isnt-trying-to-bring-down-bernie-sandersyet/607183/.

———. "Why Trump Isn't Trying to Bring Down Bernie Sanders." MSN, February 2020. https://www.msn.com/en-gb/news/world/why-trump-isnt-trying-to-bring-down-bernie-sanders/arBB10w9RZ?li=BBoPWjQ&ocid=mailsignout&pfr=1&% 2525252525253Bocid=UP21DHP.

Ross, K. "Sexism isn't to blame for Elizabeth Warren's Super Tuesday nightmare." *Washington Examiner*, March 4, 2020. https://www.washingtonexaminer.com/opinion/elizabeth-warrens-super-tuesday-nightmare-cant-be-blamed-on-sexism.

Rubin, Jennifer. "Opinion: Amy Klobuchar is out. Democrats should thank her." *Washington Post*, March 3, 2020. https://www.washingtonpost .com/opinions/2020/03/02/amy-klobuchar-is-out-democrats-should -thank-her/.

Steinhauer, J. "Bill Clinton Should Have Resigned Over Lewinsky Affair, Kirsten Gillibrand Says." *New York Times*, November 17, 2017. https:// www.nytimes.com/2017/11/16/us/politics/gillibrand-bill-clinton -sexual-misconduct.html.

Stepman, Inez. "Opinion: No, Elizabeth Warren is not a victim of sexism." *Detroit News*, March 10, 2020. https://www.detroitnews.com/story /opinion/2020/03/10/opinion-elizabeth-warren-president-sexism -victim/5000357002/.

Wang, Amy, and Annie Linskey. "Elizabeth Warren's exit raises questions about the role of women in U.S. politics." *Washington Post*, March 6, 2020. https://www.washingtonpost.com/politics/sen-elizabeth -warren-ends-presidential-campaign/2020/03/05/98921986–4d33–11ea -9b5c-eac5b16dafaa_story.html?tid=lk_inline_manual_3&itid=lk _inline_manual_3.

Chapter 18

WORKS CITED

Anderson, Cami. "Here's Why That Letter from Women Leaders to the News Media Is Such a Big Deal." *Forbes*, August 11, 2020. https:// www.forbes.com/sites/camianderson1/2020/08/11/heres-why -that-letter-from-women-leaders-to-the-news-media-is-such-a -bfd/?sh=7d2652e1493f.

Barbara Lee Foundation. Essential Guide: Substance. July 23, 2019. https:// www.barbaraleefoundation.org/politics/campaign-essentials/essential -guide-substance/.

Capehart, J. "Opinion: Val Demings says the VP talk is 'such an honor.'" *Washington Post*, March 17, 2020. https://www.washingtonpost.com /opinions/2020/03/17/val-demings-says-vp-talk-is-such-an-honor/.

Carter, C. "Without Question, Biden Needs Black Mothers to Win the 2020 Presidential Election." *Forbes*, June 4, 2020. https://www .forbes.com/sites/christinecarter/2020/06/04/without-question -biden-needs-black-mothers-to-win-the-2020-presidential-election /?sh=2edca9db22d8.

Casey Joins Senators Booker and Harris in Introducing Sweeping Police Reform Bill. June 8, 2020. https://www.casey.senate.gov/newsroom /releases/casey-joins-senators-booker-and-harris-in-introducing -sweeping-police-reform-bill.

Cory Booker and Kamala Harris Speech Transcript on George Floyd & Racial Injustice. June 3, 2020. Retrieved from https://www.rev.com /blog/transcripts/cory-booker-kamala-harris-speech-transcript-on -george-floyd-racial-injustice.

Christopher, Tommy. "Amid Campaign to Hobble Her VP Chances, Kamala Harris Tells Black Girls Lead Conference 'I Want You to Be Ambitious.'" Mediaite, August 1, 2020. https://www.mediaite.com /news/amid-campaign-to-hobble-her-vp-chances-kamala-harris-tells -black-girls-lead-conference-i-want-you-to-be-ambitious/.

Data Lounge. "There's reportedly a 'contingent' of Democrats lobbying against Kamala Harris as Biden's running mate." July 27, 2020. https:// www.datalounge.com/thread/26609184-there-s-reportedly-a -contingent-of-democrats-lobbying-against-kamala-harris-as-biden-s -running-mate.

Dillon, Jen O'Malley. Twitter, June 29, 2020. https://twitter.com /jomalleydillon/status/1288664987817381888?lang=en.

Glueck, K., J. Martin, and A. Burns. "Behind Biden's Reversal on Hyde Amendment: Lobbying, Backlash and an Ally's Call." *New York Times*, June 8, 2019. https://www.nytimes.com/2019/06/07/us/politics/biden -abortion-hyde-amendment.html.

Harris, Kamala. "To Be Silent Is to Be Complicit." *Cosmopolitan*, June 4, 2020. https://www.cosmopolitan.com/politics/a32766156/kamala -harris-black-lives-matter-protests/.

Harris, Kamala. Twitter, May 30, 2020. https://twitter.com/kamalaharris /status/1266839402724163584?lang=en.

Korecki, Natasha, Christopher Cadelago, and Marc Caputo. "'She had no remorse': Why Kamala Harris isn't a lock for VP." *Politico*, July 27, 2020. https://www.politico.com/news/2020/07/27/kamala-harris-biden-vp -381829.

Lerer, L. "Women's Groups Will Host Summit Meeting Before D.N.C." *New York Times*, March 12, 2020. https://www.nytimes .com/2020/03/12/us/politics/women-democratic-party-convention.html.

NARAL President on Biden's Comments to the DNC: We're glad he listened to the voices of millions of women. June 7, 2019. https://www .prochoiceamerica.org/2019/06/07/biden-hyde-oppose/.

Rubin, Jennifer. "Opinion: Women launch a shot across the media's bow." *Washington Post*, August 7, 2020. https://www.washingtonpost.com /opinions/2020/08/07/women-launch-shot-across-medias-bow/.

Ruiz, Michelle. "The Veep Watch: Some People Seem to Have a Problem with Kamala Harris's 'Ambition.' I Wonder Why." *Vogue*, August 3, 2020. https://www.vogue.com/article/kamala-harris-ambition-joe -biden-running-mate.

Scherer, M. "Inside Biden's unusual VP pick process: Tough questions, 11 finalists and many lawyers." *Washington Post*, August 13, 2020. https://www.washingtonpost.com/politics/inside-bidens-unusual-vp-pick-process-tough-questions-11-finalists-and-many-lawyers/2020/08/11/75511cbc-dc24–11ea-809e-b8be57ba616e_story.html.

Shultz, Connie. "Finding hope in her ambition." (n.d.) https://sanduskyregister.com/news/272432/finding-hope-in-her-ambition/.

Sotomayor, M. "Amid Floyd fallout, Clyburn says it's not the right time for Klobuchar to be named VP." NBC News, April 15, 2020. https://www.nbcnews.com/politics/meet-the-press/blog/meet-press-blog-latest-news-analysis-data-driving-political-discussion-n988541/ncrd1218681#blogHeader.

Walsh, J. "No Matter Who Biden Chooses as VP, It Will Be a Bittersweet Win for Women." *The Nation*, August 6, 2020. https://www.thenation.com/article/politics/suffrage-female-vice-president/.

Wright, J. "Harris talks ambition in women of color after personal attacks during Biden's VP search." CNN, August 3, 2020. https://www.cnn.com/2020/07/31/politics/kamala-harris-ambition-remarks/index.html.

Chapter 19

WORKS CITED

Axios. Twitter, August 19, 2020. https://twitter.com/axios/status/1296277122424754176?lang=en.

Bendery, J. "Nancy Pelosi 'Couldn't Have Been Prouder' of AOC's Response to GOP Rep's Sexism." *Huffington Post*, July 24, 2020. https://www.huffpost.com/entry/nancy-pelosi-alexandria-ocasio-cortez-ted-yoho-trump-sexism_n_5f1b4394c5b6296fbf429692.

Botel, M. "How Black women worked to secure Joe Biden's election as president." *USA Today*, December 2, 2020. https://www.usatoday.com/story/opinion/2020/12/02/how-black-women-organized-voters-secure-joe-bidens-victory-column/6475054002/?fbclid=IwAR2KCw-OdeVl9Mlauf5GH6nRKbfRu3sHhjr-SATi6BRrkufkuPokxq6lzh8.

Brownstein, R. "Trump's message collides with diversifying suburbs." CNN, July 28, 2020. https://www.cnn.com/2020/07/28/politics/trump-2020-election-suburbs-diversity/index.html.

DNC Opening Speech Kamala Harris. https://www.facebook.com/watch/?v=635431164023635.

Ian Schwartz. "AOC House Floor Speech: I Was Minding My Own Business and Rep. Yoho Called Me A 'F*cking Bitch.'" July 23, 2020. https://www.realclearpolitics.com/video/2020/07/23/aoc_house

_floor_speech_i_was_minding_my_own_business_and_rep_yoho
_called_me_a_fcking_bitch.html.

Liptak, K. "Trump pitches White suburban voters in blatantly political
White House event." CNN, July 17, 2020. https://www.cnn.com
/2020/07/16/politics/donald-trump-white-suburbs/index.html.

Palmer, E. "Everything Rush Limbaugh has said about Kamala Harris."
Newsweek, August 17, 2020. https://www.newsweek.com/rush
-limbaugh-kamala-harris-radio-show-1525554.

Rein, L. "As Trump appointees flout the Hatch Act, civil servants who get
caught get punished." *Washington Post*, August 29, 2020. https://www
.washingtonpost.com/politics/hatch-act-trump-convention/2020/08/28
/dce68a7e-e877–11ea-bc79–834454439a44_story.html.

Tavernise, S. "A New Political Force Emerges in Georgia: Asian-American
Voters." *New York Times*, November 25, 2020. https://www.nytimes
.com/2020/11/25/us/georgia-asian-american-voters.html.

Warren, M., and R. Nobles. "Trump's new line of attack on Biden is an old
campaign standby." CNN, August 4, 2020. https://www.cnn.com
/2020/08/04/politics/trump-reset-biden-ads-sanders-aoc/index.html.

Washington, Jessica, and Tiffany Arnold. "'Whatever it takes': How Black
women fought to mobilize America's voters." *The Guardian*, November
12, 2020. https://www.theguardian.com/us-news/2020/nov/12/black
-women-voters-mobilize-georgia-elections.

Woke, Be. Vote. BE WOKE.VOTE launches the "Rep Your City" Tour
in States across the Country to Mobilize Voters Leading up to the
Election. October 9, 2020. https://www.prnewswire.com/news-releases
/be-wokevote-launches-the-rep-your-city-tour-in-states-across-the
-country-to-mobilize-voters-leading-up-to-the-election-301149162.html.

Yam, K. "How Asian American 1st-time voters who helped flip GOP
district are mobilizing for Georgia runoff." NBC News, December 30,
2020. https://www.nbcnews.com/news/asian-america/how-asian
-american-1st-time-voters-who-helped-flip-gop-n1251175.

Yglesias, M. "Trump's tweets about saving the 'Suburban Lifestyle Dream,'
explained." *Vox*, August 3, 2020. https://www.vox.com/2020/8/3/21347565
/suburban-lifestyle-dream-trump-tweets-fair-housing.

Chapter 20

INTERVIEWS

Jen O'Malley Dillion, interview with author August 26, 2020

Longwell, op. cit.

Kamala Harris, interview with author September 21, 2020

WORKS CITED

Alexander, H. "Harris won the debate according to CNN Instant Poll while undecided focus group found her 'abrasive.'" *Daily Mail*, October 27, 2020. https://www.dailymail.co.uk/news/article-8817981/Harris-won -debate-according-CNN-Instant-Poll-Fox-News-viewers-abrasive.html.

Anonymous. "I Am Part of the Resistance Inside the Trump Administration." *New York Times*, September 5, 2018. https://www .nytimes.com/2018/09/05/opinion/trump-white-house-anonymous -resistance.html.

Bostock, B. "Rick Santorum cut off female co-panelist Gloria Borger while she was talking about Mike Pence interrupting Kamala Harris at the VP debate." *Business Insider*, October 8, 2020. https://www .businessinsider.com/rick-santorum-cut-off-gloria-borger-discussing -pence-interruption-video-2020–10.

Dawsey, J. "Former Pence aide says she will vote for Biden because of Trump's 'flat-out disregard for human life' during pandemic." *Washington Post*, September 18, 2020. https://www.washingtonpost .com/politics/olivia-troye-coronavirus-white-house/2020/09/17 /d3f67ede-f8ed-11ea-a510-f57d8ce76e11_story.html.

Fowers, A. "Ginsburg death set off month-long donor rush for Senate Democratic candidates." *Washington Post*, October 23, 2020. https:// www.washingtonpost.com/politics/2020/10/22/senate-democrats-rbg -donor-enthusiasm/?arc404=true.

Friedman, Roger. "A Searing Kamala Harris Trounces Mike Pence in Only Vice Presidential Debate: 'I Will Not Be Lectured.'" Showbiz411, October 8, 2020. https://www.showbiz411.com/2020/10/07/a-searing -kamala-harris-trounces-mike-pence-in-only-vice-presidential-debate -i-will-not-be-lectured.

Galofaro, C. "'Our house is on fire': Suburban women lead a Trump revolt." Associated Press, October 19, 2020. https://apnews.com/article /election-2020-virus-outbreak-race-and-ethnicity-joe-biden-donald -trump-a0e8c8f5332151cb74e6333e87eab920.

Glasser, Susan B. "The Trials of a Never Trump Republican." *New Yorker*, March 23, 2020. https://www.newyorker.com/magazine/2020/03/30 /the-trials-of-a-never-trump-republican.

Halon, Y. "Undecided voters found Harris 'abrasive, condescending' in vice presidential debate: Frank Luntz." Fox News, October 8, 2020. https:// www.foxnews.com/media/vice-presidential-debate-reaction -undecided-voters?fbclid=IwAR1mGyKRdPoRyAMeqb5GByEkEarJi8 -QCbR25OyeYgeuLQu_2-i5V5aMN4A.

Johnson, J. "They voted for him and now regret it. Why White women are turning away from Trump." *Washington Post*, September 14, 2020.

https://www.washingtonpost.com/politics/white-women-trump
-biden/2020/09/12/6764b89a-f167–11ea-999c-67ff7bf6a9d2_story.html.

Leonhardt, D. "18 Revelations from a Trove of Trump Tax Records." *New York Times*, September 27, 2020. https://www.nytimes.com/2020/09/27
/us/trump-taxes-takeaways.html.

MSNBC Video; Nicolle Wallace 'Ads Best I Have Ever Seen'. https://www
.msnbc.com/msnbc/watch/nicolle-wallace-calls-pro-biden-ad-one-of
-the-best-i-ve-seen-in-my-career-85103685748.

Shear, Michael. "Miles Taylor, a Former Homeland Security Official, Reveals He Was 'Anonymous.'" *New York Times*, October 28, 2020. https://www.nytimes.com/2020/10/28/us/politics/miles-taylor
-anonymous-trump.html.

Stein, Sam. Twitter, October 7, 2020. https://twitter.com/samstein/status
/1314049009162608645?lang=da.

Swan, B. "They tried to get Trump to care about right-wing terrorism. He ignored them." *Politico*, August 26, 2020. https://www.politico
.com/news/2020/08/26/trump-domestic-extemism-homeland
-security-401926.

Terruso, Julia. "White women in Pennsylvania are ditching Trump: 'He's a really good con.'" *Philadelphia Inquirer*, October 26, 2020. https://
www.inquirer.com/politics/election/white-women-pennsylvania
-trump-20201019.html.

Wheeler, Tarah. Twitter, October 7, 2020. https://twitter.com/tarah
/status/1314022106217107456.

Wootson, C., and D. Hawkins. "Trump's 'stand by' remark puts the Proud Boys in the spotlight." *Washington Post*, October 1, 2020. https://www
.washingtonpost.com/nation/2020/09/30/proudboys1001/.

Chapter 21

INTERVIEWS

Godfrey, op. cit.

Harris, op. cit.

WORKS CITED

ABC News Analysis Desk. Election 2016 National Exit Poll Results and Analysis. November 8, 2016. https://abcnews.go.com/Politics/election
-2016-national-exit-poll-results-analysis/story?id=43368675.

Astor, M. "Native Americans Helped Flip Arizona. Can They Mobilize in Georgia?" *New York Times*, December 4, 2020. https://www.nytimes
.com/2020/12/04/us/politics/georgia-native-american-voters.html.

Center for American Women and Politics. Statement on Kamala Harris Becoming the First Woman and First Woman of Color Elected Vice President. November 7, 2020. https://cawp.rutgers.edu/sites/default /files/resources/press-release-kamala-harris-vp-elect.pdf.

Crumpton, T. "Perspective: Black women saved the Democrats. Don't make us do it again." *Washington Post*, November 7, 2020. https:// www.washingtonpost.com/outlook/2020/11/07/black-women-joe -biden-vote/.

Ferman, M. "Donald Trump made inroads in South Texas this year. These voters explain why." *Texas Tribune*, November 13, 2020. https://www .texastribune.org/2020/11/13/south-texas-voters-donald-trump/.

Fonseca, F. "Native American votes helped secure Biden's win in Arizona." Associated Press, November 19, 2020. https://apnews.com/article /election-2020-joe-biden-flagstaff-arizona-voting-rights-fa452fbd546fa 00535679d78ac40b890.

Godfrey, E. "Revenge of the Wine Moms." *The Atlantic*, October 21, 2020. Retrieved from https://www.theatlantic.com/politics/archive/2020/10 /how-suburban-women-are-remaking-democratic-party/616766/.

"Latino Voters in the 2020 Election National Survey Results." http:// publications.unidosus.org/bitstream/handle/123456789/2096 /unidosus_latinodecisions_latinovotersinthe2020election.pdf ?sequence=1&isAllowed=y.

Merrill, Jeremy B., and Ryan McCarthy. "Trump Won Florida After Running a False Ad Tying Biden to Venezuelan Socialists." ProPublica, November 12, 2020. https://www.propublica.org/article/trump-won -florida-after-running-a-false-ad-tying-biden-to-venezuelan-socialists.

Rubio, Marco. Twitter, November 1, 2020. https://twitter.com/marcorubio /status/1322899749784211458?lang=en.

Rubin, Jennifer. "Opinion: Biden can't end GOP denialism, but Fox News might." *Washington Post*, December 8, 2020. https://www .washingtonpost.com/opinions/2020/12/08/biden-cant-end-gop -denialism-fox-might/.

———. "Opinion: What to do about America's great racial divide." *Washington Post,* November 5, 2020. https://www.washingtonpost.com /opinions/2020/11/05/what-to-do-about-race-big-divider-american -politics/.

Viglucci, Andres, David Smiley, Lautaro Grinspan, and Antonio Maria Delgado. "'People believe it.' Republicans' drumbeat of socialism helped win voters in Miami." *Miami Herald*, November 7, 2020. https://www.miamiherald.com/news/politics-government /article247001412.html.

Chapter 22

INTERVIEWS

Conway, interview with the author

Kelly Dittmar, interview with author, November 9, 2020

Lim, op. cit.

Meghan Milloy, interview with author, December 29, 2020

Sarah Longwell, interview with author, October 6, 2020

Stephanie Schriock, interview with author, November 12, 2020

WORKS CITED

Biryukov, Nikita. "GOP women's group blast Palatucci." *New Jersey Globe*, October 19, 2019. https://newjerseyglobe.com/congress/gop -womens-group-blast-palatucci/.

CAWP Staff. "Results: Women Candidates in the 2020 Elections." Center for American Women and Politics, November 4, 2020. https://cawp .rutgers.edu/election-analysis/results-women-candidates-2020 -elections.

Center for American Women and Politics. "Election 2020 Results Tracker." January 28, 2021. https://cawp.rutgers.edu/election2020-results-tracker.

Davis, Julie. "Joan Perry's Defeat in G.O.P. Primary Points Up Party's Gender Woes." *New York Times*, July 10, 2019. https://www.nytimes .com/2019/07/10/us/politics/republicans-women.html.

Fisher, Abigail. "Winning for Women? Gender and the GOP in the Trump Era." *American Political Review*, February 2, 2020. http://www .wesleyanarcadia.com/fall-2019/2020/2/2/winning-for-women-gender -and-the-gop-in-the-trump-era.

Latino Decisions. "CAP Action Fund: What Really Happened with the Latino Vote: Dec 6." December 2016. https://latinodecisions.com/polls -and-research/cap-action-fund-what-really-happened-with-the-latino -vote-dec-6/.

Republican Women for Progress. "Our 2020 Women to Watch." *Medium*, November 5, 2020. https://medium.com/republican-women-for -progress/our-2020-women-to-watch-51379f545231.

Schriock, Stephanie. "Turning the Wave into a Sea Change: EMILY's List Impact in 2020." EMILY's List, Press release, October 30, 2020. https:// www.emilyslist.org/news/entry/turning-the-wave-into-a-sea-change -emilys-list-impact-in-2020.

Winning for Women. "WFW Action Fund." Accessed on January 8, 2021. https://winningforwomen.com/action-fund-2/.

Chapter 23

INTERVIEWS

Klobuchar, op. cit.

Deborah Robinson, interview with author

WORKS CITED

Betancourt, Bianca. "Kamala Harris Honors Black Women as the 'Backbone of Our Democracy" in Victory Speech.'" *Harper's Bazaar*, November 7, 2020. https://www.harpersbazaar.com/culture/politics/a34608098/kamala-harris-vice-president-victory-speech/.

Feller, Madison, and Rose Minutaglio. "Four Years in the Front Row." *Elle*, January 17, 2021. https://www.elle.com/culture/career-politics/a35174004/women-four-years-covering-trump/?utm_medium=social-media&utm_source=twitter&utm_campaign=socialflowTWELM.

Nolan, Bridget, and Dana Bash. "Five badass women of the leading Democratic presidential campaigns: No longer 'token women' with seats at the table." CNN Politics, October 26, 2019. https://www.cnn.com/2019/10/26/politics/badass-women-citizen-democratic-campaign-operatives/index.html.

Schriock, Stephanie. "Turning the Wave into a Sea Change: EMILY's List Impact in 2020." EMILY's List, Press release, October 30, 2020. https://www.emilyslist.org/news/entry/turning-the-wave-into-a-sea-change-emilys-list-impact-in-2020.

Chapter 24

INTERVIEWS

Spanberger, op. cit.

WORKS CITED

Christiansen, Erik A. "How Are the Laws Sparked by #MeToo Affecting Workplace Harassment?" American Bar Association, May 8, 2020. https://www.americanbar.org/groups/litigation/publications/litigation-news/featured-articles/2020/new-state-laws-expand-workplace-protections-sexual-harassment-victims/.

Cooperman, Rosalyn. "Women Donors and Women's PACs Deliver for Democratic, not Republican, Women Candidates in 2018." Gender Watch 2018, November 25, 2018. https://www.genderwatch2018.org/women-donors-pacs-2018/.

EEOC Releases Fiscal Year 2018 Enforcement and Litigation Data. (n.d.).

https://www.eeoc.gov/newsroom/eeoc-releases-fiscal-year-2018
-enforcement-and-litigation-data.

Findings from the 2020 American Values Survey. https://www.brookings
.edu/wp-content/uploads/2020/10/AVS-2020-Presentation-FINAL.pdf.

Fingerhut, Hannah. "Most in US express positive views of country's
growing racial and ethnic diversity." Pew Research Center, June 14,
2018. https://www.pewresearch.org/fact-tank/2018/06/14/most
-americans-express-positive-views-of-countrys-growing-racial-and
-ethnic-diversity/.

Joe Biden speech in full: It is time for us to come together as a nation.
November 7, 2020. https://www.thenationalnews.com/world/the
-americas/joe-biden-speech-in-full-it-is-time-for-us-to-come-together
-as-a-nation-1.1107101.

Jones, Robert P. *The End of White Christian America*. New York: Simon &
Schuster, 2017.

Levy, Rose, and Martin Mattsson. "The Effects of Social Movements:
Evidence from #MeToo." July 22, 2020. https://papers.ssrn.com/sol3
/papers.cfm?abstract_id=3496903.

PRRI. "Dueling Realities: Amid Multiple Crises, Trump and Biden
Supporters See Divergent Priorities And Futures For The Country."
(n.d.). https://www.prri.org/research/amid-multiple-crises-trump-and
-biden-supporters-see-different-realities-and-futures-for-the-nation/.

Vandermaas-Peeler, Alex, et al. "Partisan Polarization Dominates Trump
Era: Findings from the 2018 American Values Survey." Public Religion
Research Institute, October 29, 2018. https://www.prri.org/research
/partisan-polarization-dominates-trump-era-findings-from-the-2018
-american-values-survey/.

Wehner, Peter. "The Exposure of the Republican Party." *The Atlantic*,
November 14, 2019. https://www.theatlantic.com/ideas/archive/2019/11
/trumps-republican-party-built-lies/601990/.

Westwood, Rosemary. "Why Is the GOP 'Losing With Women'? Leading
Female Republicans Talk About How to Get More Votes." *Pacific
Standard*, January 22, 2019. https://psmag.com/social-justice/why-is
-the-gop-losing-with-women-leading-female-republicans-talk-about
-how-to-get-more-votes.

INDEX